Structured Basic

STRUCTURED
BASIC

RICHARD M. JONES
Western Connecticut State University

ALLYN AND BACON, INC.
Boston   London
Sydney   Toronto

To my family
My children Karen and Edward, and my wife Wendy

Copyright © 1985 by Allyn and Bacon, Inc.,
7 Wells Avenue, Newton, Massachusetts 02159

Library of Congress Cataloging in Publication Data

Jones, Richard M., 1942–
    Structured basic

    Includes index.
    1. Basic (Computer program language)   2. Structured
programming.   3. Apple computer—Programming.   4. TRS-80
(Computer)—Programming.   5. IBM Personal Computer—
Programming.   I. Title.
QA76.73.B3J67   1985   001.642′4   84-9265
ISBN 0-205-08271-8

Printed in the United States of America
10 9 8 7 6 5 4 3 2   89 88 87 86 85

Contents

Preface

THE PRESENTATION OF BASIC

Three points should be made about the presentation of BASIC in this text:

1. Structured programming with BASIC is used, and students are introduced to structured programming in a logical and natural setting. The advantages of using only the four structures (sequence, looping, selection, and subprogram) are becoming well known. One pedagogical advantage is that students who take more computer courses will have an easier time of learning other structured languages.

2. Since Microsoft BASIC is one of the most popular versions of BASIC, the most common statements in the programs in this text have been written using Microsoft BASIC. Versions of Microsoft BASIC have been implemented on the Commodore, Radio Shack, IBM PC, DEC Rainbow, and Apple Macintosh computers.

While it is easier for an author to treat only one version of BASIC for one machine, this can cause difficulties for students who will be using a different computer at home or school or elsewhere to do assignments. Consequently, I have included discussion of different versions of BASIC statements, including BASIC Plus and Applesoft BASIC. Because Applesoft does not have the PRINT USING statement, I treat this statement in Appendix A. Readers who have the PRINT USING statement can use it at any time (perhaps as early as Chapter 3).

3. Because students have a tendency to confuse the use of the IF statement in the looping and the selection structures, I have presented a simple version of looping early (in Chapter 3), before selection. Although the IF statement is used here to implement the loop, you may use the WHILE . . . WEND statement if it is available on your machine.

PROGRAM DEVELOPMENT TECHNIQUES

One of the biggest problems in writing a program is not learning the language. The problem is understanding exactly what the program is supposed to do. For this reason, report forms are introduced early, in Chapter 2. The student even has the opportunity to do exercises with report forms at this time. Printer spacing charts are included when the PRINT statement is considered.

Also introduced in Chapter 2 are menus, hierarchy charts, flowcharts, and pseudocode. Throughout the text these program development tools are used in the appropriate places.

While some authors use either flowcharts or pseudocode, I use both, because flowcharts seem to be better at representing complicated selection structures, and pseudocode better at representing looping structures.

EXERCISES AND APPLICATIONS

There are many exercises in the text. Generally, each chapter has exercises at the end of important sections and also exercises at the end of the chapter. Exercises at the end of sections are appropriate for classroom discussion or homework. Since I consider program tracing an excellent learning tool, a good number of these exercises are included. Generally, exercises at the end of the chapters are suggestions for programming assignments.

Chapter 11, Computer Models and Simulations, presents a large number of programming exercises. Chapter 12 includes some more advanced exercises that use arrays.

COURSE ORGANIZATION

Two common organizations for a hands-on introductory computer course are:

1. Detailed instruction in the computer language BASIC along with substantial programming activities.

2. Instruction in BASIC along with instruction on how to use some common application packages such as a word processor, spread sheet calculator, file manager, and perhaps a statistics package.

This text has been written to be used in either type of course.

The text is appropriate for use in a course of the first type because the text contains a comprehensive treatment of structured programming in BASIC and of program development using the most common development tools.

This text also includes a number of topics that make it appropriate for use in a course of the second type. Generally, a course like this is designed to make the student a knowledgeable user of microcomputers, so that the microcomputer will become useful throughout the student's college career and beyond.

With that purpose in mind, the following topics have been included in the text.

- Operating system commands for CP/M and MS-DOS. Because the use of software packages requires the use of fundamental operating system commands, these commands for CP/M and MS-DOS are presented in Chapter 13.
- The dBASEII file manager. Since dBASE II is one of the most widely used and versatile file managers, its most useful commands are discussed in Chapter 15. In one or two class periods the student will be able to create and manipulate files.
- The connection between cursor movement on a screen and data manipulation in memory. In Chapters 16 and 17 the reader will see (by way of two relatively simple programs) how word processors and spread sheet calculators are able to do their jobs. That is, they will understand how moving the cursor around on the screen causes changes to take place inside the computer.

Since there are a wide variety of spread sheets and word processors, no specific packages are discussed. However, because students will experience menu-driven programs beginning in Chapter 9, they should be at home using menu-driven spread sheet calculators and word processors.

TEXT ORGANIZATION

The text is divided into five logical parts. All of Parts I and II must be completed in sequence before doing any other chapter. After this there is a considerable degree of freedom. For example, if the nature of the course is to emphasize programming, after completing Chapter 10 you could spend considerable time programming the models in Chapter 11. Or, if you wish to get to dBASE II as soon as possible, after completing Chapter 10 you could read Chapter 13 and then Chapter 14. The organization chart (page xii) shows the relationship of chapters.

ACKNOWLEDGMENTS

I am indebted to numerous people, who over the last ten years have influenced my teaching of programming and presentation of BASIC. First, I thank those students who knowingly and unknowingly have given me ideas for this book and its predecessor, *Introduction to Computer Applications Using BASIC*. Second, I have benefitted from the teaching experience and perceptions of my colleagues Nathan Loshin, Bruce King, Judy Grandahl, Joseph Friedman, and John Breen.

The form of this book has also been influenced by comments received from the reviewers of the first draft. I thank Paul M. Morris

☐ Text Organization Chart

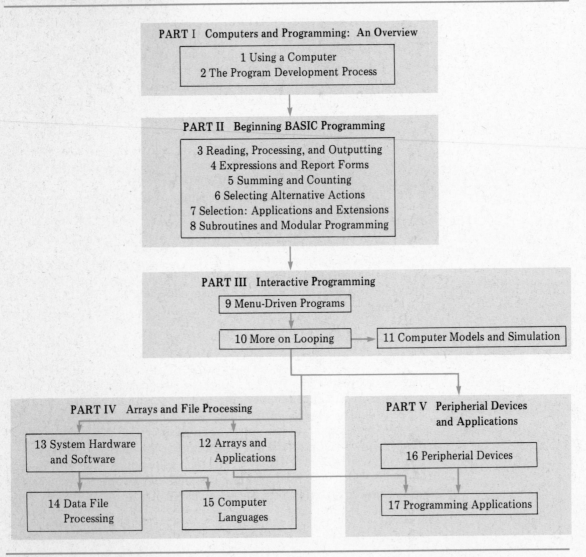

of Northeastern University, Marek Holynski of Boston University, and Yedidyah Langsam of Brooklyn College for their thoughtful suggestions.

Finally, Barbara Gracia and Carol Beal of Woodstock Publishers' Services have taken my manuscript and produced a text that conveys my ideas much better than I had thought possible. It is with grateful admiration that I express my special thanks to them for their contribution.

COMPUTERS AND PROGRAMMING: AN OVERVIEW

Using
a
Computer

INTRODUCTION TO CHAPTER 1

Every subject area—law, horse breeding, juggling, sailing, and so on—uses a certain terminology so that people can more easily discuss topics in that particular subject. Learning the terminology is a big step toward the eventual understanding of the subject. In addition, a little practical experience after some initial bookwork aids the learning process.

The same principles apply in learning about computers. The objectives of this chapter, formulated with the above two thoughts in mind, are to introduce the fundamental terminology of computers and programming and to describe (with the help of your instructor) how to enter and run an existing BASIC program on your computer system.

1.1 COMPUTERS EVERYWHERE

Computers were first commercially available in 1952. They were very expensive, and it was a common belief at that time that 50 computers would be sufficient to handle all the data processing needs of the entire country. Today computers are relatively inexpensive, and millions of computers of all types are in use performing a wide variety of jobs. Since computer costs continue to decrease while their power is increasing, their use should continue to expand.

In this section we will look at the types of computers in use today and explore their possible uses ten years from now.

Computers Today

A wide variety of computers are available today. For discussion purposes we will classify computers by cost and by their typical uses and functions.

supercomputers

Supercomputers, manufactured primarily by Control Data Corporation and Cray Research, are designed to perform 800 million instructions per second (800 mips). These speeds are required in scientific research, weather forecasting, and moviemaking. The cost of these computers is in the neighborhood of $10 million.

mainframe
computers

Mainframe computers (Fig 1.1) cost more than $1 million and execute 5 to 20 million instructions per second. They are used to process jobs where large amounts of data are involved and fast processing speeds are important. For example, computers of this size are used to process transactions for banks with 50 or more branches, to keep track of Social Security eligibility and payments, and to maintain insurance policies.

super-minicomputers

Super-minicomputers, which cost between $200,000 and $500,000, are usually time-shared computers that allow 64 or more people to use the system all at one time. They are called time-shared computers because the computer gives one person a fraction of a second of processing time, then moves on to the next person, and so on. Computers with this power are also used in education, computer-aided design, and manufacturing.

☐ **FIGURE 1.1**   **Mainframe Computer System**

Courtesy Burroughs Corporation.

minicomputers

  Minicomputers (Fig. 1.2), also called small business computers, cost between $20,000 and $80,000 and perform a wide range of office functions. These functions include all accounting functions (accounts payable, accounts receivable, payroll, inventory, general ledger) and word processing, financial planning (budgeting), and marketing applications. Minicomputers are also time-shared computers, allowing a number of office workers to do different jobs at the same time.

personal microcomputers

  Personal microcomputers (Fig. 1.3), which cost between $2000 and $10,000, can also handle all the business applications mentioned above for the minicomputer, but the microcomputer is not time-shared; that is, only one person can use the system at one time. A growing trend now is to link two, three, or more microcomputers so that they can share common information and printers, a system called a **local-area net-**

local-area network

work. A network can be constructed by periodically acquiring new computers.

  Interestingly, most programs for microcomputers are written not by the computer manufacturer but by independent software companies. Thus a whole new software industry has been created, and it has become very competitive because of the large amounts of money involved. As a result, programs for microcomputers have become very sophisticated—better than some programs run on larger computers.

home computers

  Home computers, which generally range in price from $100 to $1000 are rapidly becoming a common household item. Computer programs available for these machines allow the user to play video and

☐ **FIGURE 1.2**   **Small Business Computer, the Hewlett-Packard 9000 System**

Photo courtesy of Hewlett-Packard Company.

educational games, do financial planning and word processing, and gain access by way of the telephone to large information banks.

microprocessor   A **microprocessor** (Fig. 1.4) is a computer mounted on a single board. Microprocessors, which cost between $25 and $500, are usually dedicated to a specific task, such as monitoring various functions of automobiles, monitoring and controlling the temperature in buildings, controlling a milling machine, and controlling the actions of a robot.

Given a task of any size, there seems to be a computer to handle it—or there will be in a few months.

Computers in Ten Years

On the one hand, we can easily project some things computers will be doing for us in ten years. In areas where they are being successfully used now, they will be used to a greater extent. For example, virtually all businesses large and small will do their accounting on computers; word processors will replace typewriters; more robots will be used in factories; more movies will be made by computers; and the ordinary telephone will be replaced by a digital computer that will do what the telephone did as well as many other things.

On the other hand, we may find it difficult to imagine other things computers will be doing for us simply because of the rapid developments being made in both the hardware and the software. From John Backus, who more than twenty-five years ago headed the development of the FORTRAN programming language, comes the following state-

□ **FIGURE 1.3** **Microcomputer, an IBM Personal Computer System**

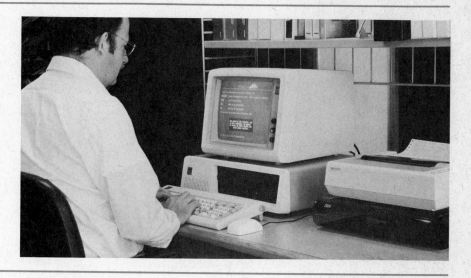

ment: "I think it's clear: There is going to be a real revolution. It's like computer science is starting all over again."

1.2 ESSENTIAL OPERATIONS AND COMPONENTS OF COMPUTERS

Even though computers come in a wide variety of shapes, sizes, and costs, they all operate essentially the same way and consist of the same major hardware components. These similar operations and components will be described in this section.

Operations

All computers execute programs. As you will see shortly, a program is a sequence of instructions, or statements, that direct the computer to perform a particular task. The computer decodes each statement and performs the specified action. Under program control a computer can do the following tasks:

- Accept data
- Process the data
- Output the results

Figure 1.5 illustrates the execution of a program after it has been loaded into memory—that is, after it has been typed in by the user

□ **FIGURE 1.4**   **Microprocessor**

Wintek 6800 Control Module, courtesy of Wintek Corporation.

and accepted by the computer. The highlighted (boldface) characters on the video display terminal (VDT) have been typed by the user. Usually, every character typed on the keyboard is displayed on the screen so that the users know whether they have hit the intended key.

Once a data value has been typed on the keyboard, it is stored temporarily in the main memory of the computer. Subsequently, program statements will direct the central processing unit (CPU) to perform some arithmetic operations and/or comparisons on the data to obtain the desired results, which are also stored in main memory. The CPU carries out the intent of the program statements; that is, it processes the data.

Program statements may then direct the computer to write results from the main memory onto the screen of a video display terminal or onto a printer.

Hardware

To execute a program, a computer needs the first four types of hardware components described below. The fifth device, secondary storage, is almost mandatory for convenience. Figure 1.6 illustrates the flow of data and information among the various components.

input device

1. **Input device:** An input device is a keyboard or some other device that captures the data. Figure 1.5 illustrates a keyboard.

☐ **FIGURE 1.5** **Microcomputer System Executing a Program with User Interaction**

Output device: Video display terminal (VDT)

```
THE CURRENT YEAR IS . . . . . ? 1984
YOUR BIRTH YEAR (0 TO STOP) . ? 1964
HAD YOUR BIRTHDAY THIS YEAR . ? Y
YOUR AGE MUST BE . . . . . . : 20
YOUR BIRTH YEAR (0 TO STOP) . ?
```

Central processing
unit (CPU)

Main (short-term)
memory

Output device: Printer

Secondary (long-term) memory:
Disk storage

Input device: Keyboard

main memory

2. Main memory: Main memory is a storage unit that holds a copy of the program being executed. Main memory also holds the data while it is being processed.

central processing unit

3. Central processing unit: The CPU carries out the instructions of the program. It performs the appropriate arithmetic operations and comparisons that produce the desired results.

output device

4. Output device: The output device receives the results of the program's actions and makes them available to the user. Video display terminals and printers are the most common devices for accepting the results from a computer. In Fig. 1.5 the output is directed to the VDT, but it could have been directed to the printer for a permanent copy of the results.

secondary memory

5. Secondary memory (disk drives): Secondary memory is a storage device that holds data and programs for an extended period of time. It acts as both an input and an output device. Data can be transferred from secondary memory to main memory and from main memory to the disk.

☐ **FIGURE 1.6**   **Flow of Data and Information Among Components**

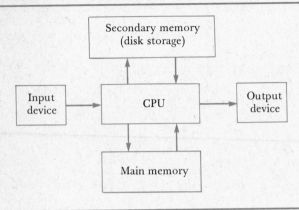

Figure 1.7 shows some of the components we have just discussed. Figure 1.7A illustrates a microcomputer as a user sees it. Inside the computer are one or more green circuit boards (Fig. 1.7B) filled with inch-long chips. One of these chips is the CPU, and others (one or more) are main memory. Some of the other chips regulate the pulses of electricity flowing through the chips, condition the power supply, route data from and to the input and output devices, and do a number of other tasks.

Figure 1.7C illustrates a typical chip, which contains an integrated electronic circuit mounted in the center. The pins at the bottom of the chip are connected to portions of the circuit. Figure 1.7D is a magnification of the electronic circuit. By reducing the size of the circuits, chip manufacturers such as Texas Instruments, Intel, NEC, and Motorola are able to put more and more circuits on an individual chip. For example, the Apple II+ had 110 chips; the enhanced Apple IIe has just 31. It is this technological advance that is causing the costs of computers to decline at the rate of about 20% per year.

1.3 ENTERING, RUNNING, AND EDITING A PROGRAM

In this section you will learn how to enter a program into main memory, to run the program, and to edit the program (that is, to correct errors in the program).

We note here, as a caution, that a program has to be written on paper before it can be entered into a computer. All programs, except for the simplest programs, are too involved for most people to just sit down and start typing them.

☐ **FIGURE 1.7**   **Exploded View of a Computer**

Photo courtesy of Digital
Equipment Corporation.

A.   MICROCOMPUTER SYSTEM

B.   CIRCUIT BOARDS INSIDE THE COMPUTER

□ **FIGURE 1.7**   (Continued)

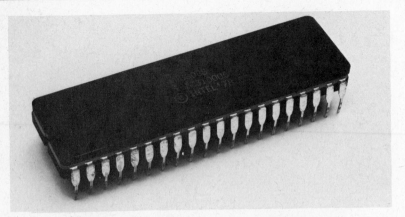

C.   THE 8088 IN AN INTEGRATED CIRCUIT (IC)

Photo courtesy of Intel
Corporation.

D.   MAGNIFIED PHOTO OF THE 8088 CHIP

Entering and Running a Program

Figure 1.8 illustrates the five steps involved in entering a BASIC program into the computer and then running it. As an aid in understanding the procedures, enter the program presented in Fig. 1.8. (You are not expected to understand all the statements in this program until you have read through Chapter 6.) We explain each step of the process below.

Step 1: Access the BASIC Language. You must first be connected with (that is, you must *access*) the BASIC language system. This step varies depending on whether you are using a microcomputer or a time-shared computer. The following list gives directions for each type:

Microcomputer	**Time-Shared Computer**
▪ Turn on the system. ▪ Insert the system disk. ▪ Press the reset button.	▪ Log into the system. This procedure usually requires entering an account number and a password.

prompt
operating system

After performing the steps in the above list, you will see a **prompt** like a > or another symbol. The prompt is an indication that you are in communication with the **operating system,** which is a program that supervises all the computer resources. This program is discussed further in Chapter 13.

Now you are ready to inform the operating system that you will be using the BASIC language, rather than some other language. To do so, type

```
> BASIC
```

Note: Apple II users are immediately in BASIC and do not need to type in this word.

Step 2: Enter the Program. At this point you can begin typing—that is, entering—the program in Fig. 1.8 into the computer. You may make some typing errors; these errors can be corrected with the techniques that will be discussed in the next subsection. Notice in Fig. 1.8 that the lines, or statements, of the program are numbered on the left. Each **line (statement)** is an instruction that the computer can carry out. When the **program**—the sequence of statements—is carried out by the computer, some specific task is accomplished. Programs will be explained in detail in later chapters.

line
statement
program

Step 3: Run the Program. By typing the word RUN—called a *command* in BASIC (see Section 1.4)—you instruct the computer to execute the individual statements in the program. As illustrated in Fig. 1.8, after we typed RUN, we entered some values where requested, and the results of the program were displayed.

☐ **FIGURE 1.8**   **Entering and Running a Program**

```
>BASIC                                        Step 1: Accessing the BASIC language.

READY
-NEW

-100 PRINT "THE CURRENT YEAR IS . . . . . ";   Step 2: Enter the program.
-110 INPUT C
-120 PRINT " "
-130 PRINT "YOUR BIRTH YEAR (0 TO STOP) . ";
-140 INPUT B
-150                             REM
-160 IF B = 0 THEN 400
-170   PRINT "HAD YOUR BIRTHDAY THIS YEAR . ";
-180   INPUT R$
-190                             REM
-200   IF R$ = "Y" THEN 250
-210     REM --- FALSE ---
-220          LET A = C - B - 1
-230          GOTO 300
-240     REM --- TRUE ---
-250          LET A = C - B
-260     REM --- ENDIF ---
-270                             REM
-300   PRINT "YOUR AGE MUST BE . . . . . . . . . . . "; A
-310   PRINT " "
-320   PRINT "YOUR BIRTH YEAR (0 TO STOP) . ";
-330   INPUT B
-340 GOTO 160
-350                             REM
-400 PRINT " "
-410 PRINT "DONE PROCESSING"
-420 STOP
-430 END
-RUN                                          Step 3: Run the program.

THE CURRENT YEAR IS . . . . . ? 1984          Notice how the data is entered after the
                                              question marks.
YOUR BIRTH YEAR (0 TO STOP) . ? 1964
HAD YOUR BIRTHDAY THIS YEAR . ? Y
YOUR AGE MUST BE . . . . . . . . . . .   20

YOUR BIRTH YEAR (0 TO STOP) . ? 0

DONE PROCESSING

READY

-SAVE "AGECALC.BAS"                           Step 4: Save the program.


READY
-BYE                                          Step 5: Terminate the session.
```

Step 4: Save the Program. You may want to run (or execute) a program at a later time. Instead of retyping the program at that time, you can save it on disk by using the word SAVE (another command) along with a name with which you choose to identify the program. (See Fig. 1.8.)

Later, when you want to use the program, you can enter the program (move a copy of the program into main memory) by typing

```
LOAD "AGECALC.BAS"
```

(*Note:* Apple users do not use quotation marks in the above commands.)

Step 5: Terminate the Session. To disconnect your communication with the computer, follow these steps:

Microcomputer	**Time-Shared Computer**
▪ Remove the disks.	▪ Type BYE or QUIT.
▪ Turn off the computer.	

Editing a Program

edit

When entering a program (Step 2), you may make typing errors. To correct the errors, you **edit** the program, following the directions given below.

Notice that each line, or program statement, in the following examples is preceded by a number. All corrections are made by referencing statement numbers in the program.

To Change a Statement. Retype the statement, including the statement number.

☐ EXAMPLE

```
200   IF R$ = YES THEN 250
210      REM --- FALSE ---
220          LET A = C - B - 1
```

At this point, suppose we recognize the mistake in statement 200. The YES should be "Y". We now retype that statement correctly:

```
200   IF R$ = "Y" THEN 250
```

To Correct a Statement While Still on the Line. Use the left arrow key (←) to erase characters to the left of the cursor (■). Then type the correct characters.

☐ **EXAMPLE**

```
200   IF RT█
```

At this point, we realize that we have incorrectly typed a T. So we press the left arrow key to erase the T. Then we continue.

To Delete a Statement. Type the statement number and press the ⟨return⟩ key. To delete several statements between statement numbers nnn and mmm, type

```
DELETE nnn, mmm
```

Note: Throughout, we will use symbols like nnn or mmm to refer to statement numbers in a general way.

☐ **EXAMPLE**

```
223   ⟨return⟩          <return> indicates the RETURN key on the keyboard
```

Deletes statement 223.

```
DELETE 223, 243
```

Deletes statements 223 through 243.

To Insert a New Statement Between Two Other Statements. Type the new statement, using a statement number that is between the other two statement numbers.

☐ **EXAMPLE**

```
240   REM --- TRUE ---
260   REM --- FALSE ---
```

At line 260, we realize that we have omitted a statement. So we type it with an in-between line number.

```
250   LET A = C - B
```

To See the Results of Making Changes. Type LIST (another BASIC command). This command instructs the computer to list all the instructions in the program in sequence by statement number.

☐ **EXAMPLE**

After making various changes in the program, we will want to see the entire program with corrections. So we type the LIST command:

```
LIST
.
.
.
200  IF R$ = "Y" THEN 250
210     REM --- FALSE ---
220        LET A = C - B - 1
230        GOTO 300
240     REM --- TRUE ---
250        LET A = C - B
260     REM --- ENDIF ---
.
.
.
```

All the statements of the program are now printed in sequence.

1.4 BASIC COMMANDS

The BASIC language has two types of instructions: commands and statements. The differences between them are described below:

command

- A **command** is not preceded by a statement number, and it is executed by the computer as soon as it is entered. LIST and RUN are examples of commands.

statement

- A **statement** is preceded by a statement number. Statements are combined to form a BASIC program.

Table 1.1 contains some of the more commonly used BASIC commands. Although you may not understand or be able to use all these commands now, they are presented here for future reference. You should be aware that all versions of BASIC do not have exactly the same names, however.

☐ **TABLE 1.1**   **Common BASIC Commands**

Command	Description
NEW	Clears the computer's main memory to allow a new program to be entered
LIST	Lists all the statements in the current program in sequence by statement number
LIST nnn, mmm	Lists all statements between statement nnn and statement mmm

(continued)

☐ **TABLE 1.1**   **(Continued)**

Command	Description
LLIST	Lists all statements in the program on the printer (Microsoft BASIC)
PR#1 LIST PR#0	Lists all statements in the program on the printer (Applesoft BASIC)
DELETE nnn, mmm	Deletes all statements between statement nnn and statement mmm
RUN	Instructs the computer to run (or execute) the program, beginning with the lowest statement number
RUN 200	Instructs the computer to start executing the program beginning with statement 200
RUN "AGECALC.BAS"	Instructs the computer to load the program with the name AGECALC.BAS from the disk and start executing it. (Apple users: Do not use quotation marks.)
SAVE "AGECALC.BAS"	Instructs the computer to save the current program in main memory on the disk under the name AGECALC.BAS. The name in quotation marks identifies the program. Most systems allow a name to consist of 8 characters with a 3-character extension. (Apple users: Do not use quotation marks.)
LOAD "AGECALC.BAS"	Instructs the computer to find the program with the name AGECALC.BAS on the disk and load it into main memory. After this command is given, the program can be edited and/or RUN. (Apple users: Do not use quotation marks.)
BYE	On time-shared systems this command terminates your interaction with BASIC. Other commonly used names for this command are QUIT and SYSTEM.

EXERCISES

1.1. Enter the program in Fig. 1.8 into your computer; fix your typing errors; RUN it; and when it works, SAVE it.

1.2. LOAD the program saved in Exercise 1.1. Then RUN it.

The Program Development Process

INTRODUCTION TO CHAPTER 2

Perhaps you have had a chance to enter and run a program like the age calculation program in Fig. 1.8. If so, you know that a program accepts data, processes it, and then outputs the results.

You saw in Fig. 1.8 that a program is merely a sequence of instructions that directs the computer through some task. However, someone had to write the program; a computer does nothing on its own. But how does someone proceed to write a program? Where does the programmer start? What does he or she do next?

The entire process of programming—from the start to the finish—is the subject of this chapter. The following five major steps in constructing a computer program are described in each chapter section:

1. Establish objectives.
2. Design the solution.
3. Develop an algorithm.
4. Code the program.
5. Test the program.

Clearly, you will not be able to use all this information until you know enough BASIC to begin writing substantial programs. But these steps are appropriate to discuss now for three reasons: (a) The discussion will give you an overview of some important topics in the text. (b) It will help condition you into thinking in a step-by-step, logical fashion. (c) It will give you some tools that you will find useful in solving problems.

2.1 ESTABLISH OBJECTIVES: REPORTS AND DATA

To complete a task (any task), you should know precisely what has to be done. Tasks such as "make this company more efficient" or "build a summer house" are too vague for anyone to act on. They must be refined and made more specific. In the first case a department manager would probably be given a specific objective to meet, such as "do the same work with 5% fewer people." In the second case a building contractor would have a set of architectural plans to work from.

In the same way that managers and builders must have established objectives, programmers must have a set of agreed-on goals or objectives to work from. The objectives for programmers are commonly expressed in the form of *report forms* and *data formats*, then later in terms of *data entry screens* and *menus* (step 2). Once you know the desired form for your reports (the objectives), you can then determine the data needed to produce the report. The example in the first subsection illustrates how to determine both the form of the report and the data you need. The succeeding two subsections explain the terminology of report and data forms.

□ **FIGURE 2.1**   **Desired Report Form**

```
                        CITY LINE TRUCK RENTAL
                             07/16/83

        TRUCK
        LICENSE NO.    CUSTOMER        DISTANCE    HOURS    CHARGE

        BG123          J. BREEN         34.5       3.5      ????
        YRZ-57         J. GRANDAHL      13.6       2.75     ????
        TS-398         E. LOVETT        24.6       4.0      ????
```

Example: Summer Truck Rentals

Suppose, because you own a pickup truck and all of your friends have
borrowed it for one reason or another, you decide to go into the business
of renting pickup trucks for the summer. You locate three other pick-
ups, which you finally put into running condition after some frustrating
weeks. With little experience for guidance, you decide that all trucks
must be returned by the end of the day with a full tank of gas and that
the rental fee schedule will be as follows:

> $5.00 per hour
> 25¢ per mile

You also decide that on each truck rental you should keep the information shown in Fig. 2.1.

So now you want to know how the distance, hours, and charge
can be determined for each customer. What data is needed to determine
these values?

To calculate the distance for customer J. BREEN, you have to
know the truck mileage before it was rented and after it was returned.
To calculate the hours, you have to know the time when the truck was
rented and when it was returned. The charge can then be determined
by finding the sum of the mileage multiplied by $0.25 and the time
multiplied by $5.00. Thus the following information is sufficient to cal-
culate Breen's charge (do this calculation):

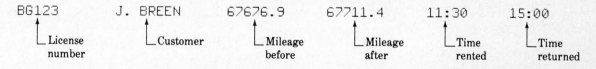

BG123   J. BREEN   67676.9   67711.4   11:30   15:00
 └License   └Customer   └Mileage   └Mileage   └Time   └Time
  number   before   after   rented   returned

Therefore the data needed for each customer should be in the
following form:

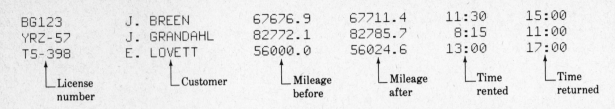

Now you know what data you need and what form your report should have. The following subsections describe reports and data in more detail.

Report Forms

reports

title
headers
detail line
summary
  information

The reports in Fig. 2.2 are typical of many reports generated by computers. Such **reports** generally have a title, headers, detail lines, and summary information, which together make the report understandable. A **title** gives a broad description of the purpose of the report. The **headers** concisely explain the significance of the data below them. Each row of data and results is called a **detail line**. **Summary information** usually consists of sums, counts, high and/or low values.

Once the report form and the required data are determined, you should verify that the report form and the data are consistent by calculating the results for a few hypothetical records.

Data Files

data file
records

fields

A set of values on one topic—like the truck rental data discussed above —is called a **data file**. A data file is subdivided into **records**. In the truck rental file each record contains the data for one customer's rental. Each record is further subdivided into a number of components called **fields**. The fields of each record in the truck rental example are as follows:

License number	Identification of the truck rented
Customer	Person renting the truck
Mileage before	Mileage before the truck is rented
Mileage after	Mileage after the truck is returned
Time rented	Time at which the truck is rented
Time returned	Time at which the truck is returned

structure

Thus our data now has a **structure**, with specific names given to parts of the structure. The structure and the names are illustrated in Fig. 2.3.

☐ **FIGURE 2.2**   **Typical Reports**

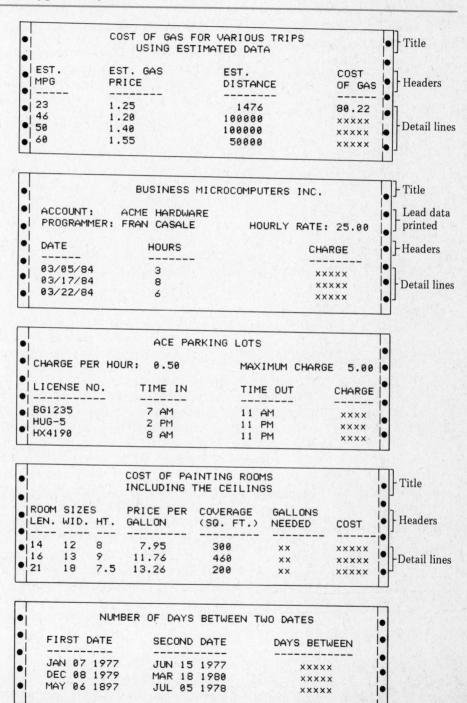

```
           COST OF GAS FOR VARIOUS TRIPS              • ⊢Title
                 USING ESTIMATED DATA

  EST.         EST. GAS          EST.          COST     • ⊢Headers
  MPG          PRICE             DISTANCE      OF GAS
  -----        --------          --------      ------
  23           1.25                 1476       80.22    • ⌐Detail lines
  46           1.20               100000       xxxxx    •
  50           1.40               100000       xxxxx    •
  60           1.55                50000       xxxxx    •
```

```
            BUSINESS MICROCOMPUTERS INC.               • ⊢Title

  ACCOUNT:      ACME HARDWARE                           • ⌐Lead data
  PROGRAMMER:   FRAN CASALE      HOURLY RATE: 25.00       ⌐printed

  DATE          HOURS                    CHARGE         • ⊢Headers
  ------        -------                  --------
  03/05/84        3                      xxxxx          • ⌐Detail lines
  03/17/84        8                      xxxxx          •
  03/22/84        6                      xxxxx
```

```
                  ACE PARKING LOTS

  CHARGE PER HOUR:  0.50          MAXIMUM CHARGE  5.00

  LICENSE NO.      TIME IN        TIME OUT      CHARGE
  -----------      -------        --------      ------
  BG1235           7 AM           11 AM         xxxx
  HUG-5            2 PM           11 PM         xxxx
  HX4190           8 AM           11 PM         xxxx
```

```
              COST OF PAINTING ROOMS                   • ⊢Title
                INCLUDING THE CEILINGS

  ROOM SIZES       PRICE PER   COVERAGE   GALLONS       • ⊢Headers
  LEN. WID. HT.    GALLON      (SQ. FT.)  NEEDED   COST
  ---- ---- ---    --------    --------   -------- ------
  14   12   8       7.95         300        xx     xxxxx •⌐Detail lines
  16   13   9      11.76         460        xx     xxxxx
  21   18   7.5    13.26         200        xx     xxxxx
```

```
          NUMBER OF DAYS BETWEEN TWO DATES

  FIRST DATE        SECOND DATE      DAYS BETWEEN
  ----------        -----------      ------------
  JAN 07 1977       JUN 15 1977        xxxxx
  DEC 08 1979       MAR 18 1980        xxxxx
  MAY 06 1897       JUL 05 1978        xxxxx
```

☐ **FIGURE 2.3**   **Data Structure Terminology**

Data file	BG123	J. BREEN	67676.9	67711.4	11:30	15:00 } Record 1
	YRZ-57	J. GRANDAHL	82772.1	82785.7	8:15	11:00 } Record 2
	T5-398	E. LOVETT	56000.0	56024.6	13:00	17:00 } Record 3
	Field 1	Field 2	Field 3	Field 4	Field 5	Field 6

In formal terms all data that is processed by a computer can be thought of as a data file.

EXERCISE

2.1. Study the reports in Fig. 2.2. Determine the structure of the data file required to calculate the desired results in the detail lines. Calculate those results.

2.2 DESIGN TOP-DOWN

Often there is no clear division between the first two steps of the program development process—(1) establishing objectives and (2) designing a solution. The process may flip-flop between these two steps many times. A question in the design step may easily cause a modification to one of the objectives.

hierarchy chart

In establishing objectives for the design of a large application, you will often hear from people who only understand their portion of the larger application. So once you have heard from everyone, you will have to get an overview of the application. This overview is obtained by constructing a hierarchy chart of the entire system. A **hierarchy chart** clearly shows the major components of the system. Hierarchy charts are explained in the first subsection that follows. The eventual design of a menu-driven application (which is described in the second subsection) generally reflects the form of the hierarchy chart.

Hierarchy Charts

The problem of calculating the charge for renting a truck is relatively easy. But how should a larger, more complex task be attacked? A commonsense way of solving a difficult problem or performing an involved task is to break it into smaller parts ("divide and conquer").

☐ **FIGURE 2.4**   **Hierarchy Charts**

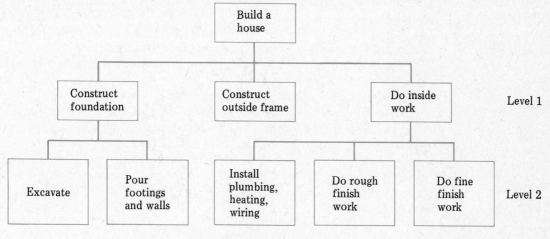

A. BUILDING A HOUSE

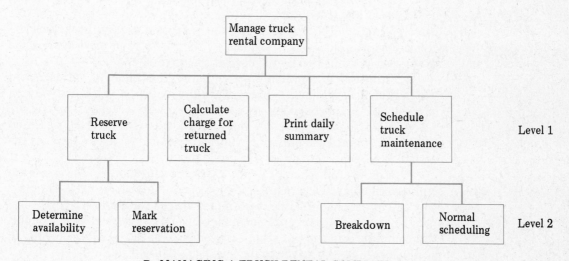

B. MANAGING A TRUCK RENTAL COMPANY

Let's consider a noncomputer example first. Suppose a house is to be built and the architectural plans have already been completed. The task of building the house can be subdivided into a number of smaller distinct tasks, as illustrated in Fig. 2.4A. This diagram is called a *hierarchy chart*. The tasks directly under (and connected to) a task are parts of the task.

top-down design

Notice that the *subtasks* (levels 1 and 2) are just parts of the larger tasks above them. Also, they specify *what* has to be done—*not how* the task is done. Notice, too, that the processes on the second level are independent. In fact, they are normally done by different people. Tasks on the second level can be further subdivided into even smaller, more manageable tasks—hence the term **top-down design.**

Programming tasks can also be broken down into manageable tasks, as you will see throughout this text.

Let's return now to your truck rental business. Suppose it has expanded into a full-time business with 75 trucks of various types and sizes and four mechanics to keep the trucks going. The hierarchy chart in Fig. 2.4B illustrates the major components in this application.

The purpose of continually breaking a task into smaller, functionally independent subtasks is to allow you to concentrate on one subtask at a time. Each task will usually require some data to produce the desired results.

Menu-Driven Applications

menu

main menu

options

Ten years ago most computer program runs were initiated by submitting a deck of IBM cards to the computer center. A few hours or days later the results would be ready. Today the execution of most programs (including word processors, spreadsheet calculators, and most application programs) is controlled by the user at the terminal.

The user is commonly presented with a **menu** of options from which a choice is allowed. Figure 2.5 illustrates an expanded version of the truck rental business as a menu-driven, interactive application. The menu at the top, called the **main menu,** is the first screen presented by the program. Depending on the response, one of the screens on the bottom level—the **options**—is presented next.

For example, suppose the user selects option 1. The program will then display the screen on the lower left side of Fig. 2.5. The user now enters data as he or she is prompted by the program.

For most programs permanent reports are printed on paper. But computer reports can also be directed to the video display terminal, as illustrated by the screen to the lower right of Fig. 2.5.

The design of an interactive, menu-driven computer application is simply a question of designing the appropriate screens, like those shown in Fig. 2.5. You will be able to write menu-driven applications after completing Chapter 9.

EXERCISE

2.2. For the modified truck rental example, what data will have to be in the truck file to accomplish what is requested in Fig. 2.5?

□ FIGURE 2.5   Menu-Driven Application

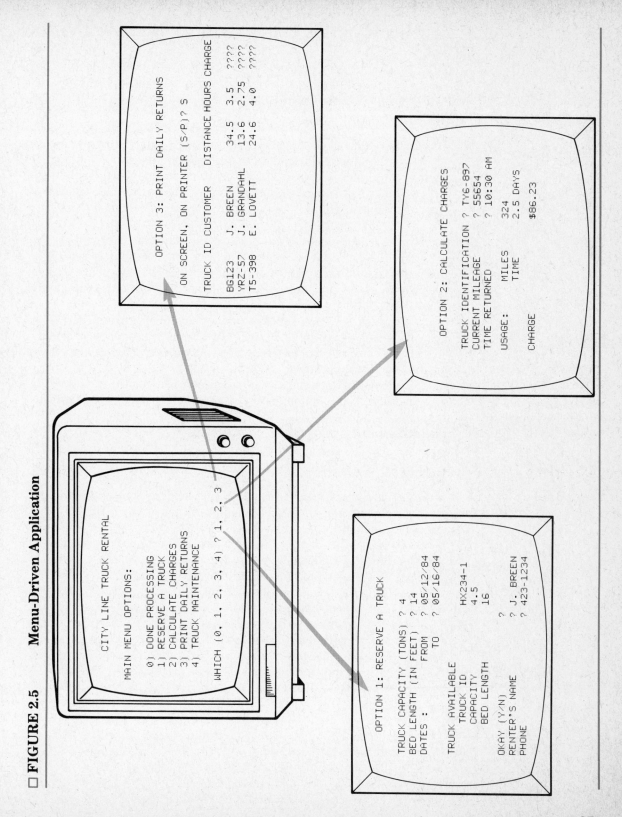

```
        CITY LINE TRUCK RENTAL

MAIN MENU OPTIONS:

      0) DONE PROCESSING
      1) RESERVE A TRUCK
      2) CALCULATE CHARGES
      3) PRINT DAILY RETURNS
      4) TRUCK MAINTENANCE

WHICH (0, 1, 2, 3, 4) ? 1, 2, 3
```

```
OPTION 1: RESERVE A TRUCK

TRUCK CAPACITY (TONS) ? 4
BED LENGTH (IN FEET)  ? 14
DATES :     FROM ? 05/12/84
            TO   ? 05/16/84

TRUCK AVAILABLE
    TRUCK ID        HX234-1
    CAPACITY        4.5
    BED LENGTH      16

OKAY (Y/N)          ? Y
RENTER'S NAME       ? J. BREEN
PHONE               ? 423-1234
```

```
OPTION 2: CALCULATE CHARGES

TRUCK IDENTIFICATION ? TY6-897
CURRENT MILEAGE      ? 55654
TIME RETURNED        ? 10:30 AM

USAGE:   MILES       324
         TIME        2.5 DAYS

      CHARGE         $86.23
```

```
       OPTION 3: PRINT DAILY RETURNS

ON SCREEN, ON PRINTER (S/P)? S

TRUCK ID CUSTOMER   DISTANCE HOURS CHARGE

BG123    J. BREEN     34.5   3.5    ????
YRZ-57   J. GRANDAHL  13.6   2.75   ????
TS-398   E. LOVETT    24.6   4.0    ????
```

2.3 DEVELOP A STRUCTURED ALGORITHM

Up to this point we have performed the following steps in developing a program:

1. Established the objectives in terms of report forms and determined the required data to produce the reports.
2. Subdivided and organized a problem into manageable subtasks, as indicated by hierarchy charts, and developed a menu of options.

The next step is to determine exactly how each subtask in the hierarchy chart is to be done. That is, what sequence of instructions is needed to accomplish each subtask? Each subtask of the hierarchy chart (or the main menu) can be considered in turn, beginning with the one at the top and working downward.

algorithm
The "how" of each subtask is handled in programming by an algorithm. An **algorithm** is a sequence of instructions that clearly specifies how you can do a particular task. In other words, an algorithm gives the steps in a procedure.

There are two common ways of expressing algorithms: *flowcharts* and *pseudocode*. The following subsections describe these two representations as well as a more precise version of each, called symbolic flowcharts and symbolic pseudocode.

Algorithms as Structured Flowcharts

flowchart
A **flowchart** is a graphical representation of an algorithm. The standard flowchart symbols and their meanings are illustrated in Fig. 2.6. For example, diamond shapes are used to show selection points of a procedure, and rectangles are used to indicate actions that are to be taken. Study the symbols and their meanings; we will use these symbols throughout this section as we develop several algorithms.

Undisciplined construction of algorithms can lead to flowcharts that look like a plate of spaghetti (Fig. 2.7). Although such an algorithm may be correct, it is hard to understand and modify. There are better, simpler ways of constructing flowcharts.

sequence
selection
looping
In 1966 two computer scientists, Bohm and Jacopini, proved that all algorithms can be expressed by using just three flow structures: **sequence**, **selection**, and **looping**. These structures are illustrated in Fig. 2.8. An important characteristic of these structures is that they have one entry point and one exit point.

From Fig. 2.8 notice that in the sequence structure, action flows from one statement to the next. In the selection structure, action on a statement is taken only after a condition is evaluated as true or false. In the loop structure a certain statement may be acted on repeatedly, depending on the results of the evaluation of a condition.

☐ **FIGURE 2.6**   **Standard Flowchart Symbols**

Shapes	Name	Use
	Start/stop	Indicates the starting and stopping points of an algorithm
	Flow lines	Indicate the sequence in which instructions are executed
	Input/output	Indicates where data are entered into the algorithm and also where results are printed
	Process	Specifies some action to be taken; for example, an arithmetic or replacement operation might be specified
True / False	Selection	Indicates a selection point. Perhaps a comparison is made or a question asked. Notice that two flow lines emanate from this shape. If the selection is true (or false), then the appropriate flow line is followed to the next symbol
	Commentary	Contains additional descriptive comments or explanatory notes as clarification

structured algorithm   A **structured algorithm** (expressed as a flowchart or in pseudocode) is one that has been constructed by using these three structures. In a structured algorithm the sequence, selection, and loop structures may be connected in series or may be nested, one within another.

Figure 2.9B illustrates a structured flowchart for calculating the truck charges and producing the report illustrated at the beginning of the chapter in Fig. 2.1. The data file is included (Fig. 2.9A) so that you can carry out the instructions on each record.

Study the flowchart in Fig. 2.9B and follow the steps in the procedure. Notice which symbol shapes are used for the different tasks. For example, rectangles are used for calculation steps, and parallelograms are used for input, print instructions, and so on.

☐ **FIGURE 2.7**   **A Spaghettilike Flowchart**

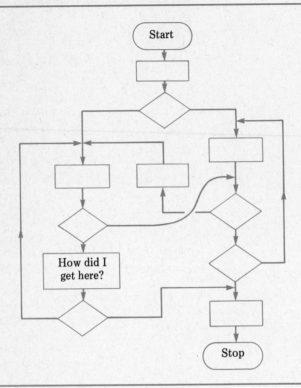

☐ **FIGURE 2.8**   **The Three Fundamental Flow Structures**

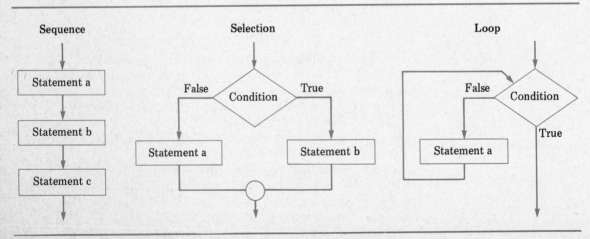

☐ **FIGURE 2.9**   **Flowchart for Calculating Truck Rental Costs**

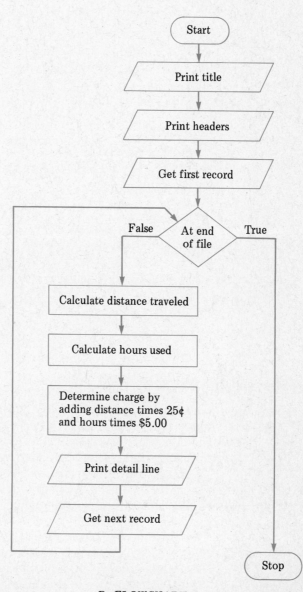

```
BG123      J. BREEN      67676.9   67711.4   11:30    15:00
YRZ-57     J. GRANDAHL   82772.1   82785.7    8:15    11:00
T5-398     E. LOVETT     56000.0   56024.6   13:00    17:00
```

A. DATA FILE

B. FLOWCHART

☐ **FIGURE 2.10**   **Pseudocode Conventions**

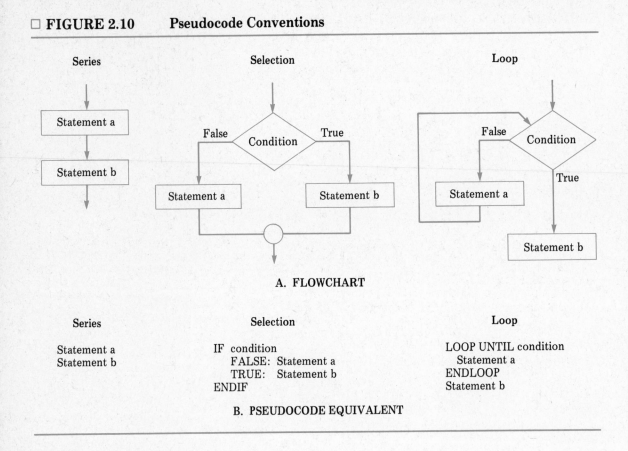

A. FLOWCHART

Series	Selection	Loop

Statement a
Statement b
	IF condition
	    FALSE: Statement a
	    TRUE: Statement b
	ENDIF
		LOOP UNTIL condition
		    Statement a
		ENDLOOP
		Statement b

B. PSEUDOCODE EQUIVALENT

Algorithms Expressed in Pseudocode

pseudocode

Pseudocode is another way of expressing structured algorithms. **Pseudocode** uses a few keywords to represent the selection and looping structures rather than the geometric shapes and arrows of flowchart language. And in pseudocode, statements in series are simply written one after another.

In Fig. 2.10B the pseudocode structures are defined in terms of flowcharts (Fig. 2.10A). Notice how compact pseudocode is compared with flowcharts. Here we use a special version of pseudocode that allows easy conversion from pseudocode to BASIC.

The pseudocode structures can be combined in series or nested, as shown in Fig. 2.11. Nesting structures are illustrated by the highlighted loop within the IF structure in Fig. 2.11.

Study both the flowchart and the pseudocode in Fig. 2.11. See whether you can follow the sequence of events or actions in both cases.

Figure 2.11 allows us to compare the strengths and weaknesses of flowcharts and pseudocode. As we can see, flowcharts express the

☐ **FIGURE 2.11**   **Flowchart and Corresponding Pseudocode**

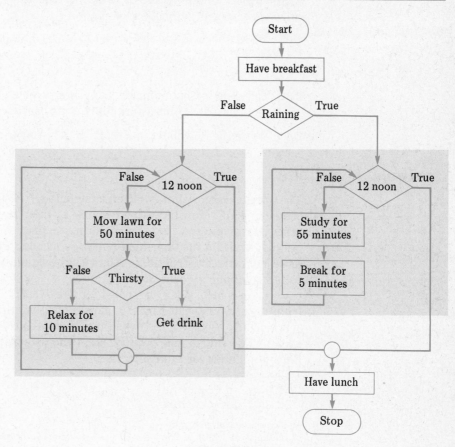

A. FLOWCHART

```
Have breakfast
IF  raining
      FALSE:  LOOP UNTIL 12 noon
                  Mow lawn for 50 minutes
                  IF thirsty
                      FALSE:  Relax for 10 minutes
                      TRUE:  Get drink
                  ENDIF
              ENDLOOP

      TRUE:  LOOP UNTIL 12 noon
                  Study for 55 minutes
                  Break for 5 minutes
              ENDLOOP

ENDIF
Have lunch
```

B. PSEUDOCODE

algorithm in such a way that people can quickly understand the algorithm. But this advantage is offset by the time it takes to draw the various geometric symbols.

EXERCISES

2.3. Take the instructions for a card game or a board game and write them as a structured flowchart or as pseudocode.

2.4. Write the flowchart in Fig. 2.9B in pseudocode.

Symbolic Algorithms

The previous algorithms written as structured flowcharts and as pseudocode can sometimes be vague because of their terse, narrative instructions. However, they can be made more precise by using a symbolic language within the flowchart and pseudocode structures in place of the terse narrative instructions. Algorithms using symbolic language are *symbolic algorithms* called **symbolic algorithms.**

As a brief example, consider the excerpt, below and left, taken from the flowchart in Fig. 2.9. This narrative direction can be written symbolically as shown on the right. The symbolic shorthand can be used in both flowcharts and pseudocode. (The asterisk in the expression on the right stands for multiplication.)

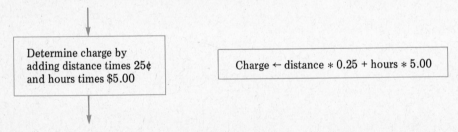

Determine charge by adding distance times 25¢ and hours times $5.00

Charge ← distance ∗ 0.25 + hours ∗ 5.00

Symbolic language consists of named boxes, which hold values (numbers and other data values), relational operators, the assignment operator, and the print instruction.

named boxes   **Named boxes** hold data values. Note that only one value can be stored in a box at one time. Box names should suggest the type of value assigned to the box.

☐ EXAMPLE

Charge	Distance	Hours	Customer
26.13	34.5	3.5	J. BREEN

relational operators   **Relational operators** are used to create the conditions in the selection and loop structures. The six standard operators are as follows:

| = equal to | > greater than | < less than |
| ≠ not equal to | ≥ greater than or equal to | ≤ less than or equal to |

☐ EXAMPLE

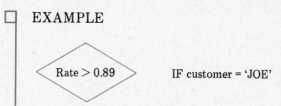

IF customer = 'JOE'

assignment operator   The **assignment operator,** which is indicated by an arrow ←, is used to assign values to a named box. The value on the right side of the arrow is assigned to the named box on the left. On the right side of the backarrow may be any number, named box, or arithmetic expression. If the right side is an expression, it is evaluated, and the value is assigned to the named box on the left. Instructions using the assignment **assignment statements** operator are called **assignment statements.**

☐ EXAMPLE

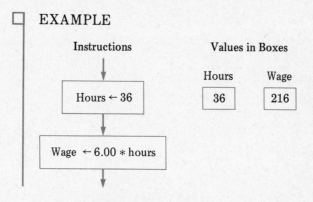

PRINT statement   The **PRINT statement** is used to print a value in a box onto a piece of paper. It can be used in flowcharts and pseudocode. For example,

Print hours, wage   Print hours, wage

causes the value in boxes hours and wage to be printed onto a piece of paper.

trace   To **trace** a symbolic algorithm, you execute each statement in the algorithm, showing exactly how the contents of the boxes change values. For example, Fig. 2.12A gives the flowchart for an algorithm; Fig. 2.12B gives the equivalent pseudocode. Then Fig. 2.12C shows the trace of the algorithm, and Fig. 2.12D shows the results that would be

☐ **FIGURE 2.12**   **Trace of a Symbolic Algorithm**

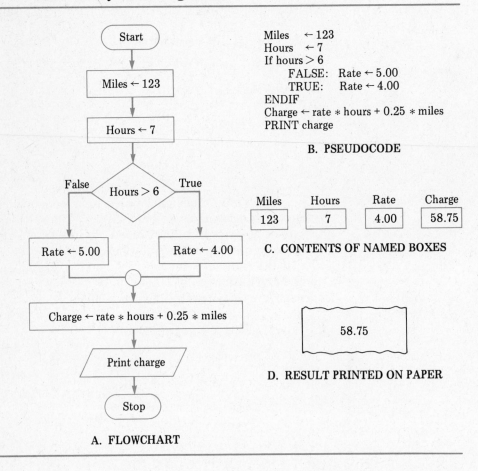

Miles ← 123
Hours ← 7
If hours > 6
         FALSE: Rate ← 5.00
         TRUE: Rate ← 4.00
ENDIF
Charge ← rate * hours + 0.25 * miles
PRINT charge

B. PSEUDOCODE

Miles	Hours	Rate	Charge
123	7	4.00	58.75

C. CONTENTS OF NAMED BOXES

58.75

D. RESULT PRINTED ON PAPER

A. FLOWCHART

printed. In this truck rental example the algorithm gives a break to the customer who rents the truck for more than 6 hours. Trace the algorithm yourself to verify the results shown in Figs. 2.12C and 2.12D.

EXERCISES

2.5. In Fig. 2.12 assume the following assignments at the beginning of the algorithm:

Miles ← 123
Hours ← 4.5

Then trace the algorithm.

2.6. Trace each of the following flowcharts, showing clearly how the contents of the boxes change.

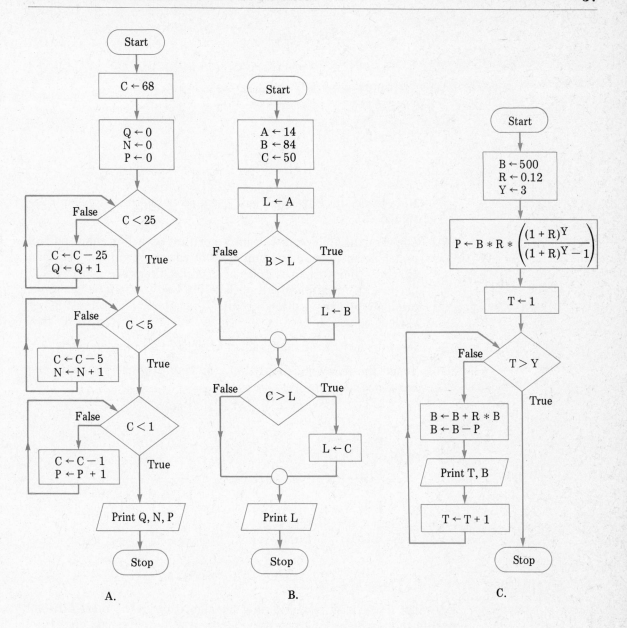

A.   B.   C.

2.7. Let the following be the names for boxes:

Hours   Holds the number of hours you have worked this week
Rate   Holds your wage rate
Wage   Holds your wages for the week

Suppose you are paid time and a half for all hours worked over 35 hours. Complete the following flowchart and pseudocode so that they calculate your wage correctly. Then trace them.

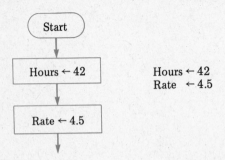

Hours ← 42
Rate ← 4.5

Now trace the flowchart and pseudocode again with hours assigned 32.

2.8. Express the following tuition algorithm as a flowchart and in pseudocode: If your total number of course credits is less than 12, then your tuition is $50 per credit. Otherwise, you pay $45 per credit. Maximum tuition is $700. Use the following names to identify boxes: tuition, credits. Trace your algorithms, using various values for credits.

2.9. Rewrite each of the flowcharts in Exercise 2.8 in pseudocode.

2.10. Trace the following algorithm, showing how the values in the boxes change.

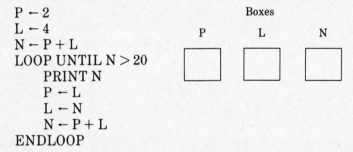

```
P ← 2
L ← 4
N ← P + L
LOOP UNTIL N > 20
    PRINT N
    P ← L
    L ← N
    N ← P + L
ENDLOOP
```

2.4 CODE THE ALGORITHM IN BASIC

Defining, developing, and refining an algorithm is the most difficult part of the programming process. Putting a well-understood algorithm into BASIC, especially if it has been written as a symbolic algorithm, is relatively simple.

Computers do not understand symbolic flowcharts or pseudocode. So algorithms written in these forms must be rewritten in a formal computer language like BASIC, Pascal, FORTRAN, or others in order for computers to understand them.

Figure 2.13 illustrates an algorithm and the corresponding BASIC program. Some informal comments follow; these comments may

☐ **FIGURE 2.13**   **Algorithm and Corresponding BASIC Program**

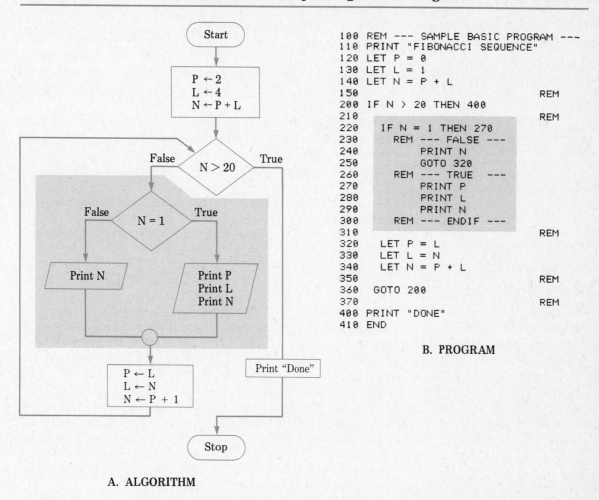

```
100 REM --- SAMPLE BASIC PROGRAM ---
110 PRINT "FIBONACCI SEQUENCE"
120 LET P = 0
130 LET L = 1
140 LET N = P + L
150                              REM
200 IF N > 20 THEN 400
210                              REM
220   IF N = 1 THEN 270
230     REM --- FALSE ---
240         PRINT N
250         GOTO 320
260     REM --- TRUE ---
270         PRINT P
280         PRINT L
290         PRINT N
300     REM --- ENDIF ---
310                            REM
320     LET P = L
330     LET L = N
340     LET N = P + L
350                            REM
360   GOTO 200
370                            REM
400 PRINT "DONE"
410 END
```

B. PROGRAM

A. ALGORITHM

answer some obvious questions. But you will not be able to completely understand this program until you have finished Chapter 6.

Note that BASIC (as well as all other computer languages) has a certain **syntax**—specific ways that statements are written. For instance, if we had written statement 200 as

syntax

```
200  IF N > 20, THEN 400
```

syntax error

we would have produced a **syntax error.** That is, in BASIC there should be no comma after the 20. We will discuss the syntax of all statements in succeeding chapters.

The following comments refer to specific lines (statements) in the program in Fig. 2.13B:

- Line 100: Every statement is numbered with a positive integer. Gaps are left between numbers in case another statement has to be inserted between two existing statements. The computer executes the statement with the lowest number first and continues in sequence.
- Lines 100, 150, 230: REM statements (REM stands for REMark) are included to make the program more understandable to you and others who read the program. They are also used to give the appearance of space between program statements, as in line 150.
- Lines 120, 130, 140: The letters are names for memory locations in the computer.
- Line 140: Notice how the assignment statements are written in BASIC:

$$N \leftarrow P + L \qquad \text{becomes} \qquad \text{LET } N = P + L$$

- Lines 200 through 360: These lines constitute a *loop*. The loop structure is implemented with the IF–THEN and GOTO statements. If the condition $N > 200$ is false, the computer proceeds to the next highest line number; that is, it continues performing the loop. Otherwise, it exits the loop by going to line 400. The loop structure is discussed in Chapter 3.
- Lines 220 through 300: These lines constitute a selection structure. The selection structure is implemented with the IF–THEN statement. If the condition is false, the computer proceeds to the next highest statement number. Otherwise, it goes to the statement number after the THEN. The selection structure is discussed in Chapters 6 and 7.
- Lines 250, 360: The GOTO statement instructs the computer to execute the statement with the indicated number. The GOTO statement is used along with the IF statement to implement the loop and selection structures.

2.5 TEST THE PROGRAM

test a program

Once the program has been entered, all syntax errors should be removed (editing the program) and all obvious logic errors should be corrected. Then the program should be tested. A programmer **tests a program** by entering data that exercises all situations that can arise in the program. It is quite embarrassing to be demonstrating the final version of a program to a customer and have errors crop up every few minutes.

We will have more to say about program testing in Chapter 6.

BEGINNING BASIC PROGRAMMING

Reading, Processing, and Outputting

INTRODUCTION TO CHAPTER 3

The purpose of this chapter is to have you understand everything about the program in Fig. 3.1A. This program implements the initial truck rental example of the previous chapter. Specifically, given the data file in Fig. 2.3, the program produces the report in Fig. 2.1, following the algorithm in Fig. 2.9B.

This complete program lets you see how various statements of BASIC described in this chapter are typically used in a program. The program will serve as a reference for many of your future programs.

The following BASIC statements are illustrated in this program and described in this chapter:

```
LET     PRINT     DATA
REM     STOP      IF
END     READ      GOTO
```

Another important part of this chapter is the explanation of the elementary loop structure, discussed in Section 3.8. The loop structure allows the program to process more than one customer record in this example.

The LET, PRINT, and IF statements can contain more complicated expressions than those discussed in this chapter. These more complex expressions are described in Chapter 4.

3.1 CONSTANTS AND VARIABLES

Many BASIC statements contain *constants* and *variables*. There are only two fundamental types of constant values that BASIC can manipulate: numbers and strings. In this section the form of these constants is explained. Then the naming of BASIC variables (which correspond to the boxes described in the previous chapter) is described.

Numeric Constants

decimal constant
integer constant

There are three types of numeric constants in BASIC: decimal, integer, and exponential. The number 0.25 in statement 330 of Fig. 3.1A is called a **decimal constant** because it has a decimal point. A number without a decimal point (such as 7 or 6000) is called an **integer constant**. Numeric constants cannot contain other symbols, like commas or dollar signs, normally used for readability. That is, 1,023,450 and $23.89 are illegal constants. A fraction like ½ is also not considered a constant.

☐ **FIGURE 3.1**   **Truck Rental Program**

```
100 REM --- DAILY TRUCK RENTAL REPORT ---
110 REM
120 PRINT "               CITY LINE TRUCK RENTAL"
130 PRINT "                    07/16/84"
140 PRINT
200 PRINT "TRUCK"
210 PRINT "LICENSE", "CUSTOMER", "DISTANCE";
212 PRINT TAB(40); "HOURS"; TAB(50); "CHARGE"
220 PRINT
240 READ L$,C$,M1,M2,T1,T2
250                             REM
300 IF L$ = "ZZZ" THEN 400
310    LET D = M2 - M1
320    LET H = T2 - T1
330    LET C = 0.25*D + 5.00*H
340    PRINT L$, C$, D; TAB(40);H; TAB(50); C
350                             REM
360    READ L$, C$, M1, M2, T1, T2
370 GOTO 300
400 PRINT " "
410 PRINT "DONE"
420 STOP
430                             REM
800 REM --- CONSTANT DATA FILE ---
810 DATA "BG123", "J. BREEN",    676.9, 711.4, 11.5,15
820 DATA "YRZ",    "J. GRANDAHL", 775.8, 785.7, 8.25,11
830 DATA "T5-398","E. LOVETT",   6000, 6224.6, 7, 19
900 DATA "ZZZ"," ",0,0,0,0
999 END
```

A. PROGRAM

```
            CITY LINE TRUCK RENTAL
                 07/16/84

TRUCK
LICENSE      CUSTOMER      DISTANCE    HOURS      CHARGE

BG123        J. BREEN      34.5        3.5        26.125
YRZ          J. GRANDAHL   9.899999    2.75       16.225
T5-398       E. LOVETT     224.6       12         116.15

DONE
```

B. OUTPUT

exponential constant

Another type of numeric constant that is occasionally used is an **exponential constant**. The general form and meaning of exponential constants are as follows:

BASIC Form   **Meaning in Arithmetic**

mEn $m * 10^n$

Here n must be an integer constant, but m can be any integer or decimal constant. The asterisk indicates multiplication. For example,

21.3E5   equals $21.3 * 10^5 = 2130000$

Table 3.1 gives examples of each type of numeric constant.

String Constants

string constant

A string of characters in quotation marks, such as "CUSTOMER" in statement 210 of Fig. 3.1A, is called a **string constant**. "DONE" and "ZZZ" are other examples of string constants in the program. Generally, a string constant may consist of up to 256 characters. String constants may also represent addresses, locations, descriptions, license plate numbers, and so on.

Variables

variable

A **variable** is a compartment in main computer memory where constants can be stored temporarily. The compartment in memory is called a variable because it can hold different values at different times. For example, at one time the variable may hold 23.45; later it may contain 101.115.

numeric variable
string variable

There are two fundamental types of variables in BASIC: numeric variables and string variables. A **numeric variable** can hold any numeric constant; a **string variable** can hold any string constant.

Variable Names

variable name

As a reference for the value in a variable, each **variable** has a **name** attached to it. In other words, a compartment in memory may look like this:

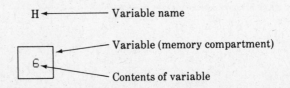

☐ **TABLE 3.1**   **BASIC Numeric Constants**

Type	Examples
Integer constants	34 −16 +758993 0 −47923 1
Decimal constants	34.67 −16.016 0.1 −0.8091 100.56
Exponential constants	21E5 2.54E−2 −4.6E+12 −67.9E−11

BASIC requires that names for numeric and string variables have different forms, as follows:

☐ **RULE**

numeric variable names

Numeric variable names consist of a letter or a letter followed by a digit.

Examples of numeric variables are

N   H1   S   Z8

☐ **RULE**

string variable names

String variable names consist of a letter followed by a dollar sign or a letter followed by a digit and then a dollar sign.

Examples of string variables are

N\$ A\$ F1\$

Numeric and string variables are used in statements 240, 340, and other statements in Fig. 3.1A.

String and numeric variable names should reflect as much as possible the kind of value that will be assigned to it. For example, for the program in Fig. 3.1A we used the following names:

Variable	Description	Type
L\$	License number	String
C\$	Customer name	String
M1	Starting mileage	Numeric
M2	Ending mileage	Numeric
D	Distance	Numeric
T1	Starting time	Numeric
T2	Ending time	Numeric
H	Hours	Numeric
C	Charge	Numeric

The rule for naming variables is one major limitation of BASIC. In large programs with many variables, names like

    C   H   T   S1

mean very little and can be confusing. Therefore many computers have extended the naming of variables in the following way:

EXTENDED RULE

[Applies to Microsoft (TRS-80 and IBM PC) and DEC BASIC-PLUS.] Numeric and string variable names may consist of any number of characters. However, only the first 31 characters are significant.
Examples of the extended rule are

AVERAGE   LENGTH   ADDRESS$ PRICE   PROFIT   CHARGE

In Apple BASIC only the first two characters are significant.

Throughout this book to emphasize that variables are in the computer, we will show variables like this, on a memory chip:

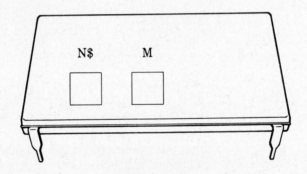

Memory Chip

3.2 THE LET STATEMENT

LET statement
assignment statement

One way to put a value into a variable is to use the **LET statement.** This statement is called the **assignment statement.** Remember from the previous chapter that a LET statement like

LET A = 34   is equivalent to   A ← 34

in our symbolic language. The value 34 is assigned to variable (box) A. In BASIC the backarrow is replaced with the equal sign.

The short program and memory chip below illustrate the action of the LET statement:

```
10   LET R$ = "KITCHEN"
20   LET L = 20
30   LET W = 9
40   LET A = L * W
```

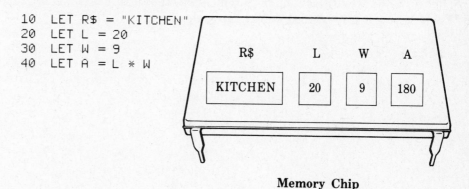

Memory Chip

Notice that in statement 10 a string constant is assigned to a string variable. In statement 20 a numeric constant is assigned to a numeric variable. String constants cannot be assigned to numeric variables and vice versa.

Statement 40 illustrates the use of a simple arithmetic expression in a LET statement. Here the computer will look for the current values in variables L and W, multiply the values, and assign the result to variable A. In effect, the BASIC processor is tracing the program in the same way we traced symbolic algorithms in the previous chapter. The values assigned to the variables during the execution of the program are illustrated in the memory chip.

In a LET statement only one variable may be on the left-hand side of the equal sign. The right-hand side can be any arithmetic or string expression. Arithmetic and string expressions will be discussed in detail in the next chapter.

In the LET statement the word LET is optional. So statements 10 and 20 above can be written as

```
10   R$ = "KITCHEN"
20   L = 20
```

In the program of Fig. 3.1A LET statements are used in lines 310, 320, and 330.

Recall from Chapter 2 that statement numbers are used to identify statements so that you can make changes to specific statements. Be sure to leave gaps in your statement numbers so that you can insert statements later, if necessary. Statement numbers are also used by the computer to control the execution sequence of the statements. When a program is RUN, the computer finds the lowest-numbered statement and executes statements in increasing sequence unless directed otherwise.

Statement numbers must be integers. The largest statement number is usually 32766 or 65535. Check your system for the details. If you enter statements at the terminal out of sequence, the BASIC processor will arrange them correctly inside the system.

EXERCISES

3.1. Show how the following sequences of LET statements change the values in the variables.

a)
```
100   LET A = 3
110   LET B = 7
120   LET C = 5
130   LET V = (A + B + C)/3
```

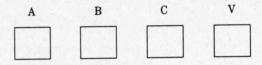

A   B   C   V

b)
```
100   LET R = 6.0
110   LET H = 45
120   LET W = R * 40 + 1.5 * R * (H - 40)
```

R   H   W

c)
```
100   LET A = 17.6
110   LET B = 43
120   LET A = B
130   LET B = A
```

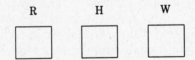

A   B

3.2. What, if anything, is wrong with the following LET statements?

a)
```
100   LET A = A + 1
```
b)
```
123   LET Q + Z = U
```
c)
```
156   LET D5 = Z45
```
d)
```
231   LET AB = A * B
```
e)
```
342   LET S = $3.45 + V
```
f)
```
456   LET B = 2X + X2
```

3.3 THE REM STATEMENT

REM statement

REM is an abbreviation for REMark. A **REM statement** contains any remark that the programmer might want at that point in the program. Examples of common uses of REM statements are given in the following list:

Use	Example
To title the program	```100 REM --- ACME PAYROLL PROGRAM```
For administrative information	```110 REM --- REVISION 1.2 02/03/84```
To explain the role of variables	```120 REM ROLE OF VARIABLES:```
	```130 REM H - HOURS```
	```140 REM N$ - NAME```
To explain an action	```230 REM - - - SUM THE COST```
	```240 LET S = S + C```

3.4 THE END STATEMENT

END statement

Every program must have exactly one END statement. The **END statement** informs the BASIC processor that there are no more statements in the program.

The END statement should be the highest-numbered statement in your program. Do not accidentally add statements after the END statement; the computer will ignore them. Notice that END statement for the program in Fig. 3.1A is in line 999.

3.5 THE PRINT STATEMENT

PRINT statement

The **PRINT statement** tells the computer to display or print information on the output device, usually a video screen or a printer. There are a number of ways that a PRINT statement can be written. They are discussed one at a time in the following subsections.

Simple PRINT Statements

The simplest form of the PRINT statement is the word PRINT followed by a constant (string or numeric, but usually a string) or a variable. This form is illustrated in statements 300 through 350 in the following program. The resulting output is shown on a video screen (p. 52); the memory chip shows the current contents of the variables.

```
100   REM   ROLE OF VARIABLES
110   REM     D$ - DAY OF WEEK
120   REM     P - PAYMENTS
130   REM     R - RECEIPTS
140   REM     G - GROSS PROFITS
150                    REM
200   LET D$ = "MONDAY"
210   LET R = 1250
220   LET P = 920
230   LET G = R - P
```

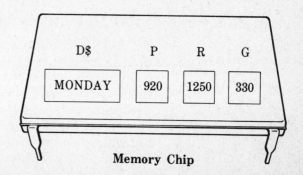

Memory Chip

```
240                          REM
300   PRINT "DAY OF WEEK:"
310   PRINT D$
320   PRINT " "
340   PRINT "GROSS PROFITS"
350   PRINT G
360                          REM
999   END
```

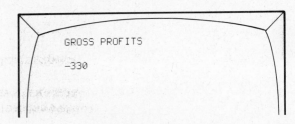

```
DAY OF WEEK:
MONDAY

GROSS PROFITS
 330
```

Notice from the video display for statements 300, 320, and 340 that when PRINT is followed by a string constant, the constant is printed exactly as it appears. Notice the space character in line 320. This PRINT statement prints a blank line.

When PRINT is followed by a variable (statements 310 and 350), the value in the variable is printed.

When a numeric value is to be printed (line 350), a space is left for the sign. If the value is positive, the sign is not printed, as in the video display above. For a negative value the minus sign is printed. For example, if gross profit were negative, then the output would look like this:

```
GROSS PROFITS

 -330
```

In the program in Fig. 3.1A simple PRINT statements are used in lines 120, 130, 400, and 410.

Print Zones and PRINT Statements with Commas

The use of punctuation in the PRINT statement causes values to be printed at various places across the screen or page, not just on the left-hand margin, as illustrated for the program in the previous subsection. But before we can discuss punctuation in PRINT statements, we have to consider a unique feature—print zones—of the BASIC processor.

print zones

The BASIC processor considers the screen and printed page to be divided into **print zones,** as illustrated in Fig. 3.2. For example, if a screen can hold 80 characters on a line, as it can in the situation illus-

□ FIGURE 3.2   **Print Zones on Screen and Printer**

Zone 1	Zone 2	Zone 3	Zone 4	Zone 5
Columns				
1 ··· 16	17 ··· 32	33 ··· 48	49 ··· 64	65 ··· 80

trated in Fig. 3.2, then there are usually five zones, with each zone containing 16 characters. The screen width is one of the major differences of computers. The specifics for some popular computers are given in Table 3.2.

PRINT statements with commas

Now we can discuss print zones and **PRINT statements with commas.**

□   RULE

When an item (variable or constant) in a PRINT statement is followed by a comma, the next item is printed in the next zone.

□ TABLE 3.2   **Zone Specifications on Common Microcomputers**

Computer Model	Number of Characters in Horizontal Line	Number of Zones	Number of Characters in Zone
IBM PC	80	5	14 in zones 1–4 24 in zone 5
Apple	40	3	16 in zones 1 and 2 8 in zone 3
TRS–80 Model I and Model III	64	4	16
TRS–80 Color Computer	32	2	16
TRS–80 Model 4 and Microsoft	80	5	16

In the program in Fig. 3.1A the PRINT statement with commas is used in lines 210 and 340. Notice the corresponding output in Fig. 3.1B.

To see how the PRINT statement with commas works, study the following two programs and corresponding output. For these programs we assume that we have a three-zone screen.

```
100 PRINT "LENGTH","WIDTH","AREA"
110 LET L = 20
120 LET W = 8
130 LET A = L * W
140 PRINT L, W, A
999 END
```

Zone 1	Zone 2	Zone 3
LENGTH	WIDTH	AREA
20	8	160

```
100 LET L = 20
110 LET W = 8
120 LET A = L * W
130 PRINT "LENGTH =", L
140 PRINT "WIDTH  =", W
150 PRINT "AREA   =", A
999 END
```

Zone 1	Zone 2
LENGTH =	20
WIDTH =	8
AREA =	160

If there are more items separated by commas than there are zones, the computer will continue printing on the next line of the screen. For example, if your screen has three zones, then a statement like

```
100  PRINT "LENGTH", "WIDTH", "AREA", "PERIMETER"
```

will produce a screen like this:

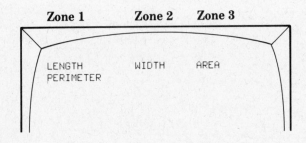

Zone 1	Zone 2	Zone 3
LENGTH	WIDTH	AREA
PERIMETER		

PRINT Statements with Semicolons

PRINT statements with semicolons　　The only other form of PRINT statement with punctuation is a **PRINT statement with semicolons.**

☐ **RULE**

A semicolon between two items in a PRINT statement instructs the computer to skip *no* spaces between the printing of the items.

The following program and output show the use of the PRINT statement with semicolons. In the printing of two numeric variables (statement 140 below), a space is always left for the sign, and a space is always printed immediately to the right of the number. Thus there are two spaces separating the 20 and 8 in the output of the following example.

```
100 PRINT "LENGTH";"WIDTH";"AREA"
110 LET L = 20
120 LET W = 8
130 LET A = L * W
140 PRINT L; W; A
999 END
```

```
LENGTHWIDTHAREA
 20  8  160
```

In the next example, notice that both commas and semicolons are included in statement 130. The semicolon causes the value of L to be printed immediately after the string "LENGTH =". The comma causes the string "WIDTH =" to be printed in the next zone.

```
100 LET L = 20
110 LET W = 8
120 LET A = L * W
130 PRINT "LENGTH ="; L, "WIDTH ="; W
140 PRINT "AREA    ="; A
999 END
```

	Zone 1	Zone 2
	LENGTH = 20	WIDTH = 8
	AREA = 160	

PRINT Statements with TABs

You can use commas only to position items at the beginning of a print zone. To print items at other specific positions on the screen, you use the **TAB( ) function** in the PRINT statement. The TAB( ) function positions the print head to the particular column that is specified in the parentheses. For example, TAB(4) in the statements

TAB( ) function

```
10  PRINT TAB(4);"HI"    or    10  PRINT TAB(4) "HI"
```

causes the computer to position the print head to column 4 so that the word HI begins at column 4. In effect, this statement says: Print HI, starting at column 4. The semicolon after the TAB is optional. We point out that some computers begin counting columns at 0, others at 1. Thus depending on the computer, the output looks like this:

DEC BASIC–PLUS
Microsoft BASIC
IBM PC BASIC
Apple II, IIe

TRS–80 Model I, Model III
TRS–80 Color Computer

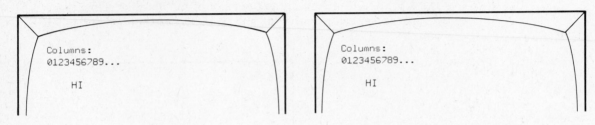

```
Columns:
0123456789...

     HI
```

```
Columns:
0123456789...

     HI
```

report-spacing chart

Suppose you want your report to look like the layout shown in Fig. 3.3A. The gridlike chart is called a **report-spacing chart.** The TAB statements that produce the desired lines are given in Fig. 3.3B. Statement 100 causes the computer to print "ACME STORES" starting at column 15. Statement 202 causes the computer to print "PRICE" starting at column 23 and "COST" starting at column 31.

Note: When a PRINT statement ends with a comma or semicolon (statement 200 in Fig. 3.3B and statement 210 in Fig. 3.1A), the print head remains on the same line and continues printing with the next PRINT statement in the program.

PRINTing to Screen or Printer

Reports and other output are automatically directed to the video display screen. But the output can also be directed to an attached printer. The procedure for this task depends, as usual, on the computer.

For IBM PC, TRS–80, and Microsoft BASIC, you direct the output to the printer by using the

```
LPRINT
```

statement. LPRINT stands for line printer.

For Apple II and IIe, you direct the output to the printer by including the statement

```
PR #1
```

in your program. This statement assumes that the printer interface card is in slot 1. All subsequent PRINT statements direct the output

☐ FIGURE 3.3   Report-Spacing Chart and Appropriate TABs

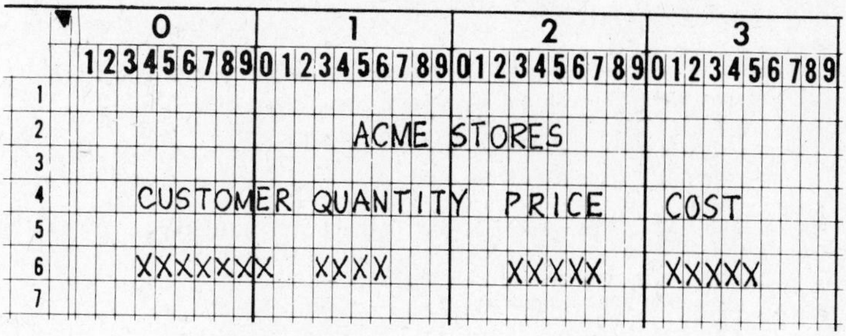

A. REPORT-SPACING CHART

```
100 PRINT TAB(15) "ACME STORES"

200 PRINT TAB(4) "CUSTOMER"; TAB(13) "QUANTITY";
202 PRINT TAB(23) "PRICE"; TAB(31) "COST"

400 PRINT TAB(4) N$; TAB(13) Q; TAB(23) P; TAB(31) C
```

B. TAB STATEMENTS

to the printer. To return output to the screen, include in your program the statement

    PR #0

EXERCISES

3.3. What will the following program print? Show how the values of the variables change.

```
100    PRINT "ATTEMPTED"
110    PRINT "PASSES", "COMPLETIONS", "PERCENT"
200    LET A = 16
210    LET C =  4
220    LET P = C/A * 100
230    PRINT A, C, P; "%"
999    END
```

3.4. The following program does not do what is intended. Fix the mistake.

```
100    PRINT "3 NUMBERS", "AVERAGE"
110    LET X = 7
120    LET Y = 14
130    LET Z = 9
300    LET A = X + Y + Z/3
310    PRINT X; Y; Z, A
999    END
```

3.5. What will the following programs print?

a)
```
100   PRINT "LENGTH"; "WIDTH"; "AREA"
110   PRINT "LENGTH"; " "; "WIDTH"; " "; "AREA"
999   END
```

b)
```
100   PRINT "GUARANTEED UNTIL IT", "BREAKS."
110   PRINT "GUARANTEED UNTIL IT",
120   PRINT "BREAKS."
999   END
```

3.6. What will the following program print? Show how the values of the variables change.
```
100   PRINT " ", "-A-", "-B-"
110   LET A = 35
120   LET B = 8
130   PRINT " ", A, B
140   PRINT "SWITCH",
150   LET H = A
160   LET A = B
170   LET B = H
180   PRINT A, B
999   END
```

3.7. Run the following two programs on your computer. They illustrate numbers printed in exponential notation.

a)
```
100   PRINT "A", "B", "A * B"
110   LET A = 7479
120   LET B = 9217
130   LET C = A * B
140   PRINT A, B, C
999   END
```

b)
```
100   LET Y = 0.0007845
110   PRINT Y
999   END
```

3.6 THE STOP STATEMENT

STOP statement

The **STOP statement** is almost self-explanatory. It instructs the computer to stop at that statement. Consider the following program and output:

```
10   LET R$ = "KITCHEN"
20   LET L = 20
30   LET W = 9
40   STOP
50   LET A = L * W
60   PRINT R$; " AREA IS";A
70   STOP
80   END
```

```
BREAK AT 40
CONT
KITCHEN AREA IS 180
BREAK AT 70
```

Notice in the video display that accompanies the program that the computer will inform us at which statement it has stopped. To resume executing statements in the program, we type CONT for continue. In the program in Fig. 3.1A the STOP is used in line 420.

3.7 THE READ AND DATA STATEMENTS

In the examples shown so far the LET statement has been used to assign values to variables. Another way to assign values to variables is to use READ statements in conjunction with DATA statements.

☐ RULE

READ statement
DATA statements

Each time the computer executes a **READ statement**, it assigns the next group of constants found in the **DATA statements** to successive variables in the READ statement.

This rule is illustrated by the program in Fig. 3.4A and the accompanying output and memory chip (Figs. 3.4B and 3.4C). The DATA statements (lines 810 through 830) provide a pool of data that is used by the READ statements (lines 300, 400, and 500). The constants in the DATA statements are sequenced; that is, there is a first value, BATH; a second value, 8; a fifth value, 14, and so on. Notice that each constant is separated by a comma in the DATA statements.

In the program of Fig. 3.4A, when the computer executes statement 300,

```
READ R$, W, L
```

the computer finds the next values in the data pool and assigns them to the variables in the READ statement. Thus the first value in the data pool, BATH, is assigned to the first variable, R$. The next value in the data pool, 8, is assigned to the next variable W. And so on.

When the computer executes another READ statement, it remembers the last value used in the DATA statements and will use the next value. Thus in the program of Fig. 3.4A, when the computer executes statement 400,

```
READ R$, W, L
```

the constant LIVING is assigned to variable R$, and so on.

The constants read by a READ statement can be in two or more successive DATA statements. Or the constants may all be in one DATA

☐ **FIGURE 3.4**   · **Use of READ and DATA Statements**

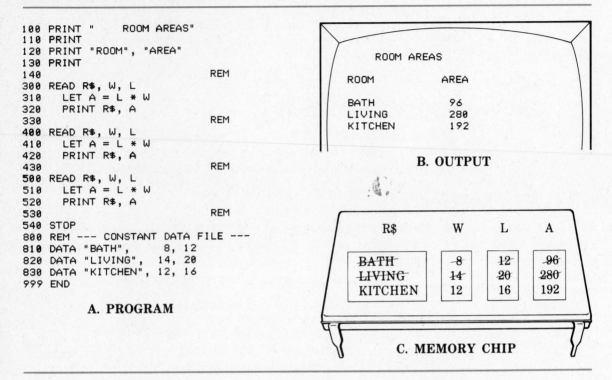

```
100 PRINT "    ROOM AREAS"
110 PRINT
120 PRINT "ROOM", "AREA"
130 PRINT
140                        REM
300 READ R$, W, L
310   LET A = L * W
320   PRINT R$, A
330                        REM
400 READ R$, W, L
410   LET A = L * W
420   PRINT R$, A
430                        REM
500 READ R$, W, L
510   LET A = L * W
520   PRINT R$, A
530                        REM
540 STOP
800 REM --- CONSTANT DATA FILE ---
810 DATA "BATH",      8, 12
820 DATA "LIVING",   14, 20
830 DATA "KITCHEN",  12, 16
999 END
```

A. PROGRAM

B. OUTPUT

C. MEMORY CHIP

statement. For example, in the program of Fig. 3.4A the data in the DATA statements could have been written like this:

```
810   DATA "BATH", 8
820   DATA 12, "LIVING", 14, 20, "KITCHEN", 12
830   DATA 16
```

EXERCISES

3.8. Suppose you had four rooms for which you had to calculate the areas. How would you modify the "ROOM AREAS" program of Fig. 3.4A to do this calculation?

3.9. What will the following program print? Show how the values of the variables change.

a)
```
200   READ A, B
210   READ C
220   READ D, E, A
230   READ E
```

```
240    PRINT A; B, C; D, E
800    DATA 4, 7, 32
805    DATA 16, 21
810    DATA 8, 9, 48, 123
999    END
```

A	B	C	D	E
☐	☐	☐	☐	☐

b) Instead of using the data statements in the program in part (a), use the statements below. What will the computer do?

```
800    DATA 15, 32
805    DATA 45, -88
810    DATA 17, 9
```

3.8 PROCESSING MORE THAN ONE DATA RECORD

Recall the terminology used in the discussion of data files in Chapter 2. The constants in all the DATA statements of a program can be thought of as a data file. If the group of values in each DATA statement has the same structure, then each group can be thought of as a record in the file. The structure of the records processed by the program in Fig. 3.4A is

room name, width, length

Suppose we were to expand the program in Fig. 3.4A to calculate the areas of ten rooms (ten records in the file). Then the program would have to have ten groups of exactly the same statements that READ, calculate, and PRINT (see, for example, lines 300–320 and 400–420 of Fig. 3.4A), a total of more than 50 statements.

However, a loop structure like that discussed in Section 2.3 (especially in Fig. 2.9) could be used to simplify the processing of these records with similar structures. Figure 3.5A illustrates the loop structure of the algorithm that can be used; the corresponding program is shown in Fig. 3.5B.

The loop structure in the flowchart is straightforward. Trace it to be sure you understand it.

In this example we want to exit from the loop after the areas of all rooms have been calculated, that is, when all the records in the file have been processed. A common way of recognizing the end of a data file is to place a dummy trailing record at the end of the file. (This record is also called a *sentinel record*.) A **dummy trailing record** is a record with the same structure as the other records in the file, but one

dummy trailing record

□ FIGURE 3.5   Algorithm and Program for Calculating Area of Ten Rooms

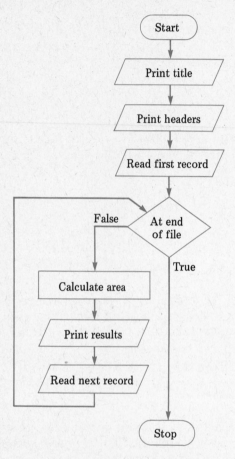

A. FLOWCHART (ALGORITHM)

```
100 PRINT "    ROOM AREAS"
110 PRINT
120 PRINT "ROOM", "AREA"
130 PRINT
140                         REM
200 READ R$, W, L
210                         REM
300 IF R$ = "ZZZ" THEN 400
310    LET A = L * W
320    PRINT R$, A
330                         REM
340    READ R$, W, L
350 GOTO 300
360                         REM
400 PRINT
410 PRINT   "DONE"
420 STOP
800 REM --- CONSTANT DATA FILE ---
810 DATA "BATH",    8, 12
820 DATA "LIVING",  14, 20
830 DATA "KITCHEN", 12, 16
900 DATA "ZZZ", 0,0
999 END
```

B. PROGRAM

---

field has a value that cannot realistically exist. In our example the dummy trailing record is

```
"ZZZ", 0, 0
```

(line 900 of Fig. 3.5B). Since there is no real room with the name "ZZZ", the computer looks for that constant in the file. When "ZZZ" is found, the end of the file has been reached (see line 300).

The loop structure in the program of Fig. 3.5B is created with the IF-THEN statement in line 300 and the GOTO statement in line 350. In line 300 the expression

```
R$ = "ZZZ"
```

condition

is called a **condition;** it can have a value of true or false depending on the current value in variable R$. If R$ contains the constant "ZZZ", then the condition is true. In this event the computer goes to the statement number following the THEN, line 400 in Fig. 3.5B. Any other value in R$ causes the condition to be false, and the computer goes to the next highest line number after 300. Then the statements within the loop are executed. Eventually, the GOTO statement in line 350 causes the computer to go back to the IF statement in line 300.

This flow of statement execution is summarized as follows:

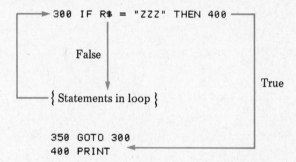

The IF statement is discussed in detail in Chapter 6. But this brief discussion should be sufficient to show you how to create a loop for processing any number of records.

Note: If the trailing record is not included in the file or if the condition never becomes true, then the computer will try to read data that is not there. An error message such as

```
OUT OF DATA IN LINE 340
```

will be printed. Line number 340 is the number of the READ statement in the program (Fig. 3.5B) that is trying to read the nonexistent data.

EXERCISES

3.10. What is wrong with the following loop structure?
```
300   READ R$, W, L
310     IF R$ = "ZZZ" THEN 400
320     LET A = L * W
330     PRINT R$, A
340   GOTO 300
400   PRINT
410   PRINT "DONE"
420   STOP
810   DATA "BATH", 8, 12
820   DATA "LIVING", 14, 20
830   DATA "KITCHEN", 12, 16
999   DATA "ZZZ", 0, 0
```

trace a program   **3.11.** Trace the following program. To **trace a program,** you execute each statement in the program as the computer would, showing how the values in the variables change and showing the printed results. Fix any errors that may exist. If you don't find any errors, enter the program into your computer and run it.

```
100   PRINT "EMPLOYEE NUMBER", "RATE", "HOURS",  "WAGE"
200   READ N, R, H
300   IF N = 0 THEN 400
310     LET W = R * H
320     PRINT N, R, H, W
330     READ N, R, H
340   GOTO 300
400   STOP
800   DATA 1005, 8.00, 30
810   DATA 1008, 10.00, 40
820   DATA 1012, 7.50, 20
900   DATA 0
```

3.12. Modify the program in Exercise 3.11 so that it prints the items where indicated on the following report-spacing chart.

3.13. Each of the following programs is supposed to determine the miles per hour. Find and correct the errors in each program.

```
a)  100   PRINT "MILES", "HOURS", "MPH"
    110   READ M, H, S
    120   IF M = 0 THEN 200
    130     LET S = M/H
    140     PRINT M, H, S
    150     READ M, H, S
    160   GOTO 120
    200   STOP
    800   DATA 300, 6, 425, 10
    810   DATA 385, 7, 300, 1/2
    999   END
b)  100   PRINT "MILES", "HOURS", "MPH"
    110   READ X, Y
    120   IF X = 0 THEN 200
```

```
130    LET S = X/Y
140    PRINT X, Y
150    READ X, Y
160   GOTO 120
200   STOP
800   DATA 6, 300
810   DATA 10, 425
820   DATA 7, 385
999   END
```

3.9 SUMMARY

The sample program at the beginning of this chapter (Fig. 3.1A) illustrates the nine statements presented in this chapter. The following comments discuss some details in the program and summarize the material covered in the chapter. The video display in Fig. 3.1B shows the output that results from the program.

In reading the following list, refer to Figs. 3.1A and 3.1B:

- Lines 100, 800: The REMark statement gives us a way to insert, within the program, remarks helpful to us and others who read the program.
- Line 140: This PRINT statement prints a space on the next line. It allows us to print a space between the title and headers (see the output).

dangling semicolon

- Line 210: Notice the **dangling semicolon** at the end of the line; it causes the next printed matter to appear on the same line.
- Lines 250, 350, 430: These indented REMark statements separate groups of related statements so that the program listing is easier to read.
- Line 240: Notice that the variable names indicate the kind of values they hold; that is, L$ represents license, C$ represents customer, and so on.
- Lines 310 through 360: Statements are usually indented to emphasize related groups of statements.
- Lines 212, 340: The TABs are used so that the hours and charge are printed closer to the other items.
- Lines 810 through 900: I prefer to put the DATA statements near the end of the program, isolated from the logic statements.
- Output: Notice that the numbers are not aligned on the right or aligned by the decimal point, making them hard to read. Integers can easily be aligned, as illustrated in Chapter 4, Section 4.4. Decimal numbers can be aligned by employing the PRINT USING statement (Appendix A) or a special routine presented in Exercise 4.23.

EXERCISES

3.14. In the sample program shown in Fig. 3.1A, suppose the following changes are made. Describe what will happen in terms of the printed report.

a) 370   GOTO 240
b) 370   GOTO 310
c) 360   GOTO 300
   370   READ L$, C$, M1, M2, T1, T2
d) 420   END

3.15. Trace the following program.

```
120 REM --- ASSUME GAS PRICE IS $1.25
130     LET P = 1.25
140 REM
150 PRINT " ","SUMMER TRIPS"
160 PRINT " "," GAS COSTS"
170 PRINT " "
200 PRINT "NAME"; TAB(10);"MPG",
202  PRINT "DISTANCE", "GAS COST"
210 PRINT " "
220                         REM
230 READ N$, M, D
240                         REM
300 IF N$ = "ZZZ" THEN 400
310    LET G = D/M
320    LET C = P * G
330    PRINT N$; TAB(10); M, D, C
340                         REM
350    READ N$, M, D
360 GOTO 300
370                         REM
400 PRINT " "
410 PRINT "DONE"
420 STOP
430                         REM
800 REM --- CONSTANT DATA FILE ---
810 DATA "TOM",   23, 2400
820 DATA "PETE",  45, 5000
830 DATA "KAREN", 30, 15000
840 DATA "KEN",   70, 4900
900 DATA "ZZZ",    0,  0
999 END
```

3.16. Modify the program in Exercise 3.15 so that the output looks like that shown below:

				GAS	FOOD	TOTAL
		SUMMER TRIP COST				
NAME	MPG	DISTANCE	DAYS	COST	COST	COST
TOM	23	2400	7	XXX	XXX	XXX
XXXXX	XX	XXXX	XX	XXX	XXX	XXX

To do this exercise, let the trip record also include the number of days each person expects the trip to take. So each record now has the following form:

name, mpg, distance, length in days

Assume it will cost $25 for food each day.

3.17. Trace the following program.

```
100 PRINT "                ACME STORES"
110 PRINT " "
120 PRINT "CUSTOMER"; TAB(11);"QUANTITY";
122 PRINT TAB(21);"PRICE";TAB(30);"COST"
130 PRINT "========"; TAB(11);"========";
132 PRINT TAB(21);"=====";TAB(30);"===="
200 READ N$, Q, P
210                     REM
300 IF N$ = "ZZZ" THEN 500
310    LET C = Q * P
320    PRINT N$; TAB(11); Q; TAB(21); P; TAB(30); C
330                     REM
340    READ N$, Q, P
350 GOTO 300
360                     REM
500 PRINT " "
510 PRINT "DONE PROCESSING"
600 STOP
800 DATA "JOE",    34, 2.34
810 DATA "KAREN", 10,   .53
820 DATA "JILL",   8,  1.23
830 DATA "ZZZ",    0,     0
999 END
```

Expressions and Report Forms

INTRODUCTION TO CHAPTER 4

The previous chapter described the structure of simple programs that process more than one record. To arrive at this point as quickly as possible, we had to curtail our presentation of arithmetic expressions. Recall that *arithmetic expressions*, like L * W, are used in LET statements such as

```
230  LET A = L * W
```

In this chapter expressions are discussed in detail. You will then use expressions to write programs that generate some of the report forms illustrated in Section 4.3.

Expressions in BASIC consist of combinations of constants (or values), variables, operations, and functions. When an expression is evaluated, it will result in a specific value—either a numeric value or a string value. Thus expressions can be classified by the values they yield. Numeric expressions yield numeric values; string expressions yield string values. A good understanding of expressions is important because they are used in LET, PRINT, and FOR statements, and they are used to form conditions in the IF statement.

While numeric expressions (consisting of numeric operations and functions) have been used for centuries, string expressions and functions have only recently become useful with the advent of computers in processing nonnumeric data. In this chapter the one string operation, concatenation, and a number of string functions are discussed. They will be more useful at a later time. We introduce them in this chapter so that you can get acquainted with them and so that Apple users can print integers right-justified.

4.1 NUMERIC EXPRESSIONS

In this section numeric operations and expressions and the order in which operations are carried out are explained. Numeric expressions may include numeric functions, which are explained in the next section.

Operations and Expressions

arithmetic operations
The five **arithmetic operations** are specified by using the symbols indicated in Table 4.1.

expression
An **expression** is a sequence of constants and variables separated by arithmetic operators. For example, $A + 2/C - Q \uparrow 3$ is an arithmetic expression.

Parentheses may also be used in arithmetic expressions. Consider the expression A * (2 + B). The parentheses have the usual meaning;

☐ **TABLE 4.1**   **Arithmetic Operations**

Operation	BASIC Symbol	Example	Comments
Addition	+	A + B	
Subtraction	−	A − B	
Multiplication	*	A * B	Do not write AB
Division	/	A/B	Do not write A ÷ B
Exponentiation	↑ or ^ or **	A ↑ B	$2 \uparrow 3$ means $2^3 = 2 * 2 * 2 = 8$ $4 \uparrow 0.5$ means $\sqrt{4} = 2$

the 2 and the contents of B are added, and then this sum is multiplied by the contents of variable A.

Parentheses are, in fact, more important in writing expressions in BASIC than in standard mathematics simply because expressions must be typed on one line. For example, the expression

$$\frac{a + b}{c}$$

must be written in BASIC as (A + B)/C.

Table 4.2 shows how some algebraic expressions are written in BASIC.

Table 4.3 shows how the illegal expressions in BASIC are corrected.

☐ **TABLE 4.2**   **Algebraic Expressions in BASIC**

Algebraic Expressions	Algebraic Expressions Written in BASIC	Comments
$7ab$	7 * A * B	Multiplication must be indicated by the *
$\dfrac{a + b + c}{3}$	(A + B + C)/3	The parentheses must be used in this case
$a + \dfrac{b}{c}$	A + B/C	
$2(a + b)$	2 * (A + B)	Do not write 2(A + B)
$d(1 + r)^y$	D * (1 + R) ↑ Y	
$\sqrt{a + b}$	(A + B) ↑ 0.5	

☐ **TABLE 4.3**   **Correcting Illegal Expressions**

Illegal Expression	Corrected	Comments
2B + 7	2 * B + 7	Multiplication must be indicated by the *
A * −6	A * (−6)	
(A + B)/C + D)	(A + B)/(C + D)	Parentheses must be used in pairs

Order of Operations

Evaluate the expressions below. Try them now.

(a) $3 + 4 * 2 = ?$ (d) $8/4/2 = ?$
(b) $3 + 4 * 2 \uparrow 3 = ?$ (e) $8/4 + 6 * 2 = ?$
(c) $8/2 * 4 - 2 = ?$ (f) $(8/4 + 6) * 2 = ?$

Now compare your answers with the correct answers given at the bottom of the page. If your answers do not agree with the answers below, an obvious problem in communication exists.

To avoid any misunderstandings, everyone—and all computers, too—should agree on the rules for evaluating arithmetic expressions. The accepted rules for evaluating expressions—that is, the rules specifying the order in which the arithmetic operations are done—are given in Table 4.4.

☐ **TABLE 4.4**   **Rules for Evaluating Expressions**

Rules	Examples Illustrating Rules
1. If an expression contains parentheses, perform the operations in the parentheses first, according to the rules in parts 2 and 3 below	$(8/4 + 6) * 2 = (2 + 6) * 2$ $= 8 * 2 = 16$
2. First, do all $\uparrow$ Second, do all * and / Third, do all + and −	$8/2 + 6 * 2 \uparrow 3 - 1$ $= 8/2 + 6 * 8 - 1$ $= 4 + 48 - 1$ $= 52 - 1 = 51$
3. If two "adjacent" operations have the same priority, perform the operations from left to right. (Some BASIC systems evaluate adjacent $\uparrow$ from left to right. Others evaluate from right to left. How does your system work?)	$8/4 * 2 = 2 * 2 = 4$ Depending on the system, $2 \uparrow 3 \uparrow 2$ can be evaluated as $(2 \uparrow 3) \uparrow 2 = 64$ or $2 \uparrow (3 \uparrow 2) = 512$

Answers: (a) 11, (b) 35, (c) 14, (d) 1, (e) 14, (f) 16

Usually, the expressions encountered in the examples and exercises in this book are very simple. If you can complete the exercises that follow, you should have no trouble with expressions found elsewhere in the book.

EXERCISES

4.1. Write the following algebraic expressions as BASIC expressions.

a) $\dfrac{a}{b} + 5$

e) a^{2b}

b) $\dfrac{a+b}{c}$

f) $(z+8)^{1/2}$

c) $\dfrac{b}{8+h}$

g) $b\left(1 + \dfrac{r}{n}\right)^{ny}$

d) $\dfrac{y+5}{h-e}$

h) $\dfrac{1}{1 - \dfrac{1}{a+b}}$

4.2. Variable A contains 3, variable B contains 2, and variable C contains −2. What are the values of the following expressions?

```
    A          B          C
  ┌─────┐   ┌─────┐   ┌─────┐
  │  3  │   │  2  │   │ -2  │
  └─────┘   └─────┘   └─────┘
```

a) A + B/2   d) 16/(A + B)   g) (A + 1)/B * C − 2
b) (A + B)/2   e) A/(B * 2) − C   h) A ↑ B * C
c) 16/A + B   f) A * 4/C + 2.9E + 2

4.2 NUMERIC FUNCTIONS

From a previous mathematics course you are probably familiar with the mathematical functions square root and absolute value. For example,

$$\sqrt{16} = 4 \qquad |8 - 17| = 9$$

The BASIC language processor allows us to use these and other functions in any numeric expression. But instead of using the familiar mathematical symbols for the functions, BASIC uses three-letter names. In this section we will look at some common numeric functions and a special function, the INT function.

Some Common Numeric Functions

numeric functions   Some common **numeric functions** are listed in Table 4.5. A complete list of numeric functions is given in Appendix C.

☐ **TABLE 4.5**   **Some Common Numeric Functions in BASIC**

Name	Description	Example
ABS(X)	Absolute value	ABS(6 − 10.3) is 4.3
SQR(X)	Square root	SQR(16) is 4
INT(X)	The greatest integer that is less than or equal to X	INT(3.45) is 3 INT(−23.45) is −24 INT(67) is 67
EXP(X)	Exponential	EXP(1) is 2.71828
LOG(X)	Logarithm ln(X)	LOG(5) is 1.6094379
RND(X)	Random number	See Chapter 11

function argument

The item in parentheses following the three-letter name of the function can be any numeric constant, variable, or expression. The expression is called the **function argument**. The argument may also contain function references, such as in

```
LET Y = SQR(3 * ABS(X − 2) + 3)
```

The BASIC processor evaluates the argument expression and then determines the function value.

In BASIC, numeric functions can be used in several ways in writing numeric expressions. Some examples of their use are given next.

☐ **EXAMPLE**

Suppose A and B are the sides of a rectangle. Then the length of the hypotenuse H is evaluated by

```
LET H = SQR(A * A + B * B)
```

Suppose that D dollars are deposited in a bank. The annual interest rate is R, and it is compounded continuously. The amount A of money in the bank after Y years is given by

```
LET A = D * EXP(R * Y)
```

Suppose one sailboat is 23 feet long and another is 45 feet long. Then the difference in length between the two boats is evaluated by the statement

```
LET D = ABS(23 − 45)
```

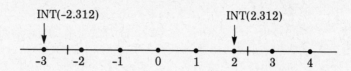

The INT Function

Of the functions listed in Table 4.5, the INT function is probably the most unfamiliar. The value of INT(X) is the greatest integer that is less than or equal to X.

To understand this definition, consider the number line and the examples shown in Fig. 4.1. From the figure and the definition we see that the greatest integer that is less than or equal to 2.312 is 2. The greatest integer that is less than or equal to −2.312 is −3. For positive numbers INT(X) is simply the integer part of the number. For negative numbers INT(X) is one less than the integer part of the number, which is the greatest integer less than the number.

The INT function is used, for example, when you may not need complete accuracy in your results or when you want your results to be clear and readable. For instance, the following output on the right is just as useful as the output on the left. But it is also more readable.

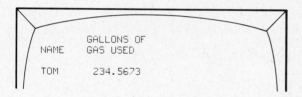
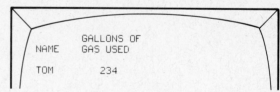

The INT function can also be used to round a value to any desired number of places. For instance,

```
LET X = INT(X + 0.5)
```

rounds a result to the nearest integer. Thus we might have

X	X + 0.5	INT(X + 0.5)
234.5673	235.0673	235

To round the value in X to the nearest penny, you can use the formula

```
LET X = INT(100 * X + 0.5)/100
```

This formula, INT(100 * X + 0.5)/100, can be included in the program in Fig. 3.1A. The modified program lines (see especially line 335) are as follows:

```
300    IF L$ = "ZZZ" THEN 400
310      LET D = M2 - M1
320      LET H = T2 - T1
330      LET C = 0.25 * D + 5.00 * H
335      LET C = INT(100 * C + 0.5)/100
340      PRINT L$, C$, D; TAB(40); H; TAB(50); C
350                                              REM
360      READ L$, C$, M1, M2, T1, T2
370    GOTO 300
```

Then notice the charges in the resulting output:

```
                    CITY LINE TRUCK RENTAL
                         07/16/84

    TRUCK
    LICENSE          CUSTOMER        DISTANCE    HOURS      CHARGE

    BG123            J.  BREEN       34.5        3.5        26.13
    YRZ              J.  GRANDAHL    9.899999    2.75       16.23
    T5-398           E.  LOVETT      224.6       12         116.15

    DONE
```

Some typical uses of the INT function are given in Table 4.6.

EXERCISES

4.3. Evaluate the following expressions:
  a) `INT(ABS(-2.34))`
  b) `ABS(INT(-2.34))`
  c) `SQR(ABS(-16))`

4.4. What will the following program print?
```
100    LET A = 2476.937
110    LET B = A - INT(A)
120    LET C = INT(A + 0.5)
130    LET D = INT(10 * A + 0.5)/10
140    LET E = INT(A/10) - 100 * INT(A/1000)
150    PRINT A, B, C, D, E
999    END
```

4.3 REPORT FORMS

Before reading this section, you might want to review the terminology used in discussing report forms in Chapter 2. This section presents several report forms. With what you have learned in Chapter 3 and the

☐ **TABLE 4.6**   **Common Uses of the INT Function**

Use	Formula	Z	X	Y
		Contents Of		
Round to the nearest integer	LET Z = INT(X + 0.5)	26	25.511	
Round to the nearest penny	LET Z = INT(100 * X + 0.5)/100	3.52	3.518	
Fractional part of X	LET Z = X − INT(X)	0.1416	3.1416	
Integer remainder when X is divided by Y	LET Z = X − Y * INT(X/Y)	4	14	5
		8	28	10

first two sections of this chapter, you should be able to write a program that generates any one of these reports or a similar report form of your own design.

How to Get Started

After you have selected a report form or designed a report form of your own, follow these four steps:

- *Step 1:* Use a report spacing chart to put the title, headers, and detail lines in the desired columns. If you are limited to 40 characters per line, you will have to modify the headers a bit.
- *Step 2:* Make sure you know how to calculate the results on paper.
- *Step 3:* Choose the names for the variables you will use.
- *Step 4:* Code the program.

☐ EXAMPLE

A newsvendor sells newspapers for \$0.25 each. He buys them whole-sale for \$0.10 each and can return unsold newspapers at the end of the day to his distributor for \$0.05 each. He has kept track of his sales each day for the last two months and wants to analyze his profit for each day.

 Step 1: The desired output on a report-spacing chart is shown in Fig. 4.2.

 Step 2: The number returned can easily be calculated as

Returned = bought − sold

The profit is

Profit = sold * 0.25 − bought * 0.10 + returned * 0.05

 Step 3: The variable names used (B represents the number

☐ **FIGURE 4.2**   **Output on a Report-Spacing Chart**

REPORT-SPACING CHART

bought, S the number sold, R the number returned, and P the profit) are circled on the report-spacing chart in Fig. 4.2.

Step 4: Some of the code for the program will look like this:

```
LET P = S * 0.25 - B * 0.10 + R * 0.05
PRINT B; TAB(13); S; TAB(23); R; TAB(37); P
```

EXERCISES

Select one of the following report forms and write a program to generate the report form. Use the steps outlined in the previous subsection to get started. The title and headers should be sufficient explanation for what is desired. In any event, do not begin writing your program before you know how to calculate the desired result.

4.5.   BATTING AVERAGES

NAME	AT BATS	HITS	AVERAGE
YAZ	526	156	XXXX
RICE	493	146	XXXX

4.6.   PAINTING COSTS OF ROOMS

ROOM SIZE LEN. WID. HT.			PAINT COST PER GALLON	COVERAGE OF GALLON	NO. GALLONS	TOTAL COST
20	15	10	15.99	300	XXX	XXX
60	26	20	12.95	250	XXX	XXX
.						
.						
.						

4.7.
MONEY SAVED IF QUIT SMOKING

SMOKER'S NAME	NO. PACKS PER DAY	COST PER PACK	AMT. SAVED PER WEEK	AMT. SAVED PER YEAR
JOE	1.5	.73	xxx	xxx
AL	.5	.80	xxx	xxx
.				
.				
.				

4.8.
COMPARISON OF REPAIR COSTS

OWNER	CAR MAKE MODEL	TIME OWNED (YR)	TOTAL COST OF REPAIRS	COST PER YEAR
KEN	BMW	4	650	xxx
BILL	VOLVO	13	800	xxx
DOUG	VW	8	200	xxx
.				
.				
.				

4.9.
COMPARISON OF SCHOOL COSTS

DISTRICT	NO. STUDENTS	NO. TEACHERS	NO. ADMINISTRATORS	BUDGET	$ PER STUDENT	$ PER ADMIN.
SHEPAUG	389	36	12	867567	xxx	xxx
REGION 8	978	50	42	197654	xxx	xxx
.						
.						
.						

4.10.
ROUND TRIP TIME AND COSTS

MPG	COST PER GALLON	ROUND TRIP DISTANCE	NO. TRIPS PER YEAR	MPH	COST OF GAS	TIME IN CAR
20	1.08	15	45	35	xxx	xxx
40	1.17	35	150	50	xxx	xxx
.						
.						
.						

4.11.
STUDENT AVERAGES

NAME	TEST 1	TEST 2	FINAL	AVERAGE
JIM	45	97	70	xxx
PETE	77	80	85	xxxx
.				
.				
.				

4.12.   BREAK-EVEN ANALYSIS

PRODUCT	FIXED COST (OVERHEAD, ETC.)	VARIABLE COST (MATERIAL & LABOR)	SELLING PRICE	NO. TO SELL TO BREAK EVEN
LTZ999	200000	7.50	15.99	xxx
L1011	75000	23.67	29.99	xxx
280Z	900000	5999.99	7899.00	xxx
.				
.				
.				

4.13.   CYCLE RANCH MOTOR CYCLES
                        ECONOMIC REORDER QUANTITY

CYCLE MODEL	DEMAND RATE PER WEEK	HOLDING COST: $ PER WEEK (INSURANCE, STORAGE, ETC.)	ORDER COST: FIXED $ PER ORDER (SHIPPING, ETC.)	NO. CYCLES TO ORDER TO MINIMIZE HOLDING AND ORDER COST
HONDA15	3	12.50	200	xxx
KAW1200	2	20.00	150	xxx
.				
.				
.				

4.14.   CONCRETE COSTS

IN FEET: LEN. WID. DEP.			CUBIC YARDS	CONCRETE AT $32/CU. YD.	LABOR AT $20/CU. YD.	TOTAL COST
20	8	.5	xx	xx	xx	xx
32	20	.25	xx	xx	xx	xx
.	.	.				
.	.	.				
.	.	.				

4.15.   COMPOUND INTEREST CALCULATIONS

AMT. DEPOSITED	ANNUAL INT. RATE	NO. TIMES COMPOUNDED PER YEAR	NO. YEARS LEFT ON DEPOSIT	AMT. IN BANK AT END
750	.0625	2	25	xxx
750	.06	365	25	xxx
.				
.				
.				

For the amount of money, a, in the bank at the end, use the formula

$$a = d * \left(1 + \frac{r}{t}\right)^{t*y}$$

where d is the amount deposited, r is the annual interest rate, t is the number of times the interest is compounded per year, and y is the number of years the money is left in the bank.

4.16.   INSTALLMENT LOAN: AMOUNT OF MONTHLY PAYMENT

AMT. BORROWED	ANNUAL INT. RATE	NO. YEARS TO REPAY	MONTHLY PAYMENT
5000	.12	5	XXX
750000	.115	35	XXX
.			
.			
.			

For the monthly payment p, use the formula

$$p = b\left(\frac{r}{12}\right) * \frac{\left(1 + \frac{r}{12}\right)^{y*12}}{\left(1 + \frac{r}{12}\right)^{y*12} - 1}$$

where b is the amount borrowed, r is the annual interest rate, and y is the number of years needed to repay the loan.

4.17.   ANNUAL RATE OF RETURN

AMT. INVESTED	NO. YEARS INVESTED	AMT. RECEIVED BACK	ANNUAL RATE OF RETURN
10000	4	15000	XXX
5	.5	8	XXX
.			
.			
.			

For the annual rate of return r, use the formula

$$r = Log(a/i)/y$$

where i is the amount invested, a is the amount received, and y is the number of years the money is invested.

☐ **FIGURE 4.3**   **Truck Rental Program with Lead Data Record**

```
100 REM               --- DAILY TRUCK RENTAL REPORT ---
110 REM
120 PRINT "              CITY LINE TRUCK RENTAL"
125 READ D$, R1, R2
130 PRINT TAB(18);"DATE: ";D$
132 PRINT "RATES:"
136 PRINT TAB(10);"PER MILE:";R1;TAB(30);"PER HOUR:";R2
140 PRINT
200 PRINT "TRUCK"
210 PRINT "LICENSE", "CUSTOMER", "DISTANCE";
212 PRINT TAB(40); "HOURS"; TAB(50); "CHARGE"
220 PRINT
240 READ L$,C$,M1,M2,T1,T2
250                                    REM
300 IF L$ = "ZZZ" THEN 400
310   LET D = M2 - M1
320   LET H = T2 - T1
330   LET C = R1 * D + R2 * H
335   LET C = INT(100 * C + .5)/100
340   PRINT L$, C$, D; TAB(40);H; TAB(50); C
350                                    REM
360   READ L$, C$, M1, M2, T1, T2
370 GOTO 300
400 PRINT " "
410 PRINT "DONE"
420 STOP
430                                    REM
800 REM --- CONSTANT DATA FILE ---
805 DATA "09/27/84", .27, 5.50
810 DATA "BG123", "J. BREEN",     676.9, 711.4, 11.5,15
820 DATA "YRZ",    "J. GRANDAHL", 775.8, 785.7, 8.25,11
830 DATA "T5-398","E. LOVETT",    6000, 6224.6, 7, 19
900 DATA "ZZZ"," ",0,0,0,0
999 END
```

A. PROGRAM

```
              CITY LINE TRUCK RENTAL
                 DATE: 09/27/84
    RATES:
         PER MILE: .27        PER HOUR: 5.5

    TRUCK
    LICENSE      CUSTOMER       DISTANCE   HOURS    CHARGE

    BG123        J. BREEN       34.5       3.5      28.56
    YRZ          J. GRANDAHL    9.899999   2.75     17.8
    T5-398       E. LOVETT      224.6      12       126.64

    DONE
```

B. OUTPUT

Lead Records and Report Forms

The data file, program, and output report form in Fig. 4.3 are somewhat similar to those of the examples we considered throughout the first part of this chapter and in Fig. 3.1 in Chapter 3. One difference between this program and the one in Fig. 3.1A is this: The first record in the data file (line 805) contains the date of the truck rentals and the truck rental rates. All the other records contain customer rental data. One reason for including the data in this way is to achieve flexibility. Now for each new date and each rate change, we need change only the first record, not several lines in the program.

Notice how the data values for the date and rates are used in the program. They are read in line 125. This record must be read before the other data is processed.

lead data record

The record in line 805 is an example of a lead data record. A **lead data record** provides additional data to the program that is needed in the report form or in calculating values in the detail lines. A number of report forms require the use of special data in the lead record.

EXERCISES

4.18. Trace the following program.

```
100 PRINT " ","ACME MARKETS"
110 PRINT " ","  PAYROLL"
120 PRINT
200 READ M$, D, Y
210 PRINT "WEEK OF:  "; M$; D; Y
220 PRINT
230 PRINT "EMPLOYEE", "RATE", "HOURS", "WAGE"
240 PRINT
250 READ N$, R, H
300 IF N$ = "ZZZ" THEN 400
310   LET W = R * H
320   PRINT N$, R, H, W
330                      REM
340   READ N$, R, H
350 GOTO 300
360                      REM
400 PRINT
410 PRINT "DONE"
420 STOP
800 REM --- CONSTANT DATA FILE ---
810 DATA "JANUARY", 26, 1986
820 DATA "ALLEN", 5.50, 40
830 DATA "GREEN", 8.00, 36
840 DATA "BAUER", 7.40, 50
850 DATA "ZZZ", 0, 0
999 END
```

4.19. Write a program that produces one of the following reports. Make sure that your data have lead data.

a)
```
                    WASHINGTON HS TRACK TEAM
                      PRACTICE PERFORMANCES

        DATE: xx/xx/xx
        EVENT: xxxxxxxxx

        NAME        THREE BEST TIMES (DISTANCES)      AVERAGE
        ----------  ----------------------------      -------

        xxxxxx        xxxx      xxxx      xxxx            xxx
        xxxxxx        xxxx      xxxx      xxxx            xxx
        xxxxxx        xxxx  .   xxxx      xxxx            xxx
```

b)
```
                 NEW PRICE LIST

        EFFECTIVE DATE: xx / xx / xx
        RATE OF INCREASE: xx

        ITEM            OLD         NEW
        DESCRIPTION     PRICE       PRICE
        -------------   -------     -------

        MILK            1.65        xxxx
        CHEESE          2.29        xxxx
        xxxxx           xxxx        xxxx
        xxxxx           xxxx        xxxx
```

c)
```
        MARTHA'S DANCE SCHOOL

        HOURLY RATE: xx

        STUDENT     HOURS       CHARGE
        ----------  -------     --------

        KAREN         7          xxx
        ALEX          9          xxx
        xxxxx        xx          xxx
        xxxxx        xx          xxx
```

d)
```
                    INFLATION

        BASE YEAR: 1975
        ITEM COST: 24.95

                            RATE OF CHANGE
        YEAR    COST        SINCE BASE YEAR
        ------  -------     ---------------

        1980    25.99       xxxx
        1981    30.54       xxxx
        1982    30.99       xxxx
        xxxx    xxxxx       xxxx
```

4.20. Write a program that produces one of the following reports. Each requires the use of lead data. What are the lead data?

a)   STANDINGS

TEAM	WON	LOST	PCT.	GAMES BEHIND
K.C.	90	72	xxx	0
OAKLAND	87	74	xxx	xx
MINN	85	77	xxx	xx
CALIF	76	86	xxx	xx

  .
  .
  .

b)   YEARLY RATES OF CHANGE

PRODUCT: HAMBURG

YEAR	PRICE	YEARLY RATE OF CHANGE
1979	1.65	
1980	2.09	xxx
1981	2.19	xxx
1982	2.22	xxx

  .
  .
  .

4.4 STRING EXPRESSIONS

numeric expressions

So far in this chapter we have thoroughly discussed and used numeric expressions. **Numeric expressions** consist of numeric constants (values), variables, operations, and functions. In this section we will consider string expressions. **String expressions** consist of string constants (values), variables, the one string operation (concatenation), and string functions. We will discuss each of these elements as well as the use of string functions.

string expressions

String Concatenation

concatenate

To **concatenate** means to link together. String constants and the contents of string variables can be concatenated, or linked together, by using the + symbol. For example, after the lines

```
10   READ F$, L$
20   LET N$ = "MR. " + F$ + " " + L$
50   STOP
80   DATA "CLIFF", "ALLEN"
```

F$	L$	N$
CLIFF	ALLEN	MR. CLIFF ALLEN

are executed, variable N$ will contain the string "MR. CLIFF ALLEN". Concatenation is frequently used in conjunction with string functions. More examples will be presented shortly.

String Functions

string function
substring

A **string function** is a function that yields a string value when the function is evaluated. A **substring** of a string is a sequence of consecutive characters that occurs in the string. For example, "ABC" is a substring of "ZZZABCXXXX". The string functions available in BASIC are listed in Table 4.7. Notice that a number of functions in Table 4.7 have values that are substrings of a string.

Some of the functions in Table 4.7 have string arguments, but when they are evaluated, they have a numeric value. Technically, these functions are numeric functions, but they are included here for convenient reference.

□ **TABLE 4.7**   **String-Related Functions in BASIC**

Function Name*	Description	Example
		Suppose A$ contains "ABCDEFGHIJ"
LEN(string)	Returns the length of the string	LEN(A$) is 10
LEFT$(string, length)	Returns the leftmost characters, of the length specified, of the string	LEFT$(A$, 3) is "ABC"
RIGHT$(string, length)	Returns the rightmost characters, of the length specified, of the string	RIGHT$(A$, 2) is "IJ"
MID$(string, position, length)	Returns a substring, of the length specified, from the string, beginning at the specified position	MID$(A$, 2, 3) is "BCD"
INSTR(position, string1, string2) (not available on Apple)	Searches for the first occurrence of string2 in string1, beginning at the specified position, and returns the position in string1 where the match is found or returns the value 0 if no match is found	INSTR(2, A$, "DE") is 4 INSTR(2, A$, "AB") is 0
STR$(number)	Converts a numeric constant to a string constant	STR$(12.34) is "12.34"
VAL(string)	Converts a string constant that has the appearance of a number into a number	VAL("12.34") is 12.34
ASC(string)	See Appendix B	
CHR$(number)	See Appendix B	

*The words in parentheses identify the information that the function argument must contain.

Uses of String Functions

String functions can be used in a number of ways. Three uses are described in the following paragraphs.

To limit the length of a string value: Because of limited room on the screen or the printer, you may want to print a limited number of characters in a string. Suppose you allocate 10 columns for last names. If variable N$ contains "HENDRICKSON", the PRINT LEFT$ (N$, 10) prints

```
HENDRICKSO
```

To insert characters into a string to make it more readable: Suppose D$ has the value 041283, which represents a date. To make this date more readable, you could insert slashes in the following way:

```
LET D$ = LEFT(D$, 2) + "/" + MID$(D$, 3, 2) + "/" + RIGHT$(D$, 2)
```

String D$ now contains "04/12/83".

To right-justify integers: An interesting application of the STR$ and VAL functions is to right-justify numbers. (Note that this operation can be done more simply on computers that have the PRINT USING statement, that is, on most non-Apple computers.) Suppose at column 24 you want to right-justify integers that are in variable X. First, you have to find the number of digits in the number in variable X. This number is given by LEN(STR$(X)). Now you can back off this number of characters. Thus

```
PRINT TAB(24 - LEN(STR$(X)) ); X
```

right-justifies the values on column 24.

EXERCISES

4.21.   Modify the sample program in Fig. 3.1A so that the calculated distance is rounded to the nearest integer and is printed right-justified.

4.22.   Trace the following program. Explain what it does.

```
100 LET B$ = "          "
200 READ N$,A
300 IF N$ = "ZZZ" THEN 400
310    LET A = INT(A)
320    PRINT LEFT$(N$ + B$,8);
330    PRINT RIGHT$(B$ + STR$(A),5)
340    READ N$,A
350 GOTO 300
```

```
360                              REM
400 STOP
800 DATA "TOM", 234.45
810 DATA "RICHARD", 12.3
820 DATA "ZZZ", 0
999 END
```

4.23. Trace the following program. Explain what it does.

```
8   PRINT "123456789012345"
10 READ X
20 IF X = 0 THEN 100
30    LET I$ = STR$(INT(X))
40    LET D$ = STR$(X - INT(X))
50    LET D1$ = MID$(D$,3,2)
60    PRINT TAB(8-LEN(I$)); I$+"."+D1$
70    READ X
80 GOTO 20
90                              REM
100 STOP
800 DATA 23.458, 72.862
810 DATA  2.3, -56.78, 675, 0
900 END
```

4.24. Trace the following program. Explain what it does.

```
4 B$ = "              "
8 PRINT "123456789012345"
10 READ X
20 IF X = 0 THEN 100
30    LET I$ = STR$(INT(X))
40    LET D$ = STR$(INT(X*100))
50    LET D1$ = RIGHT$("00"+D$,2)
60    PRINT RIGHT$(B$ + I$+"."+D1$,10)
70    READ X
80 GOTO 20
90                         REM
100 STOP
800 DATA 23.45, 162.862, 2.3
810 DATA -23.45, 0
900 END
```

Summing
and
Counting

INTRODUCTION TO CHAPTER 5

Often results that summarize the detail lines in a report are desired. The summing and counting of values are two fundamental methods for summarizing information. Other summary results frequently are combinations of these methods. For example, statistical summaries (such as the standard deviation) and financial summaries involve the summing and counting of various values.

This chapter is short but important. Here you will learn how to write programs that find sums and counts. Many of the programs in the previous chapters can be extended to incorporate sums and counts. In Chapter 7 another fundamental method of summarizing information is explained. This method involves finding the largest and/or smallest values in a set of values. These values will give us information about the best and worst situations.

The overall structure for programs that produce summary results is quite similar for all programs. This structure along with an example is given in Section 5.1.

5.1 PROGRAM STRUCTURE FOR SUMMARIES

To illustrate the typical program structure for calculating summaries, we'll consider an example. Suppose you plan to take a number of automobile trips this summer. You may want an estimated cost for each trip and to calculate the distance and cost of all the trips taken. Let's assume

☐ **FIGURE 5.1**   **Data File and Desired Report**

```
GRAND CANYON    2300
WORLD'S FAIR     800
KENTUCKY DERBY   450
```

A. DATA FILE

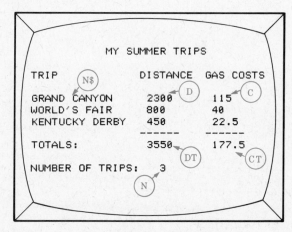

B. DESIRED REPORT

that you get 25 miles per gallon and the expected cost of gas per gallon is $1.25. The data file for this example and the desired output are shown in Fig. 5.1. Notice that on the report form (Fig. 5.1B) we have circled the names of all the variables that could be used in a program: N$ holds the trip name, D holds the distance, DT holds the total distance, and so on.

The flowchart and program in Fig. 5.2 produce the desired report shown in Fig. 5.1A. The flowchart structure shown in Fig. 5.2A is common to all programs that produce various summaries. The important aspects of the program (Fig. 5.2B) are shaded. These aspects will be discussed in subsequent sections. However, since the program has no new statements, you should be able to trace the program as suggested in Exercise 5.1.

EXERCISES

5.1.   Trace the program in Fig. 5.2B.

5.2.   Rewrite the flowchart in Fig. 5.2A in pseudocode.

5.2 ACCUMULATING SUMS

Accumulating sums or totals is a very common activity. For example:

- A bank customer   might want to know   • the balance in his account after a series of deposits and withdrawals.
- An employer   • the total wages paid to employees during the current pay period.
- A football announcer   • the total yards a team gained by passing and running the football in the last drive.

Clearly this list can go on and on.

cumulative sums
Sums are usually calculated **cumulatively**. That is, successive values are added to the previous sum to obtain the current sum so far. This method is the one you use when adding numbers on a desk calculator.

Compare cumulative summing with the usual method you use when adding a column of numbers by hand. In the manual method you add the digits in the one's column, then in the ten's column, then in the hundred's column, and so on, carrying digits to the next column when necessary.

☐ **FIGURE 5.2**   **Flowchart and Program for Report in Fig. 5.1A**

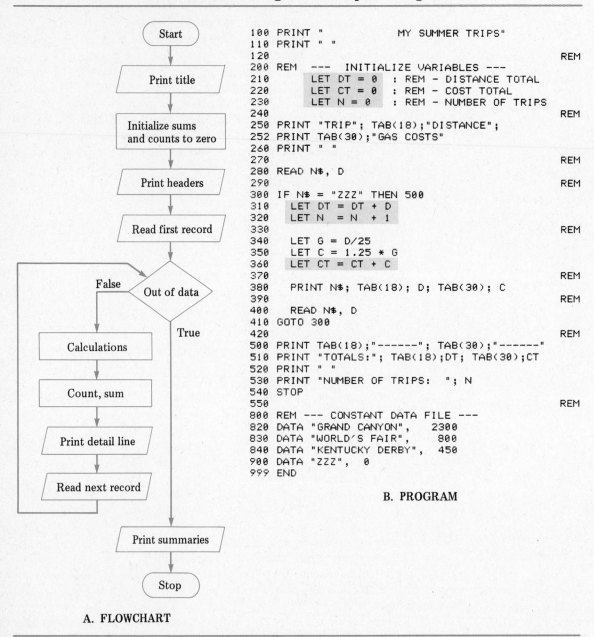

```
100  PRINT "              MY SUMMER TRIPS"
110  PRINT " "
120                                                    REM
200  REM   ---   INITIALIZE VARIABLES ---
210       LET DT = 0   : REM - DISTANCE TOTAL
220       LET CT = 0   : REM - COST TOTAL
230       LET N = 0    : REM - NUMBER OF TRIPS
240                                                    REM
250  PRINT "TRIP"; TAB(18);"DISTANCE";
252  PRINT TAB(30);"GAS COSTS"
260  PRINT " "
270                                                    REM
280  READ N$, D
290                                                    REM
300  IF N$ = "ZZZ" THEN 500
310       LET DT = DT + D
320       LET N  = N + 1
330                                                    REM
340       LET G = D/25
350       LET C = 1.25 * G
360       LET CT = CT + C
370                                                    REM
380     PRINT N$; TAB(18); D; TAB(30); C
390                                                    REM
400     READ N$, D
410  GOTO 300
420                                                    REM
500  PRINT TAB(18);"------"; TAB(30);"------"
510  PRINT "TOTALS:"; TAB(18);DT; TAB(30);CT
520  PRINT " "
530  PRINT "NUMBER OF TRIPS:  "; N
540  STOP
550                                                    REM
800  REM --- CONSTANT DATA FILE ---
820  DATA "GRAND CANYON",   2300
830  DATA "WORLD'S FAIR",    800
840  DATA "KENTUCKY DERBY",  450
900  DATA "ZZZ", 0
999  END
```

B. PROGRAM

A. FLOWCHART

The process of cumulative summing is shown in Fig. 5.3 for the calculator along with the manual methods.

Programs calculate sums in the same way that sums are calculated on a calculator—they are accumulated. Let's focus on summing

☐ **FIGURE 5.3**   **Cumulative Summing**

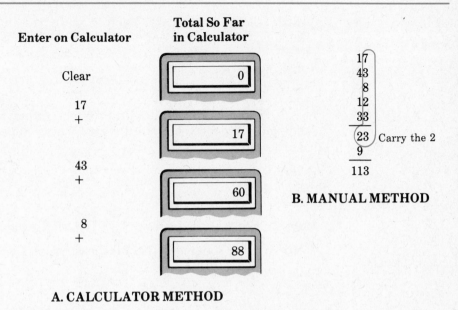

Enter on Calculator   Total So Far in Calculator

Clear   0

17
+
17

43
+
60

8
+
88

17
43
8
12
33
23 Carry the 2
9
―――
113

B. MANUAL METHOD

A. CALCULATOR METHOD

the trip distances for the example of Fig. 5.1. Assume that the data is as follows:

```
GRAND CANYON    2300
WORLD'S FAIR     800
KENTUCKY DERBY   450
```

First, as illustrated in Fig. 5.1B, we use N$ to hold the trip name and D to hold the trip distance. Second, we need a variable to hold the sum. Let's use DT for distance total. (If your computer does not allow names like DT, use D1.)

Next, we have to set the distance total (DT) to zero, which we do as follows (refer to the program in Fig. 5.2B):

```
210  LET DT = 0
```

initializes

This step **initializes** the sum to zero. We perform this step for the same reason that we clear a calculator before adding numbers.

Now, after reading the next trip distance into D, we add this distance to the total distance so far, using the statement

```
310  LET DT = DT + D
```

For example, suppose DT is currently zero, and the first value of D is 2300. Then the above statement (310) is equivalent to

```
LET DT = 0 + 2300
```

which assigns 2300 to DT. Suppose the next value of D is 800. Then statement 310 is equivalent to

```
LET DT = 2300 + 800
```

which assigns 3100 to DT.

Figure 5.4 illustrates the program, output, and memory chip for adding the trip distances. Verify that the trace illustrated in the memory chip is correct.

EXERCISES

5.3. In Fig. 5.4A, explain why DT is initialized to zero.

5.4. Suppose statement 310 of the program in Fig. 5.4A is changed to

```
310   LET DT = D
```

What will the resulting report look like?

□ **FIGURE 5.4**   **Accumulating Trip Distances**

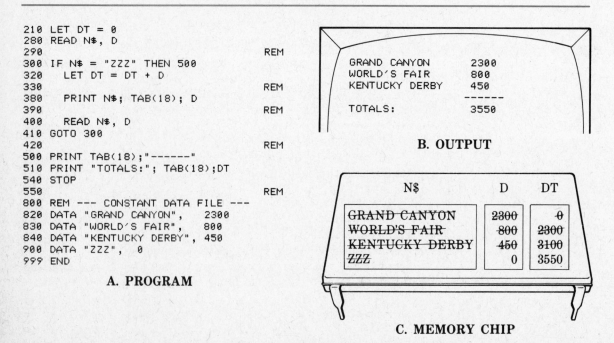

```
210 LET DT = 0
280 READ N$, D
290                       REM
300 IF N$ = "ZZZ" THEN 500
320    LET DT = DT + D
330                       REM
380    PRINT N$; TAB(18); D
390                       REM
400    READ N$, D
410 GOTO 300
420                       REM
500 PRINT TAB(18);"------"
510 PRINT "TOTALS:"; TAB(18);DT
540 STOP
550                       REM
800 REM --- CONSTANT DATA FILE ---
820 DATA "GRAND CANYON",   2300
830 DATA "WORLD'S FAIR",    800
840 DATA "KENTUCKY DERBY", 450
900 DATA "ZZZ",  0
999 END
```

A. PROGRAM

```
GRAND CANYON        2300
WORLD'S FAIR         800
KENTUCKY DERBY       450
                    ------
TOTALS:             3550
```

B. OUTPUT

N$	D	DT
GRAND CANYON	2300	0
WORLD'S FAIR	800	2300
KENTUCKY DERBY	450	3100
ZZZ	0	3550

C. MEMORY CHIP

5.5. Suppose statement 310 of the program in Fig. 5.4A is moved (changed) to

```
405  LET DT = DT + D
```

What will the resulting report look like?

5.6. Write a program that produces a printout showing the transactions of a person's checking account. Deposits can be indicated by positive numbers, withdrawals by negative numbers. The format of the desired report form is shown below.

```
     STATEMENT OF CHECKING ACCOUNT

MONTH: xxxx
CUSTOMER NAME: xxxxxxxx
INITIAL BALANCE: xxxxx

                           CURRENT
     DATE          AMOUNT  BALANCE
     ------------------    ----------    -------------
      2  7  1981      45        xxx
      2 10  1981     -36        xxx
      2 14  1981     100        xxx
      .
      .
      .
              FINAL BALANCE xxx
```

5.7. Write a program to calculate a student's quality point average, which is defined to be the total quality points divided by the total credits. The grade values are read, rather than the letter grades. Grade A is worth a 4, B is worth a 3, and so on. The quality points for a course are the number of credits times the grade value. The format of the desired report form is shown below.

```
                  THE COLLEGE

STUDENT: xxxxxxxx      SEMESTER: xxxxxxxx

COURSE      CREDITS    GRADE     QUALITY POINTS
----------    ------------    ----------    ---------------------------
CS150         4          3         xx
MAT 176       3          2         xx
ENG 207       3          3         xx
ART 100       2          2         xx
            ----------                      ----------
TOTALS        xxx                           xxx
QPA = xxx
```

5.8. Write a program that summarizes the trips you took last summer. The format of the desired report form is shown below.

```
                        TRIP SUMMARIES

  DESTINATION        MILES     GAS COST     TRAVEL HOURS
  ................   .......   ...........  .............
    MICHIGAN          756        60              15
    GRAND CANYON     1700       125              40
    KEY WEST         1200       100              30

  AVERAGE COST PER MILE = xxx
  AVERAGE SPEED = xxx
```

5.3 COUNTING

Counting, like summing, is a very common activity. Consider the following situations:

- A college registrar   might want   - freshmen have been admitted.
- A department chairman   to know   - sophomores are majoring in business.
- An employer   how many   - employees worked overtime.
- A social scientist   - college students both drink and smoke.
- An inventory clerk   - SCM Coronet XL typewriters are in stock.
- A stockbroker   - of his or her recommended stocks advanced last week.

Clearly, this list can go on and on.

Let's focus on counting the number of summer trips for our example (Fig. 5.2), assuming that the data looks like this:

```
    GRAND CANYON       2300
    WORLD'S FAIR        800
    KENTUCKY DERBY      450
```

Variables N$ and D will hold the trip name and distance, respectively.

First, we need a variable to hold the trip count. Let's use N for number of trips. The variable N is called the **counter**. Next, N should be initialized to zero before any trips are read. This step is done in line 230 of the program in Fig. 5.2B.

counter

incremented

Then after the computer reads each trip data, the counter should be **incremented** by one. That is, after data for a trip is read into memory, the count of the number of trips must increase by one. To increment the counter by one, we use the statement

```
320  LET N = N + 1
```

For example, suppose N is currently zero. After the next (first) trip data is read, statement 320 is equivalent to

```
LET N = 0 + 1
```

which assigns 1 to N. After the second trip data is read, statement 320 is equivalent to

```
LET N = 1 + 1
```

which assigns 2 to N.

Figure 5.5 illustrates the program, output, and memory chip for counting the number of trips. Verify that the trace illustrated by the memory chip is correct.

□ **FIGURE 5.5**   **Counting Trips**

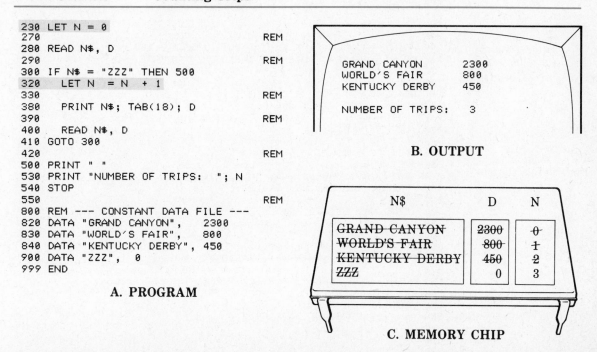

```
230 LET N = 0
270                                   REM
280 READ N$, D
290                                   REM
300 IF N$ = "ZZZ" THEN 500
320    LET N  = N  + 1
330                                   REM
380    PRINT N$; TAB(18); D
390                                   REM
400    READ N$, D
410 GOTO 300
420                                   REM
500 PRINT " "
530 PRINT "NUMBER OF TRIPS:  "; N
540 STOP
550                                   REM
800 REM --- CONSTANT DATA FILE ---
820 DATA "GRAND CANYON",   2300
830 DATA "WORLD'S FAIR",   800
840 DATA "KENTUCKY DERBY", 450
900 DATA "ZZZ",  0
999 END
```

A. PROGRAM

```
GRAND CANYON      2300
WORLD'S FAIR      800
KENTUCKY DERBY    450

NUMBER OF TRIPS:   3
```

B. OUTPUT

N$	D	N
~~GRAND CANYON~~	~~2300~~	~~0~~
~~WORLD'S FAIR~~	~~800~~	~~1~~
~~KENTUCKY DERBY~~	~~450~~	~~2~~
~~ZZZ~~	0	3

C. MEMORY CHIP

EXERCISES

5.9. Trace the following program and find the errors. The report should look like this:

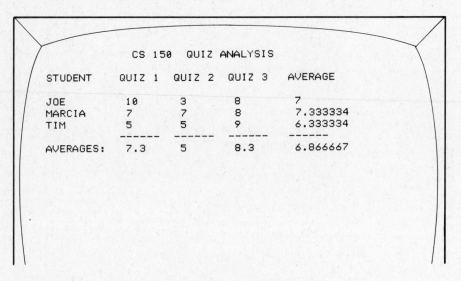

```
CS 150   QUIZ ANALYSIS

STUDENT    QUIZ 1   QUIZ 2   QUIZ 3    AVERAGE

JOE          10        3        8       7
MARCIA        7        7        8       7.333334
TIM           5        5        9       6.333334
           ------   ------   ------    ------
AVERAGES:    7.3       5        8.3     6.866667
```

```
100 PRINT "                    CS 150   QUIZ ANALYSIS"
110 PRINT
200 REM --- INITIALIZE VARIABLES ---
210     LET N = 0
220     LET A = 0
240                                         REM
250 PRINT "STUDENT"; TAB(12);"QUIZ 1"; TAB(20);"QUIZ 2";
260 PRINT TAB(28);"QUIZ 3"; TAB(37); "AVERAGE"
270 PRINT
280                                         REM
290 READ N$, Q1, Q2, Q3
300 IF N$ ="ZZZ" THEN 500
310   LET A = Q1 + Q2 + Q3/3
320   LET T1 = Q1
330   LET T2 = Q2
340   LET T3 = Q3
350   LET N = N + 1
360   PRINT N$; TAB(12);Q1; TAB(20);Q2;
365   PRINT  TAB(28);Q3; TAB(37); A
370                                         REM
380   READ N$, Q1, Q2, Q3
390 GOTO 300
400                                         REM
500 PRINT "            "; TAB(12);"------"; TAB(20);"------";
510 PRINT TAB(28);"------"; TAB(37);"------"
520                                         REM
530 PRINT "AVERAGES:"; TAB(12);T1/N; TAB(20);T2/N;
540 PRINT TAB(28);T3/N; TAB(37); (T1 + T2 + T3)/3
550 STOP
800 REM --- CONSTANT DATA FILE ---
810 DATA "JOE", 10, 3, 8
820 DATA "MARCIA", 7, 7, 8
830 DATA "TIM",    5, 5, 9
900 DATA "ZZZ", 0, 0, 0
999 END
```

5.10. Modify the program in Fig. 5.2B so that it prints the average distance of each trip. The summaries for the report should now look like this:

```
        .
        .
        .
TOTALS:                 3550    177.5

NUMBER OF TRIPS:     X
AVERAGE DISTANCE OF EACH TRIP: XXXX
```

5.11. Modify the newsvendor program on page 78 so that it prints the total profit for all days and the average profit of each day.

5.12. Modify any one of the reports on pages 78–81 and 84–85 so that it includes a sum and a count. Then write a program to produce the report.

5.13. Write a program that calculates the miles per gallon for an extended trip. At each stop the gas tank is filled. The printout might look like this:

```
        MILES-PER-GALLON CALCULATOR

                   ODOMETER      GALLONS NEEDED
        CITY       READING       TO FILL TANK
        ---------------  -------------  -------------------------

        N. HAVEN        775          13.5
        PHILADELPHIA    985          10.6
        WASHINGTON     1125          6.8
        RALEIGH        1428          11.4
        FLORENCE       1567          5.4

ACTUAL MILES-PER-GALLON   xxx
```

5.14. In addition to the common arithmetic mean, there is another mean called the geometric mean. It is used in business and economic problems when there is a need to determine the average rate of change. The **geometric mean** of n numbers is the nth root of the product of the n numbers. Write a program to calculate the yearly rate of change and then the average rate of change. The printout might look like this:

geometric mean

```
                INFLATION

                HAMBURGER        YEARLY RATE
        YEAR    PRICE/POUND      OF CHANGE
        ----------  --------------------   --------------------

        1978      1.56
        1979      1.70            0.0897
        1980      1.92            0.1294
        1981      2.13            0.1093

AVERAGE RATE OF CHANGE = 0.1083
```

The geometric mean is calculated here as

$$\sqrt[3]{1.0897 * 1.1294 * 1.1093} = (1.0897 * 1.1294 * 1.1093) \uparrow (1/3)$$

5.15. The hourly rental charge for sailboats depends on the type of boat. Write a program that generates a daily report like this:

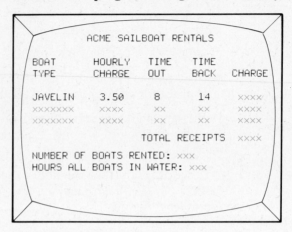

```
        ACME SAILBOAT RENTALS

BOAT       HOURLY  TIME   TIME
TYPE       CHARGE  OUT    BACK   CHARGE

JAVELIN    3.50    8      14     XXXX
XXXXXXX    XXXX    XX     XX     XXXX
XXXXXXX    XXXX    XX     XX     XXXX

                TOTAL RECEIPTS  XXXX

NUMBER OF BOATS RENTED: XXX
HOURS ALL BOATS IN WATER: XXX
```

5.16. Modify Exercise 5.15 so that minutes are included in the times. Specifically, the data should be

```
DATA "JAVELIN", 3.50, "08:00", "14:00"
```

5.17. A concrete contractor pours a number of floors in one day. The contractor wants a report that looks like this:

```
                        CONCRETE COSTS

IN FEET:            CUBIC   CONCRETE AT   LABOR AT      TOTAL
LEN. WID. DEP.      YARDS   $62/CU. YD.   $40/CU. YD.   COST

20    8    .5       XX      XX            XX            XX
32    20   .25      XX      XX            XX            XX
.     .    .        .       .             .             .
.     .    .        .       .             .             .
.     .    .        .       .             .             .
TOTALS              XXX     XXX           XXX           XXX
```

Write a program that generates such a report.

Selecting Alternative Actions

INTRODUCTION TO CHAPTER 6

In the previous chapters the IF and GOTO statements were used in most programs to create a loop so that any number of records could be processed. These programs have a common feature: Each program takes the same action on each record. Thus in a program that calculates the cost of gas for various trips, the same calculations are done with each record.

However, in many situations alternative actions must be selected for different data records (under different circumstances). For example,

IF the age is 16 or greater
   THEN can apply for automobile license

IF the inventory level of PCs is less than 25
   THEN order 50 more
   ELSE talk to the sales manager

IF the applicant shows good promise
   THEN accept application
   ELSE politely reject

In Chapter 3 the IF–THEN statement was briefly explained so that it could be used to construct the loops needed to process any number of records. In this chapter the IF–THEN statement is described in more detail so that it can be used to select alternative actions. The selected actions will depend on the values in the records. Selection is a more complicated process than looping, and we'll examine various types of selection, including selections that involve using nested IF statements. We'll also explain how to test a program that involves selecting alternative actions.

6.1 AN EXAMPLE OF SELECTION

Before explaining the details of implementing selection with IF statements, we'll describe in this section an example that involves selecting alternative actions. This example will use the flowchart and pseudocode languages described in Chapter 2.

Many state-supported colleges charge students who live out of state higher fees than those charged the in-state students. To be specific, suppose a certain Rhode Island college charges $50 per credit for all in-state students and charges $80 per credit for all out-of-state students. Using this rule, we will calculate the tuition for the students in the report shown on the following page:

The calculated tuitions for Joe and Pete are $1120 and $550 respectively.

```
        WESTERN RHODE ISLAND COLLEGE

    STUDENTS     CREDITS     STATE     TUITION

    JOE             14         CT        xxx
    PETE            11         RI        xxx
    KAREN           16         NY        xxx
```

A flowchart showing the alternative actions required by the above report is shown in Fig. 6.1. We have to select the alternative actions on the basis of whether the student lives in Rhode Island.

Now suppose the following variables are introduced:

| N\$ | Student name | S\$ | State abbreviation |
| C | Credits to be taken | T | Tuition |

Then the flowchart of Fig. 6.1 can be rewritten as shown in Fig. 6.2A and put into BASIC as illustrated in Fig. 6.2C. The pseudocode for this example is shown in Fig. 6.2B.

condition

In line 300 of Fig. 6.2C the term S\$ = "RI" looks like an assignment statement. But it is not. It is called a **condition.** Sometimes, it is called a Boolean expression [after George Boole (1815–1864), a mathe-

☐ **FIGURE 6.1**   **Flowchart for Student Tuition Charges**

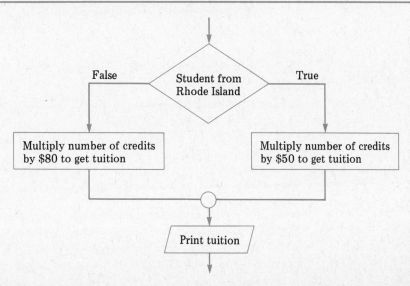

☐ **FIGURE 6.2**   **Selecting Alternative Actions**

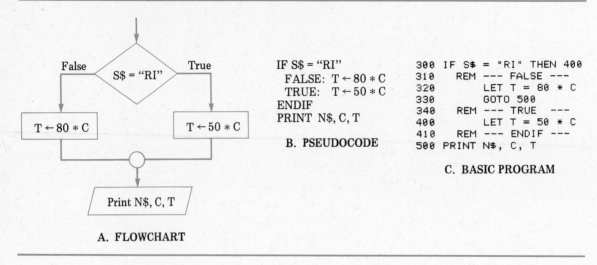

```
IF S$ = "RI"              300  IF S$ = "RI" THEN 400
   FALSE:  T ← 80 * C     310     REM --- FALSE ---
   TRUE:   T ← 50 * C     320        LET T = 80 * C
ENDIF                     330        GOTO 500
PRINT N$, C, T            340     REM --- TRUE ---
                          400        LET T = 50 * C
        B. PSEUDOCODE     410     REM --- ENDIF ---
                          500  PRINT N$, C, T
```

C. BASIC PROGRAM

A. FLOWCHART

maticin who investigated the algebra of logic]. We will refer to them simply as conditions.

Each time the computer comes to the IF statement in line 300 in Fig. 6.2C, it evaluates the condition. The condition will have the value true or false. If the condition is true, then the computer will go to statement 400, the number following THEN. If the condition is false, then the computer will continue executing the next statement, statement 310 in this program segment.

We'll explain other details of the IF–THEN statement in the following sections.

EXERCISE

6.1.   Using the BASIC code in Fig. 6.2C, write the entire program for calculating college tuition.

6.2 THE IF–THEN STATEMENT

The IF statement can be written in a few different ways. The simplest form and its meaning are discussed in this section. Other forms are discussed in the next chapter. The various types of conditions, which are a major part of the IF–THEN statement, and relational operators are also discussed in this section.

Form and Meaning

The general form of the **IF statement** is

line number   IF   condition   THEN   statement number

For example, consider the IF statement in line 300 below:

```
300   IF X = 3 THEN 400
350     LET Y = 2 * X
400   ...
```

When the computer comes upon an IF statement, it does the following: It evaluates the condition (X = 3 in the example); the condition will have a value of true or false.

- If the condition is true, then the BASIC processor goes to the statement number following THEN (400 in the example).
- If the condition is false, then the next statement (350 in the example) in the sequence is executed.

In the above example, suppose variable X contains a 3. The condition, X = 3, is true. Consequently, the computer goes to statement 400.

On the other hand, suppose X contains a 5 when the computer executes line 300. The condition X = 3 is false; so the computer goes to the next highest line number, 350 in the example.

Conditions

As you can see from the discussion and example above, the condition is a major part of the IF-THEN statement. But what, exactly, is a condition? How is it formed? These questions are answered next.

A **condition** can be either a string condition or a numeric condition. Some examples of numeric and string conditions are as follows:

Numeric Conditions	String Conditions
(A + B)/2 < 50	S$ = "F"
A > 18 + B	LEFT$(N$) < "J"
ABS(A - 30) <= 5	"BCD" = MID$(A$, 2, 3)

Notice that a condition consists of two expressions (either both numeric or both string) separated by a relational operator. (Relational operators are described in the next subsection.) The BASIC processor evaluates both the left-hand and right-hand expressions, which yields a

□ **TABLE 6.1**   **Relational Operators**

Algebraic Relational Operators	Equivalent BASIC Symbol	Example of a BASIC Condition	Interpretation of the BASIC Condition
=	=	A = B	A is equal to B
≠	<>	A <> B	A is not equal to B
>	>	A > B	A is greater than B
<	<	A < B	A is less than B
≥	>=	A >= B	A is greater than or equal to B
≤	<=	A <= B	A is less than or equal to B

value on each side of the relational operator. The processor then evaluates the condition, which has a value of true or false.

Relational Operators

relational operators

There are six **relational operators**: equal, not equal, greater than, less than, greater than or equal, and less than or equal. These operators are used to form conditions, which are used in the IF–THEN statement. The meaning of each relational operator is explained in Table 6.1.

Numeric Conditions

numeric condition

A condition with numeric expressions on both sides of the relational operator is called a **numeric condition.** (Recall that a *numeric expression* can be just a constant or a variable, or an expression with constants, variables, and functions.)

□ **TABLE 6.2**   **Evaluating String Conditions**

Condition	Value	Reason
"ABC" < "ABD"	True	C is less than D
"ABC" = "ABC "	False	Strings are not identical; a space follows the C in the string on the right
"ABC" < "ABC "	True	Nothing (the null character) is less than any other character; specifically, the null character on the right-hand side of the left string is less than the space character after the C in the string on the right side
"JOHNSON" < "JONES"	True	One string is less than another if, alphabetically, it comes before the other

Now let's see how we evaluate numeric conditions. Suppose variable A contains 3, B contains −2, and C contains 7. Then the following two conditions are evaluated as shown:

Condition	Value
C − (A + 1)/B > 4 + A	
7 − 4/(−2) > 7	
9 > 7	True
C − A − 1 <= A 2 − 2 * C	
7 − 3 − 1 <= 9 − 14	
3 <= −5	False

String Conditions

string condition

A condition with string expressions on both sides of the relational operator is called a **string condition**. Usually, the string expression on each side of the relational operator is a string constant or variable.

How are string conditions evaluated? Specifically, when is one string less than, equal to, or greater than another string? *Answer:* Strings are compared on the basis of individual characters in the strings. There is a specific order among all the characters (see Appendix B, Table B.1). The order of some of the characters is as follows:

(null) (space) # $ % * 0 1 9 ; = ? A B C Z

In this ordering a character to the left of another character is less than that character. For example, # is less than ?.

Some examples of string conditions and their values are given in Table 6.2.

EXERCISES

6.2. Trace the following program.

```
100 PRINT "SMALLEST","LARGEST"
110 PRINT
200 READ G, T
300 IF G = 0 THEN 500
310    IF G < T THEN 350
320    LET H = G
330    LET G = T
340    LET T = H
350    PRINT G, T
360    READ G, T
370 GOTO 300
```

```
500 PRINT "DONE"
510 STOP
800 DATA 16, 5
810 DATA 16, -625
820 DATA .1, .02
830 DATA 0,0
999 END
```

6.3.   Trace the following program.

```
100 PRINT "FIRST","SECOND","LARGEST"
110 PRINT
200 READ A, B
300 IF A = 0 THEN 500
310   IF A < B THEN 340
320     LET D$ = "FIRST"
330     GOTO 400
340     LET D$ = "SECOND"
400   PRINT A, B, D$
410   READ A, B
420 GOTO 300
500 PRINT "DONE"
510 STOP
800 DATA 45, -6
810 DATA -67, 35
820 DATA -3, -1
830 DATA 0,0
999 END
```

6.3   THREE TYPES OF SELECTION AND THEIR IMPLEMENTATION

Selecting alternative actions can take three fundamental forms: there can be (1) actions on both branches, (2) actions on just the false branch, and (3) actions on just the true branch. You should be able to recognize these forms and to put them into BASIC.

In this section we will illustrate how you put these forms into BASIC. You will have to use the GOTO statement in two of these forms, so the GOTO statement is discussed first.

The GOTO Statement

Recall that the form of the GOTO statement is

line number   GOTO   line number

When the computer sees this statement, it simply goes to the statement number on the right and continues executing the program from this point on.

In previous chapters the GOTO statement was used to help implement the loop structure. We saw that its role is to send the computer back to the IF statement, which controls the exit from the loop.

In the next subsection we will describe how the GOTO statement

☐ **FIGURE 6.3**   **Action on Both Branches**

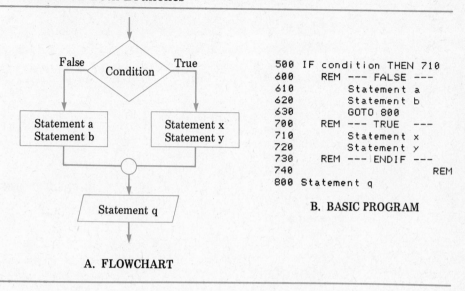

```
500 IF condition THEN 710
600     REM --- FALSE ---
610          Statement a
620          Statement b
630          GOTO 800
700     REM --- TRUE  ---
710          Statement x
720          Statement y
730     REM --- ENDIF ---
740                      REM
800 Statement q
```

B. BASIC PROGRAM

A. FLOWCHART

is used to help implement selection. As you will see, it is used to avoid (go around) statements that should not be executed.

Implementing the Three Types of Selection

Action on both branches is shown in the flowchart in Fig. 6.3A and the corresponding program in Fig. 6.3B. Notice particularly the GOTO statement in line 630. It is needed in order to go around the statements on the true branch (lines 700–720).

Action on the false branch is shown in the flowchart and corresponding BASIC program in Fig. 6.4. This is the easiest type of selection to put into BASIC. No GOTO statement is needed to go around the action on the true branch because there is no true branch.

Action on the true branch is illustrated in the flowchart and corresponding program in Fig. 6.5. The GOTO statement in line 610 is necessary in order to go around the actions on the true branch.

Notice how the GOTO statement is used in the programs in Fig. 6.3 and Fig. 6.4. It is used to send the computer around the actions on the true alternative—that is, it makes the computer skip the actions for the true alternative.

EXERCISES

6.4.   If a person's total purchase (variable T) is more than $100.00, the cost is reduced by $12.00. Write an IF–THEN statement to make this adjustment.

☐ **FIGURE 6.4**   **Action on the True Branch**

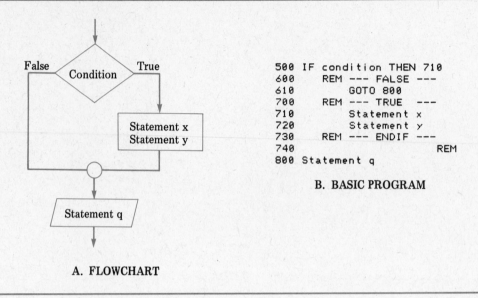

```
500 IF condition THEN 710
600     REM --- FALSE ---
610             GOTO 800
700     REM --- TRUE  ---
710             Statement x
720             Statement y
730     REM --- ENDIF ---
740                             REM
800 Statement q
```

B. BASIC PROGRAM

A. FLOWCHART

6.5. Modify the sample program in Fig. 5.2B so that it counts the number of trips that exceed 3000 miles. The format for the report summaries is shown below:

```
    .
    .
    .
    KENTUCKY DERBY          450          22.5
                          ----------   ------------
                           XXXX         XXXXX

       NUMBER OF TRIPS:              XX
       NUMBER OVER 3000 MILES:       XX
```

6.6. Suppose the state sales tax of 3% is applied only if the purchase price is $5.00 or greater. Write a program that reads the purchase price and calculates the tax, if there is one. The report should look like the form shown below:

```
CUSTOMER       PURCHASE      STATE      TOTAL
IDENT.         PRICE         TAX        COST

AB123          16.78         0.50       17.28
QF87            4.23         0.00        4.23
```

6.7. A college student who is registered for 12 or more credits is considered a full-time student. The tuition for a full-time student is $350 even if the student carries more than 12 credits. A part-time student is charged $40 per credit for tuition. The program seg-

☐ **FIGURE 6.5**   **Action on the False Branch**

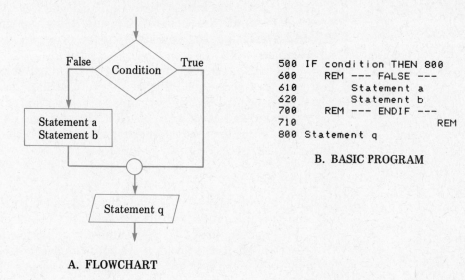

```
500 IF condition THEN 800
600     REM --- FALSE ---
610         Statement a
620         Statement b
700     REM --- ENDIF ---
710                      REM
800 Statement q
```

B. BASIC PROGRAM

A. FLOWCHART

ments below are supposed to calculate a student's tuition from this rule. Notice that N$ is the student name, C is the number of credits, and T is the tuition. What is wrong with each program?

a)
```
400   IF C < 12 THEN 420
410    LET T = 350
420    LET T = 40 * C
500    PRINT N$, C, T
510    READ N$, C
520   GOTO 300   : REM PROCESS NEXT RECORD
```

b)
```
400   IF C >= 12 THEN 440
410   IF C < 12 THEN 420
420     LET T = 40 * C
430     GOTO 500
440     LET T = 350
450     GOTO 500
500   PRINT N$, C, T
510   READ N$, C
520   GOTO 300
```

c)
```
400   IF C < 12 THEN 600
410     LET T = 350
420     PRINT N$, C, T
430     READ N$, C
440   GOTO 300
600     LET T = 40 * C
610     GOTO 420
```

6.4 PROGRAM TESTING

Once a program has been written in BASIC, all the syntax errors have been removed, and the program appears to be working, the program should be tested so that you are sure the program works properly in all situations.

Recall that a program is tested by running it with representative test data. Ideally, the test data should exercise all paths in the program. The results printed by the test run are then compared with the results the programmer knows to be correct. Usually, test data are chosen so that it is easy for the programmer to calculate the results by hand. We'll illustrate the process with an example.

☐ EXAMPLE

Suppose a corner newsvendor buys papers wholesale for 10¢ a copy and sells them retail for 30¢ a copy. At the end of the day she can return a maximum of 20 copies to the distributor for a 5¢ rebate. This return limit discourages the vendor from overordering newspapers.

For the last few months the newsvendor has kept track of how many newspapers were bought wholesale and sold retail each day. She now wants to calculate and analyze the daily profit and total profit to help her with her marketing strategy.

A test program for the newsvendor's daily profits is shown in Fig. 6.6A. Does the program work correctly? To answer the question, first calculate the daily profit with a calculator. Does your answer agree with the computer's in Fig. 6.6B. It should. Next, do the records in lines 820–850 exercise all paths in the program? Verify that they do.

6.5 NESTED IF STATEMENTS

Let's modify the tuition program of Section 6.1, where all in-state students were required to pay $50 per credit. Suppose now that a break is given to full-time (12 or more credits), in-state students. They pay $40 per credit. The logic for calculating the tuition in this situation is given by the flowchart in Fig. 6.7A and the pseudocode of Fig. 6.7B.

Notice here that another selection of alternatives is needed within one of the previous alternatives, shown by the shaded portion of the flowchart and pseudocode. This arrangement of selections is called a **nested selection**. The corresponding program segment is illustrated in Fig. 6.7C. Notice that the IF–THEN statement in line 510 is nested within the IF–THEN statement beginning at line 300.

To see how the nesting works, suppose S$ contains RI. At line 300, since the condition is true, the computer will go to line 510. Here it evaluates the condition of the nested IF–THEN statement and selects the appropriate condition.

nested selection

□ FIGURE 6.6   Program Test of Newsvendor's Daily Profits

```
100 PRINT "        NEWSVENDOR: DAILY PROFITS"
110 PRINT
120 READ Y
130 PRINT "YEAR: "; Y
140 PRINT
160 PRINT "DATE    BOUGHT","SOLD   RETURN","PROFIT"
170 PRINT
250 READ D$, B, S
300 IF D$ = "ZZZ" THEN 600
310    LET L = B - S            : REM LEFTOVER
320    IF L > 20 THEN 360
330      REM --- FALSE ---
340          LET R = L
350          GOTO 400
360      REM --- TRUE  ---
370          LET R = 20
380      REM --- ENDIF ---
390                                      REM
400    LET P = 0.30*S + 0.05*R - 0.10*B
410    PRINT D$; TAB(8) B,S;TAB(22) R, P
420                                      REM
430    READ D$, B, S
440 GOTO 300
600 PRINT
610 PRINT "DONE"
620 STOP
800 REM --- CONSTANT DATA FILE ---
810 DATA 1985
820 DATA "08/12",400, 200
830 DATA "08/13",400, 385
840 DATA "08/14", 30, 5
850 DATA "08/15", 30, 15
860 DATA "ZZZ", 0, 0
999 END
```

A. PROGRAM

```
        NEWSVENDOR: DAILY PROFITS

YEAR:  1985

DATE    BOUGHT  SOLD   RETURN   PROFIT

08/12    400    200     20       21
08/13    400    385     15       76.25
08/14     30     5      20       -.5
08/15     30     15     15       2.25

DONE
```

B. OUTPUT

□ **FIGURE 6.7**   **Logic and Program Segment for Modified Tuition Problem**

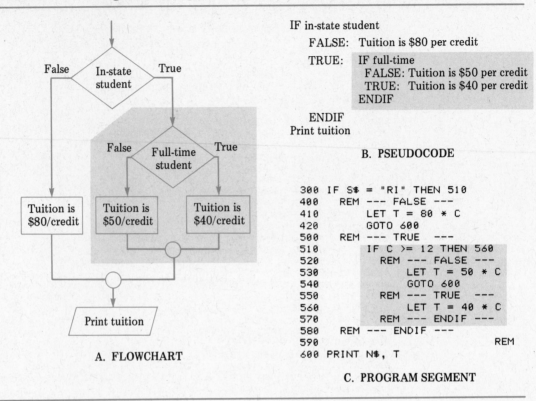

```
IF in-state student
    FALSE:  Tuition is $80 per credit
    TRUE:   IF full-time
                FALSE: Tuition is $50 per credit
                TRUE:  Tuition is $40 per credit
            ENDIF
    ENDIF
Print tuition
```

B. PSEUDOCODE

```
300  IF S$ = "RI" THEN 510
400     REM --- FALSE ---
410        LET T = 80 * C
420        GOTO 600
500     REM --- TRUE ---
510        IF C >= 12 THEN 560
520           REM --- FALSE ---
530              LET T = 50 * C
540              GOTO 600
550           REM --- TRUE ---
560              LET T = 40 * C
570           REM --- ENDIF ---
580        REM --- ENDIF ---
590                            REM
600  PRINT N$, T
```

C. PROGRAM SEGMENT

A. FLOWCHART

Nested selections are very common. For example, suppose you are planning the next day of your vacation. Your reasoning might follow the logic shown in Fig. 6.8. Here another selection is nested in each first-level alternative.

EXERCISES

6.8.   Put the modified tuition problem (Fig. 6.7) into BASIC. Test all paths in the program.

6.9.   Put the flowchart shown in Fig. 6.9 (p. 116) into BASIC. What does the flowchart do?

6.10. With regard to expressing nested selections, discuss the relative merits of using flowcharts and pseudocode.

6.11. Suppose a store has the following discount policy: On 4 or fewer of the same item the full price is paid. On 5 to 10 items there is

□ **FIGURE 6.8**   **Nested Selections**

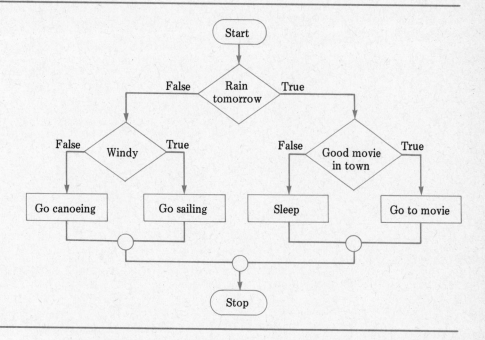

a 7% discount. On more than 10 items there is a 12% discount. Suppose Variable N contains the number of items and P contains the item price. Write a segment of BASIC code to calculate the cost.

CHAPTER EXERCISES

The object of each of the following exercises (except the last one) is to write a program that calculates a result on the basis of selection. Remember how to get started? If not, refer to Section 4.3. Also, test each program that you write. Each exercise can be extended to include various counts and sum. Extend each exercise accordingly.

6.12.   This exercise is a modification of the quantity discount pricing policy discussed in Exercise 6.11. Suppose the first four items cost the standard unit price; the fifth through tenth items cost the standard price less 7%; and all items after the tenth cost the standard price less 12%. Write a program that implements this pricing policy.

6.13.   Write a program that calculates college fees on the basis of the

□ **FIGURE 6.9**

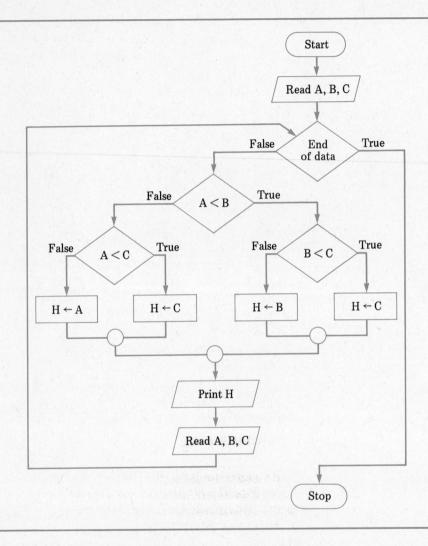

appropriate charges at your college. The printout might look like the results shown below:

```
                          COLLEGE FEES


              NUMBER     IN
NAME          CREDITS    STATE?   ROOM?    MEALS?    TOTAL
-----------   --------   ------   -----    ------    -----
PETER           16       YES      NO       YES       xxx
ROBERT          12       NO       YES      YES       xxx
  .
  .
  .
```

6.14. Determine each employee's wage given the worker's standard hourly rate and hours worked. For each hour worked in excess of 40 hours, the worker is credited with $1\frac{1}{2}$ hours. (This job can be extended as suggested in Exercise 6.22 of this section.) The report form is shown below:

```
              ACME MARKET

      DATE: xx xx xxxx

      NAME     RATE     HOURS     WAGE
      -------  -------  -------   -------
      JOE      7.47     30        xx
      AL       6.00     45        xx
```

6.15. Write a program that determines the fine for a traffic violator on the basis of the following schedule:

Offense	Point Value	Fine
SP: Speeding	5	$75.00
DK: Drunk driving	9	$300.00
RR: Running a red light	3	$30.00
RK: Reckless driving	4	$50.00

Furthermore, if the offenders accumulate more than 10 points, their licenses are suspended. The printout might look like the results shown below:

```
                  TRAFFIC FINES

              PREVIOUS    OFFENSE    CURRENT
      DRIVER  POINTS      TYPE       POINTS     FINE
      ------- ----------- ---------- ---------- -------
      TIM     6           RK         xx         xx
      WALKER  2           DK         xx         xx
```

6.16. Write a program to calculate the charges for using a parking lot. Assume that all cars have to be out of the lot by midnight. The form of the DATA statement might look like this:

```
      810  DATA "CT6775", 8, "AM", 11, "AM"
```

The form for the printout is shown below:

```
                ACME PARKING LOTS

      CHARGE PER HOUR: 0.50     MAXIMUM CHARGE: 5.00

      LICENSE NO.      TIME IN    TIME OUT    CHARGE
      --------------   --------   ---------   -------
      CT6775           8 AM       11 AM       xx
      HX4190           9 AM       10 PM       xx
```

6.17. If you find Exercise 6.16 easy, include minutes in the times. You will then have to convert the minutes to hours in order to calculate the charges. For example, a detail line might look like this:

```
CT6775     8 25 AM     11 36 AM     xxx
```

6.18. Write a program that determines people's ages in years when given the current month and year and each person's birth month and year. The report format is as shown below:

```
          AGES IN YEARS

CURRENT DATE (MONTH AND YEAR): 6     1980

NAME        BIRTH MONTH YEAR     AGE IN YEARS
...........  ............................     ......................

JAMES               5   1959     xx
THOMAS              7   1959     xx
```

6.19. If you find Exercise 6.18 easy, try to find people's ages given the current month, *day*, and year and each person's birth month, *day*, and year. Calculate the ages in either years or years and months.

6.20. Write a program that calculates the roots of a quadratic equation, using the quadratic formula. Remember: It is possible to have none, one, or two real roots.

6.21. Design a printout and write a program that calculates the charge for electricity consumption on the basis of the following schedule:

Energy Consumed	Rate per kwh
First 300 kwh	0.0449
Next 200 kwh	0.0401
All kwh over 500	0.0367

Customer monthly service charge: $4.32

You might modify the program so that it takes into account the amount of electricity consumed during peak and off-peak hours. Some utilities charge less for energy consumed during off-peak hours. In such cases the detail lines in the printout might look like this:

```
          KWH:              KWH:
NAME      PEAK HOURS        OFF-PEAK HOURS      CHARGES
.........  ....................  ............................  ...............

GERSON    645               489                 xxx
```

Devise a reasonable rule for calculating the charges for off-peak-hour consumption.

6.22. There are a number of IRS requirements that must be taken into account when determining a payroll; chief among them are withholding and the social security tax (FICA). The FICA tax rate is 6.7% of gross wages up to $32,400. Wages in excess of $32,400 are not subject to any further tax. Write a program that calculates FICA taxes. The tricky aspect of this calculation is the point where a person's wages first exceed the $32,400. Assume that the printout looks like the report shown below:

```
                                                   TAKE-
          PREV. TOTAL   THIS WEEK    GROSS  LESS   HOME
NAME      WAGES PAID    RATE HOURS   WAGES  FICA   PAY
-------   ----------    ----  -----   -----  ----   -----
FRED      22800         9.00  40      XXXX   XXXX   XXXXX
```

6.23. Here are a few more situations in which calculating results depends on first making decisions. You should determine (or make up) appropriate assumptions on which to calculate the results. Determine the form of the printout, and then write the program.
   a) Calculate salaries on the basis of commission rates for different levels of sales.
   b) Calculate local taxes on the basis of property value, use of public water and sewers, and fire protection area.
   c) Calculate automobile premiums on the basis of one insurance company's rates.
   d) Calculate energy consumption on the basis of the R value of walls, ceilings, windows, and so forth.

6.24. Trace the following program.

```
100 PRINT "        SUMMARY OF MONTHLY PREMIUMS"
110 PRINT " "
200 READ M$, Y
210 PRINT "DATE: "; M$; Y
220 PRINT " "
240 PRINT "                ", "CAR"
250 PRINT "NAME      AGE", "TYPE","PREMIUM"
260 PRINT " "
270                              REM
280 READ N$, A, T$
290                              REM
300 IF N$ = "ZZZ" THEN 700
310    IF A <= 25 THEN 510
400    REM --- FALSE ---
410        IF T$ = "HP" THEN 460
420        REM --- FALSE ---
430            LET P = 200
440            GOTO 480
450        REM --- TRUE   ---
460            LET P = 250
470        REM --- ENDIF ---
480        GOTO 600
500    REM --- TRUE   ---
510        IF T$ = "HP" THEN 560
520        REM --- FALSE ---
530            LET P = 300
540            GOTO 600
550        REM --- TRUE   ---
```

```
560            LET P = 400
570         REM --- ENDIF ---
580    REM --- ENDIF ---
590                                    REM
600    PRINT N$; TAB(10);A, T$, P
610                                    REM
620    READ N$, A, T$
630 GOTO 300
640                                    REM
700 PRINT " "
710 PRINT "DONE PROCESSING"
720 STOP
730                                    REM
790 REM --- CONSTANT DATA FILE ---
800 DATA "JULY", 1984
810 DATA "CLIFF",  23, "HP"
820 DATA "ROBERT", 18, "ST"
830 DATA "JAMES",  45, "HP"
840 DATA "CAROL",  35, "ST"
850 DATA "EDWARD", 78, "HP"
900 DATA "ZZZ",     0, "Z"
```

Selection: Applications and Extensions

INTRODUCTION TO CHAPTER 7

Two common ways of summarizing data are to accumulate sums and counts as discussed in Chapter 5. A third common way is to determine the largest or smallest of a set of values. In fact, most summary results are one of these three algorithms or a combination of them. This third algorithm, determining the largest or smallest, is explained in this chapter.

In addition to simple selection (two alternative actions) and nested selection, there is another common selection structure: the case structure, which is used to select one of multiple alternatives. In this chapter we look at some applications of this structure and its implementation.

The simple IF statement has a variety of extensions. These extensions also are described in this chapter.

7.1 FINDING THE LARGEST/SMALLEST VALUE

Finding the largest or smallest of a group of values is a common activity. For example:

■ A weather forecaster	might want	■ the hottest and coldest day on a particular date.
■ An engineer	to know	■ the least expensive way to build a product given a variety of possibilities.
■ A baseball statistician		■ the player with the best batting average.
■ A subscriber to a dating service		■ the person who best meets the subscriber's requirements.
■ A financial analyst		■ the best rate of return of various investment opportunities.
■ A consumer		■ the four-passenger car in the $8000–$12,000 dollar range with the best combined city and highway mileage.

Recall:

■ Summing requires keeping track of the sum so far.
■ Counting requires keeping track of the count so far.

In the same way, the algorithm for finding the largest (smallest) value involves keeping track of the largest (smallest) value so far. In the following subsections we examine the procedure for finding the largest (smallest) value.

The Largest Value

Consider the following sequence of numbers in variable X and observe how the largest is determined:

Value in X		Largest So Far Held in L	Action
		-999	Initialize to a small value.
45	←Compare→	-999	Compare. Since 45 is larger, assign it to L.
17	←Compare→	~~-999~~ 45	
53	←Compare→	-999 ~~45~~	Compare. Since 53 is larger, assign it to L.
26	←Compare→	~~-999~~ ~~45~~ 53	

Each time a new value is generated or read into a variable like X, it is compared with the largest so far, L. If the new value is larger, it is assigned to L.

The algorithm for this procedure is shown in Fig. 7.1A. The corresponding BASIC program is shown in Fig. 7.1B. An important part of the algorithm is assigning a small value to L (line 110) before reading any value for X. This step ensures that on the first comparison of L and X the value of X will be larger and consequently be assigned to L.

Notice that the portion of the program that keeps track of the largest value so far, lines 310–360, can be written without using the

□ **FIGURE 7.1**   **Algorithm and Program for Finding Largest Value**

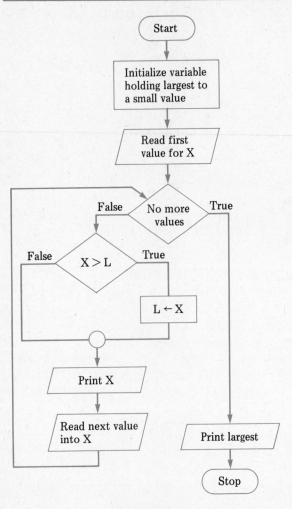

```
100 REM --- FIND THE LARGEST ---
110 LET L = -999
120 PRINT "NUMBER"
250 READ X
300 IF X = 0 THEN 500
310   IF X > L THEN 350
320     REM --- FALSE ---
330         GOTO 370
340     REM --- TRUE  ---
350         LET L = X
360     REM --- ENDIF ---
370   PRINT X
380   READ X
400 GOTO 300
410                     REM
500 PRINT
510 PRINT "THE LARGEST IS "; L
520 STOP
800 DATA  17, 34, 5, 0
999 END
```

B. PROGRAM

A. FLOWCHART

GOTO statement as long as the condition is "reversed." That is, lines 310–360 can be written as follows:

```
310   IF X < L THEN 370
320     REM --- FALSE: NEW LARGEST ---
330         LET L = X
340     REM --- ENDIF ---
370   PRINT X
```

The program in Fig. 7.2A illustrates finding the largest wage. Notice in this program that we are calculating a series of results (the

☐ **FIGURE 7.2**   **Finding Largest Wage**

```
100 PRINT "        ACME MARKETS PAYROLL"
110 PRINT
120 REM --- INITIALIZE LARGEST ---
130     LET L = -1
140                              REM
200 PRINT "NAME"; TAB(9);"HOUR","RATE","WAGE"
210 PRINT " "
250 READ N$, H, R
260                              REM
300 IF N$ = "ZZZ" THEN 600
310    LET W = H * R
320    IF W > L THEN 350
330      REM --- FALSE ---
340         GOTO 400
350      REM --- TRUE   ---
360         LET L = W
370    REM --- IF END ---
400    PRINT N$; TAB(9); H, R, W
410                              REM
420     READ N$, H, R
430 GOTO 300
440                              REM
600 PRINT
610 PRINT "LARGEST WAGE: "; L
620 STOP
800 DATA "JOE", 30, 4.50
801 DATA "MARY", 40, 5.00
802 DATA "FRAN", 30, 8.00
803 DATA "HARRY", 15, 5.00
999 DATA "ZZZ", 0, 0
```

A. PROGRAM

```
           ACME MARKETS PAYROLL

   NAME      HOUR    RATE           WAGE

   JOE        30      4.5            135
   MARY       40      5              200
   FRAN       30      8              240
   HARRY      15      5              75

   LARGEST WAGE:  240
```

B. OUTPUT

wages) and finding the largest of these values. Since variable L is used to hold the largest value, it is initialized (in line 130) to a small value before any wages are calculated. The portion of the program that keeps track of the largest wage so far is highlighted. The output for the program is shown in Fig. 7.2B.

The Smallest Value

For the program in Fig. 7.2A, suppose we want to find the smallest wage for the period. First, let's use variable S to hold the smallest wage so far. Now we replace lines 130, 320–370, and 610 in Fig. 7.2A with the following statements:

```
130   LET S = 999999

320   IF W < S THEN 350
330      REM --- FALSE ---
340          GOTO 400
350      REM --- TRUE  ---
360          LET S = W
370   REM --- IF END ---

610   PRINT "SMALLEST WAGE: "; S
```

Notice that to find the smallest values, we must initialize the variable that will hold the smallest to a very large number (line 130). Otherwise, the procedure for finding the smallest value is very similar to the procedure for finding the largest value.

EXERCISES

7.1. Trace the program in Fig. 7.2A.

7.2. Modify the program in Fig. 7.2A so that it finds the greatest overtime wages. Employees earn time-and-one-half for all time over 40 hours.

7.3. Modify the program in Fig. 7.2A so that it prints the name of the person who has the largest wage.

7.4. Modify the program written for Exercise 7.3 so that it also prints the smallest wage and the name of the person earning that wage.

7.5. Write a program that reads a list of numbers and finds the largest and how many times it occurred. For example, in the list

   42, 19, 35, 41, 42, 19, 42, 13

the largest is 42 and it occurs three times.

7.6. Explain why, when finding the smallest value, variable S must be initially assigned a very large value.

7.7. What does it mean to find the smallest string?

7.8. Write a program that finds the car with the best (most) miles per gallon. Assume that 75% of the driving done is in the city and 25% on the highway. A suggested report form follows:

```
            BEST CHOICE OF VEHICLE
                BASED ON MPG

     CITY DRIVING PERCENT 75
     VEHICLE        CITY MPG     HIGHWAY MPG
     --------------  --------------  -------------------
     CORVETTE        19           30
     NOVA            22           28
     F150            21           24
     DART            24           26

     BEST VEHICLE CHOICE:  ×××
     MILES PER GALLON:     ×××
```

7.9. The following program is supposed to find both the largest and the smallest value. Trace the program and find the problem.

```
110 LET L = -999
115 LET S = 999
120 PRINT "NUMBER"
250 READ X
300 IF X = 0 THEN 500
310   IF X > L THEN 350
320     REM --- FALSE ---
322        IF X < S THEN 326
324           GOTO 370  : REM - FALSE
326           LET S = X : REM - TRUE
330         GOTO 370
340     REM --- TRUE  ---
350        LET L = X
360     REM --- ENDIF ---
370   PRINT X
380   READ X
400 GOTO 300
410                     REM
500 PRINT
510 PRINT "THE LARGEST IS "; L
515 PRINT "THE SMALLEST IS"; S
520 STOP
800 DATA  17, 34, 5, 0
999 END
```

7.2 THE CASE STRUCTURE

case structure

The **case structure** is used when several mutually exclusive alternatives (cases) exist. In this section we will examine some situations that call for the case structure. Then we will look at two different ways of coding the case structure.

Multiple Alternatives or Cases

Recall that we examined the selection of two alternatives using the IF statement in Chapter 6. The situation when only two alternatives exist is a common one. Consider the following examples with two alternatives:

Condition True	Condition False
On time	Not on time (late)
In stock	Not in stock
Odd	Even
Day	Night
On	Off
Male	Female
Undergraduate	Graduate
Deposit	Withdrawal

You can undoubtedly think of other situations with only two alternatives. Selection of two alternatives is easily done with one IF statement, as we saw in Chapter 6.

We also studied the type of selection that requires nested selection. Again, as we saw in Chapter 6, a nested selection is dependent on the previous selection, as the following diagram suggests:

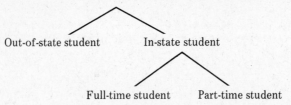

Out-of-state student   In-state student

Full-time student   Part-time student

case

Another common situation arises when there are several mutually exclusive (no overlapping) possibilities, or **cases**. The following list illustrates some typical examples:

Attribute	Cases, or Possibilities
Class	Freshman, sophomore, junior, senior
Size	Small, medium, large
Transaction	Order, return, payment
Age group	Child, teen, adult, senior citizen
Seat	Mezzanine, balcony, bleachers
Shipping	Surface, special priority, air
Membership	Single, family, full
Class	Coach, first class, ambassador
Team	Offense, defense, kicking, special
Type of sale	Cash, charge card, store charge, check
Direction	North, east, south, west
Car type	Compact, standard, high performance

For a specific example, suppose employees can be paid in one of three ways, as follows:

Method	Code	Action to Calculate Weekly Wage
Hourly wage	H	Multiply rate times hours worked
Commission	C	$100.00 + rate times sales amount
Salary	S	Yearly salary divided by 52

Also, suppose we have the following sample data:

```
"ROBERT", "H", 36, 6.00
"PETER", "C", 5400, 0.02
"ALLEN", "S", 36000, 0
```

The record format then is

		Number of hours or	Hourly wage rate or
Name	Pay code	Amount of sales or	Commission rate or
		Yearly wage	zero

and the variable names are N\$, P\$, A, and R. Notice how the interpretation of record fields 3 and 4 depends on the pay code.

The logic, expressed in flowchart and pseudocode, for selecting the appropriate alternatives (cases) is as shown in Fig. 7.3. These two representations of the algorithm suggest that when the pay code P\$ is "H", the wage is calculated one way; when P\$ is "C", it is calculated another way; when P\$ is "S", it is calculated a third way.

These two representations define the case structure. The case structure is used to select one of three or more possible alternatives or cases.

Coding the Case Structure

One way of coding the case structure is illustrated in the program in Fig. 7.4A. Two other ways are commonly used, too; one is described in the next subsection, and the second is illustrated in Section 7.4.

☐ **FIGURE 7.3**   **Case Structure: Logic for Selecting One of Three Cases**

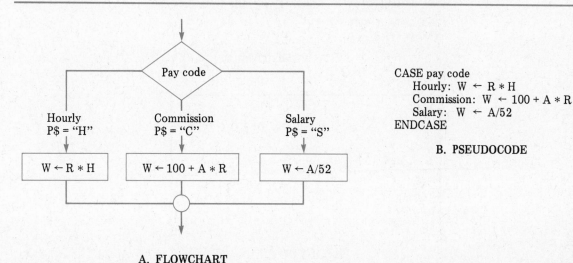

CASE pay code
    Hourly: W ← R * H
    Commission: W ← 100 + A * R
    Salary: W ← A/52
ENDCASE

B. PSEUDOCODE

A. FLOWCHART

☐ **FIGURE 7.4**   **Coding the Case Structure**

```
100 PRINT "          ACME MARKETS PAYROLL"
110 PRINT
140                                   REM
200 PRINT "          PAY", "HOUR/"
202 PRINT "NAME     CODE","AMOUNT","RATE","WAGE"
210 PRINT " "
250 READ N$, P$, A, R
260                                   REM
300 IF N$ = "ZZZ" THEN 600
310                                   REM
320   REM --- CASE-SELECTION --- ---
330       IF P$ = "H" THEN 400
340       IF P$ = "C" THEN 430
350       IF P$ = "S" THEN 470
360         PRINT "CASE ERROR"
370         STOP
400       REM -- CASE: HOURLY WAGE --
410           LET W = R * A
420           GOTO 500
430       REM -- CASE: COMMISSION  --
440           LET W = 100 + R * A
450           GOTO 500
460       REM -- CASE: SALARY      --
470           LET W = A / 52
480   REM --- ENDCASE    ---
490                                   REM
500   PRINT N$; TAB(12);P$, A, R, W
510                                   REM
520     READ N$, P$, A, R
530 GOTO 300
540                                   REM
600 PRINT
610 STOP
620                                   REM
790 REM --- CONSTANT DATA FILE ---
800 DATA "JOE",    "H", 30,    4.50
801 DATA "MARY",   "C", 5400, .02
802 DATA "FRAN",   "S", 28080, 0
803 DATA "HARRY",  "H", 15,    5.00
999 DATA "ZZZ",  "X",   0, 0
```

A. PROGRAM

```
          ACME MARKETS PAYROLL

          PAY   HOUR/
NAME      CODE  AMOUNT  RATE  WAGE

JOE        H     30      4.5   135
MARY       C     5400    .02   208
FRAN       S     28080   0     540
HARRY      H     15      5     75
```

B. OUTPUT

Notice in the program how the three IF statements (lines 330, 340, 350) are used to select the appropriate alternative. That is, the computer will be instructed to execute line 410, 440, or 470, depending on the pay code. Also note that if none of these pay codes exist, the program will print an error message and stop.

Once an alternative action is selected, a GOTO statement (lines 420 or 450) instructs the computer to go around the other alternative actions.

The output for this program is shown in Fig. 7.4B.

The ON–GOTO Statement

ON–GOTO statement The **ON–GOTO statement** in BASIC implements a limited version of the case structure. The case variable (variable X in the example below) may take on any one of the values from one to some positive integer. The form of the statement looks like this:

```
400    ON X GOTO 500, 600, 700
410    PRINT "ON-GOTO ERROR"
420    STOP
500      Statement
510      Statement
520    GOTO 1000
600      Statement
610    GOTO 1000
700      Statement
710      Statement
720      Statement
730    GOTO 1000
1000   REM --- END ON-GOTO ---
```

For this program, if X contains 1, then the processor goes to the first statement number following the GOTO. If X contains 2, then it goes to the second statement number following the GOTO. And so on. If the value in X is less than 1 or greater than the number of line numbers following the GOTO, then the processor goes to the next highest statement number, line 410 in the above example. In this event you may want to print a message to the effect that X has an unexpected value or to perform some other processing.

Again notice how the GOTO statements (lines 520 and 610) are used to go around alternative actions that are not selected.

The ON–GOTO statement will be used frequently in the following chapters in order to make select menu options.

EXERCISES

7.10. Trace the program in Fig. 7.4A.

7.11. Give two examples where three or more alternatives exist.

7.12. Explain the difference between the case structure and nested selection. (See Fig. 6.8 for an example of nested selection.)

7.3 LOGICAL OPERATORS

We have used two types of conditions so far: numeric conditions, like

$$A + B > C * 6$$

and string conditions, like

$$A\$ < B\$$$

compound conditions
logical operators

Each condition will have a value of true or false when it is evaluated. Other conditions, called **compound conditions,** may be formed by combining numeric or string conditions with the **logical operators** AND and OR. We'll illustrate their use with some examples.

☐ EXAMPLE

A student may be awarded a scholarship if her academic average (variable A) is greater than 95 or her average (A) is greater than 85 and she has earned two or more varsity letters (variable V). This compound condition can be expressed as

```
IF A > 95 OR (A > 85 AND V >= 2) THEN ...
```

☐ EXAMPLE

A customer will receive credit if he has done more than $500 worth of business (variable A holds the amount) in the last year and currently owes us (variable D is debt) no more than $100. That is,

```
IF A > 500 AND D < 100 THEN ...
```

☐ EXAMPLE

The navy will accept for submarine duty all males (variable S$ is sex) who have passed the physical (variable P$ is Y or N) and who are between the ages of 19 and 30. Thus

```
IF S$ = "M" AND P$ = "Y" AND 19 <= A AND A <= 30 THEN ...
```

These examples show that using the logical operators AND and OR is easier and simpler than using nested IF statements.

◻ **TABLE 7.1**   **Meanings of the Logical Operators**

cndt a	cndt b	cndt a AND cndt b	cndt a OR cndt b	cndt a	NOT cndt
True	True	True	True	True	False
True	False	False	True	False	True
False	True	False	True		
False	False	False	False		

AND, OR, NOT

Now let's see how the logical operators—AND, OR, and a third operator, NOT—are defined.

Suppose cndt a and cndt b stand for two conditions, condition a and condition b. Each of these, when evaluated, has a value of true or false. Then the meanings of the operators **AND, OR,** and **NOT** are defined as shown in Table 7.1.

In effect, simple conditions combined with logical operators are expressions, similar to numeric and string expressions. They have a value. The operators AND and OR and NOT are like the arithmetic operators $+$, $-$, $*$, and so on. Also, just as the arithmetic operators have a precedence in numeric expressions, the logical operators AND, OR, and NOT have **priorities,** or precedences, as shown below:

priorities

Highest priority	NOT
	AND
Lowest priority	OR

Furthermore, parentheses can be used to change the usual order in which the operations are carried out.

Thus to evaluate the expression

NOT X OR Y AND Z

where X, Y, and Z are currently false, we proceed as follows:

```
NOT false   OR   false   AND   false
     true   OR   false   AND   false   Evaluate NOT first
     true   OR           false         Evaluate AND second
                  true                  Evaluate OR third
```

But notice that

```
(NOT X       OR Y)      AND Z
(NOT false   OR false)  AND false
     true    OR false)  AND false
(       true        )   AND false
              false
```

EXERCISES

7.13. Assume that X, Y, and Z are numeric variables and U$ and V$ are string variables that contain the following values:

X	Y	Z	U$	V$
3	5	−4	"A"	"%"

Evaluate the following expressions:

a) `(X + Y > Z) OR (X − Y > 5)`
b) `NOT((16 < X) AND (X < 32))`
c) `"B" = V$ OR "B" < V$`
d) `U$ = "A" OR Z < 5 AND X = 3`

7.14. With the following different values in variables H, W, A, and S$,

	H	W	A	S$
i)	68	154	36	"M"
ii)	62	123	18	"F"
iii)	60	112	52	"F"
iv)	75	203	22	"M"

evaluate the following compound conditions:

a) `W > 150 AND S$ <> "F" OR H < 67`
b) `NOT (H < 65) OR A = 34 AND W > 124`
c) `ABS(A−20) < 3 AND S$ = "F"`
d) `A < 30 AND A > 20`

7.15. Suppose cndt 1 and cndt 2 represent any two conditions, and stmt 1 and stmt 2 represent any two statements. Are the following two program segments equivalent? Explain.

```
200  IF cndt 1 THEN 300        200  IF cndt 1 AND cndt 2 THEN 230
210    GOTO 400                210    stmt 2
300    IF cndt 2 THEN 350      220    GOTO 400
310      stmt 1                230    stmt 1
320      GOTO 400              400  ...
350      stmt 2
400  ...
```

7.16. Write the following IF statement without using any logical operator:

```
200   IF cndt 1 OR cndt 2 THEN 300
210     stmt 2
220     GOTO 400
300     stmt 1
400   ...
```

7.17. a) Suppose a and b are any compound conditions. Verify the following:

   i) NOT(a AND b) = (NOT a) OR (NOT b)
   ii) NOT(a OR b) = (NOT a) AND (NOT b)

These equivalencies are called De Morgan's rules. They are useful in simplifying Boolean expressions.

   b) Notice that

NOT((B < 0) OR (A = 8))

is equivalent to

NOT(B < 0) AND NOT(A = 8)

and is also equivalent to

(B >= 0) AND (A <> 8)

Simplify the following expressions:

   i) NOT((L < A) AND (A < U))
   ii) NOT((N >= K) AND ((X = 0) OR (T > U)))

7.4 EXTENSIONS TO THE IF STATEMENT

In this section we will discuss two useful extensions to the IF statement. These extensions will allow us to write certain selections more simply.

The IF–THEN Any Statement

Another common form of the IF statement is

IF   condition   THEN   any statement

Thus instead of being restricted to a specific statement number following THEN, the IF statement, in most versions of BASIC, may contain any BASIC statement. For example,

IF condition THEN PRINT "HELLO"
IF condition THEN LET A = B

This extension is particularly useful when we have a selection with action only on the true branch, as in the flowchart in Fig. 7.5A. With this extension we do not have to use a GOTO statement to go around the action on the true branch. (*Note:* The abbreviation stmt stands for statement.)

colon

multiple statements on a line

Notice in the code in Fig. 7.5B that there is a **colon** separating the two statements. The colon is the most common symbol to separate **multiple statements on a line.** However, different computers use different punctuation. Thus Apple, IBM PC, TRS-80, and Microsoft BASIC use the colon, as follows:

IF   condition   THEN   stmt 1 : stmt 2 : stmt 3

But BASIC–PLUS of Digital Equipment uses the back slash \ :

IF   condition   THEN   stmt 1 \ stmt 2 \ stmt 3

This form of the IF statement is particularly handy for implementing the case structure, as illustrated in the following program

---

☐ **FIGURE 7.5**   **Use of IF-THEN Any Statement**

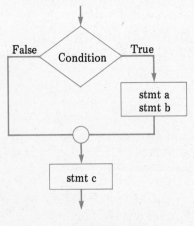

IF condition THEN stmt a : stmt b

B. CORRESPONDING BASIC

A. FLOWCHART

lines. If variable P$ contains H, the processor will execute the statement W = R * A in line 330. Then it will execute the GOTO statement, which sends the processor to the end of the case structure in line 480.

```
320   REM --- CASEBEGIN ---
330       IF P$ = "H" THEN W = R * A        : GOTO 500
340       IF P$ = "C" THEN W = 100 + R * A : GOTO 500
350       IF P$ = "S" THEN W = A / 52       : GOTO 500
360       PRINT "CASE ERROR" : STOP
480   REM --- ENDCASE   ---
```

If there are more than two statements for each alternative, the statements will not fit on the same line. So you will have to use the previous method of implementation for the case structure.

IF–THEN–ELSE

Another common extension of the IF statement (but it is not available on the Apple) is

$$\text{IF} \quad \text{condition} \quad \text{THEN} \left\{ \begin{matrix} \text{statement(s)} \\ \text{line number} \end{matrix} \right\} \text{ELSE} \left\{ \begin{matrix} \text{statement(s)} \\ \text{line number} \end{matrix} \right\}$$

If the condition is true, the statements after THEN are executed; when completed, the processor goes to the next statement. If the condition is false, the statements following ELSE are executed; when completed, the computer goes to the next statement.

This form of the IF statement is useful when there are only one or two statements for each alternative, as in the flowchart in Fig. 7.6A.

EXERCISE

7.18. Simplify the code for finding the largest value in the programs in Figs. 7.1B and 7.2A.

CHAPTER EXERCISES

7.19. Write a program like the one described in Exercise 5.7 (Section 5.2), which calculates the quality point average. However, the data record should contain the letter grade (A, B, C, D, F) rather than the numeric value (4 for A, 3 for B, and so on). The program should convert the letter grade to its numeric value (A is 4, B is 3, and so forth).

7.20. Automobile insurance premiums depend on many factors: round-

□ **FIGURE 7.6**   **Use of IF-THEN-ELSE**

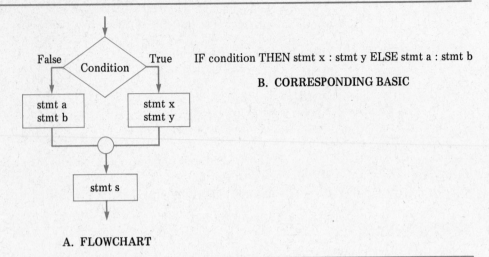

IF condition THEN stmt x : stmt y ELSE stmt a : stmt b

B. CORRESPONDING BASIC

A. FLOWCHART

trip distance to work, occupation, driving record, marital status, place of residence, and so on. However, the two most important factors are the person's age and the type of car the person owns—high performance (H), standard (S), or compact (C). To keep the problem simple, suppose premiums are calculated by using the following table:

Car Type	Person's Age	Premium
H	16–25	$400
H	Over 25	$250
S	16–25	$300
S	Over 25	$200
C	16–25	$275
C	Over 25	$225

Write a program that calculates premiums. Test the program.

7.21. Modify the program written for Exercise 7.20 so that a premium is increased by $300 if the client has had an accident in the last three years. Use the following information:

Record form   Name, age, car type, previous accident
Sample record   "JOE", 34, "H", "Y"

Subroutines and Modular Programming

INTRODUCTION TO CHAPTER 8

The programs up to this point have been quite short. They have fit nicely on one page. For this reason it has been easy to see the overall structure and purpose of the programs.

With the experience you have gained in the first seven chapters and the facility you have in using the IF statement, you are now in a position to analyze and write longer and more complicated programs. But before you attempt this task, we remind you of the advice given in Chapter 2 on program development, specifically on top-down design: Break the larger tasks into smaller, more manageable tasks. In fact, at this time you may want to review Chapter 2.

modular
programming

The purpose of this chapter is to explain the technique of **modular programming**, which makes longer programs more manageable. Essentially, in modular programming, short and well-defined tasks are implemented as a unit of code called *subroutines* (or subprograms). These subroutines are then tied together with a main control program.

This chapter expands on the student tuition program first described in Chapter 6. With this example we explain how subroutines are nested and how the output can be paged with subroutines.

The example in the final section describes the processing of groups of records and illustrates how subroutines can be used to simplify the process.

8.1 AN EXAMPLE

We'll begin our discussion with an example to illustrate a situation in which modular programming is needed. Suppose the college tuition example of Chapter 6 is expanded to incorporate room and meal charges as well as tuition. The desired report and overall program logic (flowchart) are illustrated in Figs. 8.1A and 8.1B.

Notice that in the flowchart in Fig. 8.1B we have not included the details on how to calculate the various costs. Instead, we indicate their calculation with a new symbol: a rectangle with two lines on the sides. This symbol is used to indicate a predefined or soon-to-be-defined algorithm (that is, it is defined elsewhere in another flowchart). Had we included all the details for calculating the various costs, the flowchart would have been quite a bit longer, and you would not have been able to visualize the overall structure of the entire program.

Now let's proceed with the various costs for this example. The room charge depends on the number of occupants of the room, according to the following schedule:

Room Type	Code	Charge	Room Type	Code	Charge
Triple room	T	$400	Single room	S	$700
Double room	D	$500	No room	N	$0

☐ **FIGURE 8.1**   **College Costs: Desired Report and Flowchart Logic**

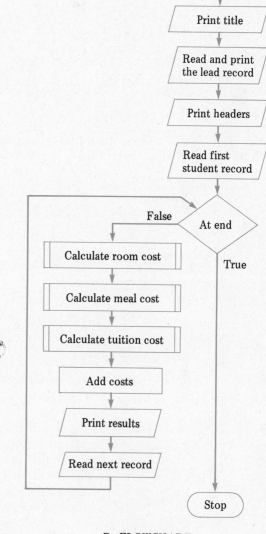

```
        WESTERN RHODE ISLAND UNIVERSITY

    SEMESTER: SPRING 1987
                                      TOTAL
    NAME    ROOM   MEALS  TUITION     FEES

    SAM     400    800    480         1680
    PETE    400    800    960         2160
    KAREN   400    0      960         1360
```

A. REPORT

B. FLOWCHART

There are three meal plans, as follows:

Plan	Code	Charge
Weekday plan	W	$800
Full plan	F	$1000
No plan	N	$0

☐ **FIGURE 8.2**   **Calculation of Specific Costs**

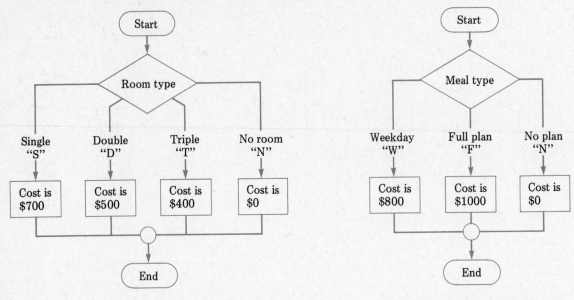

A. CALCULATION OF ROOM COST   B. CALCULATION OF MEAL COST

Finally, the tuition is calculated as explained in Section 6.5.

To produce the desired report, we should structure each data record like this:

Record structure   Name, state, room code, meal code, credits
Sample record   "JOE", "CT", "D", "W", 14

Figures 8.2A and 8.2B indicate the logic for calculating the room and meal costs. Notice that both calculations involve the case structure. As mentioned earlier, the tuition is calculated as explained in Chapter 6.

The following sections explain how the program for this modified tuition example is written.

8.2 SUBROUTINES (SUBPROGRAMS)

subroutine
subprogram

A **subroutine** or **subprogram** is a program that is executed at the request of another program. Think of the flowcharts in Fig. 8.2 as subprograms. The main program—the flowchart in Fig. 8.1B—requests that these subprograms be executed at the appropriate times to calculate room, meal, and tuition costs.

calling program

main program

The program that requests (calls for) the execution of another program is termed the **calling program**. In effect, you can think of the calling program as the one that supervises the work of the subroutines. The **main program** is the program segment that is first executed and controls the execution of the major subprograms. Thus the main program is also a calling program.

The following subsections explain how subroutines work.

GOSUB and RETURN Statements

GOSUB statement

In BASIC a program initiates the execution of a subprogram by executing a **GOSUB statement**. The form of the statement is

line number   GOSUB   line number

The GOSUB statement is illustrated in the program of Fig. 8.3 (lines 320, 340, and 360).

Let's look at the GOSUB statement in line 320. This statement causes two actions:

stack

1. The number of the next statement, 330, is saved in a stack. *Note:* A **stack** is a special memory location that can hold one or more statement numbers. Statement numbers are saved on the top and are removed from the top.

330

Stack

2. Next the computer "goes to" statement 5000, where it continues to execute that statement and the statements that follow it.

RETURN statement

Eventually, the computer comes to a **RETURN statement** (such as line 5510). At this point two more actions are taken:

3. The computer removes the statement number from the top of the stack—330 in this case.
4. The computer "returns to" statement 330 and continues executing statements in the main program.

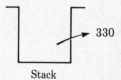

330

Stack

Hierarchy Charts

Hierarchy charts are used to show which (sub)programs request the execution of other subprograms. When you have a program with more

FIGURE 8.3 Program for Calculating College Costs

```
8000 REM --- CONSTANT DATA FILE ---
8010 DATA "SPRING", 1987
8020 DATA "SAM",   "RI", "T", "W", 12
8030 DATA "PETE",  "CT", "T", "W", 12
8040 DATA "KAREN", "CT", "T", "N", 12
9000 DATA "ZZZ",   "X", "X", "X", 0
9999 END

100 PRINT "      WESTERN RHODE ISLAND UNIVERSITY"
110 PRINT
120 READ Q$, Y
130 PRINT "SEMESTER: ";Q$;Y
140 PRINT
200 PRINT TAB(33); "TOTAL"
202 PRINT "NAME"; TAB(10);"ROOM"; TAB(16);"MEALS";
204 PRINT TAB(22);"TUITION"; TAB(33); "FEES"
210 PRINT
220                                          REM
250 READ N$, S$, R$, M$, C
260                                          REM
300 IF N$ = "ZZZ" THEN 500
310   REM --- CALCULATE ROOM CHARGE
320     GOSUB 5000
330   REM --- CALCULATE MEAL CHARGE
340     GOSUB 6000
350   REM --- CALCULATE TUITION
360     GOSUB 7000
370                                          REM
380   LET T1 = R + M + T
390   PRINT N$; TAB(10);R; TAB(16);M;
392   PRINT TAB(22);T; TAB(33); T1
400                                          REM
410   READ N$, S$, R$, M$, C
420 GOTO 300
430                                          REM
500 PRINT
510 STOP
520                                          REM
530                                          REM
```

```
5000 REM --- CALCULATE ROOM CHARGE
5010    REM --- BEGINCASE ---
5020    IF R$ = "S" THEN 5100
5030    IF R$ = "D" THEN 5200
5040    IF R$ = "T" THEN 5300
5050    IF R$ = "N" THEN 5400
5060    PRINT "ROOM ERROR"
5070    STOP
5080
5100    REM --- CASE: SINGLE ROOM ---   REM
5110    LET R = 700
5120    GOTO 5500
5200    REM --- CASE: DOUBLE ROOM ---
5210    LET R = 500
5220    GOTO 5500
5300    REM --- CASE: TRIPLE ROOM ---
5310    LET R = 400
5320    GOTO 5500
5400    REM --- CASE: NO ROOM ---
5410    LET R = 0
5420
5500    REM --- ENDCASE ---   REM
5510 RETURN
5520    REM
5530    REM
5540    REM
```

```
6000 REM --- CALCULATE MEALS COST
6010    REM --- BEGINCASE ---
6020    IF M$ = "W" THEN 6100
6030    IF M$ = "F" THEN 6200
6040    IF M$ = "N" THEN 6300
6050    PRINT "MEALS ERROR"; M$
6060    STOP                    REM
6070
6100    REM --- CASE: WEEKDAY ---
6110    LET M = 800
6120    GOTO 6500
6200    REM --- CASE: FULL PLAN ---
6210    LET M = 1000
6220    GOTO 6500
6300    REM --- CASE: NO PLAN ---
6310    LET M = 0
6320
6500    REM --- ENDCASE ---   REM
6510 RETURN
6520    REM
6530    REM
6540    REM
```

```
7000 REM --- CALCULATE TUITION
7010    IF S$ = "RI" THEN 7200
7020    REM --- FALSE ---
7030    LET T = 80 * C
7040    GOTO 7400
7200    REM --- TRUE ---
7210    IF C >= 12 THEN 7300
7220    REM --- FALSE ---
7230    LET T = 50 * C
7240    GOTO 7400
7250    REM --- TRUE ---
7300    LET T = 40 * C
7310    GOTO 7400
7320    REM --- ENDIF ---
7330    REM --- ENDIF ---
7340                           REM
7400 RETURN
7410                           REM
7420                           REM
```

□ **FIGURE 8.4**   **Hierarchy Chart for College Costs Program**

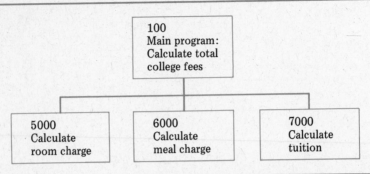

than four or five subprograms, it is almost mandatory to have a corresponding hierarchy chart in order to know what is happening. The hierarchy chart in Fig. 8.4 shows the subroutine hierarchy for the college costs example.

Each rectangle in the chart corresponds to the main program or a subprogram that carries out a particular function. The logic for the routine of each rectangle can be represented as a flowchart or as pseudocode.

The hierarchical representation of (sub)programs is similar to the command structure in the army. The main program (general) directs and supervises a number of colonels; each colonel directs and supervises a number of majors; each major directs and supervises a number of captains; and so on.

EXERCISES

8.1. Trace the program in Fig. 8.3 completely.

8.2. Modify the program in Fig. 8.3 so that it does the following:
   a) Counts all the students.
   b) Sums the tuition for all students.
   c) Counts all students with the full meal plan.
   d) Prints the number of students whose total fees exceed $3000.
   e) Counts the number of part-time students who have the full meal plan.

8.3 NESTED SUBROUTINES

A subroutine can call another subroutine. For example, a subroutine that starts at line 4000 may call another subroutine that begins at line 5000 (GOSUB 5000). In this situation we say that the subroutine beginning at line 5000 is a **nested subroutine**; it is nested within the subrou-

nested subroutine

☐ **FIGURE 8.5**   **Hierarchy Chart Showing Subroutine Calling Other Subroutines**

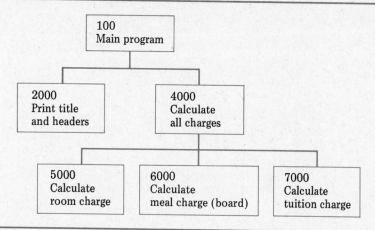

tine that begins at line 4000. This relationship between subroutines is suggested by the hierarchy chart in Fig. 8.5. Since the rectangle labeled 5000 is connected to the rectangle labeled 4000, subroutine 4000 calls subroutine 5000. Subroutine 4000 also calls subroutines 6000 and 7000.

The hierarchy chart in Fig. 8.5 corresponds to the program in Fig. 8.6, which is a modification of the program in Fig. 8.3. In Fig. 8.6 we have removed portions of the main program of Fig. 8.3 and made them into subprograms, one beginning at statement 2000 and another at statement 4000.

It is important to understand how the computer executes the GOSUB statements. The stack, mentioned previously, plays an important role. Let's trace the program in Fig. 8.6, paying particular attention to the contents of the stack. The diagrams below in the column to the right show the stack contents.

Program Trace

- The first GOSUB executed is 130 GOSUB 2000. The next highest statement number, 140, is assigned to the stack, and the computer goes to statement 2000. It then executes the subroutine in lines 2000 through 2220.

- The RETURN statement, statement 2220, causes the computer to return to the line number currently at the top of the stack, 140. This line number is then removed from the stack.

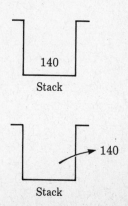

□ **FIGURE 8.6**   **Modified College Costs Program with
                          Subroutine Calling Other Subroutines**

```
100 REM --- MAIN PROGRAM: CALCULATE FEES ---
110                                               REM
120 REM --- PRINT TITLE AND HEADERS
130     GOSUB 2000
140                                               REM
250 READ N$, S$, R$, M$, C
260                                               REM
300 IF N$ = "ZZZ" THEN 500
310   REM --- CALCULATE ALL CHARGES ---
320       GOSUB 4000
330                                               REM
380   LET T1 = R + M + T
390   PRINT N$; TAB(10);R; TAB(16);M;
392   PRINT  TAB(22);T; TAB(33); T1
400                                               REM
410   READ N$, S$, R$, M$, C
420 GOTO 300
430                                               REM
500 PRINT
510 STOP
520                                               REM

2000 REM --- PRINT TITLE AND HEADERS ---
2100    PRINT "    WESTERN RHODE ISLAND UNIVERSITY"
2110    PRINT
2120    READ Q$, Y
2130    PRINT "SEMESTER: ";Q$;Y
2140    PRINT
2200    PRINT TAB(33); "TOTAL"
2201    PRINT "NAME"; TAB(10);"ROOM"; TAB(16);"MEALS";
2202    PRINT TAB(22);"TUITION"; TAB(33); "FEES"
2210    PRINT
2220 RETURN

4000 REM --- CALCULATE ALL CHARGES ---
4020    REM --- CALCULATE ROOM COST
4030        GOSUB 5000
4040    REM --- CALCULATE MEAL COST
4050        GOSUB 6000
4060    REM --- CALCULATE TUITION
4070        GOSUB 7000
4080                                              REM
4140                                              REM
4200 RETURN
4210                                              REM
```

■ When statement 320 is executed, statement
number 330 is put into the stack. Then the
computer goes to statement 4000 and executes the subroutine beginning with that
line.

330

Stack

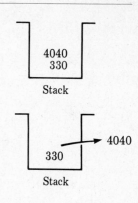

- At statement 4030 GOSUB 5000, statement number 4040 is put onto the stack. Then the computer goes to statement 5000 and continues executing that subroutine (which is not shown in Fig. 8.6; see Fig. 8.3).

- When statement 5510 RETURN (see Fig. 8.3) is executed, where does the computer return to? It pulls the statement number from the top of the stack and returns to this statement, which is line 4040. The stack now has only one statement number in it, 330.

EXERCISES

8.3. Continue tracing the program in Fig. 8.6, showing how the statement numbers in the stack change.

8.4. Describe what would happen in the stack if statement 4200 were

```
4200   GOTO 380
```

8.5. What would happen if statement 510 STOP was accidentally omitted?

8.4 PAGING THE OUTPUT

The output from all the previous programs have been limited to one page or screen. However, computer output usually consists of more than one page or screen. In this section subroutines are used to make the computer output more readable by formatting each page or screen. Specifically, the hierarchy chart in Fig. 8.5 and the program in Fig. 8.6 are modified in order to produce an output like that shown in Fig. 8.7.

Report-Paging Form

Suppose your output is being directed to a printer. Each page of the output is separated by a perforation so that the output can be put into folders. In order to make each page readable, you should include a title and a heading at the top of each page. This form for report paging is illustrated in Fig. 8.7. The figure also shows that the pages are counted in a typical report.

If the output is directed to the video display terminal (VDT), the program should pause after each screen is filled so that the user can

□ **FIGURE 8.7**   **Report-Paging Form for College Costs Program**

```
                                            PAGE 1
                  WESTERN RHODE ISLAND UNIVERSITY

             SEMESTER: SPRING 1987

                                            TOTAL
             NAME     ROOM  MEALS TUITION   FEES

             SAM      400   800   480       1680
             PETE     400   800   960       2160
             KAREN    400   800   960       2160

─ ─ ─ ─ ─ ─ ─ ─ ─ ─ ─ ─ ─ ─ ─ ─ ─ ─ ─ ─ ─ ─ ─ ─ ─ ─ ─ ─

                                            PAGE 2
                  WESTERN RHODE ISLAND UNIVERSITY

             SEMESTER: SPRING 1987

                                            TOTAL
             NAME     ROOM  MEALS TUITION   FEES

             ED       400   800   550       1750
             JIM      400   800   1200      2400
```

inspect the results. (This technique is illustrated in the next chapter.) The techniques of paging are similar for both printers and VDTs, so we will confine our discussion here to printed output.

Paging Logic

Now let's develop the overall logic for generating the output in Fig. 8.7. In order to do so, we first have to know how many detail lines can be printed per page. Let's assume that there are three detail lines per page, so we don't have to enter a lot of data. Second, we will have to count the detail lines as they are printed. Third, we will have to check to see when the line limit has been reached.

The pseudocode in Fig. 8.8A is essentially the logic for the main program given in Fig. 8.3. The pseudocode in Fig. 8.8B expands on various statements in Fig. 8.8A. Notice that printing the detail line is now the key element in the paging logic. Before the next detail line is printed, a test is made to determine if the line belongs on the page. If it does, it is printed. Otherwise, we skip to a new page, print the title and headers, and then print the new detail line.

As an aid in understanding the relationship between the various subroutines, Fig. 8.9 shows the hierarchy chart for the college costs program with paging subroutines; the program is given in Fig. 8.10.

□ FIGURE 8.8 Paging Logic

*Read semester and initialize variables
Print title and headers
Read first student record
LOOP—UNTIL no more students
    Calculate charges
    Sum charges
    *Print detail line
    Read next record
ENDLOOP
Stop

A. MAIN PROGRAM LOGIC

*Read semester and initialize variables
    Read semester
    Zero counters

*Print detail line
    IF belong on current page
        FALSE:
            Skip lines to new page
            Print title and headers
            Set line count to 0
        TRUE:
            Continue on
    ENDIF
    Add 1 to line count
    Print line

B. DETAILS OF STATEMENTS WITH ASTERISKS

The hierarchy chart (compare it with the chart in Fig. 8.5) shows that the subroutine for printing the title and headers (2000) is called from two subroutines (from 100 and from 3000). Notice the corner trim marks on the rectangles for subroutine 2000. Whenever a subroutine appears two or more times in a hierarchy chart, the corner trim mark is used to make this repetition stand out.

□ FIGURE 8.9 Hierarchy Chart Showing Paging Subroutines

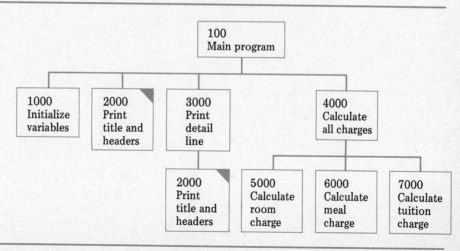

□ **FIGURE 8.10** College Costs Program with Paging Subroutines

```
100 REM --- MAIN PROGRAM: CALCULATE FEES
110                                             REM
120 REM --- INITIALIZE VARIABLES ---
130     GOSUB 1000
140                                             REM
150 REM --- PRINT TITLE AND HEADERS ---
160     GOSUB 2000
170                                             REM
250 READ N$, S$, R$, M$, C
260                                             REM
300 IF N$ = "ZZZ" THEN 500
310 REM --- CALCULATE ALL CHARGES ---
320     GOSUB 4000
330                                             REM
370     LET T1 = R + M + T
380                                             REM
390 REM --- PRINT DETAIL LINE
395     GOSUB 3000
400                                             REM
410     READ N$, S$, R$, M$, C
420 GOTO 300
430                                             REM
500 PRINT
510 STOP
520
```

```
1000 REM --- INITIALIZE VARIABLES ---
1010     READ Q$, Y :    REM - SEMESTER & YEAR
1100 LET L = 3 :         REM - # LINES PER PAGE
1110 LET L1 = 0 :        REM - LINE COUNT
1120 LET P = 0 :         REM - PAGE COUNT
1200 RETURN
1210                     REM
```

```
2000 REM --- PRINT TITLE & HEADERS ---
2010     LET P = P + 1
2020     PRINT TAB(30);"PAGE";P
2100     PRINT " WESTERN RHODE ISLAND UNIVERSITY"
2110     PRINT
2130     PRINT "SEMESTER: ";Q$;Y
2140     PRINT
2200     PRINT TAB(33);"TOTAL"
2201     PRINT "NAME"; TAB(10);"ROOM"; TAB(16);"MEALS";
2202     PRINT TAB(22);"TUITION"; TAB(33); "FEES";
2210     PRINT
2220 RETURN
2230                     REM
```

```
3000 REM --- PRINT DETAIL LINE ---
3010 REM --- STILL ON CURRENT PAGE?
3100     IF L1 < L THEN 3300
3200     REM --- FALSE: HENCE NEW PAGE ---
3210         PRINT : PRINT : PRINT
3220         GOSUB 2000
3230         LET L1 = 0 : REM - RESET LINE COUNT
3250     REM --- ENDIF ---
3300     LET L1 = L1 + 1
3400     PRINT N$; TAB(10);R; TAB(16);M;
3410     PRINT TAB(22);T; TAB(33); T1
3500 RETURN
```

```
4000 REM --- CALCULATE ALL CHARGES ---
4010     REM --- CALCULATE ROOM CHARGE
4020         GOSUB 5000
4030     REM --- CALCULATE MEAL CHARGE
4040         GOSUB 6000
4050     REM --- CALCULATE TUITION
4060         GOSUB 7000
4070 RETURN
```

The key element of paging logic—printing the detail lines—is implemented in subroutine 3000 of the program in Fig. 8.10. Compare the program's subroutine with the pseudocode in Fig. 8.8B.

Page Totals

Reports will frequently have page totals and cumulative totals. For example, a typical page may look like the page shown in Fig. 8.11. The page totals are simply totals of all detail lines on the page. Cumulative totals are totals accumulated from the beginning of the report.

EXERCISES

8.6. Modify the program in Fig. 8.10 so that it does not print the page number on the first page.

8.7. Modify the program in Fig. 8.10 so that it prints page and cumulative totals on each page.

8.5 GROUP TOTALS

Records in files can sometimes be grouped in a natural way. For example, in a large company employee records may be grouped according to the department they work in. Sometimes, it is desirable to process

☐ **FIGURE 8.11** **Paged Report with Page Totals and Cumulative Totals**

```
                                                      PAGE 5
                 WESTERN RHODE ISLAND UNIVERSITY

     SEMESTER: SPRING 1987

                                                      TOTAL
     NAME             ROOM        MEALS      TUITION    FEES

     SAM               400          800          400    1680
     PETE              400          800          960    2160
     KAREN             400          800          960    2160
      .
      .
      .

     PAGE
     TOTALS           XXXX         XXXX         XXXX    XXXX

     CUMULATIVE
         TOTALS       XXXX         XXXX         XXXX    XXXX
```

these records in groups. This section explains group processing and its logic.

Group Processing

The records in many data files are originally put in the file in sequence according to when they occurred. Then they are usually sorted into groups before reports are generated at the end of the day, week, or month. Let's look at an example to see how group processing works.

◻ EXAMPLE

Consider a small power lawn mower supply dealer. As customers come in during the month, transaction records are generated in sequence by date. At the end of the month the records will be sorted by customer and date so that complete invoices can be generated and sent to the customers and so that other reports can be generated as well.

Figure 8.12 shows such a sorted data file (part A) and a resulting report (part B). Notice that the report has a total after each group of customer records and a grand summary for all groups.

Group-Processing Logic

In a report, at the end of each group, summaries for the group are printed, as shown in Fig. 8.12B. The program can determine the end of the group by comparing the current customer identification (ID) number with the previous ID number. If they are the same, then the program is still working within the current group. If they are different, the summaries for the previous group are printed and the next group is processed.

Figure 8.13 presents the flowchart for such group-processing logic. To understand the flowchart in Fig. 8.13, you should trace it by using the sorted data file given in Fig. 8.12A.

EXERCISES

8.8.   Trace the group-processing flowchart in Fig. 8.13, using the values in the sorted data file of Fig. 8.12A.

8.9.   Write a program that implements group totals.

8.10.   Give three examples where the use of group processing is appropriate.

☐ **FIGURE 8.12**   **Group Processing for a Power Lawn Mower Supply Dealer**

```
CUSTOMER
IDENT        DATE          DESCRIPTION      AMOUNT

AC343        08/12/85      MOWER BLADE       23.45
AC343        08/13/85      OIL               12.45
AC343        08/24/85      CHAIN             31.98
BRO82        08/24/85      TIRE              37.89
BRO82        08/12/85      OIL               23.45
JR112        08/15/85      SPARK PLUG         3.45
JR112        08/17/85      TUNE-UP           51.23
  •
  •
  •
```

A. SORTED DATA FILE

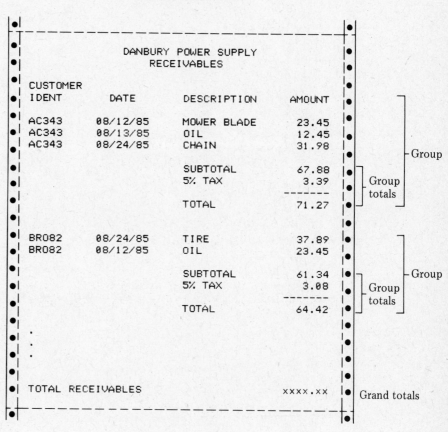

B. REPORT GENERATED

☐ **FIGURE 8.13**   **Flowchart for Group-Processing Logic**

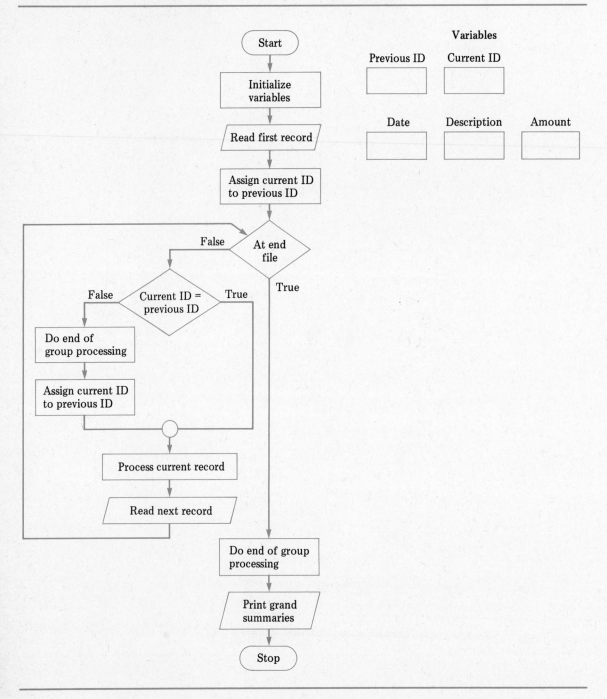

INTERACTIVE PROGRAMMING

Menu-Driven Programs

INTRODUCTION TO CHAPTER 9

Up to this point you have been exposed to only the most fundamental BASIC statements—fundamental in the sense that these statements constitute the minimum number of statements you need to process data by using the sequence, loop, selection, and subroutine control structures. The understanding of these structures is thus the first milestone in learning about programming and computers. The remaining chapters expand on the fundamental statements and present additional statements that extend the programmer's repertoire.

In previous programs the method of entering data has been limited to using the READ and DATA statements. These statements require the programmer to enter data into the program *before* the program is executed. This method has certain pedagogical advantages but has major disadvantages in real life programs. So in this chapter you will learn techniques for writing programs that allow the user to enter data from the keyboard *during* the execution of the program. We call

☐ **FIGURE 9.1**   **Main Menu from Which Options May Be Selected**

Courtesy of Digital Equipment Corporation

interactive
execution

menu-driven
program

this process **interactive execution.** Specifically, the INPUT statement, as described in Section 9.1, will let you write programs that allow data to be entered from the keyboard.

Interactive programs are usually **menu-driven.** By that we mean the user is presented with a menu of options from which he or she may select the desired processing to be done. Figure 9.1 illustrates such a menu. The ON–GOSUB statement, discussed in Section 9.2, is needed to determine the option selected. The programming details of two menu-driven applications are explained in Section 9.3. They are particularly important because they illustrate common applications.

9.1 THE INPUT STATEMENT

As mentioned in the introduction, up to this time only READ and DATA statements have been used to enter data into a program for processing. This method of entering data made program testing easier since you did not have to worry about entering data each time you tested a program. This approach also allowed you to concentrate on the control structures— series, looping, selection, and subroutines—themselves. Now by using the INPUT statement, you will be able to enter data directly from the keyboard while the program is executing.

In this section the basic forms of the INPUT statement are presented. Then we will examine several ways of making the data entry process accurate and convenient.

Basic Form of the INPUT Statement

INPUT statement

The basic form of the **INPUT statement** is

line number   INPUT   variables separated by commas

An example of a legal INPUT statement is

```
350   INPUT N$, A, R
```

To show how the INPUT statement works, we will examine the INPUT statements in the program in Fig. 9.2A. The output (Fig. 9.2B) and the contents of the appropriate variables (Fig. 9.2C) are also shown for reference.

By examining the program and the output, we see that whenever the computer comes to an INPUT statement, it prints a question mark on the screen. After it prints the question mark, the computer waits for the user to enter a value on the keyboard. You will probably see a small blinking light on the screen beside the question mark. This light is called the **cursor.**

cursor

☐ **FIGURE 9.2**   **Program Using INPUT Statements**

```
100  INPUT D$
110  INPUT P
120  INPUT Q
130  PRINT
140  PRINT "COST  "; P * Q
150  END
```

A. PROGRAM

```
RUN
? HIGHBACK CHAIR <return>
? 125. <return>
? 3 <return>

COST   375
```

B. OUTPUT

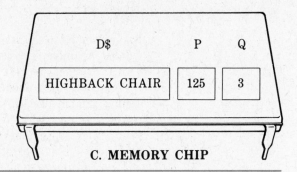

C. MEMORY CHIP

After a value is entered by the user and the <return> key is pressed, that value is assigned to the variable. For example, when <return> is pressed the first time, the string HIGHBACK CHAIR is assigned to variable D\$. When <return> is pressed the second time, the number 125 is assigned to variable P; and so on.

As illustrated in Fig. 9.2A, either a string or a numeric variable can appear in an INPUT statement.

Only one variable was used in each INPUT statement in the previous example. But more than one variable may appear in the INPUT statement. In this case the variables must be separated by commas. These commas, however, serve only to separate the variables; they have nothing to do with the print zones.

Consider the following example:

```
100  INPUT R$, L, W
110  LET A = L * W
120  PRINT "AREA = "; A
130  END
```

```
RUN
? BATHROOM, 15, 8
AREA = 120
```

When the program is RUN, data are entered, with commas separating each value. Notice that it is not necessary to put quotation marks around string values when you are entering data for INPUT statements. The first value entered, BATHROOM, is assigned to variable R$, the first variable in the INPUT statement. The second value, 15, is assigned to variable L, the second variable; and so on.

User Prompts

prompts

Whenever an INPUT statement is used in a program, the person at the keyboard should be told what type of value is being requested. That is, the person should be prompted. One way to provide **prompts** is by preceding every INPUT statement with PRINT statements, as shown in the following program. The PRINT statements identify the information the user should enter.

```
100   PRINT "ENTER":
110   PRINT "ROOM NAME, LENGTH, WIDTH"
120   INPUT N$, L, W
130   LET A = L * W
140   PRINT
150   PRINT "AREA = "; A
160   END
```

```
RUN
ENTER:
ROOM NAME, LENGTH, WIDTH
? KITCHEN, 18, 12

AREA = 216
```

Instead of all three values being entered on one line, the three values may be entered separately, as indicated in the next example. Notice that the dangling semicolons (lines 100, 120, 140) cause the question mark to occur on the same line as the printed string.

```
100   PRINT "ENTER ROOM NAME..";
110   INPUT N$
120   PRINT "LENGTH..........";
130   INPUT L
140   PRINT "WIDTH...........";
150   INPUT W
160   LET A = L * W
170   PRINT
180   PRINT "AREA = "; A
190   END
```

```
RUN
ENTER ROOM NAME .. ? KITCHEN
LENGTH .......... ? 14
WIDTH ........... ? 10
AREA = 140
```

Prompting for inputted data is so necessary that most versions of BASIC allow the prompt to be part of the INPUT statement, as illustrated in the following program:

```
100   INPUT "ENTER ROOM NAME"; N$
110   INPUT "LENGTH ........"; L
120   INPUT "WIDTH ........."; W
130   LET A = L * W
140   PRINT
150   PRINT "AREA = "; A
160   END
```

```
RUN
ENTER ROOM NAME .. ? KITCHEN
LENGTH ........... ? 14
WIDTH ............ ? 10

AREA = 140
```

Checking for Invalid Data

One reason computers sometimes give incorrect results is that the program has a logic error. Another more common reason is that the program is given incorrect data to process. Programmers refer to this error as "Garbage in, garbage out." In some ways, as discussed below, the BASIC language guards against incorrect data. But usually, the program should verify that the data is correct.

Suppose you are entering data to the following program:

```
100   PRINT "ROOM NAME, LENGTH, WIDTH"
110   INPUT N$, L, W
120   LET A = L * W
130   PRINT "AREA = "; A
```

BASIC will check for invalid data in the following situations:

1. *Too little data:* Suppose you enter just two values and then press <return>. Since the computer is expecting three values, it will ask for *more*, as shown in the output to the right.

```
RUN
ROOM NAME, LENGTH, WIDTH
? PLAYROOM, 12 (return)
MORE ?
```

2. *Too much data:* Suppose you enter four data values and press <return>. Most computers will respond with EXCESS IGNORED, as shown in the output at the right.

```
RUN
ROOM NAME, LENGTH, WIDTH
? PLAYROOM, 12, 10, 5
EXCESS IGNORED
AREA = 120
```

3. *Data of the wrong type:* Notice in the output at the right that a numeric value will be accepted as a string value. But the computer will not allow a string value to be entered into a numeric value. Most computers will ask you to REDO it with the correct value.

```
100   INPUT "ROOM NAME ..."; N$
120   INPUT "LENGTH ......"; L
130   INPUT "WIDTH ......."; W
140   LET A = L * W
```

```
RUN
ROOM NAME ... ? 9
LENGTH ...... ? JOHN
REDO
LENGTH ...... ? 9
```

There are many situations where you must include in your program a check for valid data. For example, if the values entered constitute a date, then the month must be between 1 and 12 and the day between 1 and 31. The following example illustrates how you verify that the data has one of a few specific values—in this event, a gender (male or female). In line 120 if the inputted gender is not M or F, then the computer goes to line 110 to INPUT the gender again.

```
100   INPUT "NAME ......"; N$
105   REM --- LOOP UNTIL CORRECT ---
110   INPUT "GENDER ...."; G$
120      IF NOT (G$ = "M" OR G$ = "F") THEN 110
130   INPUT "HEIGHT ...."; H
 .
 .
 .
```

```
RUN
NAME ....... ? WILLIAM
GENDER .... ? X
GENDER .... ? B
GENDER .... ? M
HEIGHT .... ? 72
```

Designing Convenient Data Input

Since valid data is an absolute necessity, programs should be designed so that data entry is as convenient as possible. In this way mistakes are reduced. One way to make data input convenient is to limit the number of keystrokes.

Let's consider the calculation of costs at a fast-food chain. One way to calculate the cost of an order is to multiply the price per unit by the quantity. Two methods of entering the data are illustrated below. Notice in Method 1 that the product type and the quantity are entered separately. The second method eliminates a keystroke by entering the product and the quantity as one string. The first character of the string is the product type.

Method 1

```
   MCDOUGS FAST-FOODS CALCULATOR

F - FRIES   H - HAMBURGERS   S - SHAKE
              X - EXIT

ENTER TRANSACTION:
   PRODUCT TYPE ....... ? H
   QUANTITY .......... ? 2
         COST ........ 2.58
```

Method 2

```
   MCDOUGS FAST-FOODS CALCULATOR

F - FRIES   H - HAMBURGERS   S - SHAKE
              X - EXIT

ENTER TRANSACTION .... ? H2
         COST IS      2.58
```

{Two hamburgers}

In the second method H2 is inputted as a string. The string then has to be taken apart by the program to isolate the product type and the quantity. This process is illustrated by the program in Fig. 9.3. Notice the use of the string function MID$ and LEFT$. (Recall that these functions were discussed at the end of Chapter 4.)

☐ **FIGURE 9.3**   **Entering Two Values with One String**

```
100 PRINT "       MCDOUGS FAST-FOODS CALCULATOR"
110 PRINT
200 PRINT "F - FRIES     H - HAMBURGER     S - SHAKE"
210 PRINT
220 PRINT "                X - EXIT"
230 PRINT
290 INPUT "ENTER TRANSACTION .... "; T$
300 IF LEFT$(T$,1) = "X" THEN 800
320    LET N$ = MID$(T$,2,3)
330    LET N = VAL(N$)
400    REM --- CASE BEGIN ---
410       IF LEFT$(T$,1) = "F"   THEN C =  .59 : GOTO 500
420       IF LEFT$(T$,1) = "H"   THEN C = 1.29 : GOTO 500
430       IF LEFT$(T$,1) = "S"   THEN C =  .79 : GOTO 500
440    REM --- CASE END   ---
500    PRINT "          COST IS        "; C * N
510                                                    REM
520    PRINT
530    INPUT "ENTER TRANSACTION .... "; T$
540 GOTO 300
800 STOP
810 END
```

EXERCISES

9.1. Refer to the program in Fig. 9.3. What will happen if a value other than F, H, S, or X is entered? Fix the program to protect against this data entry error.

9.2. Write a program segment that will accept a date as a string in the form mm/dd/yy. Check that the slashes (/) are in the proper place and that the mm and dd values are reasonable. You will have to use some of the string functions.

9.3. Write a program segment that will accept a valid time as a string in the form hh:mm:ss. Then write a main program that calculates the difference between two times.

9.4. Modify the Acme parking lots problem, Exercise 6.16, so that the times are entered interactively and are in the form hh:mm:XX, where XX is AM or PM.

9.5. Write a program that sums a series of numbers entered from the keyboard. Have the program also determine the average.

9.6. Write a program that reads a string consisting of numbers and arithmetic operators and evaluates the expression. For example,

```
?45 * 324 - 345 =
14235
```

9.7.   Write a program that acts like a calculator. For example, the program input/output may look like this:

```
VALUE      ? 234
OPERATION ? *
VALUE      ? 345
OPERATION ? -
VALUE      ? 45
OPERATION ? =
RESULT IS   80685
```

9.2 THE ON-GOSUB STATEMENT

The ON–GOSUB statement is a combination of the ON–GOTO and the GOSUB statements. The ON–GOTO statement was discussed in Section 7.2; the GOSUB statement was discussed in Section 8.2. If you do not feel comfortable with these statements, please review those sections. Then return to this section and continue on.

ON–GOSUB
statement

The form of the **ON–GOSUB statement** is

line number   ON   expression   GOSUB   line numbers separated by commas

The expression must yield an integer value.

Consider the following program segment. First, see if you can figure out how statement 400 works. Then read the explanation below.

```
390
400   ON X GOSUB 1200, 1300, 1400
410   statement
  .
  .
  .
1100   STOP

1200   ...
  .
  .
1280   RETURN

1300 ...
  .
  .
1360   RETURN

1400 ...
  .
  .
1480 RETURN
```

```
          PALACE THEATER, INC

CURRENT DATE: 06/23/84    CAPACITY: 234

              MAIN MENU

OPTIONS:

     1) INITIALIZE NEXT SHOW PRICES AND TOTALS
     2) ENTER ADMISSIONS TRANSACTIONS
     3) DISPLAY SHOW SUMMARIES
     4) DISPLAY DAILY TOTALS
     5) DONE FOR THE DAY

WHICH (1, 2, 3, 4, 5) ?
```

```
OPTION 4: DISPLAY DAILY TOTALS

DATE: 06/23/84

TOTAL DAILY REVENUE SO FAR: 345.50

PRESS <RETURN> TO CONTINUE ?
```

```
OPTION 1: INITIALIZE NEXT SHOW PRICES
              AND TOTALS

NEXT SHOW TIME . . . ? 2:30 PM
ATTENDANT NAME . . . ? DEBBIE JONES
ENTER TICKET PRICES:

     CHILD   ? 1.25
     ADULT   ? 2.75
     SENIOR  ? 2.00

PRESS <RETURN> TO CONTINUE ?
```

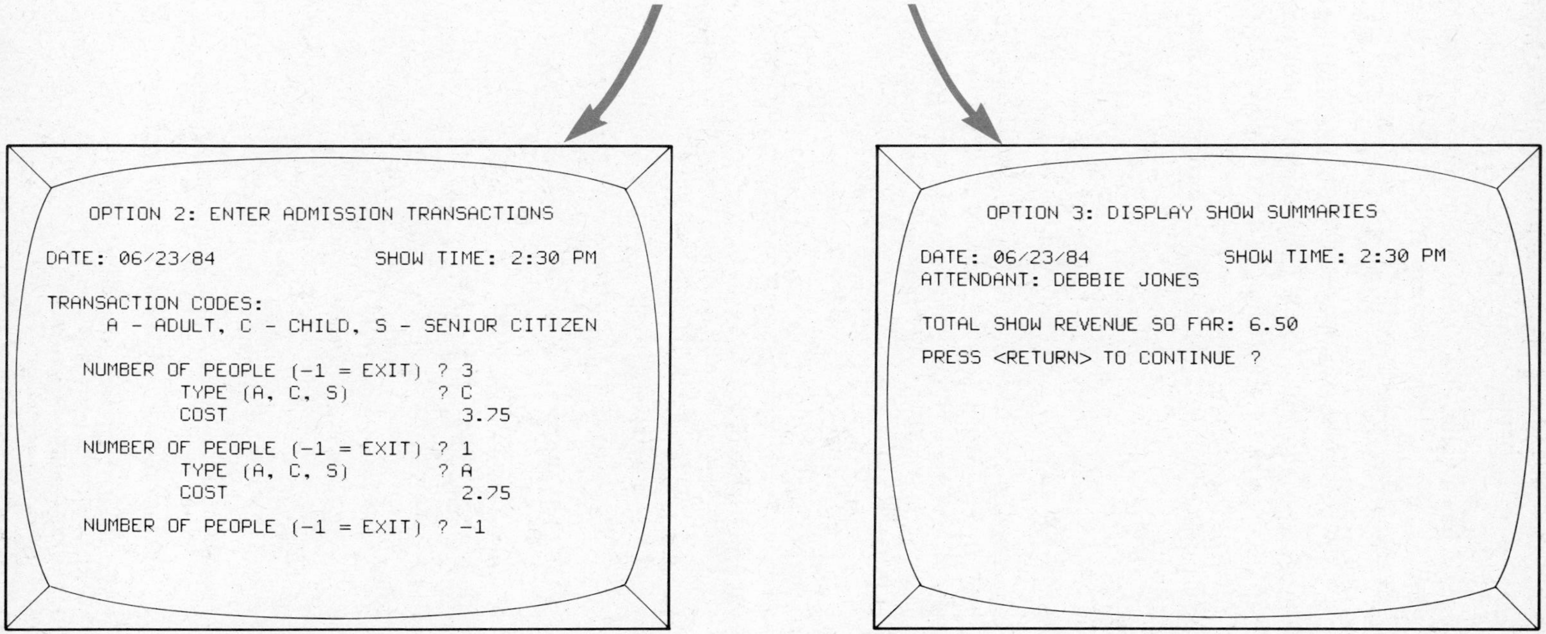

```
          OPTION 3: DISPLAY SHOW SUMMARIES

DATE: 06/23/84    SHOW TIME: 2:30 PM
ATTENDANT: DEBBIE JONES

TOTAL SHOW REVENUE SO FAR: 6.50

PRESS <RETURN> TO CONTINUE ?
```

```
          OPTION 2: ENTER ADMISSION TRANSACTIONS

DATE: 06/23/84    SHOW TIME: 2:30 PM

TRANSACTION CODES:
   A - ADULT, C - CHILD, S - SENIOR CITIZEN

NUMBER OF PEOPLE (-1 = EXIT) ? 3
     TYPE (A, C, S)          ? C
     COST                      3.75

NUMBER OF PEOPLE (-1 = EXIT) ? 1
     TYPE (A, C, S)          ? A
     COST                      2.75

NUMBER OF PEOPLE (-1 = EXIT) ? -1
```

□ **FIGURE 9.4   Menu and Options for Theater Transaction Processing**

Explanation: If X has a value of 1, then the computer will go to the subprogram beginning at line 1200, because 1200 is the first line number in the list. Eventually, when the RETURN is executed, the computer returns to line 410 and continues on. If X is 2, then the computer will execute the subroutine beginning at line 1300, because 1300 is the second line number in the list; and so on. Generally, in most versions of BASIC if X takes on a value other than 1, 2, or 3 in the above example, the BASIC processor will go to the next statement.

The ON–GOSUB statement will be needed in programs in the next section.

9.3 TWO MENU-DRIVEN APPLICATIONS

In Chapter 2 we discussed the need for menu-driven programs. (You may want to reread that discussion in Section 2.2 now.) A menu-driven application allows the user to select one of a number of processing options from the keyboard. The options and other data are accepted by the program with the INPUT statement.

□ **FIGURE 9.5**   **Palace Theater Program**

```
100 REM - - - INITIALIZE VARIABLES - - -
110                                                              REM
120 LET R = 0   : REM - - - TOTAL DAILY REVENUE
130 D$ = " "    : REM - - - DATE
140 X = 0       : REM - - - OPTION RESPONSE
150                                                              REM
160 PRINT "                    PALACE THEATER, INC"
162 PRINT
170 PRINT "ENTER THE FOLLOWING:"
172 PRINT " "
174 INPUT "      DATE (MM/DD/YY)       "; D$
176 PRINT " "
178 INPUT "      THEATER CAPACITY      "; C
180 GOSUB 10000
190                                                              REM
200 IF X = 5 THEN 500
210   GOSUB 10000
220   PRINT "                    PALACE THEATER, INC"
230   PRINT " "
240   PRINT "CURRENT DATE:  "; D$;"       "; "CAPACITY:  ";C
250   PRINT " "
260   PRINT "                    MAIN MENU"
270   PRINT " "
300   PRINT "OPTIONS:"
310   PRINT " "
320   PRINT "    1) INITIALIZE NEXT SHOW PRICES AND TOTALS"
330   PRINT " "
340   PRINT "    2) ENTER ADMISSIONS TRANSACTIONS"
350   PRINT " "
360   PRINT "    3) DISPLAY SHOW SUMMARIES"
370   PRINT " "
```

The following subsections discuss two very common menu-driven applications. After you study these examples, you should be able to write programs for similar examples.

Transaction Processing

A *transaction* is a business event such as the sale of a product, the payment of a bill, and so on. Some business transactions need only be summarized, as illustrated by the following discussion and program.

As an example of transaction processing, we will consider the needs of the Palace Theater, which wants to introduce a computer at the ticket window so that accurate revenue and counts for all the shows are maintained. The menu in Fig. 9.4 (pp. 168–169) shows the design of the system. Before the top menu in the Fig. 9.4 is produced, the program requests the current date and theater capacity.

The program that implements the Palace Theater menu and reports is given in Fig. 9.5. The overall structure of the program is illustrated in the hierarchy chart of Fig. 9.6. The main menu is implemented by the main program. Each of the options is implemented with a subroutine.

```
380     PRINT "    4) DISPLAY DAILY TOTALS"
390     PRINT " "
395     PRINT "    5) DONE FOR THE DAY"
397     PRINT " "
400     INPUT  "WHICH (1,2,3,4,5) "; X
405     GOSUB 10000
410     IF X < 5 THEN ON X GOSUB 1000, 2000, 3000, 4000
420 GOTO 200
430                                                        REM
500 STOP
600                                                        REM

1000    PRINT "    OPTION 1: INITIALIZE SHOW PRICES"
1012    PRINT "              AND TOTALS"
1014    PRINT " ": PRINT " "
1016    LET T = 0 : REM - - - INITIALIZE SHOW REVENUE
1018    INPUT "NEXT SHOW TIME . . . "; H$
1020    PRINT " "
1022    INPUT "ATTENDANT NAME . . . "; N$
1024    PRINT " "
1030    PRINT "ENTER TICKET PRICES:"
1040    PRINT " "
1050    INPUT "          CHILD     "; PC
1060    PRINT " "
1070    INPUT "          ADULT     "; PA
1080    PRINT " "
1090    INPUT "          SENIOR    "; PS
1100    PRINT
1110    INPUT "PRESS <RETURN> TO CONTINUE"; Z$
1120    RETURN
1130                                                       REM
```

☐ **FIGURE 9.5**   **(Continued)**

```
2000     PRINT "       OPTION 2: ENTER ADMISSION TRANSACTIONS"
2020     PRINT " "
2030     PRINT "DATE: "; D$;"                    SHOW TIME: "; H$
2040     PRINT " "
2050     PRINT "TRANSACTION CODES:"
2060     PRINT "     A - ADULT   C - CHILD    S - SENIOR CITIZEN"
2070     PRINT " "
2080     INPUT "   NUMBER OF PEOPLE ( -1 = EXIT) "; N
2090     IF N = -1 THEN 2500
2110        INPUT "          TYPE (A,C,S)       "; T$
2130           IF T$ = "C" THEN P = PC  : GOTO 2170
2140           IF T$ = "A" THEN P = PA  : GOTO 2170
2150           IF T$ = "S" THEN P = PS  : GOTO 2170
2160        GOTO 2110
2170        PRINT "         COST           "; P * N
2180        LET T = T + P * N : REM - ACCUMULATE SHOW REVENUE
2190        LET R = R + P * N : REM - ACCUMULATE DAILY REVENUE
2210        PRINT " "
2220        INPUT "   NUMBER OF PEOPLE ( -1 = EXIT) "; N
2230     GOTO 2090
2500 RETURN
2510                                                      REM


3000     PRINT "       OPTION 3: DISPLAY SHOW SUMMARIES"
3010     PRINT " "
3020     PRINT "DATE: "; D$;"                    SHOW TIME: "; H$
3030     PRINT "ATTENDANT: "; N$
3040     PRINT " "
3045     PRINT " "
3050     PRINT "TOTAL SHOW REVENUE SO FAR: "; T
3060     PRINT " "
3070     INPUT "PRESS <RETURN> TO CONTINUE"; Z$
3080  RETURN
3100                                                      REM


4000     PRINT "       OPTION 4: DISPLAY DAILY TOTALS"
4010     PRINT " "
4020     PRINT "DATE: "; D$
4030     PRINT " "
4040     PRINT " "
4050     PRINT "TOTAL DAILY REVENUE SO FAR: "; R
4060     PRINT " "
4100     INPUT "PRESS <RETURN> TO CONTINUE"; Z$
4110  RETURN
4200                                                      REM


10000 REM - - - CLEAR SCREEN ROUTINE - - -
10010    FOR I9 = 1 TO 10: PRINT : NEXT I9
10030 RETURN
```

☐ **FIGURE 9.6**   **Hierarchy Chart for Program in Fig. 9.5**

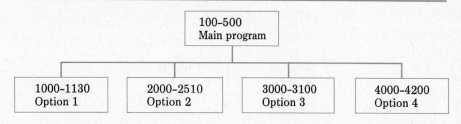

EXERCISES

9.8. Modify the Palace Theater program so that both parts of the transaction can be entered at one time. For example,

```
TRANSACTION ? A3          Means three adults
TRANSACTION ? S           Means one senior citizen
```

9.9. Modify the Palace Theater program so that it counts the number of children, adults, and senior citizens for each show and for the entire day.

9.10. Modify the Palace Theater program so that one price is generated for a group of people that come together, such as a family of 2 adults, 1 senior citizen, and 3 children. This modification might be done in the following way: When a group enters, the attendant can enter a G for group:

```
TRANSACTION? G
```

This code tells the program to accumulate the prices until some other special character is entered, perhaps another G.

9.11. Suppose you rent sailboats. You have 5 Windsurfers, 7 Hobie Cats, and 10 Sunfishes. Each rents for a specific amount per hour. Design and write a program that allows you to keep track of your daily rentals.

Finding Matching Records

A very common type of computer application consists of finding all records in a file that match certain requirements. For example, a person walks into a real estate agent's office with certain requirements for a house she wants to buy. It has to have three bedrooms and a family room, it must be located on at least 2 acres of land, and it must cost less

□ **FIGURE 9.7**   **Menu and Screens for Matching Records Application**

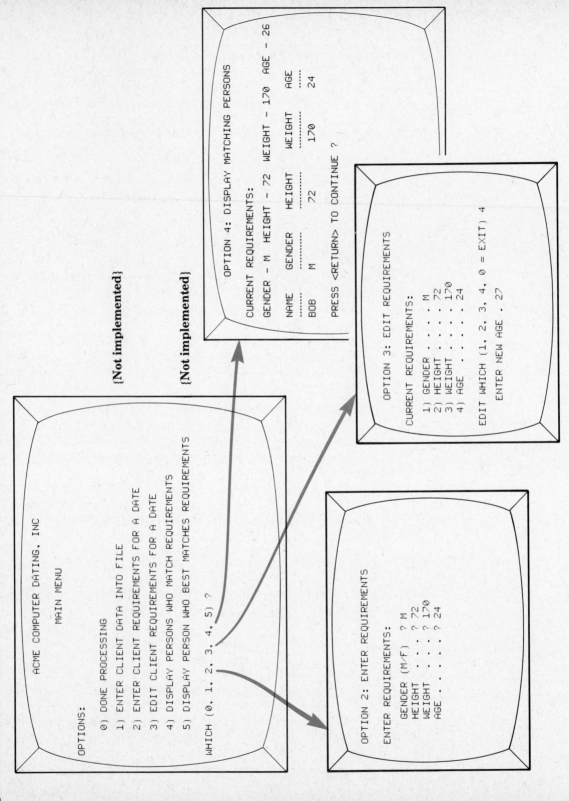

```
        ACME COMPUTER DATING, INC

              MAIN MENU


OPTIONS:

   0) DONE PROCESSING

   1) ENTER CLIENT DATA INTO FILE

   2) ENTER CLIENT REQUIREMENTS FOR A DATE

   3) EDIT CLIENT REQUIREMENTS FOR A DATE

   4) DISPLAY PERSONS WHO MATCH REQUIREMENTS

   5) DISPLAY PERSON WHO BEST MATCHES REQUIREMENTS

WHICH (0, 1, 2, 3, 4, 5) ?
```

{Not implemented}

{Not implemented}

```
OPTION 2: ENTER REQUIREMENTS

ENTER REQUIREMENTS:

   GENDER (M/F) ? M
   HEIGHT . . . : ? 72
   WEIGHT . . . : ? 170
   AGE . . . . : ? 24
```

```
    OPTION 3: EDIT REQUIREMENTS

CURRENT REQUIREMENTS:

   1) GENDER . . . :   M
   2) HEIGHT . . . :   72
   3) WEIGHT . . . :   170
   4) AGE . . . . :   24

EDIT WHICH (1, 2, 3, 4, 0 = EXIT) 4
   ENTER NEW AGE . 27
```

```
    OPTION 4: DISPLAY MATCHING PERSONS

CURRENT REQUIREMENTS:
GENDER - M HEIGHT - 72  WEIGHT - 170 AGE - 26

NAME    GENDER   HEIGHT   WEIGHT   AGE
......   ......   ......   ......   ......
BOB       M        72       170      24

PRESS <RETURN> TO CONTINUE ?
```

than $125,000. Ideally, these house requirements could be entered into a computer. Within a few minutes the program would search the entire data file and print a list of all the houses that satisfy these requirements.

There are many situations where this type of matching program is useful. A few are listed in the exercises at the end of this section.

Now let's consider a simplified computer dating program. The menu and output for the program are given in Fig. 9.7. The options operate in the following way:

- *Option 1:* This option allows you to enter, change, or delete a client's personal information from the file. (*Note:* Currently, the data file is implemented with DATA statements. To add people to the data file, you must add DATA statements. In Chapter 14 we will explain how to fully implement this option.)
- *Option 2:* This option allows you to enter a client's requirements for a date.
- *Option 3:* This option allows the client to modify his or her requirements for a date.
- *Option 4:* After requirements are entered, this option finds and lists all people who match the requirements exactly.
- *Option 5:* If no person matches the requirements, this option will select the person who best matches the requirements. (Implementation of this option is left as an exercise.)

RESTORE statement

A program for the computer dating menu is given in Fig. 9.8. The only new aspect of the program in Fig. 9.8 is the **RESTORE statement** in line 3070. This statement allows the program to reread the records in the DATA statements. In effect, it resets, or restores, all the values so that they can be read from the beginning.

Trace the program in Fig. 9.8 to be sure you understand how it operates.

EXERCISES

9.12. Modify the computer dating program of Fig. 9.8 so that you can enter the height in feet and inches. For example,

```
HEIGHT      ? 6-3
```

enters data for 6 feet 3 inches.

9.13. In the program of Fig. 9.8, implement option 5 for selecting the best match. This implementation can be done by assigning to each person a number that represents a rating. The rating might be calculated as follows:

```
LET R = ABS(H1 - H) + ABS(W1 - W) + ABS(A1 - A)
```

□ **FIGURE 9.8**   **Matching Records Program**

```
100 REM --- MAIN LOOP INITIALIZATION ---
110 LET X = 9
200 IF X = 0 THEN 500
205    GOSUB 10000
210    PRINT "            ACME COMPUTER DATING, INC"
220    PRINT " "
230    PRINT "                      MAIN MENU"
240    PRINT "OPTIONS:"
250    PRINT " "
260    PRINT "      0) DONE PROCESSING"
270    PRINT " "
280    PRINT "      1) ENTER CLIENT DATA INTO FILE"
290    PRINT " "
300    PRINT "      2) ENTER CLIENT REQUIREMENTS FOR A DATE"
310    PRINT " "
320    PRINT "      3) EDIT  CLIENT REQUIREMENTS FOR A DATE"
330    PRINT " "
340    PRINT "      4) DISPLAY PERSONS MATCHING REQUIREMENTS"
350    PRINT " "
360    PRINT "      5) DISPLAY BEST MATCH"
370    PRINT " "
400    INPUT  "WHICH (0,1,2,3,4,5) "; X
405    GOSUB 10000
410    IF X = 0 THEN 430
420     ON X GOSUB 700, 1000, 2000, 3000, 700
430 GOTO 200
440                                                  REM
500    STOP
600                                                  REM

700    PRINT "  OPTIONS 1 AND 5  NOT IMPLEMENTED YET"
710    PRINT
720    INPUT "PRESS <RETURN> TO CONTINUE "; Z$
730 RETURN
740                                                  REM

1000    PRINT "     OPTION 2: ENTER REQUIREMENTS"
1020    PRINT " "
1030    PRINT "ENTER REQUIREMENTS: "
1040    PRINT " "
1050    INPUT "      GENDER (M/F) "; G1$
1060    PRINT " "
1070    INPUT "      HEIGHT . . . "; H1
1080    PRINT " "
1090    INPUT "      WEIGHT . . . "; W1
1100    PRINT
1110    INPUT "      AGE  . . . . "; A1
1120    PRINT
1130    INPUT "PRESS <RETURN> TO CONTINUE"; Z$

2000    PRINT "     OPTION 3: EDIT REQUIREMENTS"
2020    PRINT " "
2030    PRINT "CURRENT REQUIREMENTS:
2035    PRINT " "
2040    PRINT " 1) GENDER . . . "; G1$
2070    PRINT " "
2080    PRINT " 2) HEIGHT . . . "; H1
2090    PRINT " "
2100    PRINT " 3) WEIGHT . . . "; W1
2110    PRINT " "
2120    PRINT " 4) AGE  . . . . "; A1
2130    PRINT " "
2140    INPUT "EDIT WHICH (1,2,3,4, 0 = NONE) "; Z
2150    PRINT " "
```

```
2170    ON Z GOSUB 2510, 2520, 2530, 2540
2175    PRINT
2180  IF Z <> 0 THEN 2000
2200  RETURN
2300                                            REM
2400  REM --- PROMPTS ---
2500                                            REM
2510    INPUT "ENTER GENDER . . . "; G1$
2515    RETURN
2517                                            REM
2520    INPUT "ENTER HEIGHT . . . "; H1
2525    RETURN
2527                                            REM
2530    INPUT "ENTER WEIGHT . . . "; W1
2535    RETURN
2537                                            REM
2540    INPUT "ENTER AGE  . . . . "; A1
2545    RETURN
2550                                            REM
3000    PRINT "    OPTION 4: DISPLAY MATCHING PERSONS"
3010    PRINT " "
3020    PRINT "CURRENT REQUIREMENTS:"
3030    PRINT " "
3040    PRINT "GENDER - "; G1$; "  HEIGHT -";H1,
3050    PRINT " WEIGHT -"; W1; "  AGE -"; A1
3060    PRINT
3070    RESTORE
3080    PRINT " "
3090    PRINT "NAME      GENDER   HEIGHT   WEIGHT    AGE"
3100    PRINT "========= ======   ======   ======   ==="
3110    READ N$, G$, H, W, A
3120    IF N$ = "ZZZ" THEN 3200
3130      GOSUB 3500 : REM --- DETERMINE IF MATCH ---
3140      READ N$, G$, H, W, A
3150    GOTO 3120
3160                                            REM
3200    PRINT " "
3210    INPUT "PRESS <RETURN> TO CONTINUE "; Z$
3220  RETURN
3230                                            REM
3240                                            REM
3500  REM --- DETERMINE IF MATCH AND PRINT ---
3510  IF G1$=G$ AND H=H1 AND W=W1 AND A=A1 THEN 3550
3520      REM --- FALSE ---
3530        REM - DO NOTHING
3540        GOTO 3600
3550      REM --- TRUE  ---
3560      PRINT N$; TAB(14);G$; TAB(22);H;
3570      PRINT      TAB(31);W;  TAB(38);A
3600      REM --- ENDIF ---
3610  RETURN
3620                                            REM

10000 REM - - - CLEAR SCREEN ROUTINE - - -
10010     FOR I9 = 1 TO 10: PRINT : NEXT I9
10030 RETURN

20000 REM ---- CONSTANT DATA FILE ----
20010 DATA "WENDY",  "F", 45, 123, 36
20020 DATA "ALICE",  "F", 66, 140, 54
20030 DATA "TIM"  ,  "M", 77, 187, 65
20040 DATA "RHODA",  "F", 23, 142, 68
20050 DATA "BOB"  ,  "M", 72, 170, 24
21000 DATA "ZZZ"  ,  "X", 0,  0,   0
30000 END
```

where H1 is the required height and H is the height of the person currently being read; W1 and A1 are the weight and age variables. Thus a rating (R value) of 0 means that there is a perfect match. Now as you calculate R values, keep track of the person with the lowest rating.

9.14. *Criminal justice:* Compare a witness's description of a robber with the characteristics of previous offenders "on file" in order to develop a list of possible suspects.

9.15. *Real estate:* Given a client's requirements for a house, select, from the current listing of houses for sale, the houses that meet the requirements.

9.16. *Counseling:* Given a high school student's measurable strengths, determined by the results of tests taken, course history, interests, and so on, identify some compatible courses of study and careers.

9.17. *Counseling:* Given a student's requirements for college (size, location, academic standards, specialties, and so on), select some colleges the student should apply to.

9.18. *Medicine, nursing:* Given a patient's symptoms, determine what type of illness the patient has.

9.19. *Consumer choice:* Given a consumer's requirements for a product, determine which products are acceptable from a list of products. The following list gives some examples.

Examples of Products	Important Characteristics to be Considered
Automobile	Price, capacity, mileage, etc.
Stereo receiver	Price, watts, THD, sensitivity, etc.

9.20. *Insurance:* Some independent insurance agencies subscribe to a computer service that determines the automobile premiums that all major companies charge, given the driver's characteristics (age, type of car, driving record, and so on) and the desired amount of coverage. The agent can then sell the client the least expensive policy. Visit a local independent insurance agent. Give her your characteristics and requirements and ask her to determine the premium that three different companies would charge. If she does it manually, keep track of the time involved. Implement a simplified version of the computer service, using the requirements of two or three companies.

More on Looping

INTRODUCTION TO CHAPTER 10

In previous chapters we have used loops in three primary ways:

1. To repeatedly process all the records in the DATA statements.
2. To repeatedly carry out various options in menu-driven applications.
3. To repeatedly accumulate totals of various transactions.

These loops were implemented with the IF and GOTO statements. In this chapter you will see further examples of this loop control structure and a variation of this structure.

But the main focus of this chapter is another common loop control structure: the FOR–NEXT statement. This statement allows you to perform a process a *fixed* number of times. For example, suppose you want to do one of the following tasks:

- Read the hours worked for 5 days each week.
- Print 15 asterisks.
- Add 100 numbers together.

counting loop

This type of **counting loop** is very common, and in BASIC it is implemented with the FOR–NEXT statement.

10.1 LOOP CONCEPTS

The fundamental idea of structured programming is to use "building block" control structures—such as loop structures, selection structures, and subroutines—that have only *one* entry point and *one* exit point. Programs built with these structures are easier to debug and understand.

So far, we have used only one loop structure, the loop structure that tests the exit condition at the top of the loop. This structure is called the *pretest loop*. Another loop control structure has the exit condition at the bottom of the loop; this loop structure is called the *posttest loop*. We will examine both structures in the following subsections.

Pretest Loop

pretest loop

The **pretest loop** tests the exit condition prior to executing the body of the loop. This loop structure, illustrated in Figs. 10.1A and 10.1B, is the one that has been used up to this point. The pretest loop is especially useful for processing all records up to the trailing record. Notice that if the condition is true on entry into the loop, the body of the loop is never executed.

Since the IF statement is used to implement both the loop and the selection control structures, it can cause some confusion. To distin-

□ **FIGURE 10.1**   **Pretest Loop Structure**

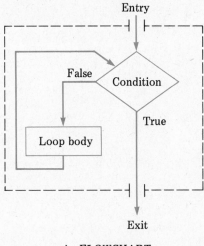

A. FLOWCHART

mmm   IF condition THEN nnn
⋮
loop body
⋮
GOTO mmm
nnn   Statement

B. PROGRAM STATEMENTS

guish the two different structures, languages developed in the past ten years have other statements (primarily the WHILE statement) to implement the loop structure. Thus some versions of BASIC (for example, DEC BASIC-PLUS and Microsoft BASIC) have available the **WHILE-WEND statement** for implementing loops in addition to the IF and GOTO statements. The WHILE-WEND statement is illustrated in Fig. 10.2. The WEND statement, which stands for While END, marks the bottom of the loop.

WHILE-WEND
  statement

Notice an important difference between the two loop structures (Figs. 10.1A and 10.2A). With the WHILE-WEND loop the loop body is executed while the condition is true. The loop terminates when the condition becomes false. That is, the test for the exit condition in the WHILE-WEND loop is the reverse of that for the IF-GOTO loop.

□ EXAMPLE

The following program segment with the WHILE-WEND loop continually processes data records WHILE variable N$ does not contain "ZZZ":

```
300   READ N$, R, H
310   WHILE N$ <> "ZZZ"
320     LET W = R * H
330     PRINT N$, R, H, W
340     READ N$, R, H
350   WEND
360   PRINT "DONE"
```

□ FIGURE 10.2   WHILE-WEND Statement

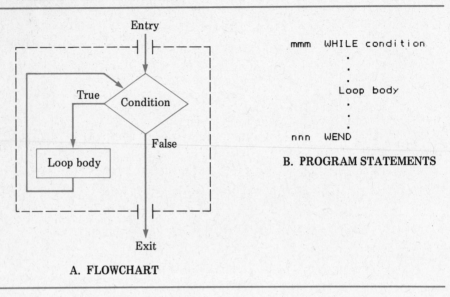

A. FLOWCHART

B. PROGRAM STATEMENTS

```
mmm    WHILE condition
         •
         •
       Loop body
         •
         •
nnn    WEND
```

Posttest Loop

posttest loop

The **posttest loop** is used in circumstances where you know you want to execute the loop body at least one time. Figure 10.3 illustrates this loop structure. Notice that the exit condition is tested after the loop body is executed.

The posttest loop can be used effectively in menu-driven applications like those in Chapter 9. The main program consists of a loop that displays the options, accepts an option selection, and then executes the option. This looping continues until the

```
OPTION 0 - DONE PROCESSING
```

option is selected. The structure of this loop is as follows:

```
mmm    PRINT "OPTION 0 - DONE PROCESSING"
       PRINT "OPTION 1 - XXXX"
       PRINT "OPTION 2 - XXXX"
       PRINT "OPTION 3 - XXXX"
       INPUT "WHICH ", R
       ON R GOSUB ln1, ln2, ln3
nnn    IF R > 0 THEN mmm
       STOP
```

The various subroutines beginning at lines ln1, ln2, and ln3 carry out the intended options.

☐ **FIGURE 10.3**   **Posttest Loop Structure**

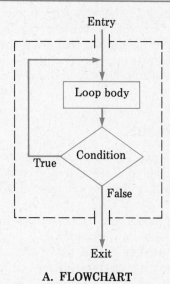

Entry

REM ---LOOP TOP ---

mmm

Loop body

nnn   IF condition THEN mmm
Statement

B. PROGRAM STATEMENTS

Loop body

Condition

True

False

Exit

A. FLOWCHART

Another effective use of the posttest loop is in programs where a computation must be done before testing the loop exit condition. For example, suppose you want to continually read and add together some numeric values until the sum first exceeds 75. The program for this operation looks like this:

```
10   LET S = 0
20   READ X
30     LET S = S + X
40   IF S <= 75 THEN 20
50   PRINT S
60   STOP
70   DATA 5, 34, 20, 14, 34, 23
100 END
```

The loop body (lines 20 and 30) is continually executed until the sum S is greater than 75.

EXERCISES

10.1.   Rewrite the main programs in Fig. 9.5 and Fig. 9.8 so that the loop is a posttest loop.

10.2.   Using a pretest loop, rewrite the program presented in this section that continually reads and adds together numeric values until the sum first exceeds 75.

10.2 THE FOR–NEXT STATEMENT

The FOR–NEXT statement is used to implement a special case of the pretest loop structure. This special pretest loop structure is illustrated in the program of Fig. 10.4A. As we will see, though, it cannot be used as a replacement for all pretest loops. The following subsections present the typical form of the FOR–NEXT statement and its use in nested loops.

Basic Form of the FOR–NEXT Statement

Before we discuss the FOR–NEXT statement, let's consider a program that uses the IF–THEN and GOTO loop. Trace the program in Fig. 10.4A. The trace values (Fig. 10.4B) and output (Fig. 10.4C) should look like those illustrated.

counter

Notice that variable I acts like a **counter**. It counts how many times the body of the loop is executed. The loop is executed until I becomes greater than 4. Also, notice that four statements are used to implement the loop: one (line 200) initializes the counter; one (line 210) tests the counter; one (line 230) increments the counter; and one (line 240) sends the computer back to the top of the loop.

The FOR–NEXT statement simplifies the implementation of the counting loop in Fig. 10.4A, as illustrated in Fig. 10.5. The FOR statement in line 210 of Fig. 10.5B essentially does the job of statements 200 and 210 of Fig. 10.5A. The NEXT statement in line 230 of Fig. 10.5B

☐ **FIGURE 10.4**   **Pretest Loop Structure That Counts**

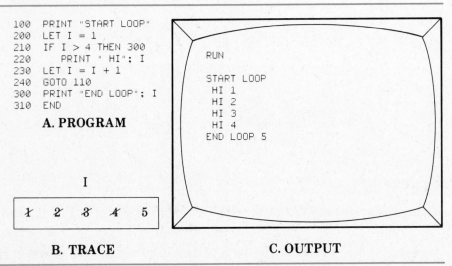

```
100   PRINT "START LOOP"
200   LET I = 1
210   IF I > 4 THEN 300
220      PRINT " HI"; I
230   LET I = I + 1
240   GOTO 110
300   PRINT "END LOOP"; I
310   END
```

A. PROGRAM

```
RUN

START LOOP
 HI 1
 HI 2
 HI 3
 HI 4
END LOOP 5
```

I

| 1̶ | 2̶ | 3̶ | 4̶ | 5 |

B. TRACE   **C. OUTPUT**

□ **FIGURE 10.5**   **FOR-NEXT Statement Implementing a Counting Loop**

```
100 PRINT "START LOOP"
200 LET I = 1
210 IF I > 4 THEN 300        210 FOR I = 1 TO 4 STEP 1
220    PRINT " HI"; I        220    PRINT " HI"; I
230 LET I = I + 1            230 NEXT I
240 GOTO 210
300 PRINT "END LOOP"; I         B. FOR-NEXT LOOP
310 END

          A.  IF-THEN LOOP
```

does the job of statements 230 and 240 of Fig. 10.5A—incrementing and sending the processor around the loop again. The STEP part of the FOR statement determines by how much the variable I is incremented.

The FOR statement is appropriately named. That is, the loop body is performed *for* I ranging from 1 to 4. When the loop is completed, the next statement (line 300) in the program is executed.

control variable

In the program of Fig. 10.5B the variable I in the FOR statement is called the **control variable**. This same variable must appear in the corresponding NEXT statement. The first value, 1 in this case, is called the **starting value**; the final value, 4 in this case, is called the **ending value**; and the 1 following the word STEP is called the **step value**. If the STEP is omitted, the step value has a **default** (automatic) **value** of 1, as in

starting value
ending value
step value
default value

```
          FOR I = 1 TO 4      STEP omitted, so I is incremented by 1
```

FOR-NEXT statements

The starting, ending, and step values may be any numeric expression, integer value, or decimal value. The general form of the **FOR-NEXT statements** is as follows:

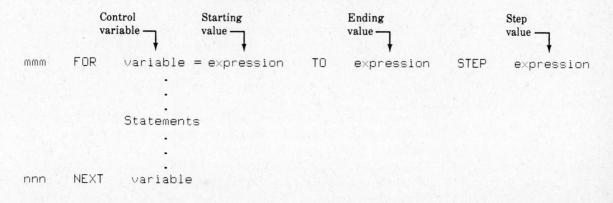

```
        Control          Starting          Ending          Step
        variable ┐       value ┐           value ┐         value ┐
                 ↓             ↓                  ↓               ↓
mmm   FOR   variable = expression   TO   expression   STEP   expression
                         .
                         .
                         .
            Statements
                         .
                         .
                         .
nnn   NEXT   variable
```

Let's trace the following program:

```
100    PRINT "START LOOP"
110    LET A = 5
120    LET B = 6
130    LET C = 2
200    FOR I = A + 1 TO 2 * B STEP C
210      PRINT " HI"; I
220    NEXT I
300    PRINT "END LOOP"; I
310    END
```

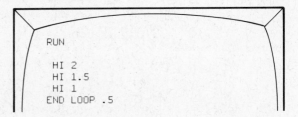

```
RUN

START LOOP
  HI 6
  HI 8
  HI 10
  HI 12
END LOOP 14
```

In line 200 the starting and ending values are 6 and 12, respectively. The step value is 2. Therefore the first value of I (the control variable) is 6; the next is 8; and so on.

Suppose in the above program that variable B is assigned 1 in statement 120. What will the program print? *Answer:* The starting value will be 6 and the ending value will be 2. On some computers the loop body will not be executed. On other computers the loop body will be executed once. Try this program on your computer to see what it does.

If the step value in a FOR statement is negative, then the control variable is decreased. When the control variable is less than the ending value, the loop is completed. The following program and its output illustrate the use of a negative step value:

```
100    FOR I = 2 TO 1 STEP -.5
110      PRINT " HI"; I
120    NEXT I
130    PRINT "END LOOP"; I
140    END
```

```
RUN

  HI 2
  HI 1.5
  HI 1
END LOOP .5
```

The FOR–NEXT statement only implements the *counting* pretest loop. It cannot be used in other circumstances where the pretest loop is used. For example, it cannot be used to process all data records until the trailing record is read. The loop exit condition here depends on testing for a specific data value, not on a count.

☐ EXAMPLE

Suppose you want to read and print a fixed number of values. That is, you want to produce a printout like the one shown in Fig. 10.6B. The hours worked on each of the five days in the week must be read. The program that reads and prints the fixed number of values is given in Fig. 10.6A. Trace the program to be sure that you understand how it operates.

☐ **FIGURE 10.6**   **Reading a Fixed Number of Values**

```
120 PRINT "            ACME DINER PAYROLL"
130 PRINT
220 PRINT "NAME    RATE  MON TUE WED THR FRI   WAGE"
230 PRINT
300 READ N$, R
310 IF N$ = "ZZZ" THEN 700
320    PRINT N$; TAB(8);R,
330    LET T = 0
340    FOR D = 1 TO 5
350     READ H
360     PRINT H;" ";
370     LET T = T + H
380    NEXT D
390    LET W = R * H
400    PRINT TAB(35); W
410                                              REM
500    READ N$, R
610 GOTO 310
620                                              REM
700 STOP
800 DATA "JOE", 4.25, 8,5,6,7,8
810 DATA "JUNE",6.36, 8,8,7,7,4
820 DATA "JIM" ,5.00, 8,7,0,8,2
880 DATA "ZZZ",0
999 END
```

A. PROGRAM

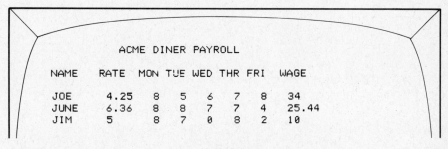

```
          ACME DINER PAYROLL

NAME    RATE  MON TUE WED THR FRI   WAGE

JOE     4.25   8   5   6   7   8    34
JUNE    6.36   8   8   7   7   4    25.44
JIM     5      8   7   0   8   2    10
```

B. OUTPUT

Nested Loops

Recall from Section 6.5 that IF statements may be nested one within another; see particularly Fig. 6.7. This arrangement occurs when, on one selection branch, another selection must be made.

nested loop

In the same manner, one loop may be nested within another loop. A **nested loop** is illustrated in Fig. 10.7A. Notice particularly that the control variables for each loop must have different names (T in line 400 and Q in line 420).

☐ **FIGURE 10.7**   **Nested FOR–NEXT Statements**

```
400    FOR T = 1 TO 2
410       PRINT "CHEER"; T
420       FOR Q = 1 TO 3
430          PRINT " GO"
440       NEXT Q
450       PRINT " TEAM"
460    NEXT T
470    PRINT "DONE"
999    END
```

A. PROGRAM

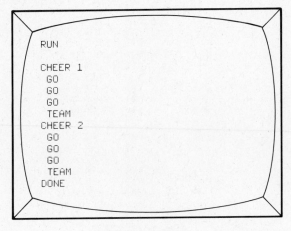

B. OUTPUT

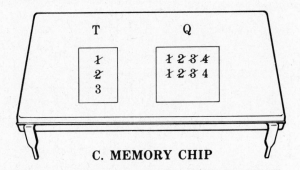

C. MEMORY CHIP

Trace the program in Fig. 10.7A and verify that the output (Fig. 10.7B) and variable values (Fig. 10.7C) are as illustrated.

Nested loops are quite common in programs. You will encounter many more of them in Chapter 11.

EXERCISES

10.3.   Trace the following program:

```
200    FOR C = 1 TO 3
210       PRINT C, "HAPPY BIRTHDAY"
220    NEXT C
230    PRINT "AND MANY MORE"
300    END
```

10.4. What will the printout in Exercise 10.3 look like if line 200 is replaced with each of the following lines?

```
a) 200 FOR C = 2 TO 10 STEP 3
b) 200 FOR C = -3 TO 2 STEP 2.5
c) 200 FOR C = 10 TO 5 STEP -.5
d) 200 FOR C = -20 TO -30 STEP -1
```

10.5. Modify the program in Fig. 10.6A so that it reads data for seven days each week.

10.6. Trace the following programs:

```
a) 200   FOR I = 1 TO 4
   220     PRINT "GO"
   240   NEXT I
   300   PRINT "GO TEAM!"
   999   END
```

```
b) 200   FOR I = 1 TO 4
   220     PRINT TAB(5 + 2 * I); "GO"
   240   NEXT I
   300   PRINT TAB(15); "G O   T E A M !!"
   999   END
```

10.7. Each of the following three programs is supposed to produce the printout on the right. But each program has a common logic error. Find the error. What does each program print?

```
a) 300   FOR Q = 1 TO 3
   320     PRINT "MARK"; Q
   340     GOTO 300
   360   NEXT Q
   999   END
```

```
MARK 1
MARK 2
MARK 3
```

```
b) 300   FOR Q = 1 TO 3
   320     PRINT "MARK"; Q
   340     LET Q = Q + 1
   360   NEXT Q
   999   END
```

```
c) 300   FOR Q = 1 TO 3
   320     IF Q > 3 THEN 999
   340     PRINT "MARK"; Q
   360   NEXT Q
   999   END
```

10.8. Find the syntax errors in each of the following programs.

```
a) 300   FOR MARK$ = 1 TO 3    b) 300   FOR I = 1 TO 3
   320     PRINT MARK$              320     PRINT "MARK"; I
   340   NEXT MARK$                340   NEXT M
   999   END                       999   END
```

10.9. Trace the following program:

```
200   PRINT "SALES- NUMBER"
202   PRINT "MAN   OF SALES";  TAB(20); "GRAPH"
204   PRINT "----- --------";  TAB(20); "-----"
300   READ N$, S
305   IF N$ = "ZZZ" THEN 400
310    PRINT N$; TAB(10); S;   TAB(20);
330     FOR C = 1 TO S
340        PRINT "#";
350     NEXT C
360      PRINT " "
365   READ N$, S
370   GOTO 300
400   STOP
800   DATA "JOE", 8
810   DATA "SANDRA", 6
820   DATA "BOB", 10
830   DATA "ZZZ", 0
999   END
```

10.10. Explain what would happen if line 360 were deleted in the program in Exercise 10.9.

10.11. Write a program to score a golf match. The printout might look like this:

```
PLAYER        NUMBER OF STROKES PER HOLE          18-HOLE TOTAL
---------      ------------------------------      -------------------

TREVINO       x  x  x  x  x  x  x  x  x
              x  x  x  x  x  x  x  x  x           xxx
CRENSHAW      x  x  x  x  x  x  x  x  x
              x  x  x  x  x  x  x  x  x           xxx
  .
  .
  .
THE WINNER IS xxxxxxxxx
```

10.12. The program below is supposed to calculate the average of a set of numbers. A sample printout should look like this:

```
        AVERAGE
HOW MANY NUMBERS? 3
NUMBERS:
?4
?5
?3
AVERAGE IS 4
```

Will this program work on your computer?

```
100   PRINT "      AVERAGE"
150   PRINT "HOW MANY NUMBERS";
160           INPUT N
```

```
200   LET S = 0
250   PRINT "NUMBERS:"
300   FOR Q = 1 TO N
310      INPUT X
320      LET S = S + X
330   NEXT Q
400   LET A = S/Q
410   PRINT "AVERAGE IS", A
420   STOP
999   END
```

10.13. Trace the following program. (This program illustrates how patterns can be produced by nested FOR–NEXT statements.)

```
100   LET K = 0
110   FOR R = 1 TO 5
120      LET K = K + 2
130      FOR S = 1 TO 6 - R
140         PRINT TAB(K + S); "*";
150      NEXT S
160      PRINT " "
170   NEXT R
999   END
```

10.14. Using the FOR–NEXT statement, write a program that multiplies the first N integers together: $1 * 2 * \cdots * N$.

10.15. Trace the following program:

```
200   LET N = 1
300   FOR D = 1 TO 7
310      IF N > 31 THEN 400
320      PRINT TAB(3 * D ); N;
330      LET N = N + 1
340   NEXT D
350   PRINT " "
360   GOTO 300
400   STOP
999   END
```

10.16. Write a program that produces a calendar for any specific month. The printout might look like this:

```
CALENDAR GENERATION

NUMBER OF DAYS IN MONTH? 31
THE FIRST DAY OF THE MONTH BEGINS
ON (1 = SUN, 2 = MON, . . . , 7 = SAT) ? 3

SUN     MON     TUE     WED     THU     FRI     SAT
-----   -----   -----   -----   -----   -----   -----
                  1       2       3       4       5
  6       7       8       9      10     ...     ...
...
```

10.17. Write a program that finds the sum of the first N terms of the series

$$\frac{1}{2} + \frac{1}{2^2} + \frac{1}{2^3} + \frac{1}{2^4} + \frac{1}{2^5} + \cdots$$

Then RUN the program for various values of N. (This program illustrates that the sum of an infinite number of certain positive fraction is equal to one!)

Computer Models and Simulations

INTRODUCTION TO CHAPTER 11

Up to this point the programs in the text have involved quite routine calculations, loops, and selections. Typically, the programs have processed a series of records in a certain way. We might characterize these programs as "data processing" applications. In these programs your main problem has been to get the computer to do something that you already knew how to do well with pencil and paper.

In this chapter you will study another type of computer application: You will use BASIC to create *computer models* for a variety of real life situations. Then by manipulating the model parameters, you will obtain results for (and consequently understand) some complicated real life problems. In effect, you will use elementary mathematics and the computer to solve problems that otherwise would require higher mathematics.

Both deterministic models and random models (using random numbers) will be explained in this chapter.

No material in this chapter is necessary for understanding any later chapters in the text. So you may move to the next chapter at any time. Some of the problems found in the later parts of this chapter are difficult, so you may wish to study the remaining parts of the text before returning to these problems.

11.1 TERMINOLOGY AND FUNDAMENTAL CONCEPTS

model

simulation

A **model** is a simplified representation of reality. A model of an object or process is another object or process that exhibits some desired characteristics of the original. A **simulation** is the activity of experimenting with a model.

In the following subsections we will examine physical models, computer models and simulations, and the rationale for using models.

Physical Models

physical model

A **physical model** is a material object that represents an existing real object or a planned object. Physical models are useful in a variety of circumstances, as the following examples illustrate.

□ EXAMPLE

scale model

Aircraft engineers usually construct a physical **scale model** of an aircraft that is planned for eventual production. The model may have the same relative shape and working control surfaces but lack all other features of the plane. By subjecting the model to airflow in a wind tunnel, perhaps in order to study the effectiveness of the control surfaces, the engineers simulate one aspect of the aircraft's flight.

☐ EXAMPLE

A developer builds a scale model of a new condominium cluster in the developmental stage of the project. The housing clusters might be movable so that different positions of the cluster can be studied to determine the optimum road placement and drainage control measures.

☐ EXAMPLE

Physical models are frequently used in teaching. To have students gain experience without actually being on a boat, a sailing instructor might recommend that the students build a model of a sailboat. This model can then be exposed to the various wind conditions that a real sailboat would experience. The three important aspects of this sailboat example—reality, physical model, and simulation—are illustrated in Fig. 11.1.

Computer Models and Simulations

mathematical model

In this chapter simple mathematical models, as opposed to physical scale models, are examined. A **mathematical model** is a set of equations and relationships that describe some object or process. For example, the equation

```
D = H - 0.5 * 32 * T * T
```

describes what happens when an object is dropped from a height of H feet above the surface of the earth. See Fig. 11.2A. After T seconds have elapsed, the object will be D feet above the ground. This model, like all models, lacks certain characteristics of the original process. In this case the model does not take into account the resistance due to air friction.

computer model

A **computer model** is simply a computer program that implements the equations and relationships embodied in a mathematical model. Figure 11.2B represents the computer model for the dropped object example.

computer simulation

A **computer simulation** is the execution of the computer model. The computer simulation for the falling object example is shown in Fig. 11.2C.

parameter

A computer model, like all good models, should be easy to *manipulate*, or experiment with. Just as the housing clusters scale models in the example presented in the previous subsection are easy to manipulate, a computer model should have parameters that can be adjusted. A **parameter** is a variable that can be initialized to different values. The different values of the parameters allow the user to evaluate various possibilities. For example, in a computer model that simulates a falling object, two parameters might be the height of the object when released and the resistance due to air friction.

☐ **FIGURE 11.1**   **Using a Physical Model in Teaching**

A. REALITY

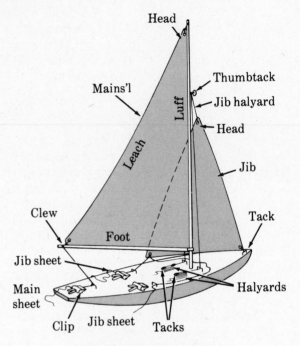

B. PHYSICAL MODEL

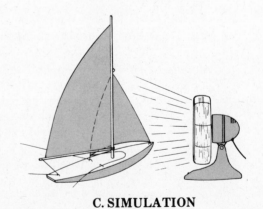

C. SIMULATION

The Need and Reasons for Using Computer Models

Computer simulation models are necessary in many situations. For example:

1. There may be no known mathematical techniques for solving a problem.

☐ **FIGURE 11.2**   **Computer Model and Simulation**

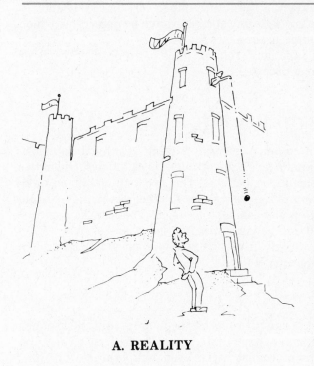

```
100  PRINT  "      ","DISTANCE"
110  PRINT  "TIME","ABOVE"
120  PRINT  "SECS","EARTH"
130  PRINT
200  FOR T = 0 TO 2 STEP .2
210    LET D = 50 - .5*32*T*T
230    PRINT T,D
240  NEXT T
300  END
```

B. COMPUTER MODEL

TIME SECS	DISTANCE ABOVE EARTH
0	50
.2	49.36
.4	47.44
.6	44.24
.8	39.76
1	34
1.2	26.96
1.4	18.64
1.6	9.039993
1.8	-1.840012

A. REALITY

C. COMPUTER SIMULATION

2. Simulation may be the only feasible method of experimenting with an object or a process. It would be foolish to experiment with the control surfaces of an aircraft only after it is completely built. What are the consequences if they do not work?
3. Computer simulations can speed up or slow down the time frame. It may be possible to experiment with a physical process, but it may take years to evaluate the results of the experiments. And again, the possibility exists that irreversible damage could be done.

There are as many reasons for using simulation models as there are for investigating a situation with any other technique. For example, simulation models might be used for the following purposes:

1. To teach, as in computer-controlled flight simulators used to train pilots.
2. To optimize, as in computer simulations used to determine what factors at what levels produce the best results.

3. To present a moving picture of events in the future. Seeing what will happen in the future under certain circumstances allows you to *evaluate* a proposed system or determine which of two competing processes is the best.
4. To establish functional relationships or to predict events or the structure of processes.

11.2 A DECISION-MAKING COMPUTER MODEL

There are a number of common decision-making problems that businesses as well as individuals face. One problem is as follows: Given two products, which one should be bought? The products could be automobiles, solar heaters, computers, and so on. Another problem is, Should I do something myself or pay someone to do it? These tasks could be painting the house, mowing the lawn, making bread, and so on.

In this section we will investigate a decision-making problem and develop the computer model for it.

The Problem: To Make or to Buy?

Suppose you like yogurt. Your curiosity has been aroused by newspaper ads for a yogurt-making machine that costs $12.95. Essentially, the machine keeps six cups of yogurt at an even temperature for eight hours. You estimate that the cost of making six cups of yogurt is $0.08 per cup. This cost includes the electricity to run the machine and the ingredients for the "starter." You also estimate that the lifetime of the yogurt maker is two years—typical for the small appliances you have purchased recently. Currently, your favorite store-bought yogurt is $0.60.

Should you buy the yogurt machine and make your own yogurt, or should you continue to buy yogurt at the grocery store?

Certainly, if you expect to eat only a few cups of yogurt in the next two years, it would be foolish to buy the machine. But suppose you eat a cup a day? What should you do then?

One way to solve the problem is to produce reports like the one shown in Fig. 11.3B. This output clearly shows the costs of both situations for consuming from 1 to 12 cups of yogurt.

The arithmetic involved in producing the report in Fig. 11.3B is as follows. Let H be the total cost of yogurt made at home. Then the home cost starts as the cost of the machine:

```
LET H = 12.95
```

Then each time another cup is bought, $0.08 is added to H:

```
LET H = H + 0.08
```

□ **FIGURE 11.3**   **Home Costs and Store Costs for Yogurt**

```
100 LET H = 12.95
110 LET R = 0
120                         REM
200 PRINT "NO. CUPS","HOME COST",
202 PRINT            "STORE RETAIL"
210 PRINT
300 FOR C = 1 TO 12
310    LET H = H + 0.08
320    LET R = R + 0.60
330    PRINT C, H, R
340 NEXT C
400 END
```

A. PROGRAM

NO. CUPS	HOME COST	STORE RETAIL
1	13.03	.6
2	13.11	1.2
3	13.19	1.8
4	13.27	2.4
5	13.35	3
6	13.43	3.6
7	13.51	4.2
8	13.59	4.8
9	13.67	5.4
10	13.75	6
11	13.83	6.6
12	13.91	7.2

B. OUTPUT

Now let R be the total retail cost of yogurt purchased. Variable R starts as zero. Then each time a cup is purchased, $0.60 is added to R:

```
LET R = R + 0.60
```

These statements are included in the program shown in Fig. 11.3A.

The Computer Model

Suppose the yogurt machine goes on sale for $9.99, an experienced friend knows the ingredient costs are actually $0.11, and the cost of your favorite yogurt goes up to $0.67. To solve this new problem, you must change parts of the program in Fig. 11.3A. Thus we now see why computer models should be easy to manipulate. In this situation the parameters—the cost of the machine, the cost of ingredients, the retail cost of a cup of yogurt, and the number of cups—should be flexible.

The menus and screens shown in Fig. 11.4 illustrate a design for this problem that allows the computer model to be manipulated. This design makes it easy for the user to enter and change the parameters. Also, the modular design allows the programmer to add other screens and related options to the current program.

Option 1 in Fig. 11.4 illustrates how parameters can be edited or fixed. You merely return to this option and make changes to the desired values (under the column labeled NEW). This type of option is especially important when there are more than a few parameters.

□ FIGURE 11.4   Menus and Screens for Make or Buy Model

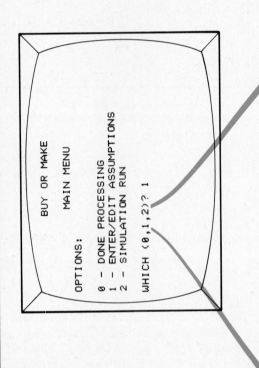

```
        BUY OR MAKE

         MAIN MENU

OPTIONS:

0 - DONE PROCESSING
1 - ENTER/EDIT ASSUMPTIONS
2 - SIMULATION RUN

WHICH ⟨0,1,2⟩? 1
```

```
OPTION 2: SIMULATION RUN

STORE COST, 1 CUP   .6

MACHINE COST       12.95
INGREDIENT COST/CUP  .08

NO. CUPS    HOME COST    STORE COST

  20         14.55         12
  21         14.63         12.6
  22         14.71         13.2
  23         14.79         13.8
  24         14.87         14.4
  25         14.95         15
  26         15.03         15.6
  27         15.11         16.2
  28         15.19         16.8
  29         15.27         17.4
  30         15.35         18

      PRESS ⟨RETURN⟩ TO CONTINUE ?
```

```
OPTION 1: ENTER/EDIT ASSUMPTIONS

        PRESS ⟨RETURN⟩
TO LEAVE ASSUMPTIONS AS IS.

                  CURRENT    NEW
STORE COST 1 CUP    .55     ? .6
MACHINE COST      12.95     ?
INGREDIENT COST     .08     ?

RANGE: NUMBER OF CUPS
  LOWER LIMIT      20       ?
  UPPER LIMIT      30       ?

  PRESS ⟨RETURN⟩ TO CONTINUE ?
```

The program that produces the output shown in Fig. 11.4 is presented in Fig. 11.5. The hierarchy chart for the program is given in Fig. 11.6. The hierarchy chart specifies which lines of the program correspond to the main menu and to the option 1 and option 2 subroutines.

The only new aspect of the program in Fig. 11.5 is the OPTION 1: ENTER/EDIT option. Notice that a nonzero value changes the value of the machine cost, starting at line 1200.

All programs in this chapter could be made more flexible by implementing a menu structure like the one in Fig. 11.4 (top). However, to conserve space and make the details of the specific models clearer, we have omitted this important feature.

□ **FIGURE 11.5**   **Computer Model for Make or Buy Problem**

```
100 REM --- INITIALIZE ASSUMPTIONS TO ZERO ---
110      LET S = 0:      REM - STORE COST OF ONE CUP
120      LET M = 0:      REM - COST OF MACHINE
130      LET I = 0:      REM - INGREDIENT COSTS, 1 CUP
140      LET L = 1:      REM - LOWER LIMIT
150      LET U = 1:      REM - UPPER LIMIT
160                                           REM
500 PRINT     "            BUY OR MAKE"
510     PRINT
520     PRINT "          MAIN MENU"
530     PRINT "OPTIONS:"
540     PRINT
550     PRINT "0 - DONE PROCESSING"
560     PRINT "1 - ENTER/EDIT ASSUMPTIONS"
570     PRINT "2 - SIMULATION RUN"
580     PRINT
600     INPUT "WHICH (0,1,2)"; X
610     GOSUB 10000   : REM CLEAR SCREEN
620     ON X GOSUB 1000, 2000
630     GOSUB 10000   : REM CLEAR SCREEN
640 IF X <> 0 THEN 500
650 STOP
660                                           REM
670                                           REM


1000 PRINT "   OPTION 1:  ENTER/EDIT ASSUMPTIONS"
1010 PRINT
1020 PRINT "          PRESS <RETURN>
1025 PRINT "     TO LEAVE ASSUMPTIONS AS IS."
1030 PRINT
1040 PRINT "               CURRENT    NEW"
1100 PRINT "STORE COST 1 CUP      ";S; TAB(30);"?";
1110 INPUT S1 :  IF S1 <> 0 THEN S = S1
1120                                           REM
1200 PRINT "MACHINE COST          ";M; TAB(30);"?";
1210 INPUT M1 :  IF M1 <> 0 THEN M = M1
1220                                           REM
1300 PRINT "INGREDIENT COST       ";I; TAB(30);"?";
1310 INPUT I1 :  IF I1 <> 0 THEN I = I1
1320                                           REM
```

(continued)

☐ **FIGURE 11.5**   **(Continued)**

```
1400 PRINT
1410 PRINT "RANGE: NUMBER OF CUPS"
1420 PRINT "  LOWER LIMIT          ";L; TAB(30);"?";
1430 INPUT L1 :  IF L1 <> 0 THEN L = L1
1440                                                   REM
1500 PRINT "  UPPER LIMIT          ";U; TAB(30);"?";
1510 INPUT U1 :  IF U1 <> 0 THEN U = U1
1600 PRINT
1610 INPUT "PRESS <RETURN> TO CONTINUE"; Z$
1700 RETURN
1800                                                   REM
2000 PRINT "       OPTION 2: SIMULATION RUN"
2010 PRINT
2020 PRINT "STORE COST, 1 CUP     "; S
2030 PRINT
2040 PRINT "MACHINE COST          "; M
2050 PRINT "INGREDIENT COST/CUP   "; I
2060 PRINT
2100 PRINT "NO. CUPS","HOME COST","STORE COST"
2110 PRINT
2120 LET H = M + L*I : REM - COST OF L CUPS
2130 LET R = L*S
2140 PRINT L, H, R
2200 FOR C = L+1 TO U
2300    LET H = H + I
2310    LET R = R + S
2320    PRINT C, H, R
2330 NEXT C
2400 PRINT
2500 INPUT "PRESS <RETURN> TO CONTINUE"; Z$
2600 RETURN


10000 FOR Z9 = 1 TO 20: PRINT : NEXT Z9
10010 RETURN
20000 END
```

☐ **FIGURE 11.6**   **Hierarchy Chart for Program of Fig. 11.5**

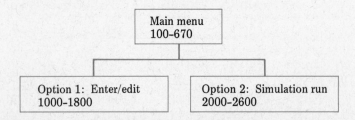

Testing a Computer Model

How do you test a computer simulation program to verify that it is working properly? Most of the previous programs in the text were tested by using test data that exercises as many possibilities as practical. The computer results are then compared with the previously determined correct results.

In computer simulations you clearly cannot do all the calculations. But you can verify that the results of the first and second steps are calculated correctly, and that the results in a few consecutive intervals are correct.

validity

While the program may work correctly, there still is a question about the **validity** of the model. That is, does the model adequately reflect the real situation? To answer this question requires experience.

EXERCISES

11.1. Modify the program in Fig. 11.5 so that option 2 allows the user to direct the report to the screen or printer. If the report is directed to the screen, there should be a pause after each full screen. Printed output should be paged.

11.2. Modify the program in Fig. 11.5 so that the program terminates when the retail cost first exceeds the home cost.

11.3. Using the following figures:

Item	Datsun Pickup	Ford Pickup
Initial cost	$6500	$5775
Miles per gallon	30	18

Assume that the cost of gas is $1.25 a gallon and is increasing at the rate of about 1¢ a month. Also, assume that you usually drive about 1500 miles a month. Determine at what point (in time and miles) the cost of buying and operating these two vehicles is the same.

11.4. Use the following facts about Volkswagen Rabbits:

Item	Gasoline Model	Diesel Model
Initial cost	$8800	$9500
Highway mileage	37	50
City mileage	24	40
Fuel cost per gallon	1.20	1.05

Further, assume that you drive 900 highway miles a month and 300 city miles a month. At what point (in miles and time) will the cost of owning and operating these vehicles be the same?

11.5. Suppose that in drawing a bath after a long, hard day, you accidentally leave the cold water on too long. The result is 40 gallons (about 7 inches of water) of 87° water in the tub, much too cold for your body, which likes the temperature to be 105°. How should you bring the tub temperature to this value?

     Possible solutions: Since the temperature of the hot water is 130°F, adding a sufficient amount of water at this temperature should raise the temperature of the water in the tub. There are at least three ways that water can be added to the tub:

Option 1	Drain X gallons from the 40 gallons of 87° water in the tub. Then add X gallons of 130° water. What value of X results in a tub temperature of 105°?
Option 2	Without draining any water from the tub, add X gallons of 130° water to the 40 gallons already in the tub. Again, what value of X results in a tub temperature of 105°?
Option 3	Simultaneously add X gallons of 130° water to the tub as X gallons are being drained from the tub. Again, what number of gallons results in a tub temperature of 105°?

Before investigating these options, make two assumptions.

- No heat in the tub is lost to the room. (This is an important assumption because the water *will* cool if left standing. You could take this cooling effect into account later on.)
- When two quantities of water with different temperatures are mixed, the resulting temperature is calculated by taking into account the *proportions* of the quantities involved. For example:

1 gallon of 90° water + 1 gallon of 70° water = 2 gallons of 80° water

3 gallons of 90° water + 1 gallon of 70° water = 4 gallons of 85° water

because $\dfrac{3}{4} \times 90 + \dfrac{1}{4} \times 70 = 85$

So   16 gallons of 92° water + 7 gallons of 68° water = ?

Setting up the proportion in the last example, you have

$$\frac{16}{16+7} \times 92 + \frac{7}{16+7} \times 68 = 84.69$$

Thus you have 23 gallons of 84.69° water.

    Which is the best option? How do you interpret the term *best?*

11.3 MODELS INVOLVING RATES OF CHANGE

Suppose that the average price of an ordinary compact car in 1984 is $10,000.00 and that new car prices are going up at the rate of 8% per year. How much will such a car cost in the year 2000 or 2018? Make a guess and then look at the simulation results in Fig. 11.7B.

This simulation of new car prices can put many other costs and values into perspective, such as the cost of a life insurance policy. The two most common types of policies are whole-life and term. Most people are sold whole-life policies because they are more profitable for the insurance companies. These policies are a combination of life insurance and a savings account. That is, if you die, your beneficiary will receive the amount of the policy. But if you reach a certain old age, perhaps 70 or 75, you will receive the amount of the policy. Common amounts of such policies are $10,000, $25,000, and $50,000. But an important question to consider is: What is the real value of $25,000 likely to be in the year 2020?

In the following subsections we will see how we can determine future costs like those produced in the printout of Fig. 11.7B. First, we will examine how to (1) calculate rates of change and (2) use rates of change to estimate future values and amounts. Then we will consider interest rates for fractional parts of a year and for loans.

Calculating and Using Rates of Change

Suppose that last year the cost of a particular car was $10,000 and that the same model this year costs $10,800. The amount of change in one year is

$$\$800 = \quad 10,800 \quad - 10,000$$

or   Amount of change = (current value) − (previous value)

The rate of change for this one year is

$$8\% = 0.08 = \frac{800}{10,000} = \frac{\text{amount of change}}{\text{previous value}}$$

Notice that the amount of change is for a one-year period. Consequently, the rate of change applies to a one-year period. The rate of change is 8% *per year*.

Suppose a dealer sells a particular vehicle for $10,800 and says that the same model next year will cost 8% more. What will the cost be then? The amount of change is

$$\$864.00 = 0.08 \times 10,800$$

or   Amount of change = (rate of change) × (current value)

☐ **FIGURE 11.7**   **Future Costs**

```
200 PRINT "     INFLATION / DEFLATION"
210 PRINT
220 INPUT "CURRENT VALUE OF ASSET   "; V
230 INPUT "RATE OF CHANGE           "; R
240 INPUT "STARTING YEAR            "; Y1
250 INPUT "YOUR CURRENT AGE         "; A
260 INPUT "YEARS INTO THE FUTURE    "; N
270 PRINT
300 PRINT "        YOUR", "VALUE OF"
310 PRINT "YEAR   AGE", "OF ASSET"
320 PRINT
330 PRINT Y1; A, V
400 FOR Y = Y1+1 TO Y1 + N
410     LET C = R*V
420     LET V = V + C
430     LET V = INT(V*100 + .5)/100
440     LET A = A + 1
450     PRINT Y; A, V
460 NEXT Y
500 END
```

A. PROGRAM

```
          INFLATION / DEFLATION

CURRENT VALUE OF ASSET   ? 10000
RATE OF CHANGE           ? .08
STARTING YEAR            ? 1984
YOUR CURRENT AGE         ? 18
YEARS INTO THE FUTURE    ? 25

          YOUR     VALUE OF
YEAR      AGE      OF ASSET

1984      18       10000
1985      19       10800
1986      20       11664
1987      21       12597.12
1988      22       13604.89
1989      23       14693.28
1990      24       15868.74
1991      25       17138.24
1992      26       18509.3
1993      27       19990.05
1994      28       21589.26
1995      29       23316.4
1996      30       25181.71
1997      31       27196.25
1998      32       29371.95
1999      33       31721.71
2000      34       34259.45
2001      35       37000.2
2002      36       39960.22
2003      37       43157.04
2004      38       46609.6
2005      39       50338.37
2006      40       54365.44
2007      41       58714.68
2008      42       63411.86
2009      43       68484.81
```

B. OUTPUT

The new value is

$$\$11,664.00 = 10,800 + 864$$

or   New value = (current value) + (amount of change)

Thus by knowing the rate of change, we can calculate the new current value in the following way:

New current value ← (current value) + (rate of change) × (current value)

Notice that this relation is used repeatedly in the program in Fig. 11.7A, in lines 410 and 420. Trace the loop a few times to be sure you understand how it works.

In addition to projecting future costs, values, and amounts assuming an initial value and a fixed rate of change, the program in Fig. 11.7A can determine annual rates of change from historical information. For example, suppose a particular house costs $73,000 in 1977 and is sold for $105,999 in 1982. What is the *annual* rate of change? This rate can be determined with mathematics. However, suppose we use the program with 10% (0.10) as a guess for the annual rate of change. The program would print the following result:

Year	Value
.	.
.	.
.	.
1982	117,567

This rate is clearly too large. Let's try again with 5% (0.05) as our next guess. The program would print the following:

Year	Value
.	.
.	.
.	.
1982	93,168

Consequently, our next guess should be between 5% and 10%. After five or six guesses the actual rate of change per year will be determined quite accurately.

EXERCISES

11.6. With appropriate assumptions, use the program in Fig. 11.7A to show how the costs, values, or amounts of the various assets or resources below will change in the future.

a) Housing costs are increasing at the rate of about 12% per year. The average cost of a new ranch house is $75,000 this year. What will it cost in 5 years?

b) A Ford Pinto was bought in 1976 for $2800. Assume that its value depreciates at a rate of 30% per year. What is its value today?

c) Some people have suggested that the cost of computing power has decreased at a rate of 25% per year. What would a computer costing $50,000 today cost in 5 years?

11.7. Modify the program in Fig. 11.7A so that it becomes less tedious to use for guessing actual rates of change. The printout might look like this:

```
                    DETERMINING RATES OF CHANGE

            STARTING YEAR AND VALUE?    1977, 73000
            ENDING YEAR AND VALUE?      1982, 105999

        RATE OF CHANGE
        GUESS                  YEAR      CALCULATED VALUE
        -----------------------         -------   ----------------------------
        ? 0.10                 1982      117567       TOO HIGH
        ? 0.05                 1982      93168        TOO LOW
          .
          .
          .
```

Once you have determined the annual rate of change quite accurately, use the program in Fig. 11.7A to project values or amounts into the future. Of course, you have no guarantee that the rate of change will actually remain the same in the future. Consider the following examples.

a) Suppose your parents bought a house in 1955 for $15,000. Today a real estate agent says it is worth $95,000. What is the annual rate of increase in value? What will the house be worth in the year 1990?

b) Use the following population figures of the United States:

Year	Population
1930	122,775,046
1950	150,697,361
1970	203,235,298

Find the annual rate of change in population between 1930 and 1950, and then between 1950 and 1970. Use one or both of the rates of change to estimate the population in 1980. How accurate are these predictions?

11.8. Suppose that for the past 5 years inflation has progressed at the rate of 7% per year. Your income has only increased at the rate of 4.5% per year. Modify the program in Fig. 11.7A to show how inflation has affected your buying power.

11.9. This exercise shows how taxes and inflation erode the value of savings. Depending on your income, the federal government will take anywhere from 14% to 50% of your income. Assume that taxes owed are paid from your savings account. Modify the program in Fig. 11.7A so that it reads your tax bracket and the current rate of inflation and prints the value of your savings account.

11.10. *Annuities:* Any set of equal payments made or received at equal intervals of time is called an *annuity*. A deposit of $500 in the bank every year is one example of an annuity. Again, modify the program in Fig. 11.7A so that it simulates the depositing of a fixed amount in a bank account at the beginning of each year. The printout might look like this:

```
                        ANNUITY

STARTING YEAR....................? 1982
YOUR AGE.........................? 22
BANK INTEREST RATE...............? .075
AMOUNT DEPOSITED EACH YEAR.......? 1000

END OF   YOUR   EARNED INTEREST   AMOUNT IN BANK
YEAR     AGE    THIS YEAR         AFTER YEARLY DEPOSIT
..........  .......  ................... ....................
1982     22    xxx               xxx
1983     23    xxx               xxx
```

11.11. Amend the program created for Exercise 11.10 so that it deducts from the account the amount owed in taxes on the earned interest. Also, include in the printout the cost of a new car so that the real value of the annuity is clearly seen.

11.12. Simulate the growth of a tax sheltered annuity, or IRA. Get some details from a local bank or insurance agent.

11.13. Suppose you expect to retire at age 65 and expect to die at age 90. During the intervening 25 years you would like to withdraw $25,000 each year from your bank account to live on. Furthermore, as soon as you withdraw the last $25,000 from your account at age 90, you want your bank account to be zero. Assuming a fixed rate of interest, how much must you begin depositing at age 25 in order to do this? The process might be visualized like this:

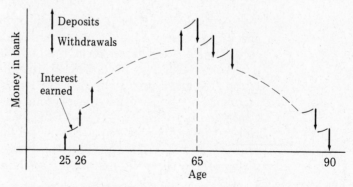

Hint: There will be two main loops in this program. One will simulate the depositing of the money; the other will simulate the withdrawing of money. The simulation is then used to guess the value that should be deposited.

Interest Rates for Fractional Years and for Loans

Given rates of change, we have seen how to determine future values in successive years. But how are interest amounts calculated for a fraction of a year? Here are two examples of this type of problem.

☐ EXAMPLE

Suppose you deposit $400 in a bank that pays 5% interest per year and you withdraw the money after 3 months. What should you receive as interest?

☐ EXAMPLE

Suppose you owe the bank $800 and it is charging you 13% interest per year. You elect to pay back the loan after 5 months. What do you owe them?

The following rule tells us how to find the interest rate for fractional parts of a year.

☐ RULE

To find the interest rate used for calculating the interest for part of a year, multiply the annual rate by the fraction of the year under consideration.

In the first example above, since 3 months is one-fourth of a year, the interest rate is $(\frac{1}{4})(0.05)$, and the amount of interest earned on your $400 is $(\frac{1}{4})(0.05)(400) = 5.00$. In the second example you owe the bank $(\frac{5}{12})(0.13)(800) = 43.33$ in interest plus the original $400.

Bank loan repayment schedules are designed so that after a specific number of equal payments are made, the amount owed becomes zero. Consider the schedule in Fig. 11.8B. Because the time between payments is usually a part of a year, the interest is calculated according to the rule given previously. That is, for this printout since there are 4 payments per year, the payments occur every 3 months, or every $\frac{1}{4}$ year. Consequently, $(\frac{1}{4})(0.12) = 0.03$ is the interest rate for each interval. Notice that at the end of the first period the amount owed is $4000, the original amount borrowed, plus the interest, $0.03(4000) = 120$, which gives $4120. After a payment of $401.85 the new balance becomes $3718.15.

The only real problem in writing a program (Fig. 11.8A) to calculate a loan repayment schedule is to determine what the payment is so that at the end of the term the amount owed is zero. For the program in Fig. 11.8A the following variable names are used:

☐ **FIGURE 11.8**   **Loan Repayment Schedule**

```
100 PRINT "    MORTGAGE ANALYSIS"
110 PRINT
200 INPUT "AMOUNT BORROWED  - - - "; B
210 INPUT "ANNUAL INTEREST RATE - "; R
220 INPUT "NUMBER PAYMTS PER YR - "; N
230 INPUT "NUMBER OF YEARS  - - - "; Y
240 PRINT
250 L1$ = "    EACH PAYMENT ######.##"
300 LET Q = (1+R/N)^(N*Y)
310 LET P = B*(R/N)*Q/(Q-1)
340 PRINT USING L1$; P
350 PRINT
400 PRINT "END          AMOUNT       NEW"
410 PRINT "PERIOD       OWED         BAL. DUE"
420 PRINT
430 L2$ = " ###      ######.##      ######.##"
500 FOR T = 1 TO N*Y
510   LET I = (1/N)*R*B
530   LET B1 = B + I
540   LET B = B1 - P
550   PRINT USING L2$; T, B1, B
560 NEXT T
570 END
```

A. PROGRAM

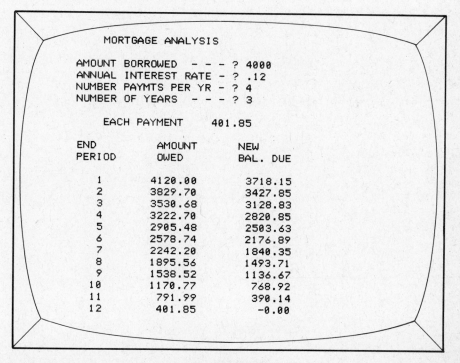

B. OUTPUT

B	Initial amount borrowed
R	Annual rate of interest
N	Number of payments per year
Y	Number of years

Then the payment for each period is

$$P = B * \frac{R}{N} * \frac{(1 + R/N)^{N * Y}}{(1 + R/N)^{N * Y} - 1}$$

According to the way interest is calculated for a fraction of the year, the interest for each period is

$$I = (1/N) * R * B$$

The balance owed after adding the interest is

$$B1 = B + I$$

The new balance owed after making the payment is

$$B = B1 - P$$

These assignments are included in the program in Fig. 11.8A; see lines 300, 310, and 510–540.

EXERCISES

11.14. Verify the first few lines of the loan repayment schedule in Fig. 11.8B.

11.15. If you have an automobile loan or house mortgage, use the program in Fig. 11.8A for calculating your loan schedule.

11.16. Modify the program in Fig. 11.8A so that it prints the cumulative interest paid.

11.17. The repayment schedule can be improved by including the month and year of each payment. For example, write a program that produces a printout like this:

```
NUMBER OF PAYMENTS PER YEAR.....?4
NUMBER OF YEARS.................?3
STARTING DATE (MONTH & YEAR)....?8, 1981

            EACH PAYMENT = 401.85

            AMOUNT      NEW BALANCE
  DATE      OWED        DUE
..........  ..........  ....................

  11  1981    4120        3718.15
  12  1982    xxx         xxx
```

11.18. Since the interest paid on a loan is a tax deduction, modify the program written for Exercise 11.17 so that the program prints the amount of interest paid for each year. Also, have the program calculate the actual amount of money saved in income taxes by having the loan. For this program you will have to input your tax bracket as an assumption.

11.19. *Compound interest:* Suppose you deposit $100.00 in your local bank at the current interest rate of 6% per year. The bank calculates (compounds) the interest four times a year, at the end of each 3-month period. According to the rule stated previously for calculating interest for part of a year, the bank uses the rate of $(\frac{1}{4})(0.06) = 0.015$ at the end of each period. Consequently, the amount of money in your account at the end of each 3-month period will be as follows:

MONTH	INTEREST AT THE START OF THE MONTH	NEW AMOUNT IN ACCOUNT
3	1.50	101.50
6	1.5225	103.0225
9	1.5453	104.5678
12	1.5685	106.1363

a) Verify the calculations above for compound interest.

b) A skeleton program for performing the calculations discussed above might look like the one that follows. Variable N holds the number of times per year the interest is calculated.

```
200  LET B = 100
210  LET R = .06
220  LET N = 4
300  FOR T = 1 TO N
320     LET I = (1/N) * R * B
330     LET B = B + I
340     PRINT T, I, B
350  NEXT T
999  END
```

Modify the program so that it will calculate compound interest for any set of initial assumptions.

11.4 CALENDAR SIMULATIONS

As you have seen, many simulations proceed through time, where time is measured in seconds, hours, days, weeks, and so on. Some simulations progress by consecutive days, where the actual dates are important.

The program in Fig. 11.9A produces consecutive dates (Fig. 11.9B). With this routine you can enhance many of the previous programs as well as do a number of interesting calculations, as suggested in the exercises for this section.

To fully understand the program, you should construct a hierarchy chart for it and then trace it (see Exercises 11.20 and 11.21).

You should be aware that the program in Fig. 11.9A does not calculate leap years correctly for centennial years, that is, those years that are divisible by 100. One exercise is to modify the program so that it fully implements the definition of a leap year, which is as follows: Every year whose number if divisible by 4 is a *leap year*, with the exception of centennial years, which are leap years only when divisible by 400.

☐ **FIGURE 11.9**   **Calculating Consecutive Dates**

```
100 PRINT "   CONSECUTIVE DATES"
110 PRINT
200 PRINT "STARTING: MONTH,DAY,YEAR"
210 INPUT "        "; M1, D1, Y1
240                                         REM
250 PRINT "  ENDING: MONTH,DAY,YEAR"
260 INPUT "        "; M2, D2, Y2
290                                         REM
300 REM --- INITIALIZE CURRENT DATE
310 LET M = M1: D = D1: Y = Y1
340                                         REM
400 GOSUB 2000 : REM - CALC DAYS IN MONTH
410                                         REM
500 REM --- LOOP UNTIL ENDING DATE ---
510 IF D=D2 AND M=M2 AND Y=Y2 THEN 600
520    PRINT M; D; Y
530     GOSUB 1000 : REM - CALC NEXT DATE
540 GOTO 510
550                                         REM
600 PRINT M; D; Y
610 STOP
620                                         REM
1000 REM --- SUB: CALC NEXT DATE       ---
1010 LET D = D + 1
1100 IF D <= N THEN 1500
1200    REM --- FALSE: NEW MONTH
1210        LET D = 1
1220        LET M = M + 1
1230        IF M <= 12 THEN 1270
1240        REM --- FALSE: NEW YEAR
1250            LET M = 1
1260            LET Y = Y + 1
1270        REM --- ENDIF ---
1280        REM - CALC DAYS IN MONTH
1290        GOSUB 2000
1300    REM --- ENDIF ---
1310                                        REM
1500 RETURN
```

(continued)

☐ FIGURE 11.9   (Continued)

```
1600                                        REM
1999                                        REM
2000 REM --- SUB: CALC DAYS IN MONTH ---
2010 REM --- N WILL HOLD DAYS IN MONTH
2020                                        REM
2030 REM --- CASE SELECTION ---
2100   IF M=4 OR M=6 OR M=9 OR M=11 THEN 2500
2110   IF M = 2                    THEN 2400
2120                                        REM
2130 REM - CASE: OTHERWISE
2300 REM -       JAN,MAR,MAY,JUL,AUG,OCT,DEC
2310     LET N = 31
2320     GOTO 2600
2330                                        REM
2400 REM - CASE: FEBRUARY
2410     IF INT(Y/4) = Y/4 THEN N=29 ELSE N=28
2420     GOTO 2600
2430                                        REM
2500 REM - CASE: APR,JUN,SEP,NOV
2510     LET N = 30
2520     GOTO 2600
2530                                        REM
2600 REM --- ENDCASE -----
2610 RETURN
2700 END
```

A. PROGRAM

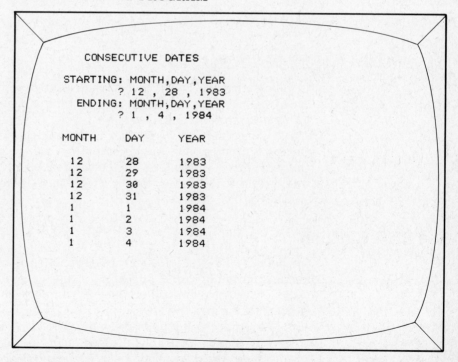

```
           CONSECUTIVE DATES

      STARTING: MONTH,DAY,YEAR
            ? 12 , 28 , 1983
        ENDING: MONTH,DAY,YEAR
            ? 1 , 4 , 1984

    MONTH     DAY     YEAR

      12       28      1983
      12       29      1983
      12       30      1983
      12       31      1983
       1        1      1984
       1        2      1984
       1        3      1984
       1        4      1984
```

B. OUTPUT

EXERCISES

11.20. Construct a hierarchy chart for the program in Fig. 11.9A.

11.21. Trace the program in Fig. 11.9A, using the dates entered in Fig. 11.9B.

11.22. Modify the program in Fig. 11.9A so that it fully implements the rule for calculating leap years.

11.23. Modify the program in Fig. 11.9A so that it prints the dates of all consecutive Fridays for the next year. *Hint:* Given the date of the first Friday, the program can print out the date every seventh time through the loop.

11.24. Write a program that prints all Fridays the 13th for the next 25 years.

11.25. Write a program that, starting from an initial date, prints the date of every seventh day. From the current day it should *calculate* the date of the day seven days later. This calculation should *not* be done as suggested in Exercise 11.23.

11.26. Write a program that produces a calendar for an entire year. The year and week day of January 1 should be INPUTted as assumptions.

11.5 RANDOM SIMULATIONS

In this section the BASIC function RND is explained and illustrated. Then we show how it can be used to simulate random processes like flipping a coin or rolling dice.

Note: The RND function is designated slightly differently on various computers. On Apple computers, use the designation RND(1). On Radio Shack computers, use the designation RND(0). In this chapter we simply refer to the function by RND, which is the way it is referenced on the IBM PC.

The RND Function

In line 320 of Fig. 11.10A the RND function is used. As you can see from the output in Fig. 11.10B, this function generates numbers between 0 and 1. The program will produce 100 numbers, but we have included only the first few.

Look at the numbers printed in Fig. 11.10B. There seems to be no way of knowing what the next number will be. For this reason the numbers are called "random." The **RND function** is a random number generator.

RND function

□ FIGURE 11.10   Generating Random Numbers

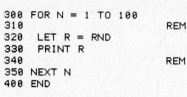

```
300 FOR N = 1 TO 100
310                    REM
320   LET R = RND
330   PRINT R
340                    REM
350 NEXT N
400 END
```

A. PROGRAM

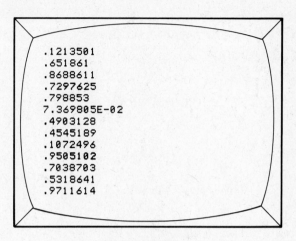

```
.1213501
.651861
.8688611
.7297625
.798853
7.369805E-02
.4903128
.4545189
.1072496
.9505102
.7038703
.5318641
.9711614
```

B. OUTPUT

uniformly distributed

Although the list of numbers is random, we do know something about the overall dispersion, or distribution, of the numbers. If "many" numbers are generated, they will be spread relatively evenly throughout the interval from 0 to 1. That is, they are **uniformly distributed** between 0 and 1. This characteristic is an essential one of the numbers generated by RND. To test the function RND for uniform distribution, we can write a program that counts the number of times a random number occurs in each $\frac{1}{10}$ interval. The printout might look like this:

```
RUN

       DISPERSION OF
      RANDOM NUMBERS

RANGE          NO. IN RANGE
-----------    ------------------
0  - .1        11
.1 - .2        9
.2 - .3        8
.3 - .4        14
.4 - .5        9
.5 - .6        10
.6 - .7        9
.7 - .8        9
.8 - .9        11
.9 - 1         10
```

☐ **FIGURE 11.11**   **Simulation of Coin Flipping**

```
300 FOR F = 1 TO 20
310  LET R = RND
320  IF R < .5 THEN D$="H" ELSE D$="T"
330  PRINT D$;
340 NEXT F
400 END
```

A. PROGRAM

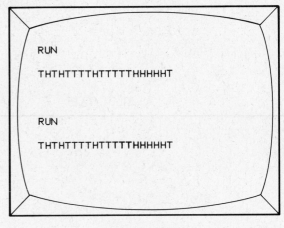

B. OUTPUT

The fact that the random numbers generated by RND are uniformly distributed is what makes the function so useful. For example, the program in Fig. 11.11A simulates the flipping of a coin. After generating a random number, the computer prints an H for heads if the number is less than 0.5. Otherwise, it prints T for tails. See Fig. 11.11B. Since the numbers are uniformly distributed, approximately half the numbers will be less than 0.5, and the other half will be greater than or equal to 0.5. Consequently, approximately half the flips will be heads and half tails. This result is what we would expect if we flipped a coin a number of times.

EXERCISE

11.27. Add statements to the program in Fig. 11.11A so that the number of heads and tails are counted.

A Coin-Flipping Game

Would you play the following game?

Each time you flip a coin, you must pay the bank $1.00. As soon as you flip three heads or three tails in a row, the game is over and the bank gives you $8.00.

Consider these two games.

Game 1   HTTHHH   Winnings $8 − $6 = $2
Game 2   HTHTTHHTHTTT   Winnings $8 − $12 = −$4

Again, would you play this game?

From the winnings columns above we see that if the average is less than eight flips a game, then it might be worthwhile to play these games. Otherwise, it would definitely not be profitable in the long run.

The average number of flips per game can be determined mathematically, but it is not easy. Instead of attempting a mathematical solution, we can decide whether or not to play a coin-flipping game by writing a computer program that imitates the play of the game. Such a program and output are illustrated in Fig. 11.12.

In the program (Fig. 11.12A) the latest three flips (since those are the important values) are held in variables A$, B$, and C$. To determine if the game is over, we simply compare these three variables. When another flip is required, a three-step process takes place: The second-to-last flip becomes the earliest flip, and the last flip is shifted to the second-to-last flip. Then the current flip becomes the last flip. This process is illustrated here:

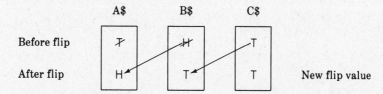

Again the question: Would you play this game? Clearly, you would not if the output in Fig. 11.11B were typical. But the short-run outcome is not necessarily what happens in the long run. To see the long-run output, you could have this program simulate the game 1000 times. To conserve paper, you would suppress the printing of the details of each game.

Testing a Random Simulation

How is a random (probabilistic) simulation program tested? Remember, data processing programs are tested by supplying carefully chosen test values that exercise as many possibilities as practical. Simulation programs that do not use the RND function (deterministic simulations) are tested by comparing a few consecutive lines of output to see that each iteration is working correctly.

Probabilistic simulation programs are a bit different. A test run generally consists of writing out everything (including the random

☐ **FIGURE 11.12**   **Simulating the Game of Flips**

```
100 PRINT "        GAME OF FLIPS"
110 PRINT
400 PRINT "GAME #   FLIPS .......";
410        PRINT    TAB(25);"AMT WON"
420 PRINT
430 FOR G = 1 TO 5
440     PRINT G; TAB(9);
450     GOSUB 1000 : A$ = F$
460     GOSUB 1000 : B$ = F$
470     GOSUB 1000 : C$ = F$
480     LET N = 3  : REM - COUNT FLIPS -
490                                   REM
500     REM --- LOOP UNTIL LAST 3 SAME ---
510     IF A$=B$ AND B$=C$ THEN 600
520        LET A$=B$
530        LET B$=C$
540        GOSUB 1000 : C$ = F$
550        LET N = N + 1
560     GOTO 510
570                                   REM
600     LET W = 8 - N
610     PRINT TAB(26); W
700 NEXT G
710 STOP
720                                   REM
1000 REM --- SUB: GENERATE FLIP AND PRINT ---
1110    LET R = RND
1120    IF R < .5 THEN F$ = "H" ELSE F$ = "T"
1130    PRINT F$;
1140 RETURN
1150                                  REM
1200 END
```

A. PROGRAM

```
        GAME OF FLIPS

GAME #     FLIPS .......  AMT WON

1          HTTT                 4
2          HHTTHHTHTTHTHTHHTTT
                              -11
3          HHH                  5
4          TTHHTTT              1
5          TTHTHTHTHHTTT       -5
```

B. OUTPUT

numbers generated) that happens in each game for 20 or 30 games and then studying this output for inconsistencies. For example, suppose the output is as shown in Fig. 11.12B. If a particular output from a game looks like this,

```
GAME #     FLIPS .......     AMT WON

45         T H T T T H T H H H
```

you know something is wrong. Why? It should have stopped after the fifth flip.

In simulation programs it is easy to make simple logic mistakes that do not readily reveal themselves. For example, wins could be counted as losses and vice versa. You must check the program carefully for such mistakes.

Once all irregularities are found and fixed, then the PRINT statements that produce all the details are removed so that just the summary results for 1000 and 10,000 games are written.

EXERCISES

11.28. Modify the program in Fig. 11.12A so that it simulates 500 games. As a summary result, it should determine the average amount of money won per game. Test the program.

11.29. Another summary result that will help you understand the game of flips is the percentage of games that end in three flips, four flips, five flips, and so on. Modify the program so that the summary results look like this:

```
NUMBER OF     % OF GAMES
FLIPS         LASTING THIS LENGTH
---------     -----------------------
3             24.67
4             21.39
5             xxxx
.
.
.
10 OR MORE    xxxxx
```

11.30. Suppose each flip of a coin costs $1. A coin is flipped successively until the number of heads is three more or three less than the number of tails. At that point the player receives $8. Would you play this game? For example, a particular game might have these results:

```
Game       HHTHTTHHTHH     (7 heads, 4 tails)
Winnings   $8-$11 = -$3
```

11.31. Suppose that at a country fair there is a booth where a man continuously flips a coin. At any time you can bet on the outcome of the next flip. If you are wrong, you lose 25¢; if you are right, you win 20¢. Your strategy for playing this game is to wait until either four heads or four tails have been flipped in a row and then bet on the opposite outcome. For example, suppose the following sequence just occurred:

```
...HTHTTTT
```

At this point you would bet that the next flip will be a head. Write a program to evaluate your strategy.

11.32. *Basketball game:* Suppose that, on the average, basketball player A makes one out of two shots at 20 feet from the basket, and player B makes one out of three shots. The game consists of the players alternating shots until someone makes the first shot. To make the game fair, player A always lets player B shoot first. Who, in general, will win the most games out of 100 played?

11.33. *Baseball game:* Suppose a baseball player that is batting .326 comes to bat exactly four times a game and never gets walked. In general, can this player expect to hit safely in 25 consecutive games during the season? Write a program that simulates 600 times at bat (approximately the number of times at bat during a season). Now do the following problem extensions:
a) Determine the length of the longest hitting streak.
b) Count the number of hitting streaks that last one game, two games, three games, and so on.
c) Make the program flexible so that the player's batting average can be READ as an assumption.
d) In general, suppose that in half the games in a season the player comes to bat four times, and in half the games he bats five times. How does this schedule affect the length of the batting streaks?
e) How "lucky" were Pete Rose and Joe DiMaggio in setting their respective records for batting streaks?

Generating Random Numbers

Notice what happened in Fig. 11.11B when the program was run twice. The same sequence of random numbers was generated, so we got the same series of flips. In real life the chance of getting the same series of flips is nil. So on most computers there is a way to get a different sequence of numbers from the RND function each time a program is run. But before we explain how this procedure works, we first give a short example showing how random numbers can be generated.

The program in Fig. 11.13A generates random numbers. Trace a few statements in the program (see Fig. 11.13B). You should get the same values given in Fig. 11.13C. Now look at the remaining values for R that are printed. They appear to be a random sequence. But they certainly are not random since we calculated them! Also, note that if we start with a different value for R in line 110, a different sequence will be generated. This initial R value is called the **seed** for obvious reasons.

seed

RANDOMIZE
statement

A number of BASIC versions (Microsoft, IBM, DEC) use the **RANDOMIZE statement**, which generates a different seed value each time a program is run. Thus if you want to get a different sequence of random numbers with each run, include RANDOMIZE as one of the first statements in the program. For example, if you run the following

□ FIGURE 11.13   Generating Random Numbers

```
100 REM --- SEED IS ---
110 LET R = .2876
120                      REM
200 FOR N = 1 TO 100
210    LET Q = 317 * R
220    LET R = Q - INT(Q)
230    PRINT R
240 NEXT N
250 END
```

A. PROGRAM

```
.1691895
.6330566
.6789551
.2287598
.5168457
.8400879
.3078613
.592041
.677002
.6096191
.2492676
1.782227E-02
.6496582
.9416504
```

B. OUTPUT

N	R	Q
	.2876	
1	.1691895	91.1691895
2	.6330566	53.6363821

C. TRACE

brief program twice, it will generate two different sequences of random numbers. Do it.

```
10  RANDOMIZE
20  FOR I = 1 TO 5
30    PRINT RND
40  NEXT I
50  END
```

In Apple BASIC you will automatically get a different sequence of random numbers with the RND(1) function. To get the same sequence each time, use RND(-1) once and thereafter use RND(1).

Expanding the Range of Random Numbers

The built-in function RND generates random numbers only between 0 and 1. This restriction might seem to be a serious one, if you happen to need random numbers between 76 and 105. However, the RND—

☐ **FIGURE 11.14**   **Expanding the Range of Random Decimal Numbers**

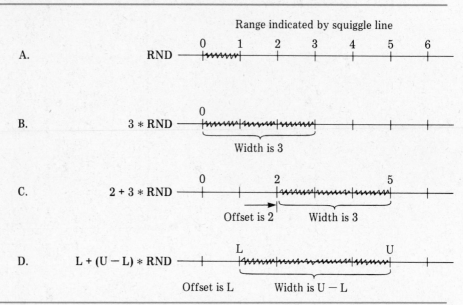

RND(1) in Apple BASIC and RND(0) in Radio Shack BASIC—function can be used in arithmetic expressions to generate random decimal numbers and random integers in any desired range, as explained below.

Figure 11.14A shows the range of the RND function. Figure 11.14B illustrates how the range of random numbers can be stretched by multiplying RND by a number (3 in this case) greater than 1. Figure 11.14C shows how the range can be *offset* from zero by adding a number to the expression (2 in this case). The expression

```
L + (U - L) * RND
```

random decimal
numbers

random integers

in Fig. 11.14D will generate **random decimal numbers** between any values you choose for L, the lower bound, and U, the upper bound.

Figure 11.15 illustrates how you can generate **random integers** between and including any two integers. The technique is quite similar to the one for generating random decimal numbers, except that the INT function is used to produce integer values. Specifically, the expression

```
INT(L + (U + 1 - L) * RND)
```

in Fig. 11.15B will generate random integers between and including any integer values you choose for L, the lower bound, and U, the upper bound.

Now let's see how we use the expression for generating random integers in a program. Suppose we wish to generate random integers uniformly between −2 and 4. Then L is −2 and U is 4. Substituting these

☐ **FIGURE 11.15**   **Generating a Range of Random Integers**

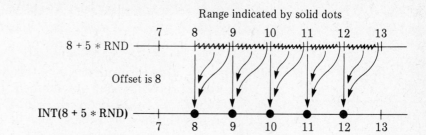

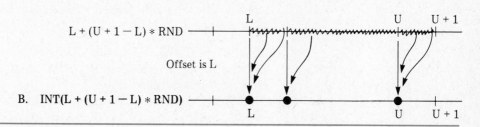

A.

B.

values in the appropriate formula for L and U (Fig. 11.15B), we get

```
INT(-2 + (4 + 1 - (-2)) * RND)      or      INT(-2 + 7 * RND)
```

The following program generates 100 such integers:

```
100  FOR I = 1 TO 100
110    LET R = INT(-2 + 7 * RND)
120    PRINT R;
130  NEXT I
```

As another example, suppose we wish to simulate the rolling of one die. Since the 6 possibilities (1, 2, 3, 4, 5, 6) are equally likely, we use the integer formula with L as 1 and U as 6.

As a final example, suppose we wish to simulate the sums obtained by rolling a pair of dice simultaneously. This simulation can be done by rolling each die independently and then adding the results, as follows:

```
LET D1 = INT(1 + 6 * RND)
LET D2 = INT(1 + 6 * RND)
LET S  = D1 + D2
```

EXERCISES

11.34. Why can't you set L = 2 and U = 12 and use the formula

```
LET D = INT(2 + (12 + 1 - 2) * RND)
```

to simulate the rolling of a pair of dice?

11.35. You want to simulate the rolling of two dice. Variable D is to hold the sum of the two dice. For each assignment statement below, explain why each expression can or cannot be used.

```
LET D = INT(1 + 6 * RND) + INT(1 + 6 * RND)
LET D = 2 * INT(1 + 6 * RND)
```

11.36. Write a program that simulates the rolling of two dice 1000 times. Have it count the number of times a 2 is rolled, a 3 is rolled, . . . , a 12 is rolled. Print the number of times each is rolled and the percentage. How do these results compare with those expected mathematically?

11.37. Craps is a casino game played with a pair of dice. The rules for playing craps are as follows:

- On the first roll 7 or 11 wins for the roller; 2, 3, or 12 is a loss for the roller; any other number is called the roller's point, and the dice are rolled again.
- On all rolls after the first one, if the point is rolled, it is a win for the roller; if a 7 is rolled, it is a loss; if any other number is rolled, the dice are rolled again.

As the roller, what are your chances of winning this game? Write a program to simulate the playing of 1000 games, counting how many times you, the roller, win. Test your program. (Compare the results of your printout with the theoretical results. A discussion of this topic can be found in *Lady Luck* by Warren Weaver.)

11.38. In roulette there are 38 possible outcomes: 00, 0, 1, 2, . . . , 36. Let the 00 be represented by a -1. Write a program that simulates the following betting system: You always bet on EVEN. Start with a $1 bet. If you lose, double your bet. (However, you can only double your bet eight times.) If you win, start again with a bet of $1. Suppose you have $500 to start with. The play stops when you go broke or win $5000. Simulate 50 encounters with the roulette wheel.

11.39. *Computer-assisted drill:* Write a program that will generate random integers, which the person at the terminal is to add, subtract, multiply, or divide. The computer will check to determine whether the response is right or wrong and print an appropriate message. The form of the questions might look like this:

```
  13
+ 36
= ?
```

There are many details that could be incorporated into the program. For instance, there could be various levels of difficulty, starting with one-digit numbers and progressing to four-digit numbers. At the end of the session the computer could summarize the student's responses. Further program suggestions: Programs could be written to test a student's ability with fractions or various common types of word problems. The word problems could be in practically any subject area—chemistry, biology, and so on.

11.6 SIMULATING REAL EVENTS THROUGH TIME

The random processes considered in the previous sections of this chapter were simulated by generating the next event. For example, in craps, as you saw in Exercise 11.37, the next event consists of rolling a pair of dice. The length of time between the events is not important.

interval of simulation

However, in some situations the time between two events is very important. Examples of time-dependent events are discussed in this section. You should notice that in each simulation in this section time is advanced in *equal steps*. This time length is called the **interval of simulation.** During each interval of simulation a random number or numbers are generated to determine what, if anything, happens in the random process.

We will now consider two time-dependent random processes. Then we will generalize the method used to simulate such events.

Traffic Arrivals at an Intersection

Figure 11.16A illustrates a traffic intersection where, in general, there are 6 cars per minute on the main street and 3 cars per minute on the side street. The accompanying simulation in Fig. 11.16C gives us a dynamic picture of the situation. The word CAR indicates that a car arrives at the intersection along either the main or the side street.

Why would we want to simulate a traffic intersection? Well, we might be interested, for example, in installing a traffic light with the lights sequenced in an optimal manner.

The interesting part of the program in Fig. 11.16B is how it determines whether or not a car arrives along one of the streets. Let's confine our attention to the main street. First, every 3 seconds (the interval of simulation) a random number is generated. The value of this number determines whether or not a car arrives. Since the interval of simulation is 3 seconds, there are $\frac{60}{3} = 20$ intervals each minute, and so 20 random numbers are generated for each minute. On the average, we want 6 of these numbers to indicate the arrival of a car. Because the random numbers are uniformly generated, approximately 6 numbers

☐ **FIGURE 11.16**   **Traffic Intersection**

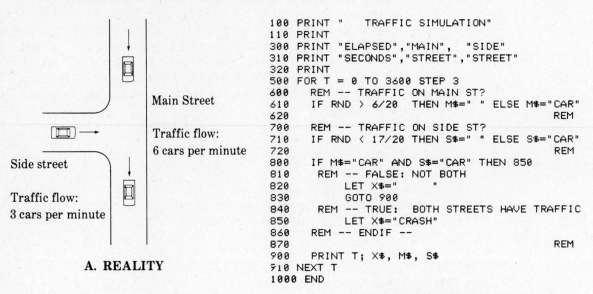

Main Street

Traffic flow:
6 cars per minute

Side street

Traffic flow:
3 cars per minute

A. REALITY

```
100 PRINT "   TRAFFIC SIMULATION"
110 PRINT
300 PRINT "ELAPSED","MAIN",  "SIDE"
310 PRINT "SECONDS","STREET","STREET"
320 PRINT
500 FOR T = 0 TO 3600 STEP 3
600   REM -- TRAFFIC ON MAIN ST?
610   IF RND > 6/20  THEN M$=" " ELSE M$="CAR"
620                              REM
700   REM -- TRAFFIC ON SIDE ST?
710   IF RND < 17/20 THEN S$=" " ELSE S$="CAR"
720                              REM
800   IF M$="CAR" AND S$="CAR" THEN 850
810    REM -- FALSE: NOT BOTH
820       LET X$="      "
830       GOTO 900
840    REM -- TRUE:  BOTH STREETS HAVE TRAFFIC
850       LET X$="CRASH"
860    REM -- ENDIF --
870                              REM
900    PRINT T; X$, M$, S$
910 NEXT T
1000 END
```

B. COMPUTER MODEL

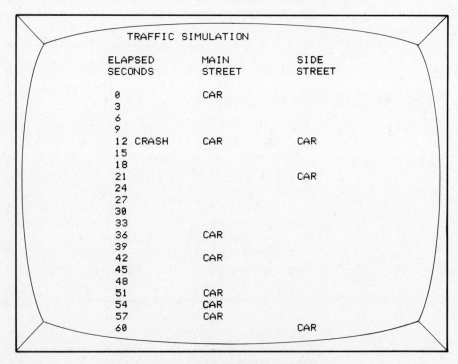

```
        TRAFFIC SIMULATION

     ELAPSED       MAIN          SIDE
     SECONDS       STREET        STREET

        0          CAR
        3
        6
        9
       12 CRASH    CAR           CAR
       15
       18
       21                        CAR
       24
       27
       30
       33
       36          CAR
       39
       42          CAR
       45
       48
       51          CAR
       54          CAR
       57          CAR
       60                        CAR
```

C. COMPUTER SIMULATION

will turn up between 0 and $\frac{6}{20}$. Consequently, when a number turns up in this interval, it is used to indicate the arrival of a car, as follows:

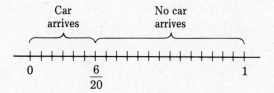

(of course, any $\frac{6}{20}$ of the unit interval could be used.)

This situation is implemented in the program with the statement

```
610  IF RND > 6/20 THEN M$=" " ELSE M$="CAR"
```

A similar argument shows that any $\frac{3}{20}$ of the unit interval can be used to indicate the arrival of a car on the side street. In our program the upper $\frac{3}{20}$ from $\frac{17}{20}$ to $\frac{20}{20}$ are used:

```
710  IF RND < 17/20 THEN S$=" " ELSE S$="CAR"
```

Customer Arrivals at a Service Facility

Suppose customers randomly arrive at a service facility at the rate of one person every 120 seconds (2 minutes), as illustrated in Fig. 11.17A. These random events can be simulated through time with the technique used in the previous example.

An interval of 20 seconds might be appropriate here. During each interval of simulation a random number is generated. Its value is used to determine whether a customer arrives. Since the interval of simulation is 20 seconds, there are 6 intervals every 120 seconds. Therefore 6 random numbers are generated. Thus any $\frac{1}{6}$ can be used to indicate the arrival of a customer, as follows:

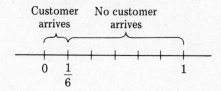

Any random number that turns up between 0 and $\frac{1}{6}$ indicates the arrival of a customer. This situation is implemented in the program in Fig. 11.17B with the following statements:

□ FIGURE 11.17   Service Facility

Clerk

Person being
served

People
waiting

Arrival time
= 1 person every 2 minutes

A. REALITY

```
100 PRINT "        SERVICE FACILITY"
110 PRINT " "
120                                                    REM
200 REM --- INITIALIZE VARIABLES ---
210     REM T  -                TIME ELAPSED, SECS
220     LET NW = 0: REM          # PEOPLE WAITING
230     LET ES = 0: REM          END OF SERVICE TIME
240     REM A$ -                 ARRIVAL STATUS
250     LET CLK$ = "    ": REM CLERK STATUS
260                                                    REM
300 PRINT "                        END     NUMBER"
310 PRINT "ELAPSED                 SERVE   PEOPLE"
320 PRINT "SECONDS  ARRIVAL?  CLERK  TIME    WAITING"
330 PRINT
400 FOR T = 0 TO 900 STEP 20
410   IF RND < 1/6 THEN 460
420   REM - FALSE: NO CUSTOMER
430        LET A$ = "    "
440        GOTO 500
450   REM - TRUE:  CUSTOMER ARRIVES
460        LET NW = NW + 1
470        LET A$ = "YES"
480   REM -- ENDIF --
490                                                    REM
500   IF T >= ES THEN 540
510   REM - FALSE: NOT END OF SERVICE TIME
520        GOTO 700
530   REM - TRUE:  END OF SERVICE TIME
540        LET CLK$ = "    "
550        IF NW >= 1 THEN 570 ELSE 600
560          REM - TRUE:  SOMEBODY WAITING
570             LET NW = NW - 1
580             LET CLK$ = "BUSY"
590             LET ES = T + 100
600          REM -- ENDIF --
610     REM -- ENDIF ---
620                                                    REM
700     PRINT T; TAB(11);A$; TAB(20);CLK$;
710        PRINT TAB(26);ES; TAB(36);NW
720 NEXT T
999 END
```

B. COMPUTER MODEL

```
410   IF RND < 1/6 THEN 460
420    REM - FALSE: NO CUSTOMER
430        LET A$ = "    "
440        GOTO 500
450    REM - TRUE:  CUSTOMER ARRIVES
460        LET NW = NW + 1
470        LET A$ = "YES"
480    REM -- ENDIF --
```

Another interesting part of this program is how the actual service is simulated. Study the output in Fig. 11.17C to be sure you under-

☐ **FIGURE 11.17** **(Continued)**

SERVICE FACILITY

ELAPSED SECONDS	ARRIVAL?	CLERK	END SERVE TIME	NUMBER PEOPLE WAITING
0			0	0
20	YES	. BUSY	120	0
40	YES	BUSY	120	1
60		BUSY	120	1
80		BUSY	120	1
100	YES	BUSY	120	2
120		BUSY	220	1
140		BUSY	220	1
160		BUSY	220	1
180		BUSY	220	1
200		BUSY	220	1
220		BUSY	320	0
240	YES	BUSY	320	1
260		BUSY	320	1
280		BUSY	320	1
300		BUSY	320	1
320		BUSY	420	0
340		BUSY	420	0
360		BUSY	420	0
380		BUSY	420	0
400		BUSY	420	0
420			420	0
440			420	0
460			420	0
480			420	0
500			420	0
520			420	0
540			420	0
560			420	0
580	YES	BUSY	680	0
600		BUSY	680	0
620		BUSY	680	0
640	YES	BUSY	680	1
660	YES	BUSY	680	2
680		BUSY	780	1

C. COMPUTER SIMULATION

stand the heading END SERVE TIME. This time is the time in the future when the current customer being waited on will leave. This technique of indicating when something happens at a future time is extremely common.

A Method for Simulating Events

In the previous two subsections we have explained how a portion of the unit interval is used to simulate the occurrence of an event. Table 11.1 systematizes the method used in the examples.

□ **TABLE 11.1**   **Fraction of the Interval Used to Indicate the Occurrence of an Event**

Situation	Rate of Occurrence: Number per Unit of Time	Unit of Time	Chosen Interval of Simulation	Number of Random Numbers per Unit of Time	Number of Occurrences	Part of Interval
Cars arriving at intersection on main street	6	60 sec (1 min)	3 sec	20	6 out of 20	$\frac{6}{20}$
	7	120 sec (2 min)	5 sec	24	7 out of 24	$\frac{7}{24}$
Persons arriving at a counter to be served	1	120 sec (2 min)	20 sec	6	1 out of 6	$\frac{1}{6}$
Machinery breakdowns at a factory	3	60 min (1 hr)	5 min	12	3 out of 12	$\frac{1}{4}$
	3	60 min (1 hr)	6 min	10	3 out of 10	$\frac{3}{10}$

Consider the first situation. The rate of occurrence is 6 cars (the number) per 60 seconds (the unit of time). Divide the chosen interval of simulation (3 seconds) into the unit of time (60 seconds) to get the number of random numbers (20) to be generated per unit of time. That is, 6 out of 20 random numbers should indicate a car arriving. Now if a random number is between 0 and $\frac{6}{20}$, we assume a car arrives.

EXERCISES

11.40. How do you determine the length of the interval of simulation?

11.41. Simulate the action of a traffic light at the traffic intersection. The output might look like this:

```
                    TRAFFIC SIMULATION

        SECONDS IN SIMULATION = 10000
        SECONDS IN LIGHT CYCLE =        40
        SECONDS GREEN ON MAIN STREET? 25

        ELAPSED      NEXT LIGHT      MAIN STREET      SIDE STREET
        SECONDS      CHANGE          LIGHT    CAR     LIGHT    CAR
        ...........  ...............  .......  ......  .......  ......
             0          25             G        X      RED
             3          25             G               RED
             6          25             G               RED
             9          25             G               RED       X
            12          25             G               RED
```

```
        15          25          G           X       RED
        18          25          G           X       RED         X
        21          25          G                   RED
        24          25          G                   RED         X
        27          40          RED                 G
        30          40          RED         X       G
        33          40          RED                 G
        36          40          RED         X       G
        39          40          RED                 G           X
        42          65          G                   RED
```

11.42. Modify Exercise 11.41 so that it counts the number of cars stopped. Then experiment with the program, varying the length of time the light is green on the main street. Observe the total cars stopped in each case.

11.43. Modify the program in Fig. 11.17B so that it keeps track of the clerk's free time as well as the cumulative total time waited by all customers. Include some of the summary results indicated below. A test printout might look something like this:

```
                                    NUMBER      CUMULATIVE      CUMULATIVE
TIME                                PEOPLE      FREE TIME:      WAIT TIME:
SEC     ARRIVAL?    CLERK           WAITING     CLERK           CUSTOMERS
-------- ----------- ----------     ------------- ----------------- ------------------
0                                   0           20              0
20      YES         BUSY            0           20              0
40                  BUSY            0           20              0
60      YES         BUSY            1           20              20
80                  BUSY            1           20              40
100     YES         BUSY            2           20              80
.
.
.
3600
```

Summary results:

```
NUMBER OF ARRIVALS          XXX
 ACTUAL ARRIVAL RATE        XXX
CLERK FREE TIME             XXX
CUMULATIVE WAIT TIME        XXX
AVERAGE TIME WAITED
  BY CUSTOMER               XXX
MAXIMUM LENGTH OF
  LINE                      XXX
AVERAGE LENGTH
  OF LINE                   XXX
```

11.44. Modify the program in Fig. 11.17B so that the arrival rate and service rate can be inputted.

11.45. A person is to be hired to repair machines that break down at an average rate of 3 per hour. Breakdowns are distributed randomly through time. When a machine is down, it costs the company $20 per hour in lost revenue. The company has the option of hiring one of two applicants for the position. One is slow but cheap; the other is fast but expensive. The following data summarizes the information about the applicants:

Applicant	Required Compensation	Repair Speed
Slow but cheap	$6.00 per hour	One machine in 15 minutes
Fast but expensive	$9.00 per hour	One machine in 10 minutes

Which applicant should be hired? Decide on the form of your test printout first!

11.46. Suppose you own a gas station located on a superhighway. The arrival and service rates are indicated in the accompanying diagram. Because of space limitations, only three cars can wait for gas. Suppose your profit per customer is $2.50.

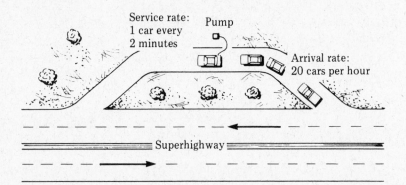

a) What is your profit per hour?
b) How much are you losing per hour because of lack of space?

11.47. Suppose a machine in a factory requires two delicate springs for its operation. The spring breaks down randomly after 30 to 100 hours. The spring replacement policies are as follows:

a) *Current policy:* Each time a spring breaks, it is replaced at a cost of $130. The cost of the spring is small. The $130 cost reflects the cost of labor and downtime.

b) *Suggested new policy:* Each time one spring breaks, both springs are replaced. The cost is less than twice the cost of replacing one—namely, $200.

c) *Modification of policies (a) and (b):* When a spring breaks, instead of replacing just that one [policy (a)] or always replacing both springs [policy (b)], suppose the company replaces the unbroken one if it is old. For example, if the unbroken spring has been used for 50 hours and 50 hours is considered old for a spring, then it is replaced when the broken one is replaced. *Note:* If old is considered to be 1 hour, then this policy is essentially policy (a). If old is considered to be 100 hours, this policy is policy (b). What is the best interpretation of old?

d) *Planned replacement:* Every 70 hours from the last replacement, both springs are replaced. Since this time is planned, there is an additional savings involved. The cost of such a replacement is $175. If a spring breaks before 70 hours, both springs are replaced at the usual cost of $200.

Evaluate these replacement policies by using computer simulations. Again, it is important to decide on the form of the test printout first.

As in the other examples and exercises in this chapter, time is an important aspect of this process. The simulation should mark time but not necessarily in equal time intervals. This situation illustrates a class of simulations in which it is more convenient to **generate the time of the next event** and advance the simulation to that time. For example, suppose the last time a spring broke was at hour 375 into the simulation. The next time to be considered is the time of the next break. *Hint:* To determine the time of the next spring break, use the following procedure: Each time a spring is replaced, a new spring life is generated; it must be between 30 and 100 hours. This time is added to the current time to give the *time in the future when it breaks.* You will need two such variables, one for each spring. Does this use of variables seem familiar? (It should.)

generate the time of
the next event

ARRAYS AND FILE PROCESSING

Arrays
and
Applications

INTRODUCTION TO CHAPTER 12

In previous chapters we have used numeric and string variables to hold data, calculated results, and various summary results. Those variables might be represented like this:

Numeric Variables   **String Variables**

Z7   D   J3   P$ Q6$ M$

Each variable can hold one numeric or string value. These variables are
simple variables   called **simple variables.** In this chapter we discuss variables that hold
more than one value at a time. These variables are called arrays.

array   An **array** is a variable that can hold several values—that is, it
has a number of compartments. For example, there are five compart-
ments for array H below:

H(1)   H(2)   H(3)   H(4)   H(5)

| 43 | 12 | 43 | 45 | 98 |

One of the more difficult aspects of arrays is knowing when to
use them. The following guideline will become clear as you read this
chapter: *An array is used when you need to hold two or more values of
the same type in memory at the same time.* These values can be data that
is read, calculated results, or summary results. Section 12.1 explains
how to create arrays as well as when to use them.

Section 12.2 describes various common array-processing routines.
Be sure to read this section carefully. Sections 12.3 through 12.5 describe
various ways in which arrays are commonly used. Section 12.6 presents
some computer models that require the use of arrays. Some of the
models are quite complex. So you may want to return to this section
after you have covered the remaining chapters in the book. In Section
12.7 two-dimensional arrays are described.

12.1 USING ONE-DIMENSIONAL ARRAYS

In this section the use of arrays is introduced. Then a typical problem
is described, followed by a discussion of why some variables in a program should be arrays. The program is further refined in the next
section.

Creating an Array

one-dimensional
array

subscript

A **one-dimensional array** is a variable that has a fixed number of compartments. Each compartment can hold one value. The compartments are named with the array name followed by the compartment number in parentheses. This number is called a **subscript.** For example, numeric array H below has five compartments, as does string array N$:

**One-Dimensional
Numeric Array H**   **One-Dimensional
String Array N$**

H(1) H(2) H(3) H(4) H(5)   N$(1) N$(2) N$(3) N$(4) N$(5)

You must inform the computer how many compartments an array has before you actually use the compartments of an array. For example, if you wish to use the above two arrays in a program, you must use the statement

```
100  DIM H(5), N$(5)
```

DIM is short for DIMension. The number in parentheses gives the size (dimension) of, or number of components in, each array. The form of the **DIM statement** is

DIM statement

line number   DIM   array names and sizes in parentheses

Once an array has been created, you can use the individual components in all the ways that simple variables are used, except that they may not be used as the control variable for a FOR-NEXT loop. (Some of these uses are illustrated later in the program in Fig. 12.2.)

When to Use Arrays

Suppose you want to write a program with an output like that shown in Fig. 12.1. Notice that management wants a summary of the total hours worked each day by all employees.

You should be able to write a program to produce this output without using arrays. In such a program you might use the following variables:

Name	Rate	Monday	Tuesday	Wednesday	Thursday	Friday	Wage
N$	R	M	T	W	TR	F	W2

Total Hours Worked by All Employees On

Monday	Tuesday	Wednesday	Thursday	Friday
M1	T1	W1	R1	F1

For instance, for employee JOE the values would be assigned to the variables as follows:

N$	R	M	T	W	TR	F	W2
JOE	4.00	8	5	6	7	8	140

However, since variables M, T, W, TR, and F are used to hold the same type of values, employee hours on each day, these variables may be replaced by the compartments of an array such as array H (for hours). Similarly, the daily totals can be held in an array T (for Totals). In this event the variables used in the program are as follows:

				Hours On			
Name	Rate	Monday	Tuesday	Wednesday	Thursday	Friday	Wage
N$	R	H(1)	H(2)	H(3)	H(4)	H(5)	W

Total Hours of All Employees On

Monday	Tuesday	Wednesday	Thursday	Friday
T(1)	T(2)	T(3)	T(4)	T(5)

Each array compartment can now be used as if it were a simple variable.

The program shown in Fig. 12.2 produces the output shown in Fig. 12.1. Notice the DIM statement in line 100. Since the compartments of array T hold sums, they are initialized (lines 200-208). Think of each component of the arrays as a simple variable and trace the program.

In this section we combined various simple variables into arrays. So far we have not gained anything by using arrays. But in the next section you will see how the program in Fig. 12.2 is simplified.

☐ **FIGURE 12.1**   **Payroll Output**

```
          ACME MANUFACTURING: PAYROLL

                    HOURS:
 NAME   RATE   MON   TUE   WED   THR   FRI   WAGE

 JOE    4.00    8     5     6     7     8    ???
 JUNE   6.00    8     8     7     7     4    ???
 JIM    5.00    8     7     0     8     2    ???

 DAILY HOURS    24    20    ?     ?     ?

                          TOTAL PAYROLL   ????
```

☐ **FIGURE 12.2**   **Program for Calculating Wages and Daily Totals**

```
100 DIM H(5), T(5)
120 PRINT "       ACME DINER PAYROLL"
130 PRINT
200 LET T(1)=0
202 LET T(2)=0
204 LET T(3)=0
206 LET T(4)=0
208 LET T(5)=0
220 PRINT "NAME    RATE  MON TUE WED THR FRI  WAGE"
230 PRINT
300 READ N$, R, H(1), H(2), H(3), H(4), H(5)
310 IF N$ = "ZZZ" THEN 700
320    LET H = H(1) + H(2) + H(3) + H(4) + H(5)
330    LET W = R * H
400    LET T(1) = T(1) + H(1)
410    LET T(2) = T(2) + H(2)
420    LET T(3) = T(3) + H(3)
430    LET T(4) = T(4) + H(4)
440    LET T(5) = T(5) + H(5)
500    PRINT N$; TAB(8);R;
510    PRINT TAB(16); H(1); H(2); H(3); H(4); H(5);
520    PRINT TAB(35); W
530                                          REM
600    READ N$, R, H(1), H(2), H(3), H(4), H(5)
610 GOTO 310
620                                          REM
700 PRINT
710 PRINT "DAILY HRS    ";T(1);T(2);T(3);T(4);T(5)
720 STOP
800 DATA "JOE", 4.00, 8,5,6,7,8
810 DATA "JUNE",6.00, 8,8,7,7,4
820 DATA "JIM" ,5.00, 8,7,0,8,2
880 DATA "ZZZ",0,0,0,0,0,0
999 END
```

12.2 MANIPULATING ONE-DIMENSIONAL ARRAYS

Arrays are not used simply to name a sequence of related values. An important reason for the use of arrays is the way the compartments can be referenced and manipulated. Common ways of manipulating arrays are discussed in this section.

Using Variable Subscripts

Suppose that the compartments of array H have the following values assigned to them:

H(1)   H(2)   H(3)   H(4)   H(5)

21	17	9	12	4

Now suppose the following segment of code is executed:

```
720   LET I = 2
730   LET J = 1
740   LET A = H(I) + H(J + 2)
```

Variables

I	J	A
2	1	?

Notice in statement 740 that array H involves variable subscripts I and expression $J + 2$. But what are $H(I)$ and $H(J + 2)$?

To determine which compartment is being referenced, we must evaluate the subscript. Since I is 2, $H(I)$ is $H(2)$, which holds the value 17. Since J is 1, then $H(J + 2)$ is $H(3)$, which holds the value 9. In summary, then, expression $H(I) + H(J + 2)$ becomes

```
LET A = H(I) + H(J + 2)
      = H(2) + H(1 + 2)
      = H(2) + H(3)
      = 17 + 9
      = 26
```

Variable subscripts are used to simplify the processing of arrays. This idea will be expanded on in the next subsection.

Common Array-Processing Routines

Many array-processing routines make use of the FOR–NEXT statement and the fact that array subscripts can be a variable or an expression. When you have a repetitive sequence of statements in your program involving array components, the FOR–NEXT statement can usually be used to make the program shorter and more flexible.

For instance, suppose that array A has 8 compartments:

A(1)   A(2)   A(3)   A(4)   A(5)   A(6)   A(7)   A(8)

The following examples illustrate some typical routines that process array A. In each example the program segment in the right column uses a FOR–NEXT statement to simplify the statements in the program segment in the left column.

☐ EXAMPLE

The following program segments initialize the array compartments to zero:

```
100   LET A(1) = 0              100   FOR Q = 1 TO 8
102   LET A(2) = 0              102     LET A(Q) = 0
 .                              104   NEXT Q
 .
 .
114   LET A(8) = 0
```

☐ EXAMPLE

The following program segments read data into the compartments:

```
100   READ A(1), A(2), A(3), A(4)    100   FOR Y = 1 TO 8
102   READ A(5), A(6), A(7), A(8)    102     READ A(Y)
                                     104   NEXT Y
```

☐ EXAMPLE

The following segments input data into the compartments:

```
100   INPUT A(1)               100   FOR Z = 1 TO 8
102   INPUT A(2)               102     INPUT A(Z)
 .                             104   NEXT Z
 .
 .
114   INPUT A(8)
```

EXAMPLE

The following segments sum the contents of the compartments:

```
400   LET S = 0                  400 LET S = 0
402   LET S = S + A(1)           402 FOR U = 1 TO 8
404   LET S = S + A(2)           404    LET S = S + A(U)
.                                406 NEXT U
.
.
414   LET S = S + A(8)
```

EXAMPLE

The following segments find the largest number in the array:

```
400   LET L = -999               400   LET L = -999
410   IF A(1) < L THEN 414       410   FOR I = 1 TO 8
412      LET L = A(1)            420      IF A(I) < L THEN 440
414   IF A(2) < L THEN 418       430      LET L = A(I)
416      LET L = A(2)            440   NEXT I
.                                450   PRINT L
.
.
438   IF A(8) < L THEN 450
440      LET L = A(8)
450   PRINT L
```

EXAMPLE

The following segments print the array:

```
500   PRINT A(1); A(2); A(3); A(4);     500   FOR Z = 1 TO 8
510   PRINT A(5); A(6); A(7); A(8)      510      PRINT A(Z);
                                        520   NEXT Z
```

EXAMPLE

The following segments print the array, using TABs:

```
500   PRINT TAB(5); A(1); TAB(10); A(2);    500   FOR I = 1 TO 8
502   PRINT TAB(15); A(3); TAB(20); A(4);   502      PRINT TAB(I * 5); A(I);
504   PRINT TAB(25); A(5); TAB(30); A(6);   504   NEXT I
506   PRINT TAB(35); A(7); TAB(40); A(8)
```

It should be clear from these examples that the use of the FOR–NEXT statement reduces the number of lines that have to be written in a program. If you have any doubt about this claim, consider an array A that has 80 compartments instead of just 8. Now determine how each sequence of statements would be modified to accommodate the change.

□ **FIGURE 12.3**   **Use of Arrays and FOR–NEXT Statements to Simplify the Program in Fig. 12.2**

```
100 DIM H(5), T(5)
120 PRINT "        ACME DINER PAYROLL"
130 PRINT
200                                            REM
202 FOR I = 1 TO 5
204   LET T(I)=0
206 NEXT I
210                                            REM
220 PRINT "NAME    RATE  MON TUE WED THR FRI  WAGE"
230 PRINT
300 READ N$, R, H(1), H(2), H(3), H(4), H(5)
310 IF N$ = "ZZZ" THEN 700
320    LET H = H(1) + H(2) + H(3) + H(4) + H(5)
330    LET W = R * H
400                                            REM
410    FOR I = 1 TO 5
420      LET T(I) = T(I) + H(I)
430    NEXT I
440                                            REM
500    PRINT N$; TAB(8);R;
510    PRINT TAB(16); H(1); H(2); H(3); H(4); H(5);
520    PRINT TAB(35); W
530                                            REM
600    READ N$, R, H(1), H(2), H(3), H(4), H(5)
610 GOTO 310
620                                            REM
700 PRINT
710 PRINT "DAILY HRS    ";T(1);T(2);T(3);T(4);T(5)
720 STOP
800 DATA "JOE", 4.00, 8,5,6,7,8
810 DATA "JUNE",6.00, 8,8,7,7,4
820 DATA "JIM" ,5.00, 8,7,0,8,2
880 DATA "ZZZ",0,0,0,0,0,0
999 END
```

The program in Fig. 12.3 illustrates how—by using some of the array-processing routines just discussed—we can simplify the program in Fig. 12.2. For instance, notice that lines 200–208 in Fig. 12.2 correspond to lines 202–206 in Fig. 12.3. Lines 400–440 in Fig. 12.2 correspond to lines 410–430 in Fig. 12.3.

EXERCISES

12.1. Consider the program in Fig. 12.3. Suppose the diner employees work seven days a week. What changes would have to be made to the program?

12.2. Use the FOR–NEXT statement to manipulate the array components in statements 300, 320, 510, 600, and 710 of the program in Fig. 12.3.

12.3.   Trace the following program:

```
100   DIM X(6)
120   FOR I = 1 TO 4
130      READ X(I)
140      PRINT X(I);
150   NEXT I
200   LET S = 0
210   FOR I = 1 TO 4
220    LET S = S + X(I)
230   NEXT I
240   PRINT "SUM ="; S
250   STOP
800   DATA 4, 9, 3, 2
999   END
```

12.4.   The following short program initializes the array B with six numbers:

```
100 DIM B(6)
200 FOR I = 1 TO 6
210    READ B(I)
220  NEXT I
250  DATA 3, 9, 17, 4, 18, 36
```

B(1)	B(2)	B(3)	B(4)	B(5)	B(6)
3	9	17	4	18	36

Explain or trace each of the following sequences of statements, assuming that the above constants are in array B.

a)
```
300   FOR I = 1 TO 6
310      PRINT B(I),
320   NEXT I
999   END
```

b)
```
300   FOR I = 1 TO 6
310      PRINT TAB(I * 4 - 4); B(I);
320   NEXT I
999   END
```

c)
```
300   LET M = 10
310   LET K = 0
330   FOR J = 1 TO 6
340    IF B(J) > M THEN 350
342      LET K = K + 1
350   NEXT J
360   PRINT K
999   END
```

d)
```
300   FOR Q = 1 TO 6
302    IF Q <> 3 THEN 306
304    PRINT " "
306    PRINT B(Q),
308   NEXT Q
999   END
```

e)
```
300  FOR I = 2 TO 6
310    IF B(I - 1) <= B(I) THEN 320
312    PRINT "OUT OF SEQ"; B(I)
314    STOP
320  NEXT I
330  PRINT "IN SEQUENCE"
999  END
```

f)
```
300  READ X
310  FOR I = 1 TO 6
320    IF X = B(I) THEN 350
330  NEXT I
340  PRINT "NOT FOUND"
345  GOTO 300
350  PRINT "FOUND"
355  GOTO 300
800  DATA 18, 7, 9
999  END
```

12.5. Write a program whose printout will look like this:

```
                    SURVEY RESULTS
                 RESPONSES TO QUESTIONS:


            1     2     3     4     5     6     7     8
          ----- ----- ----- ----- ----- ----- ----- -----
            Y     Y     Y     N     N     Y     Y     Y
            N     Y     N     Y     Y     N     N     Y
            .
            .
            .
            Y     N     N     N     Y     Y     N     N
  TOTALS  ----- ----- ----- ----- ----- ----- ----- -----
    YES:    xx    xx    xx    xx    xx    xx    xx    xx
     NO:    xx    xx    xx    xx    xx    xx    xx    xx
```

12.6. Write a program whose printout will look like this:

```
ANALYSIS OF HEIGHTS
   MALE AND FEMALE

SEX    HEIGHTS (IN.)
-----  -------------------------
M       ·72
F        65
.
.
.
F        63
```

```
RANGE           FEMALE      MALE
---------------  ----------- --------
UNDER 60         XX          XX
60-63            XX          XX
64-67            XX          XX
68-71            XX          XX
72-75            XX          XX
ABOVE 75         XX          XX
```

12.7. *Marketing study:* A soap company has developed three products, brand X, brand Y, and brand Z. The brands have been test-marketed for three months, and a survey has been conducted. The company feels that there are two distinct markets: people aged 25 and under, and those over 25. The company wants to find the most popular brand in each category. Write a program for the company, with a printout that looks like this:

```
     BRAND PREFERENCES


DATA:
AGE          BRAND CHOICE
----------   -----------------------
?23,         Z
?45,         Y
?30,         X
  .
  .
  .
?-1,          *


             NUMBER OF    PREFERENCE BY PERCENTAGE:
GROUP        RESPONDEES  BRAND X   BRAND Y   BRAND Z
----------------------  ----------  ------------  ------------  ------------
25 AND UNDER  XXX          XX        XX        XX
OVER 25       XXX          XX        XX        XX
```

12.8. Write a program whose printout will look like this:

```
     MULTIPLE-CHOICE TEST CORRECTOR

QUESTION NO.    1 2 3 4 5 6 7 8 9 10
CORRECT ANS.    3 4 2 2 4 3 1 1 2 2

STUDENT                               NUMBER
NAME            RESPONSES             CORRECT
----------------  ------------------------------------  -------------
WAYNE           3 2 2 4 4 1 1 2 2 3     XX
JEAN            1 2 3 4 1 2 3 4 4 3     XX
  .
  .
  .
```

12.9.   Suppose two people wish to determine a possible meeting time for a particular day. Write a program that accepts individual free times and then finds common free times. The input/output might look like this:

```
FREE TIME
PERSON A:     FROM       TO
              ----------  ----------
                 9 AM     10 AM
                 1 PM      3 PM
                 7 PM      9 PM

PERSON B:     FROM       TO
              ----------  ----------
                11 AM      2 PM
                 3 PM      5 PM
                 8 PM     11 PM

COMMON FREE TIMES:
              FROM       TO
              ----------  ----------
                 xxx       xxx
                 xxx       xxx
```

When the times are read in, they can be temporarily stored in two one-dimensional arrays, as follows. *Note:* Times are converted to 24-hour time.

```
A(1)   A(2)   A(3)   A(4)   A(5)   A(6)  A(7)...
+-----+-----+-----+-----+-----+-----+-----+
|  9  | 10  | 13  | 15  | 19  | 21  | ... |
+-----+-----+-----+-----+-----+-----+-----+

B(1)   B(2)   B(3)   B(4)   B(5)   B(6)  B(7)...
+-----+-----+-----+-----+-----+-----+-----+
| 11  | 14  | 15  | 17  | 20  | 23  | ... |
+-----+-----+-----+-----+-----+-----+-----+
```

There are at least two different ways to determine the free times. Come up with one method and implement it as a program.

12.10.   Extend Exercise 12.9 so that the free time for any number of people can be found.

12.3 A SIMPLE CALCULATOR USING ARRAYS

One major problem with using a hand calculator is that you can easily enter an incorrect value without noticing it before you hit <enter>. Thus the ability to edit a sequence of numbers entered into a calculator

☐ **FIGURE 12.4**   **Simple Calculator with Memory**

```
100 PRINT "   CALCULATOR WITH MEMORY"
110 PRINT
120 PRINT "OPTIONS:"
130 PRINT " A - APPEND VALUES  E - EDIT"
140 PRINT " C - CALC TOTAL     Q - QUIT"
160                               REM
200 DIM X(200)
210 LET L = 0 :   REM -- CURRENT LIST LENGTH
220                               REM
300 PRINT
400     INPUT "WHICH OPTION (A,E,C,Q) ";Z$
410     PRINT
500     IF Z$="A" THEN GOSUB 1000 : GOTO 700
520     IF Z$="E" THEN GOSUB 2000 : GOTO 700
530     IF Z$="C" THEN GOSUB 3000 : GOTO 700
700     IF Z$ <> "Q" THEN 300
800 STOP
810                               REM
1000 PRINT "APPEND VALUES (0 EXITS)"
1010    PRINT "IDENT   VALUE"
1110    LET L = L + 1
1120      PRINT L; :  INPUT "      "; X(L)
1130    IF X(L) <> 0 THEN 1110
1140    LET L = L -1
1150    RETURN
1160                              REM
2000 PRINT "EDIT A SPECIFIC VALUE"
2100     PRINT
2110     INPUT "IDENT   "; P
2120       IF P < 1 OR L < P THEN 3110
2200     PRINT "CURRENT VALUE: "; X(P)
2210     INPUT "NEW VALUE      "; X(P)
2300     RETURN
2400                              REM
3000 PRINT "PRINT & CALCULATE TOTAL"
3010     PRINT
3020     PRINT "IDENT","VALUE"
3030     PRINT
3040     LET T = 0
3100     FOR I = 1 TO L
3110      LET T = T + X(I)
3120      PRINT I, X(I)
3130     NEXT I
3140     PRINT
3200     PRINT "TOTAL  = ", T
3300     RETURN
9999 END
```

A. PROGRAM

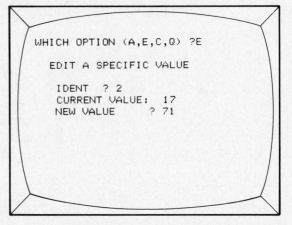

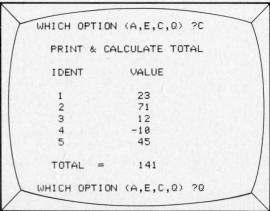

B. OUTPUT

would be very convenient. In a few years, perhaps, calculators will have enough memory so that the user will be able to review and correct values.

In the meantime, the program in Fig. 12.4A provides us with this editing capability. Look at a run of the program (Fig. 12.4B). Notice the one-line menu (WHICH OPTION) and that we can select one of four options.

Option A allows us to append values to the end of the list. Notice how variable L keeps track of the number of numbers in the array. Option E allows us to edit any specific value. The IDENTification number allows us to specify the number we wish to edit. The IDENT number is merely the subscript of array X, which holds the value to be edited (see lines 2000–2210 of the program). Option C allows us to calculate the sum of the values in the array. Option Q allows us to stop the program.

The program in Fig. 12.4A can be modified to provide other necessary functions, such as saving the data for later use. (This task will be done in Chapter 14.) The program can also be tailored for a specific application.

EXERCISES

12.11. Modify the program in Fig. 12.4A so that it does the following:
   a) Prints on the printer or screen with paging.
   b) Computes the average.

12.12. Modify the program in Fig. 12.4A so that each number can have a corresponding description. With this modification the output from the PRINT & CALCULATE option should look something like this:

```
   PRINT & CALCULATE TOTAL

 IDENT     DESCRIPTION     VALUE

   1       RENT            134.56
   2       UTILITIES        89.90
   3       FOOD            234.89

           TOTAL           459.35
```

12.13. Modify the program of Fig. 12.4A so that a title can be entered and printed on all outputs.

12.14. Modify the program of Fig. 12.4A so that a value can be deleted. There are two ways this deletion can be done:
   a) The values above the number to be deleted can be shifted

down one position onto the deleted value. Then the list length
can be reduced by one.

b) The value at the end of the list can be moved to the position
of the value to be deleted. Then the list length can be reduced by one.

12.4 THE TABLE LOOKUP ROUTINE

Consider the process of looking up a person's telephone number in your
personal phone book. This task consists of searching for the person's
name in one column and then using the value (phone number) in the
corresponding position of the other column.

For example, suppose the following names and numbers are in
your personal phone book:

Name	Telephone Number
Barbara	988-0098
Bob	987-2232
Carl	765-8543
Diane ⟶	875-9987
Joe	345-9897
Karen	897-4532
Larry	879-3345

To find Diane's phone number, you search the column on the left for her
name. Her name is found in the fourth position; so you use the phone
number in the fourth position in the right-hand column.

The purpose of such a search process is to convert a value of one
type (name) found in a table to another corresponding value (telephone
number). Here are some other table lookup processes where a value of
one type is converted to a value of another type:

Convert	To
Dollar sales or volume	Sales commission
Distance and weight	Postage
Quantity bought	Discount percent
Age and sex	Life insurance premium
Computer connect time	Charge
Telephone connect time	Charge

The following subsections explain how to put the table lookup
routine into BASIC.

Implementation of the Table Lookup Routine

Suppose you want to computerize the telephone lookup process. If the list consists of only two or three values, then the process can be done by using the case structure (see Section 7.2), as follows:

```
500  INPUT "PERSON'S NAME"; N$
510  IF N$ = "ZZZ" THEN 600
520  PRINT "PHONE NUMBER: ";
530  IF N$ = "DIANE" THEN PRINT "875-9987": GOTO 560
540  IF N$ = "BOB" THEN PRINT "987-2232": GOTO 560
550  PRINT "NOT FOUND"
560  INPUT "PERSON'S NAME"; N$
570  GOTO 510
```

But if you have more than a few values, it is easier to put the two lists of values into two arrays and then do a table lookup. This operation is done in the program in Fig. 12.5A. The values are put into the arrays in statements 210 through 230. Then the table lookup begins at line 500.

In the program, array N$ holds the names and array T$ holds the phone numbers (see the DATA statements in lines 900–906). These arrays look like this:

N$(1)	BARBARA	988-0098	T$(1)
N$(2)	BOB	987-2232	T$(2)
N$(3)	CARL	765-8543	T$(3)
N$(4)	DIANE	875-9987	T$(4)
N$(5)	JOE	345-9897	T$(5)
N$(6)	KAREN	897-4532	T$(6)
N$(7)	LARRY	879-3345	T$(7)

Note: Since statements 510–570 in the program are repetitious, we can use the following segment of code to simplify the program:

```
510  FOR I = 1 TO N
520     IF D$ = N$(I) THEN P$ = T$(I) : GOTO 660
570  NEXT I
```

☐ **FIGURE 12.5**   **Table Lookup Routine**

```
100 DIM N$(20), T$(20)
110                                  REM
120 LET N = 7
130                                  REM
200 REM --- INITIALIZE TABLE ---
210 FOR I = 1 TO N
220    READ N$(I), T$(I)
230 NEXT I
240                                  REM
400 REM --- READ PERSON'S NAME ---
410 INPUT "PERSON'S NAME (ZZZ ENDS) "; D$
420 IF D$ = "ZZZ" THEN 800
430                                  REM
500    REM --- BEGIN TABLE LOOKUP ---
510        IF D$ = N$(1) THEN P$ = T$(1) : GOTO 660
520        IF D$ = N$(2) THEN P$ = T$(2) : GOTO 660
530        IF D$ = N$(3) THEN P$ = T$(3) : GOTO 660
540        IF D$ = N$(4) THEN P$ = T$(4) : GOTO 660
550        IF D$ = N$(5) THEN P$ = T$(5) : GOTO 660
560        IF D$ = N$(6) THEN P$ = T$(6) : GOTO 660
570        IF D$ = N$(7) THEN P$ = T$(7) : GOTO 660
600        REM --- NOT FOUND ---
610            PRINT "NAME NOT FOUND"
620            GOTO 700
650        REM --- FOUND     ---
660            PRINT "TELEPHONE IS "; P$
670    REM --- END TABLE LOOKUP ---
680                                  REM
700    PRINT
710    INPUT "PERSON'S NAME (ZZZ ENDS) "; D$
720 GOTO 420
730                                  REM
800 STOP
900 DATA "BARBARA",  "988-0098"
901 DATA "BOB",      "987-2232"
902 DATA "CARL",     "765-8543"
903 DATA "DIANE",    "875-9987"
904 DATA "JOE",      "345-9897"
905 DATA "KAREN",    "897-4532"
906 DATA "LARRY",    "879-3345"
999 END
```

A. PROGRAM

```
PERSON'S NAME (ZZZ ENDS) ?KAREN
TELEPHONE IS 897-4532

PERSON'S NAME (ZZZ ENDS) ?DAVID
NAME NOT FOUND

PERSON'S NAME (ZZZ ENDS) ?LARRY
TELEPHONE IS 897-3345

PERSON'S NAME (ZZZ ENDS) ?ZZZ
```

B. OUTPUT

Table Lookup with Ranges of Values

In a number of situations you may want to do a table lookup on a range of values. For example, suppose a salesperson's base wage can be increased by a bonus determined by the level of sales, as follows:

Weekly Sales	Bonus Value	Weekly Sales	Bonus Value
0–4,999	100	12,000–24,999	300
5,000–7,999	140	25,000– ···	700
8,000–11,999	175		

In this case the upper-limit values of sales can be put into an array S and the bonus values can be put in array B:

```
                    S(1)  ┌─────────┐   ┌─────────┐
                          │  4999   │   │  100    │  B(1)
              A     S(2)  ├─────────┤   ├─────────┤
           ┌────────┐     │  7999   │   │  140    │  B(2)
           │  9765  │ S(3)├─────────┤   ├─────────┤
           └────────┘     │ 11999   │   │  175    │  B(3)
                    S(4)  ├─────────┤   ├─────────┤
                          │ 24999   │   │  300    │  B(4)
                    S(5)  ├─────────┤   ├─────────┤
                          │ 999999  │   │  700    │  B(5)
                          └─────────┘   └─────────┘
```

Suppose A holds the amount of sales. Then the search routine to find the bonus, B, will look like this:

```
FOR I = 1 TO 5
   IF A <= S(I) THEN B = B(I): GOTO ...
NEXT I
```

EXERCISES

Write a program that creates one of the printouts below.

12.15.   The program required here is a standard summary result program if the grade is read as a value, that is, 4, 3, 2, 1, 0. In this case you read the letter grade. It then has to be "changed" to the appropriate value (B = 3) in order to multiply by the credits to get the quality points.

```
              GRADE POINT AVERAGE

STUDENT: xxxxxxxxxxxxx

COURSES      CREDITS      GRADE     QUALITY PTS
..........   .........    ......    ..........
MAT107       4            B         xx
ENG243       3            C         xx
  .          .            .
  .          .            .
  .          .            .
TOTALS       xxx                    xxx
QUALITY POINT AVERAGE xxxxx
```

12.16. Use the following data to determine the letter grade:

Total Points	Letter Grade
360–400	A
310–359	B
270–309	C
230–269	D
Below 230	F

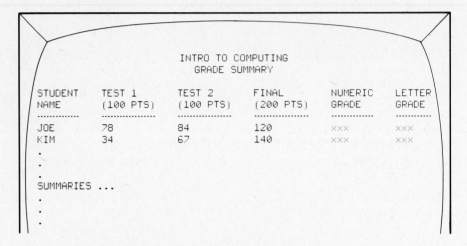

```
                    INTRO TO COMPUTING
                      GRADE SUMMARY

STUDENT     TEST 1      TEST 2      FINAL       NUMERIC    LETTER
NAME        (100 PTS)   (100 PTS)   (200 PTS)   GRADE      GRADE
...........  ........... ........... ........... ......... .........
JOE         78          84          120         xxx        xxx
KIM         34          67          140         xxx        xxx
.
.
.
SUMMARIES ...
.
.
.
```

12.17. Use the following data to determine the fine:

Offense	Point Value	Fine
Drunk	8	200
Speed	6	50
Reckless	5	100
Red light	2	25

Also, license is revoked if current total points exceed 10.

```
                  TRAFFIC VIOLATION REPORT

                         PREV     CURRENT
         NAME   OFFENSE   POINTS   TOTAL POINTS    FINE
         ....   .......   ......   ............    ....
         JOE    SPEED     4        xxx             xxx
         DAN    RKLESS    1        xxx             xxx
         SUE    DRUNK     3        xxx             xxx
         AL     REDLGT    8        xxx             xxx
```

12.18. Use the following data to determine each person's income tax:

Range Between	Base	Percent in Excess of Lower Bound
Under 5,000	0	0
5,000–9,999	700	20.
10,000–14,999	1,700	22.
15,000–19,999	2,600	23.5
20,000–29,999	3,775	25.
30,000–50,000	6,275	30.
Over 50,000	12,275	50.

For example, suppose Allen's income is between $15,000 and $19,999. Then the tax is

$$\$2600 + 0.235 * (16{,}789.56 - 15{,}000)$$

or

Base + percent * (excess over lower bound)

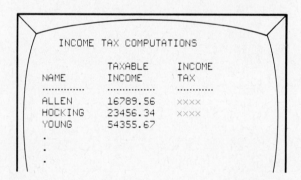

```
INCOME TAX COMPUTATIONS

                TAXABLE       INCOME
 NAME           INCOME        TAX
 ...........    .............  ...........
 ALLEN          16789.56      xxxx
 HOCKING        23456.34      xxxx
 YOUNG          54355.67
 .
 .
 .
```

12.5 SORTING TECHNIQUES

sorting

Sorting is a procedure that arranges data into either ascending or descending order. There are hundreds of methods (really) available for sorting data. In this section we explain a simple, but rather slow, method for sorting, called the Bubble Sort.

Before examining the Bubble Sort, let's consider the three-step procedure for interchanging the contents of two variables. Suppose variable X contains 33 and variable Y contains 17. Let H be a temporary holding variable. The procedure works like this:

	Variables			Program Segment

X   Y   H

33	17	7
		17
	33	
17		

Initial contents of variables

```
662  LET H = Y
664  LET Y = X
666  LET X = H
```

Thus after line 666 has been executed, X holds the value 17 and Y holds 33.

Bubble Sort

To illustrate the **Bubble Sort,** suppose the five numbers in array A are to be arranged in ascending order. Figure 12.6 explains the Bubble Sort algorithm for arranging values into ascending order, from smallest to largest. The BASIC statements on the right of each step implement the required actions. Trace the program sequence from statements 420 to 450.

Notice that each pass through the data requires the same sequence of steps. Because of the repetition, all program segments can be put into a loop, as illustrated in the program in Fig. 12.7, lines 420 through 470.

To arrange values from largest to smallest, you can reverse the operator $<=$ in statement 430 of the program in Fig. 12.7 to

```
A(J) >= A(J + 1)
```

EXERCISES

12.19. Extend the calculator program in Fig. 12.4A so that it has the option to sort the numbers in either increasing or decreasing order.

12.20. Write a program to sort the following information by last name:

			Sales	
Last Name	First Name	1982	1983	1984
EARLES	JIM	56334	44234	15678
ALLEN	KAREN	34231	44323	43233
DUSEK	AL	13432	54112	8765
BROWN	TIM	23112	31112	51222
L$( )	F$( )	A( )	B( )	C( )

☐ **FIGURE 12.6**   **Bubble Sort Method**

Beginning Sequence

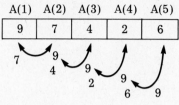

First Pass:
Moving from the first to the last compartment, compare adjacent compartments. Interchange adjacent compartments if the number on the left is larger than the number on the right. At the end of the first pass the last compartment contains the largest number. Therefore it need not be compared in the remaining passes. At the end of the first pass the sequence is as shown at the right.

```
420 FOR J = 1 TO 4
        IF A(J) <= A(J+1) THEN 450
        LET        H = A(J)
        LET        A(J)= A(J+1).
        LET A(J+1) = H
450 NEXT J
```

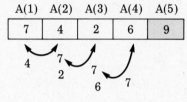

Second Pass:
Moving from the first to the next-to-last compartment, compare adjacent compartments and interchange if necessary. At the end of the second pass the second largest number is in the second-to-last compartment. At the end of this pass the sequence is as shown at the right.

```
520 FOR J = 1 TO 3
        IF A(J) <= A(J+1) THEN 550
        LET        H = A(J)
        LET        A(J)= A(J+1)
        LET A(J+1) = H
550 NEXT J
```

Third Pass:
Continue with the procedure. At the end of the third pass the sequence is as shown at the right.

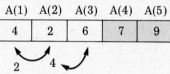

```
620 FOR J = 1 TO 2
        IF A(J) <= A(J+1) THEN 650
        LET        H = A(J)
        LET        A(J)= A(J+1)
        LET A(J+1) = H
650 NEXT J
```

Fourth Pass:
Continue with the procedure. At the end of the fourth pass the sequence is as shown at the right.

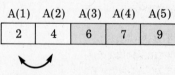

```
720 FOR J = 1 TO 1
        IF A(J) <= A(J+1) THEN 750
        LET        H = A(J)
        LET        A(J)= A(J+1)
        LET A(J+1) = H
750 NEXT J
```

Notice that if you want to keep the corresponding information together, whenever compartment values in the L$ array are exchanged, the corresponding compartments in the other arrays must also be exchanged. Thus part of the sorting routine will look like this:

□ **FIGURE 12.7**   **Bubble Sort Program**

```
100 DIM A(100)
200 REM ---    READ N VALUES INTO ARRAY    ---
210 LET N = 5
220 FOR I = 1 TO N
230    READ A(I)
240 NEXT I
250 REM ---        PRINT ARRAY         ---
260 PRINT "ORIGINAL ARRAY:"
270 GOSUB 700
280 PRINT
290                                      REM
390 REM --- SORT N COMPARTMENTS OF ARRAY ---
392 REM ---    E IS THE END COMPARTMENT  ---
394 REM ---    COMPARED ON EACH PASS.    ---
400 LET E = N
410 REM -- LOOP TOP --
420    FOR J = 1 TO E-1
430     IF A(J) <= A(J+1) THEN 450
440        LET      H = A(J)
442        LET    A(J) = A(J+1)
444        LET A(J+1) = H
450    NEXT J
460    LET E = E - 1
470 IF E >= 2 THEN 410
480 REM -- LOOP BOTTOM --
490                                      REM
500 REM ---      PRINT SORTED ARRAY      ---
510 PRINT "SORTED ARRAY:"
520 GOSUB 700
530 STOP
540                                      REM
700 REM --- PRINT THE CURRENT ARRAY      ---
710 FOR I = 1 TO N
720    PRINT A(I);
730 NEXT I
740 RETURN
800 DATA 9, 7, 4, 2, 6
999 END
```

```
430   IF L$(J) <= L$(J + 1) THEN 450
```

Exchange L$(J) and L$(J + 1)
Exchange F(J) and F(J + 1)
Exchange A( ) and A(   )   } 15 statements required
Exchange B( ) and B(   )
Exchange C( ) and C(   )

12.21. In the Bubble Sort method, if a pass is completed without any compartments being exchanged, then the array is sorted. Modify the program in Fig. 12.7 so that it recognizes whether or not an exchange is made. *Hint:* Insert the statement

```
415  LET X$ = "N"
```

Then if an exchange is made, assign "Y" to X$. At the end of the pass, test X$.

12.6 COMPUTER MODELS WITH ARRAYS

In Section 11.5 we introduced computer models that require use of the random number generator. The computer models described below and in the exercises for this section also require random numbers, as well as the use of arrays.

The model we will describe here involves simulating card games. One reason for simulating card games is to evaluate playing strategies. In order to simulate card games, you must first know how to represent a deck of cards and shuffle them. This representation and the shuffling procedure are illustrated in the program in Fig. 12.8A. In this program notice that we hold the deck of cards in an array K of 52 compartments (see lines 1110–1120).

The shuffling of the deck is an interesting process (see lines 3000–3260). First, card K(1) is exchanged with some randomly chosen card; then the second card is exchanged with a randomly chosen card; and so on for all 52 cards.

A hierarchy chart for the program is shown in Fig. 12.9. The output for the program is shown in Fig. 12.8B.

EXERCISES

12.22. Suppose there are 100 different baseball cards in a bubble gum series. In general, how many packages of gum must you buy in order to get all 100 different cards? *Hint:* Number the cards from 1 to 100. Set up 100 counters in a one-dimensional array. To buy a pack of gum, generate a random integer between 1 and 100 and add one to the appropriate counter.

12.23. *Birthday problem:* Suppose there are 20 people in a room. What are the chances that at least two people were born on the same day of the year (but not necessarily the same year)? *Hint:* Look at many rooms each containing 20 people. For each person in the room, generate a random integer between 1 and 365—that is their birth date. Put these 20 numbers into a list: S(1), . . . , S(20). Does any number in the list appear twice?

12.24. Write a program that deals five cards to a player by putting the cards into a one-dimensional array. Now have the program replace a maximum of three cards in the hand with cards from the deck. Only those cards with values less than 8 should be replaced, the smallest ones being replaced first.

☐ **FIGURE 12.8**   **Shuffling a Deck of Cards**

```
100 DIM K(52)                          1160                            REM
110 PRINT "    CREATE AND SHUFFLE DECK" 2000 REM --- PRINT DECK ---
120 PRINT                               2100 FOR I = 1 TO 52
200 PRINT "ORIGINAL DECK:"              2110    PRINT K(I);
210 GOSUB 1000                          2120    IF INT(I/13) = I/13 THEN PRINT
220 GOSUB 2000                          2130 NEXT I
230 PRINT                               2140 RETURN
300 PRINT "SHUFFLED DECK:"              2150                            REM
310 GOSUB 3000                          3000 REM --- SHUFFLE DECK ---
320 GOSUB 2000                          3100 FOR I = 1 TO 52
400 PRINT                               3110    LET R = INT(1 + 52*RND)
410 STOP                                3120    LET H    = K(I)
420                        REM          3230    LET K(I) = K(R)
1000 REM --- CREATE DECK ---            3240    LET K(R) = H
1100 LET V = 2                          3250 NEXT I
1110 FOR I = 1 TO 52                     3260 RETURN
1120    LET K(I) = V                    3270                            REM
1130    IF V < 14 THEN V=V+1 ELSE V = 2 9999 END
1140 NEXT I
1150 RETURN
```

A. PROGRAM

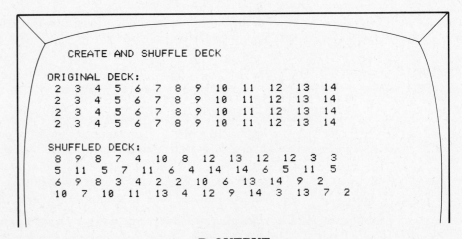

```
      CREATE AND SHUFFLE DECK

ORIGINAL DECK:
   2   3   4   5   6   7   8   9  10  11  12  13  14
   2   3   4   5   6   7   8   9  10  11  12  13  14
   2   3   4   5   6   7   8   9  10  11  12  13  14
   2   3   4   5   6   7   8   9  10  11  12  13  14

SHUFFLED DECK:
   8   9   8   7   4  10   8  12  13  12  12   3   3
   5  11   5   7  11   6   4  14  14   6   5  11   5
   6   9   8   3   4   2   2  10   6  13  14   9   2
  10   7  10  11  13   4  12   9  14   3  13   7   2
```

B. OUTPUT

12.25. Write a program that simulates the game of keno. The game involves integers between 1 and 80. The player pays $1 and then selects ten integers of his choice. (These values are read into the program.) The "bank," the computer, then randomly selects 20 numbers from 1 to 80. If there are 5 or more matches, the bank pays according to this schedule:

☐ **FIGURE 12.9**   **Hierarchy Chart for Creating and Shuffling a Deck of Cards**

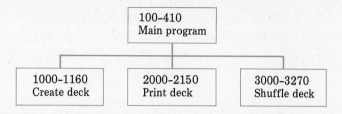

Number of Numbers That Match	Bank Pays
5	$ 2
6	18
7	180
8	1,800
9	2,600
10	25,000

After playing this game a few times (where the player is allowed to select his ten numbers), modify the program so that his ten numbers are randomly selected. Simulate the playing of this game 1000 times. Have your program print the total amount won and the average amount won per game as summary results.

12.26. Write a program that will play and score a Yahtzee dice game.

12.27. Simulate the playing of the child's game Chutes and Ladders. In general, how many rolls of a die will it take to reach square 100?

12.28. Write a program that analyzes a five-card poker hand and determines the value of the hand: four of a kind, full house, three of a kind, two pairs, one pair, and no pairs.

12.29. There are a number of ways to specify the suit value of a card as well as the value. Here three methods are explained. Use one of the methods to create a deck of cards. Then shuffle and print the new deck.
   a) The value of the cards can be put in a one-dimensional array K, and the suits—club, heart, diamond, spade—can be put into the corresponding compartments of another one-dimensional array S$. A card now consists of corresponding compartments from each array.
   b) A 2 of clubs can be represented by C2, and a jack of diamonds can be represented by D11. Similarly, each card can be represented by one of the letters C, H, D, S and an appropriate numeric value that together form a character string.

These character strings can be stored in a one-dimensional array. With use of the string functions these character strings can be pulled apart to deal with the suit and value separately.

c) The cards (suit and value) can be represented by the following numeric scheme:

0–12	Represent the 2 through ace of clubs
13–25	Represent the 2 through ace of hearts
26–38	Represent the 2 through ace of diamonds
39–51	Represent the 2 through ace of spades

To determine the suit of a particular number X, use the expression $INT(X/13)$. If the value of this expression is 0, then the suit is clubs; if the value is 1, the suit is hearts; and so on. Now use a table lookup to convert the suit number to the actual suit. To determine the actual value of the card (2 through 14), use the expression $X - 13 * INT(X/13) + 2$. For example, if X is 28, then $28 - 13 * INT(28/13) + 2$ is 4.

12.30. Write a program that imitates a blackjack dealer.

12.7 TWO-DIMENSIONAL ARRAYS

Fortunately, two-dimensional arrays are not twice as difficult as one-dimensional arrays. In this section we briefly introduce them, explaining the reasons for using two-dimensional arrays and the way we reference their components.

Reasons for Using Two-Dimensional Arrays

Whenever two or more one-dimensional arrays are being used to hold the same type of data, it is usually convenient to have an array of arrays. For example, consider yearly sales (in thousands) of salespeople. On the left in the arrays on page 267, the sales for each person in an individual year are in the same array. However, these three vertical arrays on the left can be made into one **two-dimensional array** on the right.

two-dimensional array

Like one-dimensional arrays, two-dimensional arrays must be DIMensioned. The size of the array is given by the number of rows and the number of columns in the array. For example, for the two-dimensional array S above, an appropriate DIMension statement is

```
100 DIM S(4,3)
```

The general form of the statement is

line number   DIM   array name (maximum rows, maximum columns)

Last Name	**Sales** 1982	1983	1984	S(1,1)	S(1,2)	S(1,3)
EARLES	56	44	15	56	44	15
ALLEN	23	31	51	23	31	51
DUSEK	13	54	8	13	54	8
BROWN	34	44	43	34	44	43
L$	A(4)	B(4)	C(4)		S(2,3)	

Referencing Components

Notice how the array compartments are referenced in the two-dimensional array S above. The left subscript is the row, and the right subscript is the column. By varying the left (row) subscript, we move from one row to another. By varying the right (column) subscript, we move from one column to another. As you will see below, it is a good practice to use R as the row subscript and C as the column subscript.

The FOR–NEXT statements are used in a program to vary the subscripts appropriately. The following program segments give some common processing routines.

- Read values into the array:

```
READ S(1, 1), S(1, 2), S(1, 3)
READ S(2, 1), S(2, 2), S(2, 3)
READ S(3, 1), S(3, 2), S(3, 3)
READ S(4, 1), S(4, 2), S(4, 3)
```

Or
```
FOR R = 1 TO 4
  READ S(R, 1), S(R, 2), S(R, 3)
NEXT R
```

Or
```
FOR R = 1 TO 4
  FOR C = 1 TO 3
    READ S(R, C)
  NEXT C
NEXT R

DATA 56, 44, 15
DATA 23, 31, 51
DATA 13, 54,  8
DATA 34, 44, 43
```

■ Print the array row by row:

```
FOR R = 1 TO 4
   PRINT S(R, 1), S(R, 2), S(R, 3)
NEXT R
```

Or   FOR R = 1 TO 4
```
      FOR C = 1 TO 3
         PRINT S(R, C);
      NEXT C
      PRINT    : REM  FINISH THE LINE
   NEXT R
```

■ Sum all the elements in the array:

```
LET T = 0
LET T = T + S(1, 1)
LET T = T + S(1, 2)
   .

   .

   .
LET T = T + S(4, 3)
```

Or   LET T = 0
```
   FOR R = 1 TO 4
      FOR C = 1 TO 3
         LET T = T + S(R, C)
      NEXT C
   NEXT R
```

EXERCISES

For Exercises 12.31–12.36, assume that a two-dimensional array H has been dimensioned as DIM H(3, 4).

12.31. Assuming the existence of the DATA statements below, what is the effect of the two sequences of statements? How do they differ?
Available DATA statements:
```
800   DATA 3.5, -17, 20, 16
802   DATA 82, -32, 14, 30
804   DATA 16, 80, -77, -65
```

a)
```
200  FOR R = 1 TO 3
202    FOR C = 1 TO 4
204      READ H(R, C)
206    NEXT C
208  NEXT R
```
b)
```
200  FOR C = 1 TO 4
202    FOR R = 1 TO 3
204      READ H(R, C)
206    NEXT R
208  NEXT C
```

12.32. Write a sequence of statements that will count the number of negative numbers in H.

12.33. Write a sequence of statements that will find the smallest number in H.

12.34. Write a sequence of statements that will print the row number of H with the largest sum.

12.35. Explain precisely what the following sequence of statements does.

```
400   FOR R = 1 TO 3
402    FOR C = 1 TO 4
404     PRINT TAB((C - 1) * 8); H(R, C)
406    NEXT C
408    PRINT " "
410   NEXT R
```

12.36. Explain what the following sequence of statements does.

```
350   FOR C = 1 TO 4
352    LET T = H(3, C)
354    LET H(3, C) = H(1, C)
356    LET H(1, C) = T
358   NEXT C
```

12.37. Survey responses can be tabulated in a number of different ways. For example, write a program that produces a printout like this:

```
                    SURVEY ANALYSIS

      RESPONSES ARE: Y = YES, N = NO, U = UNDECIDED

                    QUESTION NUMBERS

          1     2     3     4     5     6     7     8
        ------ ------ ------ ------ ------ ------ ------ ------
        ?Y,   N,    N,    U,    U,    N,    N,    Y
        ?Y,   U,    U,    U,    N,    Y,    Y,    N
         .
         .
         .
TOTALS: ------ ------ ------ ------ ------ ------ ------ ------
     Y:  xxx   xxx   xxx   xxx   xxx   xxx   xxx   xxx
     N:  xxx   xxx   xxx   xxx   xxx   xxx   xxx   xxx
     U:  xxx   xxx   xxx   xxx   xxx   xxx   xxx   xxx
```

12.38. Write a program that classifies people's heights in certain ranges according to sex. The printout might look like this:

```
                  ANALYSIS OF HEIGHTS
                   MALE AND FEMALE

   SEX, HEIGHT
   -------------------
   ?M,  68
   ?F,  65
   .
   .
   .
   ?0   0

   RANGE OF        NUMBER        NUMBER
   HEIGHTS(IN)     OF MALES      OF FEMALES
   -------------   ------------  --------------
    00-60            XX            XX
    61-64            XX            XX
    65-68            XX            XX
    69-72            XX            XX
    72-90            XX            XX
```

System Hardware and Software

INTRODUCTION TO CHAPTER 13

This chapter is optional. You can easily move on to the next chapter on file processing and to subsequent chapters without any loss of continuity. However, this chapter does provide a background on some fundamentals of computer systems that may enhance your understanding of later chapters.

Learning a programming language—as you have been doing in the previous 12 chapters—is a good first step to understanding computers. In this way you get firsthand use of the system hardware and the system software, the two fundamental computer components.

hardware

Computer **hardware** consists of all the physical components of a computer—the wiring, chips, video display, disk drives, and printer. In this chapter we will take a close look at these components.

However, the computer system's hardware must be controlled in order for the computer to be useful. This necessary control is provided by programs. Another name for programs is **software**. There are two types of software: *system software* and *application software*.

software

application software

Application software consists of programs that perform specific tasks of interest to the computer user, tasks such as business accounting functions, financial modeling, engineering calculations, and the like. The BASIC programs you have written belong to the class of application software.

system software

System software consists of programs that directly control and manage all the computer hardware resources. A major part of system software is called the *operating system*. Although computer users are primarily concerned about the results obtained from their applications programs, users must use and hence understand the role of the operating system in order to effectively employ a computer system. In this chapter we examine common features of all operating systems.

13.1 MEMORY, THE CPU, AND MACHINE INSTRUCTIONS

Before reading this section, you may want to read Appendix B. In that appendix you can review the binary number system and learn how the ASCII code is used to represent data in main memory. On the other hand, you may skip immediately to Section 13.2 without losing continuity.

The hardware backbone of any computer is its memory and central processing unit (CPU). A detailed view of each component is given in this section. We will also consider the relationship between machine instructions and BASIC statements.

Memory Organization

At the highest level there are two types of computer memory: main memory, which we discuss in this section, and disk memory, which is discussed in Section 13.2.

The BASIC statement

```
LET Y = X
```

main memory

illustrates the two major functions provided by a computer's **main memory:** (1) A value may be *retrieved* from a memory compartment (X), and (2) a value may be *stored* in a memory compartment (Y). In BASIC when we manipulate variables, we are referencing main memory.

Computer memory is composed of memory chips, as described and illustrated in Chapter 1. If we were able to peer into these chips, we would see that memory is organized as shown in Fig. 13.1.

Figure 13.1 illustrates the following features of computer memory:

- Memory is partitioned into individual compartments.
- Each compartment has an address, so it can be identified and referenced individually.

bit

byte

- Each compartment can hold a fixed number of bits. A **bit** is either a 0 or a 1. The memory compartments of most microcomputers hold 8 bits. Eight bits of information is called a **byte.** Other computers hold 16, 32, 48, or 64 bits in each compartment.

□ **FIGURE 13.1**   **Logical Organization of Computer Memory**

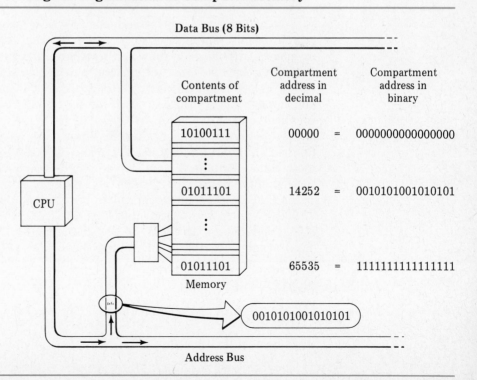

address bus

▪ The **address bus** leading into memory is an arrangement of parallel wires. The binary value (combination of 0s and 1s) on the bus determines the address of the memory compartment being referenced. The number of parallel wires in the address bus determines the maximum number of compartments in memory. For example, 16 wires will carry 16 bits at a time. With 16 places the smallest binary number is

0000000000000000   decimal 0

The largest binary number is

1111111111111111   decimal 65,535

data bus

▪ The **data bus** is a parallel arrangement of wires used to transfer data into and out of the selected memory compartments. The data bus has as many wires as there are bits in each memory compartment.

The bit values stored in a memory compartment can represent one of the following values:

▪ The binary representation of a number (see Appendix B).
▪ The binary code for a character (see Appendix B).
▪ A machine instruction or portion of a machine instruction.

Notice that both instructions and data are stored in memory compartments. The idea of storing both instructions and data in main memory is attributed to John Von Neumann, who developed this idea in 1945. This concept is still the structure used in most computers today.

A portion of memory in all computers can only be read. That is, you can assign no values to these compartments. This part of memory is called **read only memory (ROM).** The ROM contains a program that is executed when the computer is switched on. In some computers the program in ROM reads a disk drive and loads the operating system. In most home computers (that is, computers without disk drives) ROM consists of the BASIC interpreter. This interpreter program may occupy 16,000 (16K) compartments or more. In a 32K computer (approximately 32,000 memory compartments), this 32K memory may include the BASIC interpreter in ROM. So the usable memory (for programs and data) on such a computer may be less than 16K.

read only memory (ROM)

The Central Processing Unit

central processing unit (CPU)

The **central processing unit (CPU)** is the part of the computer that executes machine instructions. The instruction execution cycle is a three-step process:

1. The CPU fetches the next instruction from memory.
2. The CPU decodes the instruction.
3. The CPU executes the instruction.

registers

All CPUs contain **registers**, which are similar to memory compartments of main memory. In microcomputers, registers hold 8- or 16-bit values. To perform the instruction execution cycle, CPUs use the following four registers: an accumulator (abbreviated AC), an instruction register (IR), a program counter (PC), and an address register (AR). Most CPUs have a variety of other registers (labeled R0, R1, R2, ...) for specialized operations. These registers are represented in Fig. 13.2.

accumulator (AC)

- The **accumulator (AC)** is a register in which arithmetic operations are performed. For example, a value from memory can be assigned to the AC and then other values can be added to and subtracted from it.

instruction register (IR)

- The **instruction register (IR)** holds the next instruction to be executed. While waiting in the IR, the instruction is decoded by the circuitry in the decoder, and then signals are sent to various circuits to accomplish the execution of the instruction.

address register (AR)

- The **address register (AR)** holds the memory address of the next memory compartment to be accessed. For example, an

□ **FIGURE 13.2**   **Conceptual Organization of a CPU**

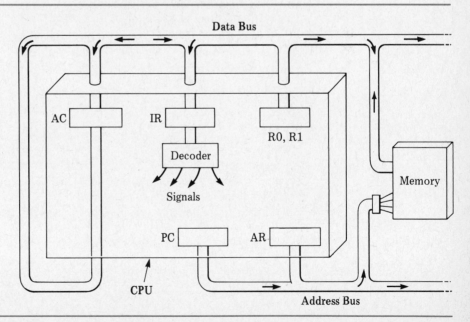

☐ **TABLE 13.1**   **Chip Manufacturers, CPUs, and Computer Systems**

Manufacturer	CPU	Computer CPU Is Used In
Intel	8080	Many systems prior to 1981
	8088	IBM PC, DEC Rainbow, Victor, and others
	8086	IBM Displaywriter, NEC APC (Nippon Electric Co.)
	iAPX 286	Future systems
MOS Technology	6502	Apple II, IIe, Commodore
Zilog	Z80	Radio Shack, Zenith, DEC Rainbow
Motorola	6809	Radio Shack Color Computer
	68000	Apple Lisa, Macintosh

instruction might require a value from memory. So the desired address is put into the address register.

program counter (PC)

- The **program counter (PC)** holds the memory address of the next instruction in the program. After an instruction is executed, the address in the PC is incremented to the memory address of the next instruction in the program.

Most large computers, like the IBM 4300, DEC VAX, Cray, CDC 68000, and Data General MV10000, have CPUs that are custom-designed and manufactured by the individual computer manufacturer. But most microcomputer CPUs are designed and manufactured by chip manufacturers like Motorola and Intel. These CPUs are then bought by the various computer companies, which design and manufacture complete computer systems around the CPU. Table 13.1 lists some of the common chip manufacturers, their CPU, and the computers that use that CPU.

CPU Instruction Sets

Computer (CPU) instructions can be put into two broad categories: memory reference instructions and CPU register-to-register instructions.

memory reference instruction

A **memory reference instruction** accesses data from a memory compartment. Instructions of this type take significantly longer to execute than register-to-register instructions. Memory reference instructions must specify an address as part of the instruction. A typical memory reference instruction may have this form:

Operation	Memory Address
8 bits	16 bits
11001101	0001010000010001

The first 4 bits specify the particular operation, and the last 16 bits specify the memory compartment being operated on. For example, one instruction may be: Store the contents of the AC in a particular memory compartment. Another instruction may be: Move the contents of a particular memory location into the AC.

register-to-register instructions

Register-to-register instructions manipulate data within the registers of the CPU. For example, one instruction may be: Increase the PC by 2. Another might be: Move the contents of one register into another. Some register-to-register instructions can have the following form:

Operation	Register	Register
8 bits	4 bits	4 bits
01110110	0011	0101

Most instructions can also be put into one of the following five categories:

data movement instruction

1. **Data movement instruction:** Data may be moved from memory to a CPU register. Or data may be moved from a CPU register to a memory compartment.

arithmetic instruction

2. **Arithmetic instruction:** The value in a memory component or a CPU register is added to, divided into, subtracted from, or multiplied times the value in the accumulator.

logical operation and shift instructions

3. **Logical operation and shift instructions:** Logical operations like AND, OR, and NOT are carried out bitwise between two registers. Here 1 is true, 0 is false.

transfer-of-control instruction

4. **Transfer-of-control instruction:** Depending on the value in a register, the program counter can be assigned different addresses. In this way the program executes different branches in a program.

input and output operations

5. **Input and output operations:** Instructions in this category select a device by sending a signal down the address bus. Data is then sent to or received from the selected device. *Note:* Computers with the same CPU can handle these operations in a variety of ways.

The Execution of a Program

As mentioned previously, there are three steps in the execution of a machine instruction:

1. The fetch process begins with the address of the next instruction in the program counter (PC). This address is sent along the address bus. The instruction in the appropriate compart-

ment is returned along the data bus to the instruction register.
2. In the instruction register the instruction is decoded.
3. After the instruction is decoded, various signals are then sent
   to appropriate CPU components to carry out the execution of
   the instruction. If the instruction is a memory reference instruction, an address is sent to the address register (AR).
   From here it is routed along the address bus to memory,
   where the appropriate compartment is selected. Then the
   value is returned along the data bus to the appropriate register, where the instruction is completed.

Machine Language Programs and BASIC

As explained previously, a computer will only execute binary instructions that the particular CPU understands. But there are difficulties
in writing programs in machine language. For example:

- The binary sequence that represents an instruction is not easy
  to remember and use.
- It takes anywhere from 2 to 50 machine instructions to do
  what can be done in one BASIC statement.
- Machine instructions differ from one CPU to another. So you
  have to know the machine intimately.

Thus to simplify the programming process, artificial, high-level
languages, such as BASIC and Pascal, have been developed. Algorithms
are written in these languages, which are easy for human beings to
understand.

Now once a program is written in BASIC or Pascal, how is the
program converted into instructions a computer understands? There
are two methods:

interpreter

1. BASIC programs can be interpreted (traced) by a program
   written in the machine language of the computer. Such a
   program is called an **interpreter**. Really, an interpreter just
   traces the program as we do. For an interpreter to execute
   (or carry out the intent of a BASIC statement), it has to get
   the next instruction, understand what type of instruction it is,
   and then carry out the intent of the instruction. To interpret
   one BASIC statement may require more than 100 machine
   statements.

compiler

2. The statements in a BASIC program can be translated (compiled) into machine instructions. A program does the transla-
   tion process, and it is called a BASIC **compiler**. Once the
   BASIC program is translated into machine language, it can
   be run over and over again without being retranslated.

Since a BASIC statement is typically translated into between 2 and 20 machine instructions, a compiled BASIC program executes at least five times faster than the interpreted version.

13.2 DISK STORAGE DEVICES

Auxiliary storage devices like the floppy-disk drive (Fig. 13.3A) and the hard-disk drive (Fig. 13.3C) are used to hold *data files* and *program files*. (You will be able to create disk data files after reading Chapter 14.

program file

A **program file** is just a program that has been saved on a disk. You have saved programs already with the BASIC SAVE command.)

floppy-disk drives

For **floppy-disk drives**, files are stored on a flexible (floppy) disk that is inserted into the drive. After its use, the disk should be removed from the drive. Since you can use any number of floppy disks on a drive (but only one at a time), your storage capability is essentially unlimited. The disadvantage of floppy drives is that they store and retrieve files at a much slower rate than hard-disk drives.

hard-disk drive

The disks of the **hard-disk drive** (also called a Winchester drive) in Fig. 13.3C are fixed and cannot be removed. But removable-pack, hard-disk drives have been commonly used on large computers since 1965. Hard-disk drives like these are now becoming available for microcomputers.

Today the fierce competition of disk drive manufacturers is causing rapid advances in disk performance. More and more data can be stored and retrieved at a faster rate.

In this section we will discuss the need for disk storage devices and the physical characteristics of such devices.

The Need for Disk Storage

There are two reasons why disk storage is needed:

1. The capacity of main memory is limited. There is simply not enough room to store all the data and programs that a computer will manipulate and execute.
2. Even if there were enough memory, the electrical nature of memory (except ROM) is such that the values in the memory components are lost when the electrical power is switched off.

Let's consider the first reason in more detail. Main memory of most computers is usually limited to 64K, 256K, 512K, or 1000K memory compartments. Many individual data files can easily exceed this number of characters.

To put these quantities into perspective, suppose one page in a book has 65 characters (letters, symbols, and spaces) per line and 40

□ **FIGURE 13.3**   **Floppy- and Hard-Disk (Winchester) Drives**

A.   FLOPPY-DISK DRIVE

B.   FLOPPY DISK

C.   HARD-DISK (WINCHESTER) DRIVE
Photo C courtesy of Vertex Peripherals.

☐ **TABLE 13.2**   **Number of Characters and Equivalent Values**

Number of Characters (Bytes)	Equivalent Pages	Equivalent Books
64,000 = 64K	25	
128,000 = 128K	50	
256,000 = 256K	100	0.25
512,000 = 512K	200	0.5
1,000,000 = 1,000K = 1Mb	400	1
5,000,000 = 5,000K = 5Mb	2,000	5
40,000,000 = 40,000K = 40Mb	16,000	40

lines per page. So one page is equivalent to 40×65 or 2600 characters. Thus 64K (65,536) memory components hold approximately

$$\frac{65,536}{2600} = 25 \text{ pages}$$

of characters. Table 13.2 converts various quantities of characters into equivalent numbers of pages and books. Note that one million bytes or characters (actually 1,048,576) is usually abbreviated as 1Mb, one megabyte.

Physical Characteristics of Disks

Floppy- and rigid-disk platters are the most common auxiliary storage media. The surface of these disks is composed of an iron oxide whose particles can be magnetized in one direction (↑) or another (↓) by a recording head, similar to the head on a tape recorder. One direction can be considered 1 and the other 0. Thus we have a way of representing information with binary digits.

read/write head

As illustrated in Fig. 13.4, the disk rotates under a **read/write head**. The read/write head can move toward the center of the disk and retract to the edge. With the head in a fixed position and with the disk rotating, a circular portion of the disk passes under the head. This portion is called a **track**. The outermost track on the disk is called track

track

00. A disk may have 36, 40, 80, 96, 400, or more tracks on a surface. The concentric circles on the disk in Fig. 13.4 indicate the form of such tracks. However, there are no boundaries between the tracks on the metal oxide.

On the disk individual characters of information, called bytes, are stored as a coded sequence of seven or nine spots (the number depends on the code used by the computer). Figure 13.4 shows how the characters 8, 9, A, and B may be stored on the disk. Some spots are magnetized in one direction and some in another direction, depending

☐ **FIGURE 13.4**   **Conceptual View of Disk Storage**

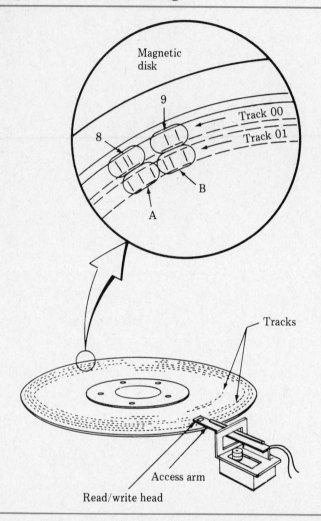

on the specific code for the character. The code for each character is recorded along the tracks. The read/write head then reads (or writes) information as the track passes under the head.

The diameter of most disks is either 8 or 5 inches. But recently, 3- and 3.5-inch disks have become popular. The reason for the great variety of disk drives is that people have different requirements for capacity, access speed, and price. Table 13.3 gives some current disk specifications.

capacity
disk density

The **capacity** of a disk and disk drive system (Table 13.3) depends on the physical size (the diameter) and the density. **Disk density** is measured by the number of bits stored per inch of track (bpi) and

□ **TABLE 13.3**   **Disk Specifications**

Disk Type	Number of Tracks	Capacity, One Side	Transfer Rate	Average Access Speed	Drive Price
5.25 inches, floppy	80	500K bytes	250K bits/second	6 milliseconds	$400
5.25 inches, hard	500 tpi	10 Mb	800K bytes/second	3 milliseconds	$2000

the closeness of the tracks—that is, the tracks per inch (tpi). Given the distance the head will travel, the tracks per inch, and the characters per track, one can calculate the capacity of the disk.

transfer rate
The **transfer rate** (Table 13.3) is the number of characters per second that can be transferred between the disk and main memory. The

average access speed
average access speed is the time it takes the drive head to be positioned over a record and read it into main memory.

formatted
Before data is written onto a disk, the disk must be **formatted** (initialized). During this process certain types of reference information are written on the disk. Also, at this time the *disk directory* (see Section 13.3) is created. All this information is used to assist the computer in locating data on the disk.

When a disk is read, the system reads a block of consecutive characters at a time. The number of characters varies; it might be 128, 256, 512, or 1024 characters at a time.

13.3 THE OPERATING SYSTEM: FUNDAMENTAL TASKS

Some computers have only a cassette deck for storing programs and data. (These computers are usually called *home computers*, and they cost less than $400.) Besides being very slow, the cassette is awkward to use because you have to keep track of where the programs and data are stored on the cassette tape. If you want to save a program, you must position the tape so that you don't write over an existing program or data file. Deleting one program on the tape involves copying all the programs you want onto a new tape.

On the other hand, a computer with a disk storage device re-
operating system
quires the use of a program called an **operating system**. One of the fundamental tasks of an operating system is to manage the program and data files stored on disks.

When a disk-oriented computer system is turned on, a program in ROM loads the operating system into memory. Then the operating system begins execution. The operating system gives the user a message letting the user know that the system is available.

There are a number of different operating systems used on microcomputers today. In this section we discuss the basic tasks of these operating systems and show that they all have similar functions.

Specifically, they allow us to manage program and data files stored on disks and allow us to load and execute programs from the disk. Other common tasks are discussed in the next section.

File Naming and Disk Directories

To manage program and data files, each operating system must have a way of naming and referencing the files on specific disk drives. Thus if your computer system has at least two disk drives, the operating system will allow you to specify a particular one.

Naming files on disks varies according to the operating system. But most allow up to eight characters followed by a three-character extension, which identifies the type of file. For example, we might use the following file names:

ASSIGN1.BAS	A BASIC program
JOE2.LET	A letter sent to Joe
ENG1.TXT	An English paper
CUSTOMER.DAT	A customer data file

Table 13.4 illustrates typical drive and file names for four common operating systems.

disk directory

Each formatted disk has a **disk directory** for all the files stored on the disk. The directory is usually located on track 00, and it is maintained by the operating system. When a program or data file is first saved on the disk, the operating system puts the name of the file and other information about the file in the directory, specifically, on which track the file begins. Later on, when the file is requested, the operating system searches the directory for the name and where the file is located.

Figure 13.5 illustrates a typical two-drive system. Notice drive A and drive B. Since program PAYROLL.COM is on drive A, it is referenced as A:PAYROLL.COM. Since program AR.BAS is on drive B, it is referenced as B:AR.BAS.

☐ TABLE 13.4   Operating System, Drive, and File Names

Operating System Name	Drive Name	File Name
TRS DOS (Radio Shack)	0, 1, ...	CUST.JUL:0
Apple DOS	D1, D2, ...	D1:PAYROLL.BAS
CP/M	A, B, C, ...	A:PAYROLL.BAS
MS-DOS	A, B, C, ...	B:CUST.AUG

☐ **FIGURE 13.5**   **Computer System**

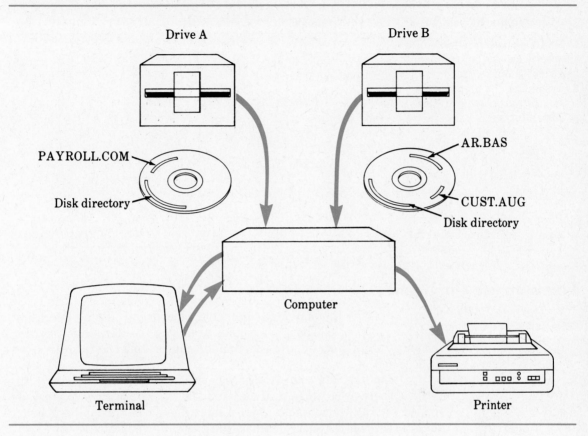

EXERCISES

13.1.   On your system, try the following command:

```
LOAD "PROG1.BAS"
```

If you have never saved a program with that name, how does your system respond?

13.2.   On your system, suppose you were to try the following command:

```
SAVE "FIRST.PRG"
```

If you had previously SAVEd a program with such a name, how would your system respond?

☐ **TABLE 13.5**   **Common Operating System Commands**

Description of Command	Apple DOS	TRS DOS	CP/M	MS-DOS
1. Getting a directory for a disk; specify drive after command	CATALOG	DIR	DIR	DIR
2. Deleting a file	DELETE	KILL	ERA	DEL ()
3. Displaying the contents of a file on the screen or printer	LIST	LIST	TYPE	TYPE
4. Renaming a file	LOAD SAVE DELETE	RENAME	REN	REN
5. Copying a file with a new name	LOAD SAVE	COPY	PIP	COPY
6. Format a disk prior to use	INIT HELLO	FORMAT	FORMAT	FORMAT
7. Copy a disk onto another disk		BACKUP	COPY	DISKCOPY

Common File Commands

There are some fundamental commands that practically all operating systems respond to. These commands are listed in Table 13.5. In order to carry out its function, each command requires that the disk directory be accessed.

The first five commands are carried out by relatively short programs. These programs are always in memory. The last two commands (called *external commands*) require more than a few machine instructions, so these programs remain on the disk until requested.

We point out that the commands for Apple DOS only work on BASIC programs.

Executing Machine Language Programs

As we mentioned earlier in this chapter, a program must be in machine language (0s and 1s) in order to be executed directly by the computer. Most operating systems LOAD a program into memory and RUN it when the program name is typed after the operating system's prompt. For example, suppose you have a BASIC program called PAYROLL.BAS. If you compile it into a machine language that you now call PAYROLL.COM and it is stored on drive A, you can run it by typing

```
>A:PAYROLL
```

If you have a computer with a disk drive, you know by now that in order to run a BASIC program, you must first LOAD the system by typing BASIC after the prompt. The following list gives some examples:

TRS-80	CP/M	MS-DOS	APPLE DOS
DOS READY	A>BASIC	A>MBASIC	See note below
BASIC	{Message}	{Message}	

What you actually are doing here is loading and starting the execution of the BASIC interpreter, a machine language program that allows you to enter and execute your own BASIC programs.

Note: The Apple II and IIe computers are unconventional in that the BASIC interpreter is part of the operating system.

13.4   OTHER TASKS OF OPERATING SYSTEMS

The previous section discussed the major functions (commands) that you should expect from any operating system—saving, renaming, deleting files, and so on. The computer user takes an active part in using these functions of the operating system. When you enter a command to the operating system, a portion of the operating system called the **console command processor (CCP)** reads and carries out the command. To do the required task, it will usually call on a subroutine in the **BDOS, the basic disk operating system,** which is a portion of the operating system.

console command
processor (CCP)
BDOS, basic disk
operating system

But all operating systems do a number of things without specifically being asked to by the user. In this section we briefly consider some of these so-called hidden tasks. Specifically, operating systems provide a bridge between our programs and the hardware, and as a result, we can write programs without having to know too much about the hardware. Also, multiple-user and network operating systems allow many people to share common computer resources.

Providing a Bridge Between Hardware and Software

Besides implementing the commands discussed in the previous section, the operating system performs common routines necessary for controlling various input and output devices. Here is a list of some of these common processes:

> Accept a character from the keyboard.
> Print a character on the screen.
> Print a character on the printer.
> Read a block of values from a disk file.
> Write a block of values to a disk file.

drivers
drive

These and other similar subroutines are called **drivers** because they **drive** (or control) the appropriate hardware device, video display,

☐ **FIGURE 13.6**   **Operating System: Command Processor and Drivers**

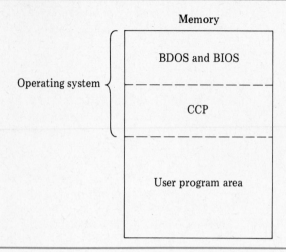

printer, disk drive. Someone who writes a machine language program can now use the equivalent of GOSUBs to go to the appropriate subroutine when that process is needed.

Thus a typical operating system has the structure illustrated in Fig. 13.6. That is, it consists of the command processor (CCP) along with the basic disk operating system (BDOS) and the various drivers, which are called the **BIOS, basic input/output system.**

Note that the Apple DOS and TRS DOS operating systems will run only on the Apple and Radio Shack computers, respectively. Other operating systems like CP/M–80, CP/M–86, MS–DOS, UNIX, Xenix, and others are designed to be used with compatible hardware. Only their drivers must be tailored to fit the particular machine.

BIOS, basic input/ output system

Sharing Computer Resources

In the 1960s computers were very expensive, the most expensive parts being the CPU and the memory. Also, at that time programs were run one at a time, from start to finish. This process created lines of people waiting to run their programs. Between program runs the CPU was idle for much of the time, waiting for program and data cards to be read by slow card readers.

time-shared computer systems

Time-shared computer systems (Fig. 13.7) solved both problems. In a time-shared system users do not have to wait long to have their jobs run, and there is no idle CPU time since usually there are a number of partially completed jobs that can use the CPU. Within a short period of time the computer allocates, in turn, a fraction of a second to process each user's program. Since the switching from one program to all the others occurs in such a short time, each user is unaware that the computer has interrupted the processing of his or her program.

☐ FIGURE 13.7   Concept of Time-Sharing

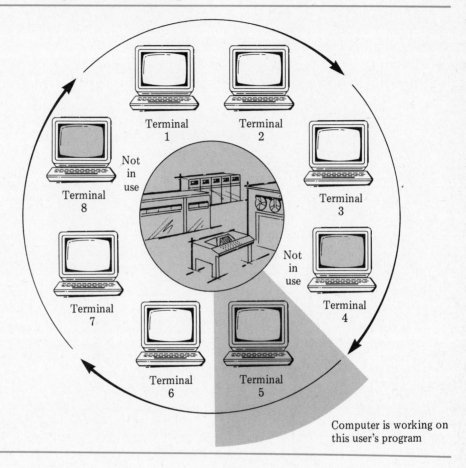

Terminal 1

Terminal 2

Not in use

Terminal 8

Terminal 3

Terminal 7

Not in use

Terminal 4

Terminal 6

Terminal 5

Computer is working on this user's program

An added benefit of time-shared computers is that the users can share information.

In addition to providing the processing of various file commands and device drivers, a time-shared operating system must also schedule the various jobs waiting for execution. For example, when it is time for the next job, the operating system must find and load the job into memory, remember where it previously left off, begin executing the job, stop after a fraction of time, save the status of various variables, and so on. Then it must load the next job, and so on.

The first commercially successful time-shared operating system was GECOS, which ran on the GE 625/635 computer in 1963. Between 1965 and 1980 most data processing was done in a time-sharing environment.

Today because of the current low cost of CPUs and memory, time-sharing is no longer a financial necessity. However, people still have the need to share information. Networked computer systems also

FIGURE 13.8   **Networked Computer System for Sharing Information and Resources**

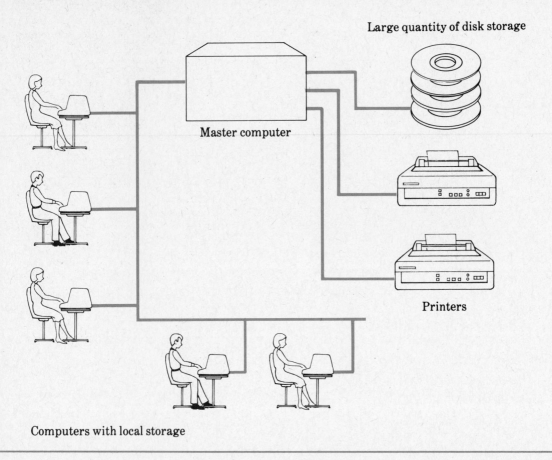

Large quantity of disk storage

Master computer

Printers

Computers with local storage

networked computer
system

allow users to share data and resources. A **networked computer system** consists of a number of microcomputers (each with CPU, memory, disk, and operating system) physically linked by cable. Important features of the operating system are the subroutines that allow the computers to pass data back and forth.

A common network structure (Fig. 13.8) includes a master computer. This computer controls a large amount of disk storage, which holds common program and data files. Also, such a system will usually have a variety of output devices (dot matrix printers, full character printers, plotters, and so on) that can be used by any computer user on the network.

Today networked computer systems are not prevalent. But many computer forecasters believe that such systems will be in widespread use in the future.

Data File Processing

INTRODUCTION TO CHAPTER 14

The essence of business data processing is record keeping. Usually, large numbers of records are processed—numbers far exceeding the capacity of main memory. Furthermore, these records are not processed just once and discarded. They are processed again and again, with important changes, additions, and deletions being made over an extended period of time. Another term for record keeping is **data file processing.**

data file procesing

data file

A **data file** is a collection of records. In earlier chapters we implemented data files with DATA statements. The problem with these files is that information in the file cannot be changed. Using DATA statements is an artificial method of creating a data file; but we used DATA statements to get us programming as quickly as possible. In this chapter we consider the creation and processing of real life data files.

There are four fundamental operations that are performed on a data file:

1. Creating a file (putting a file name in the disk directory).
2. Adding records to the file.
3. Deleting records.
4. Changing the values in any record field.

We will consider these four operations in this chapter.

There are two standard types of data files, sequential files and direct-access files.

Sequential files are easy to create and process, so we consider them first. Since other tasks on sequential files—like adding, deleting, and changing records—are awkward processes, we only consider adding additional records.

Direct-access files are presented in more detail because they are more useful. The program illustration in Section 14.4 performs all four fundamental operations. After studying the program, you should be able to modify it so that it manipulates a data file structure of interest to you.

Note to Apple users: The file programs in this chapter are written in Microsoft BASIC. But necessary changes for the programs so that they will run on Apple computers are clearly indicated. Because Microsoft BASIC can be indented, I think you will find it is easy to understand the overall program structure in this form.

14.1   SEQUENTIAL FILES

sequential file

A **sequential file** is a file that has to be created and processed sequentially. This concept will become clear at the end of the next section. In this section we describe a data processing example and the BASIC

☐ **FIGURE 14.1**   **Main Menu for a Sequential File**

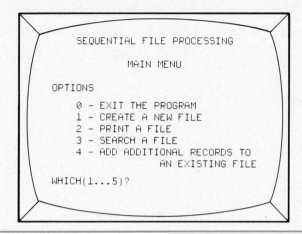

```
        SEQUENTIAL FILE PROCESSING

               MAIN MENU

     OPTIONS

         0 - EXIT THE PROGRAM
         1 - CREATE A NEW FILE
         2 - PRINT A FILE
         3 - SEARCH A FILE
         4 - ADD ADDITIONAL RECORDS TO
                     AN EXISTING FILE

     WHICH(1...5)?
```

statements needed to process sequential data files. In the next section we describe how such a file is created and processed sequentially.

First, we'll consider the example.

☐ **EXAMPLE**

To illustrate the programming of sequential file processes, let's suppose we want to maintain a file of records that looks like this:

```
ALLEN          CLIFF        921.45
JOHNSON        SYLVIA       -34.90
MIKOLAYCIK     MELISSA      34.56
```
      └─ Last name   └─ First name └─Amount due

By putting together the various routines discussed in Section 14.2, you will have a program that executes the processes suggested in the main menu in Fig. 14.1. This task of combining the routines is left as an exercise.

In the following subsections we describe the BASIC statements for processing sequential files.

File-Processing Statements

There are essentially four file statements that can be combined with other statements to implement the standard file-processing routines. Below, we describe the four statements. In the following two subsections we give specific details for Microsoft and Applesoft BASIC. In Section 14.2 we discuss four file-processing routines that comprehensively illustrate these statements.

☐ **FIGURE 14.2**   **Records Stored on a Disk Track**

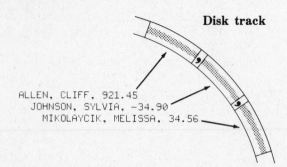

OPEN statement
- The **OPEN statement** informs the computer system that our program wants to use a particular file. The computer then makes preparations to use the file. Essentially, it will search the disk directory to see if the file exists. If it does, the read/write head of the disk drive is positioned to the track of the first record. If the file does not exist, the file name is entered into the directory.

PRINT (WRITE) statement
- The **PRINT (WRITE) statement** prints (or writes) the values in the variables in the statement into the next position on the disk. All individual data values must be separated by commas in the file. Thus the data on the disk looks very much like data in the data statement (Fig. 14.2). Each PRINT statement automatically puts a comma between each group of printed values (that is, each record).

INPUT (READ) statement
- The **INPUT (READ) statement** inputs (or reads) the next available data values from the disk into the desired variables. As in reading from a DATA statement, the computer remembers the position of the last value read. The commas between the values delimit each value. You must be sure that string values are read into string variables. As with the DATA statement, if a string value is read into a numeric variable, the computer will give a runtime error.

CLOSE statement
- The **CLOSE statement** informs the computer that the program no longer needs a particular file. At this time the computer makes sure that all values have been put into the file.

Microsoft BASIC Statements

Microsoft's implementation of the file statements has become a standard. It is the most widely used BASIC on Radio Shack computers, the IBM PC, and other computers with the MS–DOS and CP/M operating sys-file buffer

tems. Their method is also very similar to that of Digital Equipment Corporation's BASIC–PLUS.

The **file buffer** mentioned below is an area of memory where the data is held before it is written onto a file or where the data is held immediately after it is read from the file.

The four fundamental file-processing statements in Microsoft are described below.

☐ OPEN Statement

Description   The OPEN statement creates and/or makes a file available for use. A buffer number is assigned to the file. The buffer number is also used to identify the file.

Form   nn   OPEN   file type, buffer number, file name

Explanation

File type   This string constant or variable must have the value "O" or "I". An "O" indicates that data values are to be printed onto (outputted to) the file. An "I" indicates that data values are to be inputted from the file into variables in main memory.

Buffer number   This numeric constant or variable must have a value between 1 and 4 or 16, depending on the computer. This integer is used to identify the file in subsequent statements.

File name   This string constant or variable is the name of the data file to be processed. The file name consists of the drive name, file, and extension.

☐   EXAMPLES

```
OPEN "I", 3, "CLIENT.DAT"
OPEN "O", 4, F$
OPEN "I", 2, "A:CUST.DAT"
OPEN "O", 2, "CUST.DAT"
```

☐ PRINT Statement

Description   The PRINT statement prints values in the next available position in the file. The file is designated by the buffer number.

Form   nn   PRINT   buffer number, var1; ","; var2; ","; var3

Explanation   The buffer number corresponds to the buffer number of the file described in the OPEN statement. For example, given

```
OPEN "O",3, "CUST.DAT"
```

then the statement

```
PRINT #3, N2$;",";N1$
```
writes the values from the variables N2$ and N1$ into the next position of the file CUST.DAT. Notice that a comma is placed between each value printed on the disk.

☐ INPUT Statement

Description   The INPUT statement retrieves data from the next positions in the file and places them into the specified variables.

Form   nn   INPUT   buffer number, var1, var2, var3, var4

Explanation   The buffer number corresponds to the buffer number of the file described in the OPEN statement. For example, given

```
OPEN "I", 3, "CUST.DAT"
```

then the statement

```
INPUT #3, N2$, N1$
```

retrieves two values from the file and places them in variables N2$ and N1$.

☐ CLOSE Statement

Description   The CLOSE statement informs the computer that a particular file is no longer needed by the program.

Form   nn   CLOSE   buffer number

Explanation   The file that is closed is the one whose name is associated with the buffer number in the OPEN statement.

Applesoft BASIC Statements

All disk file operations in Applesoft BASIC are implemented with the PRINT statement. Each time the computer executes a statement like this,

```
PRINT CHR$(4);      {string indicating operation and file}
```

all subsequent PRINT and INPUT statements refer to the disk. The string at the end of the statement indicates the type of operation and the desired file. For the computer to resume printing on the screen and accepting input from the keyboard, another

```
PRINT CHR$(4)
```

statement must be executed. In effect, we toggle disk activity on and off with the PRINT CHR$(4) statement. This disk PRINT statement can be simplified a bit by using the following statements:

```
LET D$ = CHR$(4)      (This statement used once.)
PRINT D$;....
```

In the statement descriptions below, assume D$ has been initialized to CHR$(4).

The programs in the following sections will comprehensively illustrate the use of the following fundamental file-processing statements.

☐ OPEN Statement

Description	The OPEN statement creates and/or makes a file available for use.
Form	nn PRINT D$;"OPEN "; file name
Explanation	The file name can be a string constant or variable.

☐ EXAMPLE

```
100   PRINT D$;"OPEN ";"CUST.DAT"
100   PRINT D$;"OPEN CUST.DAT"
100   PRINT D$;"OPEN ";F$
100   PRINT D$;"OPEN ";"D1:CUST.DAT"
```

☐ WRITE Statement

Description	The WRITE statement writes values in the next available positions in the file.
Form	PRINT D$;"WRITE "; file name {Activate PRINT to disk}
	PRINT var1;","; var2; ","; var3 {Print to disk}
	PRINT D$ {Restore PRINT to screen if desired}

☐ EXAMPLE

```
500   PRINT D$;"WRITE ";"CUST.DAT"
510   PRINT N2$;",";N1$;",";A
520   PRINT D$
```

☐ READ Statement

Description   The READ statement reads data values from the next positions in the
                  file and places them into the specified variables.

Form   PRINT D$;"READ ";   file name   {Activate READ from disk}
                  INPUT   var1, var2, var3, var4   {Read/input from disk}
                  PRINT D$ {Restore INPUT from keyboard if desired}

☐ EXAMPLE

```
600   PRINT D$;"READ ";"CUST.DAT"
610   INPUT N2$, N1$, A
620   PRINT D$
```

☐ CLOSE Statement

Description   The CLOSE statement informs the computer that the program no
                  longer plans to use the file.

Form   PRINT D$;"CLOSE ";   file name

☐ EXAMPLE

```
800   PRINT D$;"CLOSE "; "CUST.DAT"
```

14.2 PROGRAMS FOR SEQUENTIAL FILE PROCESSING

Each of the programs given in the following subsections can be run
independently or can be combined as subroutines to a main program.
These programs create, read and print, and search a sequential file and
also add records to an existing file.

Creating a Sequential File

When the program in Fig. 14.3A is executed, it produces a screen like
the one shown in Fig. 14.3B. The indicated interaction with the program
creates a data file with the name CUST.DAT, as follows:

ALLEN, CLIFF, 34.56	,	JOHNSON, SYLVIA, -2.45	,	ZZZ, Z, 0

The program puts the trailing record

☐ FIGURE 14.3   Creating a Sequential File

```
2000 PRINT "      OPTION 1: CREATE A FILE"
2110 PRINT                                        Applesoft File Statements
2120 INPUT "NAME OF FILE "; F$
2130 PRINT                                        ⎰ LET D$ = CHR$(4)
2140 OPEN "O", #3, F$  ←────────────────────────  ⎱ PRINT D$;"OPEN ";F$
2150                                   REM
2200 INPUT      "LAST NAME (ZZZ EXITS) . ";N2$
2210 IF N2$="ZZZ" THEN 2400
2220     INPUT "FIRST NAME  . . . . . . "; N1$
2230     INPUT "AMOUNT OWED . . . . . . "; A      ⎧ PRINT D$;"WRITE ";F$
2240     PRINT #3, N2$;",";N1$;",";A  ←─────────  ⎨ PRINT N2$;",";N1$;",";A
2250     PRINT                                    ⎩ PRINT D$
2260     INPUT "LAST NAME (ZZZ EXITS) . "; N2$
2270 GOTO 2210
2300                                   REM         ⎰ PRINT D$;"WRITE ";F$
2400 PRINT #3, "ZZZ";",";"Z";",";0  ←──────────── ⎱ PRINT "ZZZ";",";"Z";",";0
2500 CLOSE #3  ←─────────────────────────────────
2700 END                                          ⎰ PRINT D$;"CLOSE ";F$
```

A. PROGRAM

```
        OPTION 1: CREATE A FILE

NAME OF FILE   ? CUST.DAT

LAST NAME (ZZZ EXITS) . ? ALLEN
FIRST NAME  . . . . . . ? CLIFF
AMOUNT DUE  . . . . . . ? 34.56

LAST NAME (ZZZ EXITS) . ? JOHNSON
FIRST NAME  . . . . . . ? SYLVIA
AMOUNT DUE  . . . . . . ? -2.45

LAST NAME (ZZZ EXITS) . ? ZZZ
```

B. OUTPUT

```
ZZZ, Z, 0
```

into the file so that we can recognize the end when reading the file. The
end of the file can also be detected with the EOF function, as suggested
in Exercise 14.6 at the end of this section.

Note that the statements needed in Applesoft are given to the
right in Fig. 14.3A.

☐ **FIGURE 14.4**   **Reading and Printing Contents of a Data File**

```
4000 PRINT "    OPTION 2: PRINT A FILE"
4100 PRINT
4120 INPUT "FILE NAME "; F$                          Applesoft File Statements
4130 PRINT
4140 OPEN "I", #3, F$  ←──────────────               ⎧ LET D$ = CHR$(4)
4150                                      REM         ⎨ PRINT D$;"OPEN ";F$
4200 PRINT "LAST NAME", "FIRST NAME", "AMOUNT DUE"
4210 PRINT
4300 IF N2$ = "ZZZ" THEN 4400                        ⎧ PRINT D$;"READ ";F$
4310    INPUT #3, N2$, N1$, A  ←──────               ⎨ INPUT N2$, N1$, A
4320    PRINT N2$, N1$, A                            ⎩ PRINT D$
4330 GOTO 4300
4340                                      REM
4400 CLOSE #3  ←──────────────────────               ⎰ PRINT D$;"CLOSE ";F$
4500 END
```

A. PROGRAM

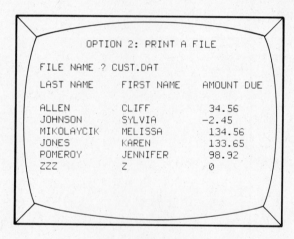

```
        OPTION 2: PRINT A FILE

FILE NAME ? CUST.DAT

LAST NAME      FIRST NAME    AMOUNT DUE

ALLEN          CLIFF           34.56
JOHNSON        SYLVIA          -2.45
MIKOLAYCIK     MELISSA        134.56
JONES          KAREN          133.65
POMEROY        JENNIFER        98.92
ZZZ            Z               0
```

B. OUTPUT

Reading and Printing a File

The program in Fig. 14.4A requests the user for a file name and then reads and prints each record in the file. A typical report is illustrated in Fig. 14.4B.

Searching a Sequential File

The program in Fig. 14.5A requests the user to enter an amount, as suggested by the screen in Fig. 14.5B. Then the program prints the name of everyone whose amount exceeds this value.

☐ **FIGURE 14.5**   **Searching a Sequential File**

```
4000 PRINT "       OPTION 3: SEARCH A FILE "
4010 PRINT
4100 INPUT "FIND CUSTOMERS WITH AMOUNT DUE > "; L
4110 PRINT                                              Applesoft File Statements
4120 INPUT "NAME OF FILE "; F$
4130 PRINT                                              ⎰ LET D$ = CHR$(4)
4140 OPEN "I", #3, F$  ◄────────────────────────        ⎱ PRINT D$;"OPEN ";F$
4150                                          REM
4200 PRINT "LAST NAME", "FIRST NAME", "AMOUNT DUE"
4210 PRINT                                              ⎧ PRINT D$;"READ ";F$
4300 IF N2$ = "ZZZ" THEN 4400  ◄───────────            ⎨ INPUT N2$, N1$, A
4310    INPUT #3, N2$, N1$, A  ◄───────────────         ⎩ PRINT D$
4320    IF A > L THEN PRINT N2$, N1$, A
4330 GOTO 4300
4340                                          REM
4400 CLOSE #3  ◄────────────────────────────           { PRINT D$;"CLOSE ";F$
4500 END
```

A. PROGRAM

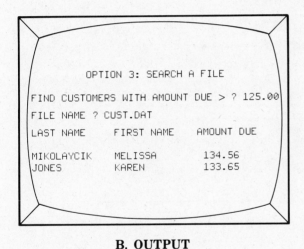

```
          OPTION 3: SEARCH A FILE

FIND CUSTOMERS WITH AMOUNT DUE > ? 125.00

FILE NAME ? CUST.DAT

LAST NAME      FIRST NAME      AMOUNT DUE

MIKOLAYCIK     MELISSA          134.56
JONES          KAREN            133.65
```

B. OUTPUT

Adding Records to an Existing File

Whenever a sequential file is modified in any way (a record is added, deleted, or changed), an entirely new file must be created. The program in Fig. 14.6A illustrates this procedure. First, look at the screen in Fig. 14.6B. Notice here that the program requests two file names—the name of the existing file, CUST.DAT, and the name of a new file, CUST1.DAT. All the records in the file CUST.DAT are first copied into the file CUST1.DAT. Then new records are added to the file CUST1.DAT.

```
8000 PRINT " OPTION 4:   ADD RECORDS"
8100 PRINT "          TO EXISTING FILE"
8110 PRINT
8120 INPUT "EXISTING FILE NAME . "; F$
8125 OPEN "I", #3, F$
8130 INPUT "NEW FILE NAME  . . . "; F1$
8135 OPEN "O", #2, F1$
8140 PRINT
8170                              REM
8200 REM - - - COPY RECORDS TO NEW FILE - -
8205 PRINT "       COPYING RECORDS "
8210 INPUT #3, N2$, N1$, A
8300 IF N2$ = "ZZZ" THEN 8350
8305    PRINT ".";
8310    PRINT #2,  N2$ "," N1$ "," A
8320    INPUT #3,  N2$ , N1$ , A
8330 GOTO 8300
8340                              REM
8350 CLOSE #3
8360 PRINT : PRINT
8400 REM - - - INPUT RECORDS INTO NEW FILE - -
8405 PRINT "NOW ADD NEW RECORDS:"
8410 PRINT
8420 INPUT    "LAST NAME (ZZZ EXITS) . "; N2$
8430 IF N2$="ZZZ" THEN 8600
8440    INPUT "FIRST NAME . . . . . . "; N1$
8450    INPUT "AMOUNT OWED . . . . . . "; A
8460    PRINT #2, N2$;",";N1$;",";A
8470    PRINT
8480    INPUT "LAST NAME (ZZZ EXITS) . "; N2$
8490 GOTO 8430
8500                              REM
8600 PRINT #2, "ZZZ";",";"Z";",";0
8700 CLOSE #2
8710 PRINT "NOTE: UPDATED FILE IS NAMED ";F1$
8800 END
```

Applesoft File Statements

```
{ LET D$ = CHR$(4)
{ PRINT D$;"OPEN ";F$

{ PRINT D$;"OPEN ";F1$

{ PRINT D$;"READ ";F$
{ INPUT N2$, N1$, A
{ PRINT D$

{ PRINT D$;"WRITE ";F1$
{ PRINT N2$;",";N1$;",";A
{ PRINT D$

{ PRINT D$;"CLOSE ";F$

{ PRINT D$;"WRITE ";F1$
{ PRINT N2$;",";N1$;",";A
{ PRINT D$

{ PRINT D$;"WRITE ";F1$
{ PRINT "ZZZ";",";"Z";",";0

{ PRINT D$;"CLOSE ";F1$
```

A. PROGRAM

```
           OPTION 4: ADD RECORDS
              TO EXISTING FILE

   EXISTING FILE NAME . ? CUST.DAT
   NEW FILE NAME  . . . ? CUST1.DAT
             COPYING RECORDS

   NOW ADD NEW RECORDS:

   LAST NAME (ZZZ EXITS) . ? BROMLEY
   FIRST NAME . . . . . . ? JANET
   AMOUNT DUE . . . . . . ? 34.56

   LAST NAME (ZZZ EXITS) . ? PERCY
   FIRST NAME . . . . . . ? MARY
   AMOUNT DUE . . . . . . ? -2.45

   NOTE: UPDATED FILE IS NAMED CUST1.DAT
```

B. OUTPUT

The reason a new file must be created is that at any one time a sequential file can be opened only as an input file ("I") or as an output file ("O"). It cannot be opened both ways.

Notice in the program that two files are opened (lines 8125 and 8135), and each has a file number. Thus you must keep track of the file numbers to know which file is being referenced.

Once the records are added to CUST1.DAT, the old file CUST.DAT can be deleted with the appropriate operating system command.

To modify a field of a record or to delete a record in a sequential file, you must again create a new file. As mentioned earlier, these processes are awkward, so the details are not discussed here.

EXERCISES

14.1. Write a program that creates a main menu and links together the programs in this section.

14.2. *Note:* This exercise assumes that you have linked the programs with a main menu. Portions of two subroutines add a record to a file. Make a subroutine out of these two subroutines. *Hint:* You will have to make the buffer number a variable and assign it a value before you enter the subroutine.

14.3. Modify OPTION 2: PRINT A FILE so that the first names are adjacent to the last name. They should look like this:

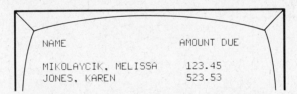

```
NAME                    AMOUNT DUE

MIKOLAYCIK, MELISSA      123.45
JONES, KAREN            523.53
```

14.4. Extend the computer dating illustration on page 174 so that clients can be put into a data file.

14.5. Implement a small file-processing application of interest to you.

14.6. What will happen on your system if you try to create a file that has already been created? Investigate the ON ERROR statement for your system. How can it be used to prevent some problems?

14.7. a) Describe an algorithm for deleting a record from a sequential file. *Note:* As with OPTION 4 in Fig. 14.6A, you will have to create a new file.
b) Describe an algorithm for deleting more than one record at a time.
c) Write a program to implement your algorithm for part (b).

14.8. The **end-of-file function, EOF,** has a value of false if the end of the file has not been reached. It becomes true when the end of the file has been reached. This function can be used in programs to recognize the end of the file. Read about the EOF function and the LINE INPUT # statement in your system manual. To demonstrate these features, enter and run the following program:

```
100    PRINT "THIS PROGRAM READS AND'
110    PRINT "'LISTS' A PROGRAM OR DATA FILE"
120    PRINT
200    INPUT "NAME OF THE FILE "; F$
210    PRINT
300    OPEN "I", #3, F$
310    IF EOF(3) THEN 500
320       LINE INPUT #3, L$
330       PRINT L$
340    GOTO 310
500    END
```

14.9. Write a program that will add, delete, and edit records of a sequential file.

14.10. Run the following program. Explain how it works.

```
100 OPEN "O",3,"GREETING.BAS"
200 INPUT "ENTER YOUR NAME"; N$
210 LET Q$ = CHR$(34) + "HELLO " + N$ + CHR$(34)
220 PRINT "HERE IS A BRIEF MESSAGE"
230 PRINT Q$
240                                              REM
300 FOR I = 1 TO 10
310    PRINT #3,   STR$(10*I)+" PRINT " + Q$
320 NEXT I
400 PRINT #3, STR$(800)+" END"
410 CLOSE #3
420                                              REM
500 PRINT
600 PRINT "FOR AN EXPANDED MESSAGE"
610 PRINT "TYPE   RUN 'GREETING'"
700 END
```

14.11. The program in Exercise 14.10 creates another program. The program in Exercise 14.8 reads another program. Give some examples of how a program could usefully process other programs.

14.3 DIRECT-ACCESS FILE PROCESSING

You should now have a pretty good idea of what the term *sequential file processing* means. You have seen that the programs in Figs. 14.3 and 14.6 create the files CUST.DAT and CUST1.DAT sequentially; that is, one record after another is written into the file. The programs in Figs. 14.4 and 14.5 process (read) the files sequentially, from the beginning to end.

The disadvantages of processing files sequentially is one of speed. We cannot go directly to a particular record; we have to read

direct-access files   over every record in front of it. **Direct-access files** allow direct (immediate) access to any record in the file. They have the same advantages over sequential files that books have over Egyptian scrolls, phonograph records have over cassette tapes, and video disks have over movie films—you can go directly to the information you want.

The following subsections describe the concepts and the statements involved in direct-access files.

Concepts

Records in a direct-access file are arranged consecutively, and each record is identified with an integer, starting with 1. To give you a rough idea of how the computer can go directly to a particular record in a direct-access file, let's assume the following:

- The first record of a file is stored on track 10 of a disk and the file records spill over into consecutive tracks through track 36.
- Each record contains 128 characters.
- Each track holds 2560 characters, so there are 20 records per track.

Now, the question is, which track will record 117 be stored on? The answer is, Track 15. The reason:

Records 1–20 are on track 10.
Records 21–40 are on track 11.
Records 41–60 are on track 12.
And so on.

Thus we see how the computer can calculate the track where any particular record is located.

To get more specific, computers do not usually read an entire disk track at one time. They read a *sector* of the disk. Suppose each sector holds 256 characters, and there are 10 sectors per track, for a total of 2560 characters on a track. On which sector of track 15 will record 117 be found? *Answer:* Sector 9.

As you can see from the above discussion, it is absolutely necessary that each record be the same length for direct-access files. In contrast, with sequential files the values in any field can be any length.

File Statements

Depending on the particular version of BASIC, there are four (or five) statements for direct-access file processing. When combined with other statements, these file-processing statements can be used to do a variety of things with direct-access files. The fundamental statements are described on the following page.

☐ **FIGURE 14.7**   **Microsoft File Buffers and Statements**

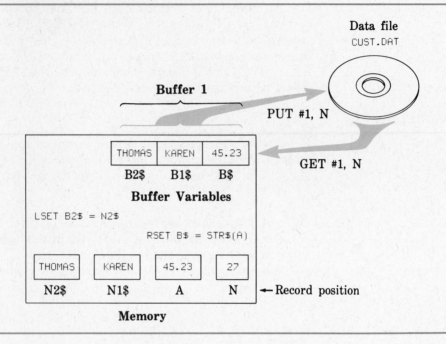

OPEN statement
: ▪ The **OPEN statement** specifies the file to be used and the length of all records in the file.

FIELD statement
: ▪ The **FIELD statement** defines the length of the records and the length and type of the individual field variables. (This statement is not used in Applesoft BASIC.)

PUT (WRITE) statement
: ▪ The **PUT (WRITE) statement** puts (writes) some values from main memory onto the disk at a particular record position within the file. The record position is specified in this statement. To add records to a direct-access file can be tricky. The program has to keep track of the position of the last record in the file.

GET (INPUT) statement
: ▪ The **GET (INPUT) statement** gets the values from a particular record position in the file and assigns them to variables in main memory.

CLOSE statement
: ▪ The **CLOSE statement** informs the computer that the file is no longer needed by the program.

Microsoft BASIC Statements

To understand the individual file-processing statements in Microsoft BASIC, consider Fig. 14.7. It shows the role that the buffer variables play in transferring information to and from the disk. All data must go through the buffers. The buffers and each of the file statements are discussed below. (Applesoft BASIC does not use buffers.)

☐ OPEN Statement

Description	The OPEN statement creates and/or makes a file available for use. A buffer number is assigned to each file. The buffer number is also used to identify the file in all file statements.
Form	nn OPEN "R", buffer number, file name, record length

Explanation

"R"	This variable names the file type; "R" indicates it is a random (direct-access) file.
Buffer number	This numeric constant or variable must have a value between 1 and 4 or 16, depending on the computer. This integer is used to identify the file in subsequent statements.
File name	This string constant or variable is the name of the data file to be processed. The file name consists of the device name, file, and extension.
Record length	This numeric constant or variable gives the length of each record in the file.

☐ EXAMPLE

```
100   OPEN "R", #1, "CUST.DAT",30     {See Fig. 14.7}
100   OPEN "R", Q, N$, L
```

☐ FIELD Statement

Description	The FIELD statement defines the length of each buffer variable in the buffer.
Form	nn FIELD buffer number, len1 AS var1, len2 AS var2, ...

Explanation

Buffer number	The buffer number is an integer variable or constant. A buffer number is assigned to each file. By referencing the buffer number with other statements, you can manipulate the correct file.
len1 AS var1	Each buffer variable is given a length at this point. For example, len1 is length of field variable var1.

☐ EXAMPLE

```
100   FIELD #1, 10 AS B2$, 10 AS B1$, 10 AS B$
```

☐ PUT Statement

Description   The PUT statement takes the current values in the buffer variables and assigns them to a particular position in the file.

Form   nn   PUT   buffer number, record position

Explanation   Since the buffer number is assigned to a file in the OPEN statement, the values in the appropriate buffer variables are put into the file at the specified record position.

☐ EXAMPLE

```
100 PUT #1, 45
100 PUT #2, N
```

☐ LSET and RSET Statements

Description   These LET statements assign string values, left- (L) or right- (R) justified, into the buffer variables.

Form   nn   LSET   buffer variable = string expression
                  nn   RSET   buffer variable = string expression

Explanation   The LSET and RSET assignment statements are the only way to move values into the buffer variables. LSET left-justifies the string value in the buffer variable. RSET right-justifies the string value in the buffer variable.

☐ EXAMPLE

```
234   RSET Q$ = STR$(T+45*G)
542   LSET N$ = "DESCRIPTION"
```

☐ GET Statement

Description   The GET statement moves a copy of a particular record position in the file to the buffer variables.

Form   nn   GET   buffer number, record position

Explanation   Since the buffer number is assigned to a file in the OPEN statement, the record at the specified record position is assigned to the appropriate buffer variables.

☐ EXAMPLE

```
100  GET #1, 45
100  GET #2, N
```

☐ CLOSE Statement

Description   The CLOSE statement informs the computer that the file is no longer needed by the program.

Form   900   CLOSE   buffer number

Applesoft BASIC Statements

Applesoft BASIC statements for direct-access files are similar to the statements for sequential files. No buffers are used. The string in the statement

```
PRINT CHR$(4);      string
```

specifies the file operation. The fundamental statements are described below.

☐ OPEN Statement

Description   The OPEN statement creates and/or makes a file available for use. It also defines the length of each record in the file.

Form   nn   PRINT D$;"OPEN   file name, Lxx"

Explanation

File name   The file name is any string of characters denoting a file.

xx   This constant indicates the length of each record in the file.

☐ **EXAMPLES**

```
100   PRINT D$;"OPEN CUST.DAT, L30"
100   PRINT D$;"OPEN ";F$;",L";30
100   PRINT D$;"OPEN ";"D1:CLIENTS.DAT,";"L35"
```

☐ WRITE Statement

Description   The WRITE statement writes values at a particular record position in the file.

Form   PRINT D$;"WRITE   file name, R"; record position {Activate PRINT to disk}
               PRINT   var1;","; var2;","; var3   {Print to disk}
               PRINT D$ {Restore PRINT to screen if desired}

Explanation   The record position value specifies to which record position the data is written. The record position can be an integer constant or a variable.

□ **EXAMPLE**

```
500   PRINT D$;"WRITE CUST.DAT, R"; N
510   PRINT N2$;",";N1$;",";A
520   PRINT D$
```

□ READ Statement

Description
The READ statement reads data values from a specific record position in the file and places them into the specified variables.

Form
PRINT D$;"READ file name, R"; record position
{Activate READ from disk and record position}
INPUT var1, var2, var3, var4   {Read/input from disk}
PRINT D$ {Restore INPUT from keyboard if desired}

□ **EXAMPLE**

```
600  PRINT D$;"READ CUST.DAT,R", N
610  INPUT N2$, N1$, A
620  PRINT D$
```

□ CLOSE Statement

Description
The CLOSE statement informs the computer that the program no longer plans to use the file.

Form
PRINT D$;"CLOSE   file name"

□ **EXAMPLE**

```
800  PRINT D$;"CLOSE CUST.DAT"
```

14.4 A DIRECT-ACCESS FILE PROGRAM

In this section we give a complete, menu-driven, direct-access file program. It processes records that have the same form as those in the sequential file example. The record form is

Last name First name Amount due

The operations that can be performed on the file are illustrated by the various screens in Fig. 14.8.

Lines 100–420

```
    DIRECT-ACCESS FILE PROCESSING
      CUSTOMER FILE: CUST.DAT

HAVE YOU PREVIOUSLY ENTERED DATA
INTO THE FILE (Y/N) ? Y

EXISTING FILE: COUNTING RECORDS
...
THERE ARE 3 RECORDS IN THE FILE

  PRESS <RETURN> TO CONTINUE ?
```

Lines 2000–2360

```
   OPTION 2: LIST CONTENTS OF FILE

   LAST NAME    FIRST NAME  AMOUNT DUE

1 MIKOLAYCIK   MELISSA      65.74
2 JONES        KAREN       123.23
3 BROMLEY      JILL         34.24
4 BROMLEY      KAREN       123.45
5 ZZZ                        0

PRESS <RETURN> TO CONTINUE ?
```

Lines 420–660

```
    CUSTOMER FILE: CUST.DAT

         MAIN MENU

OPTIONS:

  0 - EXIT THE PROGRAM
  1 - ADD RECORDS TO THE FILE
  2 - LIST ALL RECORDS
  3 - DISPLAY / EDIT / DELETE RECORDS

WHICH ? 1 2 3
```

Lines 1000–1560

```
OPTION 1: ADD RECORDS TO THE FILE

LAST NAME (ZZZ EXITS) . ? BROMLEY
FIRST NAME  . . . . . . ? JILL
AMOUNT DUE  . . . . . . ? 34.24

LAST NAME (ZZZ EXITS) . ? BROMLEY
FIRST NAME  . . . . . . ? KAREN
AMOUNT DUE  . . . . . . ? 123.45

LAST NAME (ZZZ EXITS) . ? ZZZ
```

Lines 3000–3990

```
   OPTION 3: DISPLAY/EDIT/DELETE RECORDS

5 RECORDS CURRENTLY IN THE FILE
ENTER RECORD NUMBER (0 EXITS) . ? 3

  1)  LAST NAME . . . BROMLEY
  2)  FIRST NAME  . . JILL
  3)  AMOUNT DUE  . . 34.24

OPTIONS:

  E - EDIT, D - DELETE, <RETURN> CONTINUES? E

  EDIT WHICH FIELD (1,2,3) ? 3

  AMOUNT DUE . ? 12.34

ENTER RECORD NUMBER (0 EXITS) . ? 0
```

The top screen asks if we are creating a brand new file or are going to use an existing one. If we are using an existing file, then we must read the entire file to count the number of records currently in the file. This way we know where to start adding additional records. Variable N always holds the number of records currently in the file.

The trailing record

ZZZ	.	0

is used to mark the end of the file. The EOF function could have been used. But a specific trailing record makes checking for the end of file more concrete.

The line numbers above the screens indicate the lines of the program that implement the action in the screen. The program is shown in Fig. 14.9.

Here are a few general comments on the program:

- Variable use:

Record Fields	Description	Buffer Variables
N2$	Last name	B2$
N1$	First name	B1$
A	Amount due	B

  Variable N contains the number of records currently in the file.
- To delete a record, you put the last record in the file on top of the record to be deleted. Then the file length is reduced by one.

EXERCISES

14.12. Construct a hierarchy chart for the program in this section.

14.13. Under what circumstances are direct-access files more appropriate than sequential files?

4.14. Modify the edit routines (Fig. 14.9D) so that it is like the edit routine in Section 11.2.

14.15. Introduce an identification field to the file discussed in this section, like this:

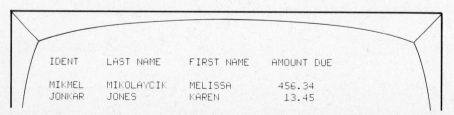

```
IDENT      LAST NAME     FIRST NAME     AMOUNT DUE

MIKMEL     MIKOLAYCIK    MELISSA          456.34
JONKAR     JONES         KAREN             13.45
```

Modify the OPTION 3 subroutine (Fig. 14.9D) so that to find an individual, the user can enter the IDENTification code.

□ FIGURE 14.9   Direct-Access File Program

Applesoft File Statements

```
100 REM       --- INTIALIZE RECORD STRUCTURE ---
105 OPEN "R", #1, "CUST.DAT",30                        ◄────  ⎧ LET D$ = CHR$(4)
110 FIELD #1, 10 AS B2$, 10 AS B1$, 10 AS B$           ⎨ PRINT D$;"OPEN CUST.DAT, L30"
120                                           REM
130 PRINT "    DIRECT-ACCESS FILE PROCESSING"
135 PRINT "      CUSTOMER FILE: CUST.DAT"
140 PRINT
150 PRINT "HAVE YOU PREVIOUSLY ENTERED DATA"
155 INPUT "INTO THE FILE (Y/N) "; Z$
160 PRINT
170 IF Z$ = "Y" THEN 300
200   PRINT "NEW FILE: INSERTING TRAILING RECORD"
210       LSET B2$ = "ZZZ"
220       LSET B1$ = "."             ◄────────────┐
230       RSET B$ = "0"                            │
240       LET N = 1                                │
250       PUT #1, N              ◄─────────────────┤   ⎧ PRINT D$;"WRITE CUST.DAT, R";N
260       GOTO 400                                     ⎨ PRINT "ZZZ";".";".":0
300   PRINT "EXISTING FILE: COUNTING RECORDS"          ⎩ PRINT D$
310       LET N = 0
320       LET N = N + 1                                 ⎧ PRINT D$;"READ CUST.DAT, R";N
330         GET #1, N          ◄──────────────────     ⎨ INPUT N2$, N1$, A
340         PRINT ".";                                  ⎩ PRINT D$
350       IF LEFT$(B2$,3) <> "ZZZ" THEN 320
360       PRINT
370       PRINT "THERE ARE";N; "RECORDS IN THE FILE"
380   REM --- ENDIF ---
400 PRINT
410 INPUT "     PRESS <RETURN> TO CONTINUE "; Z$
420 GOSUB 10000
430    PRINT "        CUSTOMER FILE: CUST.DAT"
440    PRINT
450    PRINT "            MAIN MENU"
460    PRINT
470    PRINT "OPTIONS:"
480    PRINT
490    PRINT " 0 - EXIT THE PROGRAM"
500    PRINT " 1 - ADD RECORDS TO THE FILE"
510    PRINT " 2 - LIST ALL RECORDS"
520    PRINT " 3 - DISPLAY / EDIT / DELETE RECORDS"
600    PRINT
610    INPUT "WHICH "; X
620    GOSUB 10000
630    IF X > 0 THEN ON X GOSUB 1000, 2000, 3000
640 IF X > 0 THEN 420
650 CLOSE #1
660 STOP
```

A. LINES 100–650

(continued)

☐ **FIGURE 14.9**   (Continued)

```
1000 PRINT " OPTION 1: ADD RECORDS TO THE FILE"
1110 PRINT
1120 INPUT    "LAST NAME (ZZZ EXITS) . "; N2$
1130 IF N2$ = "ZZZ" THEN 1500
1200    INPUT "FIRST NAME  . . . . . . "; N1$
1210    INPUT "AMOUNT DUE  . . . . . . "; A
1220                                               REM
1300     LSET B2$ = N2$
1310     LSET B1$ = N1$
1320     RSET B$  = STR$(A)
1330     REM --- PUT ON TOP OF TRAILING RECORD ---
1340     PUT #1, N
1350     LET N = N + 1
1360     PRINT
1400     INPUT "LAST NAME (ZZZ EXITS) . "; N2$
1410 GOTO 1130
1420                                               REM
1500 REM --- PUT TRAILING RECORD IN N'TH PLACE ---
1510     LSET B2$ = "ZZZ"
1520     LSET B1$ = "."
1530     RSET B$  = "0"
1550     PUT #1, N
1560 RETURN
```

Applesoft File Statements

```
{ PRINT D$;"WRITE CUST.DAT, R";N
{ PRINT N2$;",";N1$;",";A
{ PRINT D$
```

```
{ PRINT D$;"WRITE CUST.DAT, R";N
{ PRINT "ZZZ";",";".";0
{ PRINT D$
```

B. LINES 1000–1560

```
2000 PRINT "  OPTION 2: LIST CONTENTS OF FILE"
2110 PRINT
2200 PRINT "# LAST NAME","FIRST NAME", "AMOUNT DUE"
2210 PRINT
2300 FOR R = 1 TO N
2310    GET #1,R
2320    PRINT R; TAB(4); B2$, B1$, B$
2330 NEXT R
2340 PRINT
2350 INPUT "PRESS <RETURN> TO CONTINUE"; Z$
2360 RETURN
```

Applesoft File Statements

```
{ PRINT D$;"READ CUST.DAT, R";R
{ INPUT N2$, N1$, A
{ PRINT D$
{ PRINT R; TAB(4); N2$, N1$, A
```

C. LINES 2000–2360

```
3000 PRINT "OPTION 3: DISPLAY/EDIT/DELETE A RECORD"
3010 PRINT
3020 PRINT N; "RECORDS CURRENTLY IN FILE"
3030 PRINT
3100 INPUT "ENTER RECORD NUMBER (0 EXITS) . "; R
3110 IF R < 0 OR R > N THEN 3100
3120 IF R = 0 THEN 3500
3130     PRINT
3200     GET #1, R
3300     PRINT
3310     PRINT " 1)  LAST NAME . . .   "; B2$
3320     PRINT " 2)  FIRST NAME . .   "; B1$
3330     PRINT " 3)  AMOUNT DUE . .   "; B$
3340     PRINT
```

Applesoft File Statements

```
{ PRINT D$;"READ CUST.DAT, R";R
{ INPUT N2$, N1$, A
{ PRINT D$
```

```
{ N2$
{ N1$
{ A
```

☐ FIGURE 14.9   (Continued)

```
3350    PRINT "OPTIONS:"
3360    PRINT
3370    INPUT "E - EDIT,  D - DELETE,  <RETURN> - CONTINUE"; Q$
3380    PRINT
3390    IF Q$ = "E" THEN GOSUB 3700
3392    IF Q$ = "D" THEN GOSUB 3900
3394    PRINT
3400    INPUT "ENTER RECORD NUMBER (0 EXITS) . "; R
3410    IF R < 0 OR R > N THEN 3400
3420 GOTO 3120
3500 RETURN
3510                                            REM
3520                                            REM
3700 INPUT "EDIT WHICH FIELD (1,2,3) "; Z$
3710 PRINT
3720 IF Z$="1" THEN INPUT " 1) LAST NAME . . ";N2$ : LSET B2$=N2$       ←─┐ Omit
3730 IF Z$="2" THEN INPUT " 1) FIRST NAME  . ";N1$ : LSET B1$=N1$       ←─┘
3740 IF Z$="3" THEN INPUT " 3) AMOUNT DUE  . ";A   : RSET B$=STR$(A)
3750 PUT #1,R
3770 PRINT
3780 RETURN
3790                                            REM
3900 PRINT "DELETING ABOVE RECORD"
3910 GET #1, N-1 ◄────────: REM - - LAST RECORD
3920 PUT #1, R   ◄────────: REM - - PUT IN R'TH POSITION
3930                                            REM
3940 GET #1,N    ◄────────: REM - - TRAILING RECORD
3950 PUT #1, N-1 ◄────────: REM - - MOVE BACK 1 POSITION
3960 LET N = N - 1        : REM - - ADJUST NUMBER OF RECORDS
3970 RETURN
3980                                            REM
3990                                            REM
```

Applesoft File Statements

```
{ PRINT D$;"READ CUST.DAT, R"; N-1
{ INPUT N2$, N1$, A

{ PRINT D$;"WRITE CUST.DAT, R"; R
{ PRINT N2$;",";N1$;",";A

{ PRINT D$;"READ CUST.DAT, R"; N
{ INPUT N2$, N1$, A

{ PRINT D$;"WRITE CUST.DAT, R"; N-1
{ PRINT N2$;",";N1$;",";A
{ PRINT D$
```

D. LINES 3000-3990

```
10000 REM - - CLEAR SCREEN ROUTINE - - -
10010    FOR I9 = 1 TO 10 : PRINT : NEXT I9
10030 RETURN
11000 END
```

E. Lines 10000-11000

14.16. Write a routine for the program in this section that automatically generates an identification code for each record after the individual's data is entered. You might use the first three characters of the first and last names. After the code is generated in this way, the program should check the file for duplicate IDENT code. What action should be taken if the code already exists?

14.17. Write a subroutine for the program in this section that will sort the records alphabetically by last name. *Note:* You can do this task by writing the entire file into arrays in main memory. Then sort the data, and write the records back to the file.

14.5 INDEXING A FILE

In Exercise 14.17 at the end of the previous section you were asked to write a subroutine that sorts the file alphabetically by last names. To do this task, we suggested that you first move the record fields into arrays in main memory, as follows:

L$( )	F$( )	A( )
MIKOLAYCIK	MELISSA	65.74
JONES	KAREN	123.23
BROMLEY	JILL	34.24
YOUNG	SARAH	-3.12

Now you can use the Bubble Sort technique (Section 12.5) to sort the array by last names. Then you can copy this information back into the file. But every time you exchange two last names, you must exchange the corresponding first names and amounts. If the records contain many fields, this task results in a lot of data movement.

Another way to do this task with less data movement is to create another array named P( ), which is called a **pointer** or **index array**. This array is initialized so that P(1) is 1, P(2) is 2, and so on.

Now we can perform the sort "through" the array P so that at the end of the sort the P( ) array looks like Fig. 14.10.

Notice that the number in P(1) "points to" the first name in the sorted list of names. Also, L$(P(1)) is L$(3), which is BROMLEY. What does the following routine do?

```
1400   FOR I = 1 TO N
1410     PRINT L$(P(I)), F$(P(I)), A(P(I))
1420   NEXT I
```

It prints the names alphabetically.

pointer
index array

☐ **FIGURE 14.10** **Example of a Pointer Array**

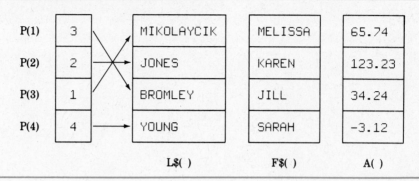

The sort routine below with pointers only moves pointer values. The routine is a slight modification of the Bubble Sort.

```
370   REM --- N IS THE NUMBER OF ELTS
372   REM --- IN THE ARRAYS L$, F$, A
374                               REM
380   REM --- INITIALIZE P( ) ---
382   FOR I = 1 TO N
384      LET P(I) = I
386   NEXT I
388                               REM
400   LET E = N
410   REM --- LOOP TOP --
420      FOR J = 1 TO E - 1
430        IF A(P(J)) <= A(P(J + 1)) THEN 450
440          LET       H = P(J)
442          LET     P(J) = P(J + 1)
444          LET P(J + 1) = H
450      NEXT J
460      LET E = E - 1
470   IF E >= 2 THEN 410
480   REM -- LOOP BOTTOM --
```

Once the pointer sort is completed, the P( ) array can be put into a disk file, which might be called LNAME.NDX. This file provides an index to the CUST.DAT file. You could also create an AMOUNT.NDX file, which is an index to the file on the *amount* field.

EXERCISE

14.18. Extend the direct-access, file-processing program given in Fig. 14.9 so that you can index on the last name. The list file routine, OPTION 2, can be extended to ask if an index file should be used.

Computer Languages

INTRODUCTION TO CHAPTER 15

Once you have learned the structured approach to programming in a particular language, as you have in this text, you should find learning other languages quite easy. The reason is that most languages share fundamental concepts that you now understand. Most languages have variables, constants, and statements (commands). And most have the following familiar program structures, or extensions of them:

- Sequence of statements
- The loop structure
- The IF-THEN-ELSE structure
- The subroutine structure

In this chapter we will explain why a variety of languages have been developed and why you should expect to see many new languages developed in the future. Then we explain the major elements of a currently popular file management language called dBASE II. By seeing the features of this language, more modern than BASIC, you will better understand why programming languages evolve.

The introduction to dBASE II is brief. You will learn how to use a number of the more common dBASE II commands. But you will not be expected to write complete dBASE II programs.

15.1 EVOLUTION OF COMPUTER LANGUAGES

Suppose this world was inhabited only by people who wanted to do various simple arithmetic calculations, find cumulative sums and counts, and find largest and smallest values in a set of numbers. Then I would bet that FORTRAN and BASIC would be the only programming languages in existence today. Since these two languages do these arithmetic processes well, there would be no need for another language.

A new computer language evolves (or an existing one is extended) because there are objects, represented by data, that have natural ways of being manipulated or processed that are not conveniently expressed in an existing language. For example, can you imagine writing a BASIC program for (a) controlling a robot, (b) manipulating geometric shapes in three dimensions, (c) simulating specialized human thought processes, or (d) playing chess? I doubt that you could. On the other hand, if you had a language with statements like GRASP, ROTATE WRIST, ROTATE BODY, ELBOW ANGLE, you might find it at least conceivable that a program could be written to have a robot weld seams.

There is a hypothesis in linguistics that states that the structure of the language defines boundaries of thought. Thus with regard to computers, if you want to think new thoughts or do new things with a computer, you need new languages. And new languages there are and will continue to be.

In the following subsections we will consider various kinds of computer languages—assembly, general-purpose, special-purpose, and database languages—and how they have evolved.

Assembly Language

machine language

The first computers (around 1950) were programmed in what is called **machine language.** Four statements in a machine language program might look like this:

```
010111010100
100101001011
010010010000
011100110101
```

Each one of these instructions directs the computer to take particular action on a memory compartment or a CPU register or both. Can you imagine the difficulties in writing modest 200-line programs with this method? It once took me four months of full-time work to write such a program.

The writing of programs was made easier in 1953 by allowing the programmer to write instructions symbolically. Each machine instruction had a symbolic representation. And memory compartments could be given symbolic names. Thus the program segment above could now be written like this:

```
CLA
LOAD A
ADD B
STORE C
```

assembly language
programming

assembler

This code is called **assembly language programming.** Of course, the program has to be translated into machine language (0s and 1s) to be executed by the computer. The translating program is called an **assembler.**

One major problem with writing in assembly language is that we have to have intimate knowledge of the particular machine we are using. Another disadvantage is that the program cannot be run on a machine with a different CPU.

General-Purpose, High-Level Languages

low-level language

Assembly language is usually referred to as a **low-level language** because it is at or very close to the level of the machine. The programming of a number of common actions, such as

> Comparing two values
> Assigning the value of one variable to another
> Controlling a loop
> Printing a value

in assembly language requires 4, 6, or 10 instructions.

high-level languages

On the other hand, **high-level languages** are designed to eliminate the tediousness of low-level programming by specifying these common actions with one or a very few statements. A **general-purpose, high-level language** is a language that is capable of expressing the most common actions on the most common data. Today this definition means a language that can do arithmetic computation, some text processing, and some graphics processing.

general-purpose, high-level language

FORTRAN

FORTRAN (FORmular TRANslator), the first major, high-level language, was developed in 1955 by an IBM team headed by John Backus. In the early to mid 1950s computers were being used primarily for scientific and engineering applications. So FORTRAN was especially good for expressing arithmetic calculations. A FORTRAN compiler translates FORTRAN statements into machine language.

BASIC

BASIC (Beginners' All-purpose Symbolic Instruction Code) is probably the most widely used general-purpose, high-level language today. It evolved in the following way: In the early sixties the most expensive part of computers was their central processing unit and memory. A problem in working with computers in those days was that only one person at a time could use the computer. So time-shared operating systems were developed. Each person was able to sit at a terminal and use it. What was needed now was a language system where people would not have to wait for program compilations. This need led to the development of BASIC, the first interactive, high-level, interpreted language. As used on microcomputers today, BASIC is not time-shared. But it has been expanded to include graphics and sound generation operations.

Pascal

Pascal, a language designed in 1969, is now fighting to become a dominate, general-purpose, high-level language. Its virtue is that it has all the flow structures built into the language. And the language is easily extended by defining new procedures.

Both BASIC and FORTRAN are evolving by taking on some of the structured elements found in Pascal.

Special-Purpose, High-Level Languages

LISP

LISP (list processor), developed between 1958 and 1960, was one of the first special-purpose, high-level languages. The objects processed by LISP are lists. It is widely used in programming for artificial intelligence applications where the interrelationships of data and information must be represented.

special-purpose
languages

Other **special-purpose languages** were developed, as you might suspect, because of special needs. For instance, in the mid to late 1950s computers were being used for data processing applications. These applications required less mathematical computation than scientific applications but more moving of data between main and auxiliary storage units. This data movement was not one of FORTRAN's strengths. Another problem with FORTRAN was that each manufacturer had a slightly different version of FORTRAN. Thus programs had to be converted to the proper FORTRAN version before being run on another machine. The U.S. government (the largest purchaser of computers at the time), not wanting to be locked into a specific manufacturer because

COBOL

of the high code conversion costs, mandated the development of **COBOL** (COmmon Business Oriented Language). Two characteristics of this language were to be as follows: (1) It would consider records and files as the primary data objects, and (2) COBOL programs written for one machine should be able to run on any other machine. Thus the U.S. government, with a large investment in programs, could theoretically switch from Honeywell to Univac computers and still run all their programs.

VAL
LOGO

VAL is a special-purpose, high-level language for writing programs to control robots. **LOGO** is a special-purpose, graphics-oriented language whose major purpose is to teach mathematics by actively engaging the user in writing programs.

Database Language Systems

During the sixties, when computers became somewhat cheaper, more and more file-processing applications were being put on the computers. Previously, application programs were rather simple in that they processed data from one or two files. For example, a payroll program would only process data in a payroll file. Now applications became much more complicated—processing data from 2, 3, or perhaps 15 different data files. Any reduction of low-level programming detail was very welcome.

Consider the following very common low-level detail. A hospital has two files, a patient file and a doctor file. The structures of the records in the two files are as follows:

Patient File

Patient ID	Name	Room	Doctor ID	Other data

Doctor File

Doctor ID	Name	Phone	Other data

☐ **FIGURE 15.1**   **Database System Handling File-Accessing Requests**

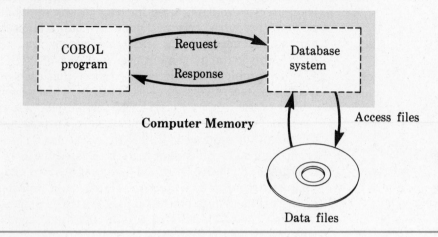

Now suppose you want to find the phone number of the doctor of patient XYZ. (*Question:* How would you do it in BASIC?) Operations such as this one are easily done by the programmer. But they are so routine that there should be a generalized program that produces such results on the basis of the structure of the files and their interrelationships. For example, it should be able to respond to questions like

```
FIND DOCTOR PHONE OF PATIENT XYZ
FIND ALL PATIENTS OF DOCTOR ABC IN A FIFTH FLOOR ROOM
```

database language
system

Thus the **database language system** evolved to satisfy this need.

Figure 15.1 illustrates the essence of what a database language system does. Within a COBOL program the programmer includes special commands to request information from the database system, which actually retrieves data from the file.

15.2 THE dBASE II LANGUAGE

dBASE II language

The **dBASE II language** is a file-processing language available for microcomputers based on the Zilog Z80 CPU or the Intel 8080 or 8088 CPU. It runs under either the CP/M or MS–DOS operating system. There must be at least 48K of available memory and two floppy-disk drives, with each drive containing at least 180K. The language is marketed by Ashton-Tate. It can be purchased for between $375 and $700.

As you will see, this language allows you to execute one statement (command) at a time or to combine the commands into a program. The creating of programs is discussed in the next section. In this section we will explain dBASE II by demonstrating some of its more useful commands. You will quickly see how much easier it is to write file-processing programs in dBASE II than in BASIC.

First, let's look at an example.

☐   EXAMPLE

Let's suppose you sell real estate. One of your main jobs is to get listings, that is, to find houses for sale and get permission from the owner to allow you to show it. Your other main job is to find clients, people interested in buying property, and then match the clients with the houses. A computer program could help you do this matching.

First, you could create a house file, where each record contains the following fields of information about each house (the number of fields is limited here for simplicity):

Owner's last name	First initial	Telephone	Town	Acres	Number of bedrooms	Price

Eventually, a dBASE II program will be written that generates screens like those in Fig. 15.2. This program could also be written in BASIC by using direct access files, but with more difficulty.

The menu in Fig. 15.2A gives the user three options. If you select option M, then the screen in Fig. 15.2B is generated. The first record in the file will be displayed beside the field names.

Notice the menu in the lower half of the screen of Fig. 15.2B, below the dashed line. If you select F, the next record forward in the file will be displayed. Selecting B causes the program to move backward in the file and display the previous record. By selecting the search option S, you may enter a person's last name; the program will then go to the first record with the appropriate last name.

As you can see in Fig. 15.2B, you can select options that allow you to add, edit (change), and delete records. Editing is easily done by typing over the values in appropriate fields.

Before discussing the program for the screens of Fig. 15.2, we will first describe some dBASE II commands.

Commands for Creating and Listing a File

Suppose you now have a copy of dBASE II on your operating system disk. To execute dBASE, type

```
>DBASE
```

The screens that follow show you how to create a file, add records to the file, and list records from the file satisfying various conditions. (The

☐ **FIGURE 15.2** **Screens for dBASE II Program**

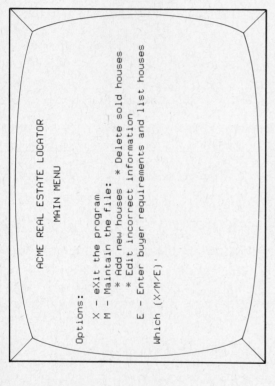

```
         ACME REAL ESTATE LOCATOR
              MAIN MENU




    Options:

        X - eXit the program
        M - Maintain the file:
            * Add new houses   * Delete sold houses
            * Edit incorrect information
        E - Enter buyer requirements and list houses

    Which (X/M/E)'
```

A. MAIN MENU

```
       OPTION M: MAINTAIN HOUSE FILE

    Current record available --- in window

Last name . . . . : HOFFMAN
Initial . . . . . : D
Telephone . . . . : 354-2233
Town . . . . . . . : ROXBURY
Acres . . . . . . : 23.4
Bedrooms . . . . . : 12
Price . . . . . . : 1287900

Movt in File  :  F - Forward   B - Back   S - Search
Update Codes  :  A - Add       E - Edit   D - Delete
Exit          :  X - eXit to main menu'

Select option : :
```

B. OPTION M

```
     Option E: ENTER BUYER REQUIREMENTS,
               THEN LIST HOUSES

Enter Requirements:

                   Min.        Min.        Maximum
                   Acres       Bedrooms    Price
Town
:ROXBURY :      : 1.0:       : 2:        : 500000:


    [All houses matching description will be printed]
```

C. OPTION E

☐ **FIGURE 15.3** **The CREATE Command**

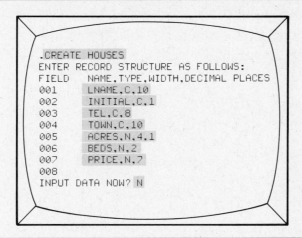

```
.CREATE HOUSES
ENTER RECORD STRUCTURE AS FOLLOWS:
FIELD    NAME,TYPE,WIDTH,DECIMAL PLACES
001      LNAME,C,10
002      INITIAL,C,1
003      TEL,C,8
004      TOWN,C,10
005      ACRES,N,4,1
006      BEDS,N,2
007      PRICE,N,7
008
INPUT DATA NOW? N
```

data in these screens is data that was entered in the program to be discussed in Section 15.3.)

CREATE command

The first screen (Fig. 15.3) shows how a file is defined by using the **CREATE command.** The name HOUSES, which follows the command, is the name of the new file. Subsequently, each field in the file is named and typed (either C for a character field or N for a numeric field); then the field length is specified. So that you can see what has been displayed by the computer and what I typed, my responses are highlighted (shaded) on the screen.

Pressing a <return> for the field name informs the system that we have completed our record definition.

USE command

As suggested by the previous screen (Fig. 15.3), we could have begun entering data at the INPUT DATA NOW point. The screen in Fig. 15.4 describes a more general procedure. First, to use one particular file of many that may have been defined, you employ the **USE command,** followed by the file name. All subsequent file commands refer to that file. The period at the beginning of many lines is the dBASE II prompt.

APPEND command

The **APPEND command** prompts the user to enter values for each field. The colons remind the user of the length of the fields.

LIST command

The **LIST command** (Fig. 15.5) lists the entire file or the portion that satisfies a specific condition. Conditions are built with the usual relational operators and Boolean operators (AND, OR, NOT). The five-digit number on the left side of the record is the physical position of the record in the file. This number is used in the EDIT and DELETE commands to be discussed shortly.

☐ **FIGURE 15.4**   **Appending Data**

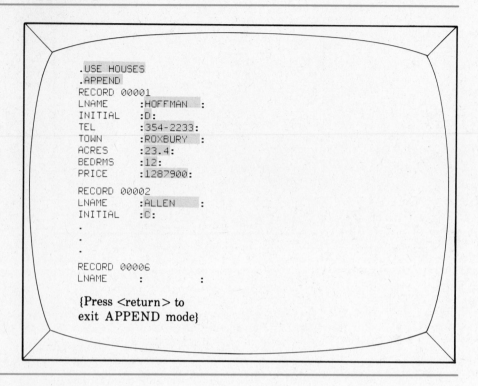

```
.USE HOUSES
.APPEND
RECORD 00001
LNAME        :HOFFMAN  :
INITIAL   :D:
TEL          :354-2233:
TOWN         :ROXBURY   :
ACRES     :23.4:
BEDRMS    :12:
PRICE     :1287900:

RECORD 00002
LNAME        :ALLEN     :
INITIAL   :C:
.
.
.
RECORD 00006
LNAME        :         :

{Press <return> to
exit APPEND mode}
```

☐ **FIGURE 15.5**   **The LIST Command**

```
.LIST

00001 HOFFMAN      D    354-2233    ROXBURY      23.4   12   1287900
00002 ALLEN        C    265-3325    BRIDGEWATE    3.6    2    103000
00003 SHAIL        D    567-3422    ROXBURY       7.8    4    234000
00004 FRIEDMAN     S    342-4455    DANBURY       1.4    3    187000
00005 JOHNSON      S    443-8899    BRIDGEWATE   31.5    9    563000
.LIST FOR BEDRMS >=3 .AND. PRICE < 300000

00003 SHAIL        D    567-3422    ROXBURY       7.8    4    234000
00004 FRIEDMAN     S    342-4455    DANBURY       1.4    3    187000
```

☐ **FIGURE 15.6**   **Editing and Deleting Records**

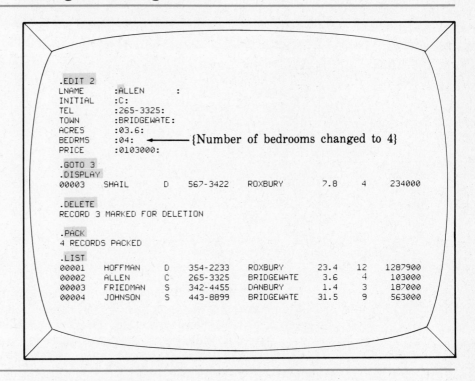

```
.EDIT 2
LNAME       :ALLEN       :
INITIAL     :C:
TEL         :265-3325:
TOWN        :BRIDGEWATE:
ACRES       :03.6:
BEDRMS      :04:   ←————— {Number of bedrooms changed to 4}
PRICE       :0103000:

.GOTO 3
.DISPLAY
00003    SHAIL      D    567-3422    ROXBURY        7.8    4    234000

.DELETE
RECORD 3 MARKED FOR DELETION

.PACK
4 RECORDS PACKED

.LIST
00001    HOFFMAN    D    354-2233    ROXBURY       23.4   12   1287900
00002    ALLEN      C    265-3325    BRIDGEWATE     3.6    4    103000
00003    FRIEDMAN   S    342-4455    DANBURY        1.4    3    187000
00004    JOHNSON    S    443-8899    BRIDGEWATE    31.5    9    563000
```

Commands for Modifying a File

Any records in a file can be edited or deleted. To do the editing or deleting, you have to GOTO the record first.

EDIT command

When you are editing a record (like record 2 in Fig. 15.6) with the **EDIT command,** the cursor is automatically set to the first character of the first field—the A in ALLEN, in this case. To make no changes, press <return>; otherwise, you type over the existing characters to make changes.

DELETE command
PACK command

The **DELETE command** is applied to the current available record. The **PACK command** completes the deletion of all the records you have marked for deletion.

Commands for Sorting and Indexing a File

sorting

Sorting a file by any field is easily done in dBASE II. Suppose you want to list the houses in alphabetical order by owners' last names. This task is done as illustrated in the screen in Fig. 15.7.

After the sort is completed, there are now two files: HOUSES.DBF and SORTFILE.DBF. Notice that SHAIL is still assumed to be in the file (see Fig. 15.6).

☐ **FIGURE 15.7**   **Sorting a File**

```
.USE HOUSES
.SORT ON LNAME TO SORTFILE

5 RECORDS SORTED

.USE SORTFILE
.LIST

00001 ALLEN      C  265-3325  BRIDGEWATE   3.6    4    103000
00002 FRIEDMAN   S  342-4455  DANBURY      1.4    3    187000
00003 HOFFMAN    D  354-2233  ROXBURY     23.4   12   1287000
00004 JOHNSON    S  443-8899  BRIDGEWATE  31.5    9    563000
00005 SHAIL      D  567-3422  ROXBURY      7.8    4    234000
```

Sorting requires a lot of data movement. As explained in Section 14.5, **indexing** provides another way of rearranging the file. The next screen (Fig. 15.8) shows how easily indexing is done in dBASE II.

indexing

After the indexing is completed, there are two files: the original file, HOUSES.DBF, and the index file, HOUSLNAM.NDX. You can now treat the file HOUSES.DBF without using the index by invoking the command

```
USE HOUSES
```

☐ **FIGURE 15.8**   **Indexing a File**

```
.USE HOUSES
.INDEX ON LNAME TO HOUSLNAM

5 RECORDS INDEXED

.USE HOUSES INDEX HOUSLNAM
.LIST

00002 ALLEN      C  265-3325  BRIDGEWATE   3.6    4    103000
00004 FRIEDMAN   S  342-4455  DANBURY      1.4    3    187000
00001 HOFFMAN    D  354-2233  ROXBURY     23.4   12   1287000
00005 JOHNSON    S  443-8899  BRIDGEWATE  31.5    9    563000
00003 SHAIL      D  567-3422  ROXBURY      7.8    4    234000
```

Or you can access it through the index file HOUSLNAM by invoking the command

```
USE HOUSES INDEX HOUSLNAM
```

Once a file is put into use with an index, all subsequent commands use the index file to access the main file.

Creating a Report

report form

Creating a report requires a program when you use BASIC. In dBASE II you can create a report "form" by answering a series of questions. Then whenever the report is needed, it is merely mentioned by name. The screen in Fig. 15.9 shows you how a **report form** is created. Figure 15.10 shows what the actual report looks like. Notice that a report is generated when the following command is given:

```
REPORT FORM HOUSELST
```

15.3 A dBASE II PROGRAM

Even when you are limited to using one command at a time, it should be clear that dBASE II has considerable power. In fact, some complete file-processing applications can be implemented this way. However, dBASE II commands can be combined to create programs. Given complete control, a programmer can construct easier-to-use, menu-driven application programs with attractive, more complete reports.

The dBASE II programs can be written by using your system editor (ED for CP/M systems, EDLIN for MS–DOS systems) or by using a word processor. Each program should have the extension CMD in CP/M system and the extension PRG in MS–DOS system, which indicates a command file. Thus dBASE II programs may have names like MENU.CMD, MAINTAIN.CMD, PROCESS.CMD, or MENU.PRG, etc.

The extensions DBF and NDX indicate database files and index files, respectively.

In the following subsections we discuss the control structures for dBASE II and the complete real estate program we have been leading up to throughout this chapter.

Programming Structures

The commands discussed in the previous section plus other commands can be combined to form programs. Commands can be put together in series or be nested one within the other.

□ **FIGURE 15.9**   **Creating a Report Form**

```
.USE HOUSES
.REPORT FROM HOUSELST
ENTER OPTIONS, M=LEFT MARGIN, L=LINES/PAGE, W=PAGE WIDTH
PAGE HEADING? (Y/N) N
ENTER PAGE HEADING: HOUSES CURRENTLY ON FILE
DOUBLE SPACE REPORT? (Y/N) N
ARE TOTALS REQUIRED? (Y/N) Y
SUBTOTALS IN REPORT? (Y/N) N

COL     WIDTH,CONTENTS
001     12, TRIM(LNAME)+', '+INITIAL
ENTER HEADING: <Owner

002     10, TEL
ENTER HEADING: <Phone

003     10, TOWN
ENTER HEADING: <Town

004     7, ACRES
ENTER HEADING: >Acres
ARE TOTALS REQUIRED? (Y/N) y
```

```
005     10, BEDRMS
ENTER HEADING: >Bedrooms
ARE TOTALS REQUIRED? (Y/N) n

006     8, PRICE
ENTER HEADING: >Price
ARE TOTALS REQUIRED? (Y/N) y

007 ■
```

□ **FIGURE 15.10**   **The Created Report**

```
.REPORT FORM HOUSELST
PAGE NO. 00001

                    HOUSES CURRENTLY ON FILE

Owner           Phone       Town          Acres    Bedrooms     Price

HOFFMAN, D      354-2233    ROXBURY        23.4          12    1287900
ALLEN, C        265-3325    BRIDGEWATE      3.6           2     103000
SHAIL, D        567-3422    ROXBURY         7.8           4     234000
FRIEDMAN, S     342-4455    DANBURY         1.4           3     187000
JOHNSON, S      443-8899    BRIDGEWATE     31.5           9     563000
** TOTAL **

                                          67.7                2374900
```

control structures

The dBASE II language has the following **control structures:**

Selection	Case	Loop
IF condition	DO CASE	DO WHILE condition
...	CASE condition	...
...	...	...
ELSE	...	...
...	CASE condition	ENDDO
...	...	
ENDIF	...	
	ENDCASE	

In the selection structure, if the condition is true, then the statements between the IF and ELSE are executed. If the condition is false, then the statements between the ELSE and ENDIF are executed.

The case structure is very convenient. See the program given later in Fig. 15.12 for a natural example.

The loop structure is similar to the WHILE statement in extended BASIC. While the condition is true, the statements within the loop are executed.

The Real Estate Program

The programs in Figs. 15.11 through 15.13 implement the real estate example discussed in the previous section and illustrated in Fig. 15.2.

□ **FIGURE 15.11**   **Program XMENU.CMD, the Main Menu Program**

```
*       acme real estate system
*       calls xmaint.cmd  and   xlisth.cmd
*
USE houses.dbf INDEX houslnam.ndx
SET TALK OFF
STORE T TO again
DO WHILE again
    ERASE
    ?                        ACME REAL ESTATE LOCATOR'
    ?
    ? '                           MAIN MENU'
    ? 'Options:'
    ?
    ? '  X  -  eXit the program'
    ?
    ? '  M  -  Maintain the file: '
    ?
    ? '           * Add new houses   * Delete sold houses'
    ? '           * Edit incorrect information'
    ?
    ? '  E  -  Enter buyer requirements and list houses'
    ?
    ? 'Which (X/M/E)'
    WAIT TO resp

    DO CASE
      CASE !(resp) = 'X'
          STORE F TO again

      CASE !(resp) = 'M'
          DO xmaint.cmd

      CASE !(resp) = 'E'
          DO xreqlst.cmd

    ENDCASE
ENDDO
QUIT
```

The programs assume that the database file HOUSES.DBF (note the use of lowercase terms in the program) and the index file HOUSLNAM.NDX have been created, as illustrated in that section.

DO command   This entire program, like most dBASE II programs, consists of a number of subprograms. The **DO command** causes the execution of a particular program. For example,

```
DO XMENU.CMD
```

causes the program XMENU.CMD (Fig. 15.11) to be executed. Within this program the command

```
DO XMAINT.CMD
```

causes the execution of the subprogram XMAINT.CMD (Fig. 15.12). Notice the RETURN command in program XMAINT.CMD. It directs the computer to return to the next statement in the XMENU.CMD program. Thus RETURN in dBASE II plays the same role as RETURN in BASIC.

Although we cannot explain everything about each of the subprograms in these figures, we can explain enough to give you a feel for the language so that you can compare it with BASIC.

Figure 15.11 implements the main menu in Fig. 15.2A. Here are the most important details:

- The question mark command (?) directs the computer to print the following items (constants or variables). Notice in Fig. 15.11 that all ?s are followed by string constants.

□ **FIGURE 15.12   Subprogram XMAINT.CMD**

```
* xmaint.cmd
ERASE
a 02,03 SAY '        OPTION M: MAINTAIN HOUSE FILE'
a 04,03 SAY '    Current record available --- in window'
a 06,03 SAY 'Last name . . . .'
a 07,03 SAY 'Initial . . . . .'
a 08,03 SAY 'Telephone . . . .'
a 10,03 SAY 'Town . . . . . .'
a 11,03 SAY 'Acres . . . . . .'
a 12,03 SAY 'Bedrooms . . . .'
a 13,03 SAY 'Price . . . . . .'
a 15,03 SAY '----------------------------------------------'
a 16,03 SAY 'Movt in File  : F - Forward   B - Back   S - Search'
a 17,03 SAY 'Update Codes  : A - Add       E - Edit   D - Delete '
a 18,03 SAY 'Exit          : X - eXit to main menu'
a 20,03 SAY 'Select option'

GOTO TOP

STORE T TO more
DO WHILE more
    a 06,23 SAY lname
    a 07,23 SAY initial
    a 08,23 SAY tel
    a 10,23 SAY town
    a 11,23 SAY acres
    a 12,23 SAY bedrms
    a 13,23 SAY price

    STORE ' ' TO action
    SET CONFIRM OFF
    a 20,17 GET action PICTURE '!'
    READ
    CLEAR GETS
    SET CONFIRM ON
    a 20,20 SAY '
```

(continued)

□ **FIGURE 15.12**   (Continued)

```
DO CASE
    CASE action = 'X'
        STORE F TO more

    CASE action = 'F'
        SKIP

    CASE action = 'B'
        SKIP - 1

    CASE action = 'S'
        STORE '            ' TO mlname
        @ 20,24 SAY 'Last name ' GET mlname PICTURE '!!!!!!!!!!!'
        READ
        STORE TRIM(mlname) TO mlname
        FIND &mlname
        IF # = 0
            @ 20,42 SAY '* Not found *'
        ENDIF

    CASE action = 'D'
        DELETE
        @ 20,40 SAY 'Deleting record. Now indexing'
        PACK
        INDEX ON lname TO houslnam.ndx
        USE houses.dbf INDEX houslnam.ndx

    CASE action = 'E'
        * Since file indexed by last name, it cannot
        *        be edited.@ 07,22 GET initial  PICTURE '!'
        @ 08,22 GET tel       PICTURE '999-9999'
        @ 10,22 GET town      PICTURE '!!!!!!!!!!!'
        @ 11,22 GET acres     PICTURE '99.9'
        @ 12,22 GET bedrms    PICTURE '99'
        @ 13,22 GET price     PICTURE '9999999'
        READ
        CLEAR GETS

    CASE action = 'A'
        APPEND BLANK
        @ 06,22 GET lname     PICTURE '!!!!!!!!!!!'
        @ 07,22 GET initial   PICTURE '!'
        @ 08,22 GET tel       PICTURE '999-9999'
        @ 10,22 GET town      PICTURE '!!!!!!!!!!!'
        @ 11,22 GET acres     PICTURE '99.9'
        @ 12,22 GET bedrms    PICTURE '99'
        @ 13,22 GET price     PICTURE '9999999'
        READ
        CLEAR GETS

    ENDCASE
ENDDO
RETURN

    A>
```

- The command

```
WAIT TO resp
```

is similar to

```
INPUT resp
```

where resp is a variable.
- The ! function is the uppercase value of the character. Thus !('a') is 'A'.

The subprogram in Fig. 15.12 allows you to add new houses to the file, edit existing house data, and search for a particular house in the file, using the owner's last name. This program is an all-purpose program that, with modifications, can be used on most files. Some of the important elements of the program are as follows:

- Commands that begin with

```
@ rr,cc SAY '...'
```

first position the cursor at row rr and column cc of the screen and then print (SAYS) the item values.
- A new record is added to the file by the command APPEND BLANK. This command actually appends a record of spaces to the file. Later, when values are moved into the field variables, the values are incorporated into the file. There is no PUT or WRITE statement as you are accustomed to in BASIC.
- The GET and READ commands work together. Notice that the GET command contains a PICTURE string, which specifies the type of data that may be assigned to the variable. A '9' represents a digit. Therefore, at most, two digits can be assigned to the BEDRMS field. A '!' represents an uppercase value. Thus a last name entered as 'allen' will be taken as 'ALLEN'.

The program in Fig. 15.13 accepts the buyer's requirements and lists all houses satisfying those requirements. The interesting command in the program is

```
LIST FOR &condt
```

What is the & in the item &CONDT? *Answer:* Since the compound condition is rather long, it is created in pieces as a string constant. Then it is assigned to string variable CONDT (lowercase used in the program). The & in front of the variable CONDT merely informs the computer that &CONDT is not really the condition but that it should look inside the variable CONDT to find the condition to be evaluated.

□ **FIGURE 15.13**   **Subprogram XLISTH.CMD**

```
* xreqlst.cmd
*
ERASE
    @ 01,03 SAY '    Option E: ENTER BUYER REQUIREMENTS,'
    @ 02,03 SAY '                    THEN LIST HOUSES'
    @ 04,03 SAY 'Enter Requirements:''
    @ 06,03 SAY '              Min.      Min.                 Maximum'
    @ 07,03 SAY ' Town         Acres     Bedrooms     Price        '
    STORE '          '    TO mtown
    STORE 00.0           TO macres
    STORE 0              TO mbedrms
    STORE 0              TO mprice
    @ 09,02 GET mtown    PICTURE '!!!!!!!!!!!'
    @ 09,18 GET macres   PICTURE '99.9'
    @ 09,27 GET mbedrms  PICTURE '99'
    @ 09,39 GET mprice   PICTURE '9999999'
    READ
    CLEAR GETS
    GOTO TOP
    IF mprice = 0
        STORE 9999999 TO mprice
    ENDIF

    ? '            HOUSES SATISFYING THE REQUIREMENTS'
    ?
    STORE          '(acres )= macres) .AND. '    TO condt
    STORE condt + '(bedrms )= mbedrms) .AND. '   TO condt
    STORE condt + '(price <= mprice)'            TO condt
    IF mtown = ' '
        SET PRINT ON
        LIST FOR &condt
        SET PRINT OFF
    ELSE
        STORE '(town = mtown) .AND. ' + condt TO condt
        SET PRINT ON
        LIST FOR &condt
        SET PRINT OFF
    ENDIF
wait to resp
RETURN

A>
```

PERIPHERAL DEVICES AND APPLICATIONS

Peripheral Devices

INTRODUCTION TO CHAPTER 16

programmed

Computers are general-purpose machines. That is, a computer can be a file processor, a word processor, a spreadsheet calculator, a teaching machine, or practically any other machine. What makes this variety possible is that computers can be **programmed** to do these different tasks.

Another reason for a computer's flexibility is the wide range of peripheral—input and output—devices that can be attached to computers. That is, in addition to the keyboard, there are other ways of entering data into the computer. And in addition to the display terminal and printer, there are other output devices that can be controlled by computers.

In this chapter we describe in some detail the variety of both input and output devices currently available for home computers.

16.1 CONVERTERS AND CONTROLLERS

Figure 16.1 illustrates some of the peripheral devices that can be attached to computers. Important parts of each connection are the converter and the controller, which lie between the device and the computer. When buying a peripheral device for a computer, you generally have

☐ **FIGURE 16.1**   **Input/Output Devices**

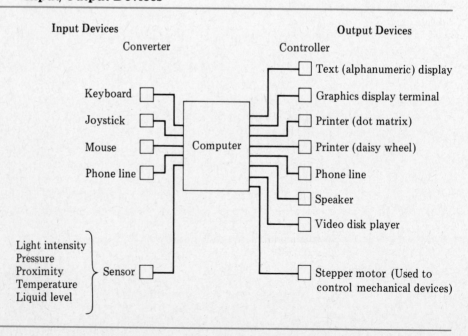

☐ **FIGURE 16.2**   **Role of Converters for Input Devices**

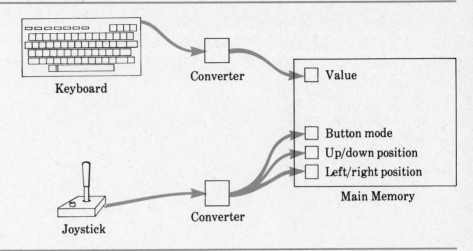

to pay for these additional pieces of equipment, which seemingly do nothing. But these electronic devices make it easier for the programmer and computer to access the data or to control a device.

The following subsections discuss each device in detail.

Converters

converter

The role of the **converter** is to convert some condition, value, or action into a binary value. This binary value is then routed to a specific memory compartment. To process this value with a BASIC program, you use a special function like PDL(X) or JOYSTICK(X) or PEEK(X). The particular function name depends on the computer. **PEEK(X)** returns the contents (in decimal) of the byte with address X. The decimal value will generally range between 0 and 255.

PEEK(X)

An input device converter may return one or more values into memory, as illustrated in Fig. 16.2. The keyboard returns the code for the last key pressed. But a joystick returns three values. One value indicates whether the button is pressed. The second value is the up/down position of the stick. The third is the left/right position of the stick. Thus you may have to look into three locations to "read" and process the joystick status.

Controllers

controller

A **controller** receives a binary value from the computer and "processes" it—that is, it takes some action in controlling the attached device. For example, a value (control code) sent to a printer controller may instruct

☐ **FIGURE 16.3**   **Components of Video Display Screen**

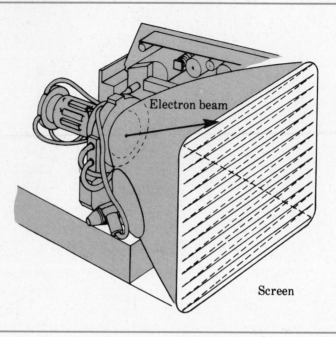

the controller to configure the printer so that it prints 12 characters per inch rather than the usual 10. A controller may take a variety of codes to set a particular condition.

Controller boards may be part of the device itself, or they may be attached to an available slot on the computer bus. To send a value to a particular device controller, you can send it to the particular slot. Because of the convenient way Applesoft BASIC can send a value to a particular slot—with PR#1, PR#2, PR#3, and so on—it is a popular computer for controlling laboratory equipment and other devices.

16.2 VIDEO DISPLAY TERMINALS

Video display terminals are becoming very complex output devices and consequently need powerful controllers to manage all the variety of outputs.

As illustrated in Fig. 16.3, a video display consists of a glass panel covered with dots of phosphor and an electron beam directed toward the panel. The electron beam scans the screen, starting in the upper left-hand corner and moving horizontally to the right. During this movement the energy in the beam is modulated. High energy at one point causes the phosphor to glow. Once the beam reaches the right, it is blanked and repositioned to the left and down one row; then it continues scanning. American televisions produce 525 horizontal scan lines.

alphanumeric (text)
screen
graphics terminal

There are two types of video displays that are commonly used with microcomputers. One is called an **alphanumeric (text) screen.** It has special circuits that generate crystal-clear alphabetic characters, digits, and special symbols. The other is called a **graphics terminal.** It generates images that are composed of tiny dots called *pixels* (picture elements). Its strength is in displaying colored pictures, graphs, and animated scenes. Graphics screens can generate characters, but they are not as clear as on alphanumeric screens. In the following subsections we will discuss both types of displays and programs that generate various types of outputs.

When purchasing a computer system, you should select the type of display (text or graphics) required by your major application. Most inexpensive screens are either one type or the other. Some manufacturers are combining the features of both into one terminal, but these terminals are expensive.

Text (Alphanumeric) Displays

Some of the major electronic characteristics of text displays are display format, available characters and formation, and visual attributes. These characteristics and others are described below.

Display Format. This characteristic defines the number of characters that can be displayed on a horizontal line (80 characters is common) and the number of vertical lines on the screen (24 is the most common). This format is illustrated below. Each position represented by a box can hold one character.

Available Characters. Text display terminals differ in the characters that can be displayed. There are 96 displayable ASCII characters. (See Table B.1 in Appendix B.) Some inexpensive terminals display fewer than these. Other, more expensive ones can display additional characters, including some graphics characters, such as

Since each of these symbols has an ASCII code, they can be displayed by using a statement like PRINT CHR$(206). The ASCII code 206 corresponds to the symbol

Visual Attributes. Each character at a position on the screen can take on various visual attributes. For example, it can be displayed in the following ways:

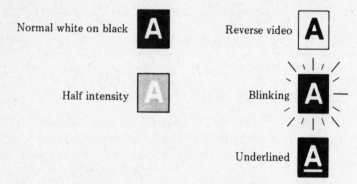

A character at a screen position may take on various attributes at one time. For example, the letter A may be in half intensity, reverse video, underlined, and blinking.

Screen Wraparound. Video displays act like sequential devices in that when you print one character after the next, the characters are displayed in successive positions on the screen. As soon as a character is displayed in column 80, the terminal positions the cursor at the start of the next line. This positioning is done electronically; the programmer does not have to count characters.

Screen Scrolling. When characters are written on the last line of a display and then more characters are written on the next line, the electronics of the terminal moves all lines up one position. This action is called **scrolling**. Scrolling allows the user to always see the last 24 lines.

scrolling

Cursor Positioning. When characters are written on a screen, the cursor automatically advances one position. However, most video displays can be sent a code that instructs it to move the cursor to a specific position on the screen.

☐ **TABLE 16.1**   **Controlling Text Display Characteristics**

Characteristics	IBM PC	Radio Shack	Apple
Clear screen and home cursor	CLS	CLS	HOME
Start flashing	COLOR 18, 0		FLASH
End flashing			NORMAL
Start reverse video	COLOR 0, 2		INVERSE
End reverse video	COLOR 2, 0		NORMAL
Cursor movement:			
Up	CHR$(30)		CHR$(27) + "D"
Down	CHR$(31)		CHR$(27) + "C"
Left	CHR$(29)	CHR$(24)	CHR$(27) + "B"
Right	CHR$(28)	CHR$(25)	CHR$(27) + "A"
Position cursor at row R, column C	LOCATE (R, C)	PRINT @ 64 * R + C;" "	VTAB R HTAB C
"Read" current position of the cursor:			
Row (vertical)	CRSLIN		PEEK(37)
Column (horizontal)	POS(0)		POS(0)

Programming Text Displays

The BASIC language makes it easy for the programmer to use the electronic characteristics of video displays. But the details generally depend on the computer and the terminal being used. Video display characteristics are set in two ways: (1) A BASIC statement is executed that controls the characteristic—like the statement FLASH on Apple computers; or (2) special control characters are sent to the terminal—like PRINT CHR$(27) + "[" + "A", which moves the cursor up one row for some displays. Most control character sequences begin with CHR$(27). Remember, this code designates the character (which happens to have no graphic representation) whose ASCII code is 27.

Table 16.1 lists the codes for controlling various screen characteristics and attributes for the IBM PC, Radio Shack computers, and Apple computers. In the next chapter we will write a program that makes use of some of these capabilities. For now, try a few of these codes in some programs you have already written to see how they work.

Graphics Displays

pixels

screen resolution

Images on a graphics screen are composed of small dots called **pixels** (for **PI**cture × **EL**ements). The **screen resolution** is the number of pixels per row (horizontally) and the number of pixels per column (vertically).

☐ **FIGURE 16.4**   **Bit-Mapped Graphics**

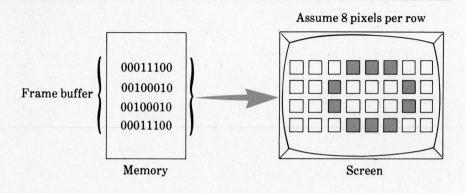

Screen resolution varies from computer to computer and also according to the number of colors being displayed.

An important electronic aspect of a graphics terminal is that the images are taken directly from a portion of memory. Thus a change in this portion of memory causes an immediate change in the screen image. This type of output is called memory-mapped or **bit-mapped output** (Fig. 16.4). The portion of memory that is mapped to the screen is called the **frame buffer**. Thirty times a second the contents of the frame buffer are written to the screen to refresh the fading phosphors.

bit-mapped output

frame buffer

With black and white graphics terminals each bit of each memory compartment in the frame buffer is mapped into one pixel location on the screen. Consider the IBM PC, which has a resolution of 640 × 200 pixels in its high-resolution mode. A pixel can be either black or white. Since there are a total of 128,000 = 640 × 200 pixels and each requires one bit, and since there are 8 bits in a memory compartment, a total of 128,000/8 = 16,000 memory compartments are required for the frame buffer.

Color graphics requires that more than one bit be mapped to a pixel. For example, the medium-resolution graphics mode of the IBM PC allows four colors at any one time. Each color can be represented by two bits: 00, 01, 10, 11. Since the resolution is 320 × 200 = 64,000 pixels, a total of 64,000 × 2 = 128,000 bits are required. Again, 128,000/8 = 16,000 memory compartments are needed for the frame buffer. In general, if the number of memory compartments allocated to the screen is fixed, then more colors mean less resolution.

Some graphics-oriented computers have more than one segment of memory (called pages) that can act as the frame buffer. Thus while one page (the frame buffer) is being displayed, an image on another page can be created. When completed, this new page can be made by the frame buffer. By using these graphics pages, the programmer can create motion on the screen.

Surprisingly, some inexpensive home computers (like Commodore, Atari, Radio Shack Color Computer) have better graphics capabilities than some of the more expensive personal computers (like the Apple IIe and IBM PC). But these graphics capabilities are still very limited. Powerful graphics presentations with motion require enormously fast processing speeds and much memory allocated for graphics pages, features generally not available with the inexpensive home computers. Thus Lucasfilms, Ltd. (producers of the Star Wars films), uses one of the most powerful computers (the Cray II) to produce its graphics screens.

Programming Graphics Displays

text mode
low-resolution mode
high-resolution mode

Graphics-oriented computers usually have at least three modes: a **text mode,** which allows characters to be displayed; a **low-resolution mode,** which allows a good variety of colors; and a **high-resolution mode,** which allows a limited number of colors. The various modes are entered (or activated) by using the appropriate statement; these statements are given in Table 16.2. In the low- and high-level graphics modes you can use the LINE, CIRCLE, DRAW, and PAINT statements, which are also described briefly in Table 16.2.

Table 16.2 lists some of the common graphics statements for the IBM PC and the Radio Shack Color Computer. Since Microsoft wrote the BASIC interpreter for both computers, the commands for both are quite similar. Table 16.3 lists some of the graphics statements for the Apple II and IIe computers.

In these tables the letter v is the vertical position and the letter h is the horizontal position of a pixel. The letter c represents the color.

The purpose of Tables 16.2 and 16.3 is to give you an idea of the structure of the BASIC statements for controlling graphics. You should consult your computer manual for complete details for your system. Then try some of the statements in a program of your own.

16.3 PRINTERS AND OTHER ELECTROMECHANICAL DEVICES

Printers, plotters, and a number of other devices require both electrical and mechanical components. Stepper motors are commonly used to produce motion. Controllers are required to control the stepper motor and other actions of these devices. The following subsections describe these devices in some detail.

Stepper Motors

stepper motor

A **stepper motor** from the outside looks like an ordinary electric motor. However, each time a stepper motor receives a signal, it will rotate only a fraction of one full revolution (take one step). The resolution of a

☐ **TABLE 16.2**   **IBM PC and Radio Shack Color Computer Graphics Statements**

IBM PC	Radio Shack Color Computer	Statement or Function Description
SCREEN 0	SCREEN 0, N (N = color set)	Puts the computer into text mode. The statements applicable in this mode are discussed in Table 16.1.
COLOR f, b	COLOR f, b	Selects the foreground (f) and background (b) colors. This statement is the only statement of the ones described below that can be used in text mode.
SCREEN N Resolution: 1 = 320 × 200 2 = 640 × 200	SCREEN 1 PMODE N, P	Puts the computer into a particular graphics mode.
PSET(v, h, c)	PSET(v, h, c)	Sets a pixel to a specific color.
PRESET(v, h)	PRESET(v, h)	"Resets" a pixel to the background color.
POINT(v, h)	PPOINT(v, h)	Returns the color number of the pixel.
LINE(v1, h1) - (v2, h2), c, BF		Draws a line between the two points. If B is used, a box is drawn. If F is used, the box is filled in with the color c.
CIRCLE(v, h), r, c		Draws a circle.
DRAW "BM128, 96; U25; R25; D25; L25"		Draws a "line" according to the commands in the string. This statement is very useful for drawing your own shapes. Consult your manual for details on the available commands.
PAINT(v, h), c, b		"Paints" a portion of the screen with the color c, starting at the pixel (v, h) and stopping at a border that is of color b.
GET		Saves a portion of the screen in an array.
PUT		Puts the contents of an array onto the screen.

stepper motor is the number of steps in one complete revolution. Two hundred and 400 steps are quite common. These steps can be geared up or down, depending on the application. Two stepper motors are illustrated in Fig. 16.5; these motors are producing the movement of the platen and of the print head.

Printers

printers

Printers are rather complex devices and require complex controllers. One of my current printers (an NEC 5530) has more chips than my computer!

All printers produce two types of movement: The platen rotates to move the paper, and the printing head moves horizontally across the page to position characters appropriately. This movement is produced by stepper motors, as illustrated in Fig. 16.5. The stepper motors can

☐ **TABLE 16.3**   **Apple II and IIe Graphics Statements**

Statement or Function	Description
TEXT	Puts the computer into text mode. The statements applicable in text mode are discussed in Table 16.1.
Low-resolution graphics:	
GR	Puts the computer into the low-resolution graphics mode: 40 × 40 pixels with four lines of text at the bottom.
COLOR = c	Sets the current active color: $0 <= c <= 15$.
PLOT h, v	Sets the pixel with coordinates (h, v) to the current active color.
SCRN h, v	Returns the color value of the pixel with coordinates (h, v).
VLIN v1, v2 AT h	Draws a vertical line at horizontal coordinate h from vertical coordinate v1 to vertical coordinate v2.
HLIN h1, h2 AT v	Draws a horizontal line at vertical coordinate v from horizontal coordinates h1 to h2.
High-resolution graphics:	
HGR	Sets the computer to high-resolution graphics, page 1. Resolution is 160v × 280h, with four lines of text at the bottom of the screen.
HGR2	Sets the computer to high-resolution graphics, page 2. Resolution is 192v × 280h.
HCOLOR = c	Sets the current active color: $0 <= c <= 7$.
HPLOT h, v	Sets the pixel with coordinates (h, v) to the current active color.
HPLOT h, v TO h1, v1	Draws a line with the current active color between the two pixels.
Shapes	Various shapes can be created and manipulated in the high-resolution graphics mode. This topic is too involved to describe here. Consult your Apple manual.

☐ **FIGURE 16.5**   **Printer Movement Produced by Stepper Motors**

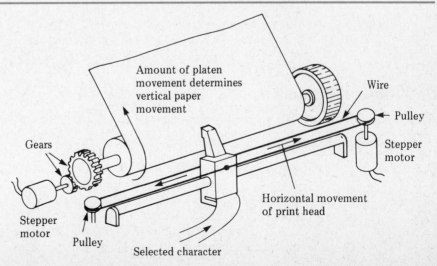

☐ **FIGURE 16.6**   **Print Mechanism for Daisy Wheel and Dot Matrix Printers**

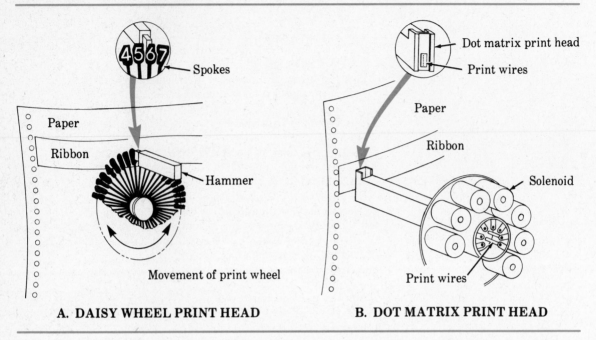

A. DAISY WHEEL PRINT HEAD   **B. DOT MATRIX PRINT HEAD**

take such small steps that the resolution of most printers is 120 vertical positions per inch and 144 horizontal positions per inch.

There are two common types of printers today. One is the *daisy wheel printer* (Fig. 16.6A), which produces "letter quality" output. In the daisy wheel printer each spoke (see Fig. 16.6A) has a raised character, which hits the ribbon when the spoke is struck by a hammer. The second type of printer is the *dot matrix printer* (Fig. 16.6B), which produces characters consisting of small dots. In this printer the wire elements in the printhead strike the ribbon to form a character. Both types of printers are described in more detail in the following subsections.

Daisy Wheel Printers

daisy wheel printer

The printing mechanism of a **daisy wheel printer** (see Fig. 16.6A) consists of a rotating wheel of characters and a hammer. (The wheel looks like the petals of a daisy.) In the printing of a particular character, the wheel is first rotated into position. Then the hammer hits the character, producing the printed character. The maximum speed of a daisy wheel printer is about 60 characters per second. Less expensive daisy wheel printers print at the rate of about 10 characters per second.

Daisy wheel printers have a good amount of intelligence built into them—which is the reason for all the chips in my NEC 5530. One

☐ **FIGURE 16.7**   **Daisy Wheel Printer Output**

```
      This text illustrates boldface
printing, 12 characters per inch, and
a ragged right margin.
```

A. BOLDFACE

```
   This text illustrates proportional
spacing of characters. That is,
narrower characters take up less space
than wide ones.
   Also notice that the right margin is
justified. Justified right is achieved
by the adjustment of spacing between
characters.
```

B. PROPORTIONAL SPACING

way this intelligence is used is to control the force of the hammer in striking a character. For example, it hits the character "." with less force than it uses for a capital H.

Because of the precise movement control of the print head, daisy wheel printers can print text in a number of ways. Figure 16.7A shows boldface characters. The printer produces boldface by first printing the character, then moving the print head a small fraction of an inch to the right and printing the same character again. In this text 12 characters are printed in every inch. Figure 16.7B illustrates proportional spacing of characters. Here the letter i does not take up as much room as other letters, like an h.

The various features of printers are controlled in the same way video screens are controlled—by printing a sequence of control characters, usually beginning with CHR$(27). For example, to have my NEC 5530 advance $\frac{1}{120}$ of an inch, I have to execute the statement

```
LPRINT CHR$(27); "]"; "A"
```

Printer control codes vary widely from printer to printer. Check your manual to see how your printer is controlled.

Dot Matrix Printers

dot matrix printers   The print head mechanism of **dot matrix printers** (see Fig. 16.6B) consists of a number of pins that act as small hammers. In the printing of a character, a particular sequence of pins have to be selected.

□ **FIGURE 16.8**   **Dot Matrix Printer Output**

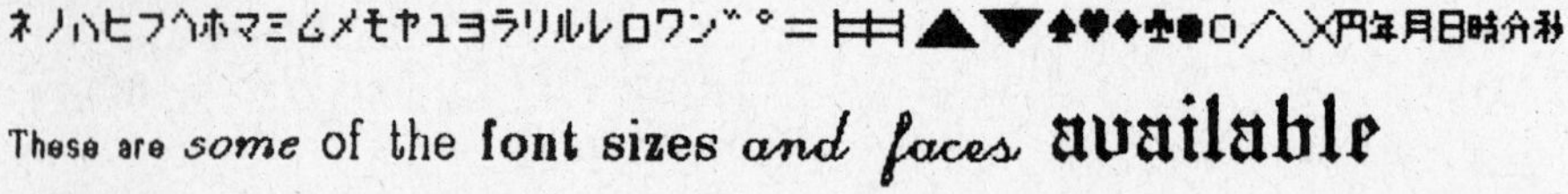

ネノハヒフヘホマミ厶メモヤユヨラリルレロワン゛゜＝Ⅲ▲▼♠♥♦♣●○／＼✕円年月日時分秒

These are *some* of the font sizes *and faces* 𝔞𝔳𝔞𝔦𝔩𝔞𝔟𝔩𝔢

Since there is no daisy wheel to rotate, dot matrix printers are considerably faster than daisy wheel printers. Also, because print head movement and individual print pins can be controlled precisely, the programmer can produce a variety of outputs. Some are illustrated in Fig. 16.8.

Programming Printers

Printer characteristics are controlled by the executing program. Sequences of control characters are sent to the printer, as illustrated by the program in Fig. 16.9, lines 400–440. Since a wide range of printers can be attached to a computer, and since each printer recognizes different control codes, you must read your printer manual to determine the control sequences that control different characteristics.

□ **FIGURE 16.9**   **Program for Setting Printer Characteristics**

```
100 LET R = 1
110 IF R = 0 THEN 1000
200  PRINT "THIS PROGRAM SETS PRINT FORMAT"
210  PRINT
220  PRINT "OPTIONS:"
230  PRINT " 0 - EXIT"
240  PRINT " 1 - PICA PITCH"
250  PRINT " 2 - ELITE PITCH"
260  PRINT " 3 - COMPRESSED, 17 CPI"
270  PRINT " 4 - BOLD SET"
280  PRINT " 5 - BOLD CLEAR"
300  INPUT "WHICH";R
400  IF R = 1 THEN LPRINT CHR$(27); CHR$(78)
410  IF R = 2 THEN LPRINT CHR$(27); CHR$(69)
420  IF R = 3 THEN LPRINT CHR$(27); CHR$(81)
430  IF R = 4 THEN LPRINT CHR$(27); CHR$(33)
440  IF R = 5 THEN LPRINT CHR$(27); CHR$(34)
500 GOTO 110
600 END
```

□ **FIGURE 16.10**   **Pen Plotter**

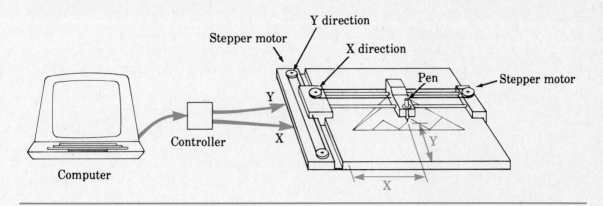

Note that the differences in printer control codes can be a problem in purchasing a word processing program. The word processor must be flexible enough to be given the control codes for your printer.

Plotters

pen plotter

A **pen plotter** is controlled by two stepper motors, as illustrated in Fig. 16.10. In addition to moving in the X and Y directions, the pen can be lifted off the page. Sending specific codes to the plotter causes short steps to be taken in the X and/or Y directions, producing a vertical, a horizontal, or a diagonal line. Two important characteristics of plotters are the resolution (the shortest movement in the X and Y directions) and the speed with which a line can be drawn.

If the computer you are using has a plotter, check the user manual. The manual will list the control codes needed to drive the plotter. Some manuals have listings of BASIC subroutines that can be called to perform various common jobs such as printing pie charts and bar graphs.

16.4 SOUND GENERATION

Speakers for sound generation are becoming popular peripheral devices. Some versions of BASIC (primarily Microsoft BASIC) have specific statements for sending commands to the speaker controller. These statements are listed in Table 16.4.

Controllers and speech generation boards can be attached to computers so that a fixed range of words can be spoken. Again, words are selected by sending the controller a sequence of control characters. Since this application is not used very often, we will not go into the details here.

□ TABLE 16.4   **Statements for Generating Sound in Microsoft BASIC**

Statement	Description
SOUND tone, duration	Generates a sound of a particular tone (0–255) of duration (0–255).
PLAY string	Plays music according to the commands given in the string. The music can be a specified note (A–G or 1–12), octave (O), volume (V), note length (L), tempo (T), and pause (P).

16.5 DATA INPUT DEVICES

The keyboard is probably the most widely used data input device. But there are many other devices that can capture data and send it to a computer, ranging from TV cameras to universal product code scanners at supermarket checkout counters. Also, a variety of sensors can be used to measure the following:

- Counts
- Flow rates
- Force
- Humidity
- Light intensity
- Liquid level
- Moisture
- Motion: linear and circular
- Position
- Pressure
- Proximity
- Radiation
- Temperature
- Thickness
- Time
- Torque

A few of the more common data input devices are described in the following subsections.

Keyboard Input

In BASIC the most common method of entering data is with the INPUT statement. A question mark is displayed on the screen, and then a complete number or string value can be entered. But for some keyboard input this method is not appropriate (see the programs in Chapter 17).

Another way of entering keyboard data is with the INKEY$ (Microsoft BASIC) or the GET (Applesoft BASIC) function. This function accepts the next character typed on the keyboard. The good feature of this method of input is that the key value is not echoed (displayed) on the screen. Consequently, if a graphics image is on the screen, it will not be disturbed. However, if you want to enter an integer, you must "read" the digits one at a time and then construct the final value yourself (see lines 1010–1120 in the program of Fig. 17.3, for example).

□ **FIGURE 16.11**   **Converting Joystick or Mouse Coordinates to Cursor Coordinates on the Screen**

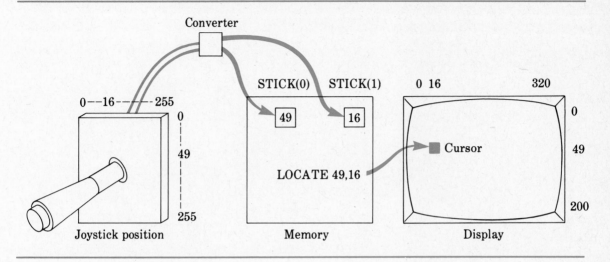

Joystick and Mouse Input

The primary use of joystick and mouse input devices is to pinpoint a position on the screen. As the joystick or mouse is moved up, down, left, and right, a program can read the joystick or mouse coordinates by using the STICK(N), JOYSTK(N), or PDL(N) functions. The program can position the cursor at a corresponding location on the screen by using the LOCATE, PRINT @, or VTAB and HTAB statements on the IBM PC, Radio Shack, or Apple computers, respectively.

Figure 16.11 illustrates the conversion of joystick coordinates to screen coordinates. For example, suppose the joystick is positioned as illustrated in Fig. 16.11 and that this position causes the two joystick functions STICK(0) and STICK(1) to have the values 16 and 49. On the IBM PC the statement

```
LOCATE STICK(0), STICK(1)
```

will cause the cursor to be positioned at column 16 and row 49 on the screen.

You may have noticed one problem with the conversion method illustrated in Fig. 16.11. The joystick coordinates do not correspond exactly to the screen coordinates. Therefore two mathematical functions must be developed that assign horizontal joystick coordinates 0...255 to screen coordinates 0...320 and vertical joystick coordinates 0...255 to screen coordinates 0...200. These two functions are incorporated in the following LOCATE statement:

☐ **FIGURE 16.12** **TV Camera Input**

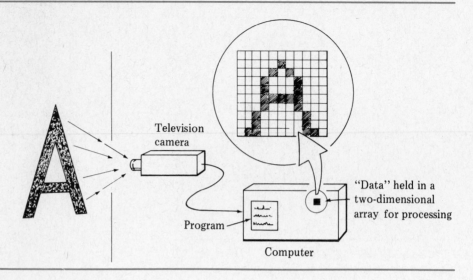

```
LOCATE .78 * STICK(0), 1.255 * STICK(1)
```

TV Camera Input

Figure 16.12 illustrates the process involved in TV camera data input. Converters take the camera signal and route it to an array in main memory. Here a program processes the image by analyzing the compartments of the array in any number of ways. For instance, the program might determine the height of the object, or it might try to determine what letter of the alphabet is being scanned.

Programming
Applications

INTRODUCTION TO CHAPTER 17

Two of the most common types of programs used on microcomputers are spreadsheet calculators (like Visicalc, Multiplan, and Lotus 1,2,3) and word processors (like Easywriter, Peachtext, and Wordstar). In the last three years the sophistication of these programs has increased dramatically. Perhaps your introductory computer course has included some instruction on how to use programs like these.

In this chapter we explain two BASIC programs. One program performs some operations of a spreadsheet calculator. The other performs some operations of a word processor. In both programs cursor positioning plays an important role. It indicates where on the screen the action is to happen. You will see in these programs how the cursor position on the screen is "attached" to values in memory.

17.1 A CURSOR-DIRECTED CALCULATOR

spreadsheet
calculator

A **spreadsheet calculator** is a program that allows the user to modify the values in the cells of a rectangular grid on the screen. Each time a value in a cell is changed, various other values (such as sums, counts,

□ **FIGURE 17.1**   **Initial Screen**

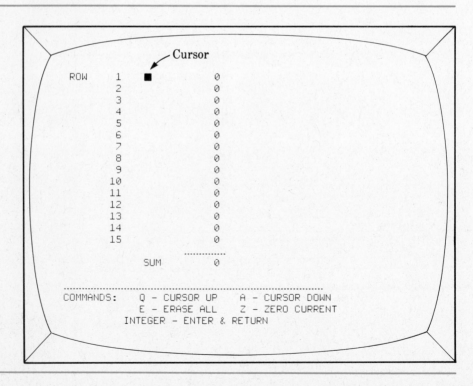

☐ **FIGURE 17.2**   **Program Hierarchy Chart**

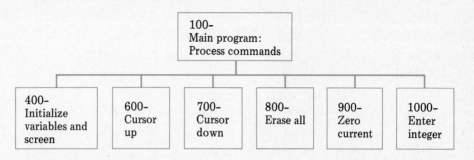

or averages) are recomputed. Organization budgets, for example, can easily be created and modified by using a spreadsheet calculator. Each time a category amount is changed, the various totals are changed.

The following subsections discuss the use and the details of the cursor-directed, spreadsheet calculator.

Using the Program

The screen in Fig. 17.1 is produced by the program given in the next subsection (Fig. 17.3). Let's explain what can be done with this screen.

After the initial screen is displayed, the cursor is positioned at row 1, as indicated in Fig. 17.1. From this point on you can move the cursor up or down. At any point you may enter a command or an integer followed by a RETURN.

An integer is entered at the current position of the cursor, replacing the current value in the row. After the value is entered, the SUM (at the bottom of the screen) is adjusted to be the sum of the values in the column.

When key E is pressed, all elements are zeroed (erased) so that the user may begin on a new total.

When key Z is pressed, the value at the current cursor position is zeroed.

Program Details

The overall structure of the program is illustrated by the hierarchy chart in Fig. 17.2. As shown in the chart, the subroutine beginning at line 400 initializes the variables and the screen. Cursor movement is provided by the subroutines beginning at lines 600 and 700. Other subroutines erase the values, zero the current values, and let the user enter integer values.

The cursor-directed calculator program is given in Fig. 17.3. In the program the screen layout is displayed in lines 470–560. After the

□ **FIGURE 17.3**   **Cursor-Directed Calculator Program**

```
70 REM --- CURSOR CONTROL CHARACTERS ---
80 UP$ = CHR$(30)    : REM CURSOR UP CODE
90 DN$ = CHR$(31)    : REM CURSOR DOWN CODE
95                                                          REM
100 GOSUB 400       : REM -- INITIALIZE VARIABLES AND SCREEN
110                                                         REM
120 REM --------    BEGIN MAIN LOOP    --------
130 Z$ = INKEY$
140 REM -- CASE --
150    IF Z$ = "" THEN 130
160    IF Z$ = "Q" THEN GOSUB 610 : GOTO 220
170    IF Z$ = "A" THEN GOSUB 710 : GOTO 220
180    IF Z$ = "E" THEN GOSUB 810 : GOTO 220
190    IF Z$ = "Z" THEN GOSUB 910 : GOTO 220
200    IF "0" <= Z$ AND Z$ <= "9" THEN GOSUB 1010 : GOTO 220
210    IF Z$ = "X" THEN STOP
220 GOTO 130
230                                                         REM
400 REM --- INITIALIZE VARIABLES AND SCREEN ---
410    DIM X(15)
420    FOR I = 1 TO 15
430       LET X(I) = 0
440    NEXT I
450    SUM = 0
460                                                         REM
470    CLS
480    LOCATE 1,1  : PRINT "ROW";
490    FOR I = 1 TO 15
500       LOCATE I,8   : PRINT I;
505       LOCATE I,20  : PRINT USING "#####"; X(I);
510    NEXT I
515    LOCATE 16,20    : PRINT "------";
520    LOCATE 17,10    : PRINT "SUM";
525    LOCATE 17,20    : PRINT USING "#####"; SUM;
530    LOCATE 20,0
535    PRINT "---------------------------------------------"
540    PRINT "COMMANDS: Q - CURSOR UP, A - CURSOR DOWN"
550    PRINT "          E - ERASE ALL, Z - ZERO CURRENT"
560    PRINT "          INTEGER - ENTER AND RETURN";
570                                                         REM
575    LOCATE 1,12
580    LET P = 1 : REM INITIALIZE POSITION
585 RETURN
590                                                         REM
600 REM --- CURSOR UP ---
610  IF P = 1 THEN 640
620     LET P = P - 1
630     PRINT UP$;
640   RETURN
```

computer clears the screen, characters are printed at specific positions by using the LOCATE command (in Microsoft and IBM PC BASIC). For example, LOCATE 2, 3 positions the cursor at vertical (row) 2 and horizontal (column) 3. To obtain these results on TRS-80 computers, you would use the PRINT @ statement. On Apple computers you would use the VTAB and HTAB statements.

☐ **FIGURE 17.3**   **(Continued)**

```
650                                          REM
700 REM --- CURSOR DOWN ---
710   IF P = 15 THEN 740
720     LET P = P + 1
730     PRINT DN$;
740   RETURN
750                                          REM
800 REM --- ERASE ALL ---
810   FOR I = 1 TO 15
812     LET X(I) = 0
814       LOCATE I,20  : PRINT USING "#####"; X(I);
816   NEXT I
820   SUM = 0
840   LOCATE 17,20   : PRINT USING "#####"; SUM;
850   LOCATE 1,12
860   LET P = 1
880 RETURN
890                                          REM
900 REM --- ZERO CURRENT POSITION ---
910   LET SUM = SUM - X(P)
920   LET X(P) = 0
930     LOCATE P,20   : PRINT USING "#####"; X(P);
940     LOCATE 17,20  : PRINT USING "#####"; SUM;
950     LOCATE P,12
960 RETURN
970                                          REM
1000 REM --- ENTER DIGITS ---
1010  VL = VAL(Z$)
1020  PRINT Z$;
1025  Z$ = ""
1030  Z$ = INKEY$
1040  IF Z$ = "" THEN 1030
1050  IF Z$ < "0" OR "9" < Z$ THEN 1200
1060    PRINT Z$;
1070    VL = 10*VL + VAL(Z$)
1100    Z$ = INKEY$
1110    IF Z$ = "" THEN 1100
1120  GOTO 1050
1130                                         REM
1200  SUM = SUM - X(P)
1210  X(P) = VL
1220  SUM = SUM + X(P)
1230  LOCATE P,20  : PRINT USING "#####"; X(P);
1240  LOCATE 17,20 : PRINT USING "#####"; SUM;
1250  LOCATE P,12  : PRINT "         ";
1260  LET P = P + 1
1270  LOCATE P,12
1280 RETURN
2000 END
```

The array X( ) holds the 15 different integer values. Notice that this array is initialized to zero at line 430.

All commands and integers are entered by way of the INKEY$ function. (The GET statement would be used in Applesoft BASIC.) Notice that commands are read in line 130 and decoded in lines 150–210.

As you can see, once the command is recognized, a subroutine is performed to carry out the intent of the command. For example, if a Q is entered, this value is recognized in line 160, whereupon the subroutine at line 610 is executed. Notice that the current cursor position in the array is decreased by one (line 620), and then the statement PRINT UP$ is executed. The variable UP$ has been initialized in line 80 to hold the control code that moves the cursor up one position.

All cursor movement causes an adjustment in variable P, which points to the current array component. In this way the program keeps track of which array component is being referenced.

Notice how the program reads an integer (lines 1000–1120). It reads one digit at a time. Each digit is converted to its integer form and added to the current value of the integer entered so far.

EXERCISES

17.1. Explain how the program in Fig. 17.3 converts a sequence of digits to an integer. Can you think of another way to convert digits to a number?

17.2. Modify the program in Fig. 17.3 so that it will accept negative integers.

17.3. Modify the program in Fig. 17.3 so that two columns of values may be entered. Dimension X to X(15, 2).

17.4. Modify the program in Fig. 17.3 so that it will accept decimal numbers.

17.5. Modify the program in Fig. 17.3 so that you can enter up to 100 numbers in the array. You will have to make the program display the "active" portion of the array.

□ **FIGURE 17.4**   **Line Processor Screen**

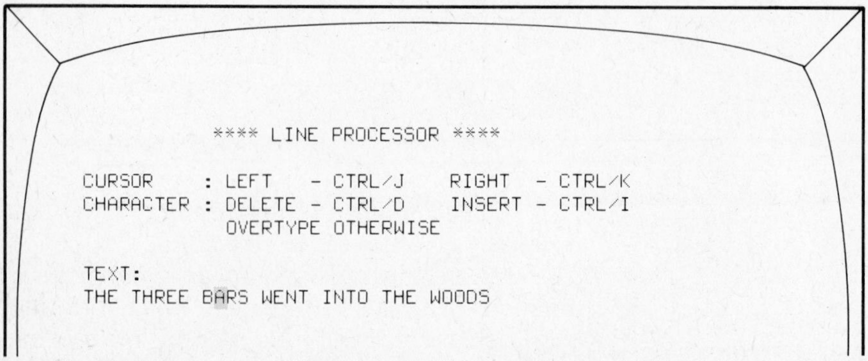

```
            **** LINE PROCESSOR ****

CURSOR    : LEFT   - CTRL/J    RIGHT  - CTRL/K
CHARACTER : DELETE - CTRL/D    INSERT - CTRL/I
            OVERTYPE OTHERWISE

TEXT:
THE THREE BARS WENT INTO THE WOODS
```

17.6. Add additional commands to the program in Fig. 17.3 so that you can save data to a data file and then retrieve it.

17.2 A LINE PROCESSOR

word processor

A **word processor** is a program that allows the user to create, edit, and then print practically any form of text, such as a letter, poem, report, or even a full-length book. In the following subsections we describe a short program that allows you to create and edit a line of text. This program will give you some idea of how a word processor performs its magic.

Using the Program

The line-processing program (presented in the next subsection) assists you in creating a line of text. By positioning the cursor to a particular point in the line, you can make a change. You may either overtype the current character, delete the character, or insert a character.

The screen in Fig. 17.4 shows a typical screen for the program. In this screen the word BARS is incorrect (it should be BEARS). So the cursor has been positioned over the A in BARS. Pressing CTRL/I shifts the line from this point to the right one position. The E can then be typed. If you want to change THREE to FOUR, you can position the cursor over the T of THREE and then type FOUR. To delete the dangling E, type CTRL/D.

Program Details

The structure of the program is illustrated by the hierarchy chart in Fig. 17.5. Again, subroutines initialize the variables, move the cursor, and allow the user to edit and correct text lines.

The line processor program is given in Fig. 17.6. In the program the primary data structure is the array L$( ), line 510, which holds up to 75 characters in the line. Variable P (line 710) points to the current array compartment referenced by the cursor. Variable N (line 560) holds the number of characters currently in the line array L$.

As in the previous program, the LOCATE statement (line 660) positions the cursor to the appropriate positions for printing.

The commands are again read by the INKEY$ function (line 120) and recognized in lines 140–190. The forms of the commands are necessarily a bit complicated, for the following reason: On most computers the arrow keys generate two character control codes, which are impossible to read with the INKEY$ function. Thus the alternative of holding down the CTRL key and pressing another key is used. This manipulation generates a single-character control code. The ASC func-

□ **FIGURE 17.5**   **Program Hierarchy Chart**

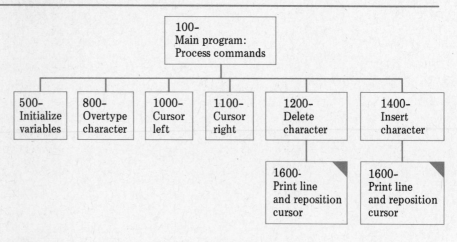

tion is then used to convert the control code to its corresponding ASCII code representation.

On the IBM PC, holding down the CTRL key and pressing the following letters produces characters that have the following ASCII code:

CTRL/CHAR	Corresponding ASCII Code
CTRL/J	10
CTRL/K	11
CTRL/D	4
CTRL/I	9

Thus to recognize the command, the program looks for the above ASCII codes in lines 140–190.

If the next character read lies between a space and Z, then this character indicates an overtype situation. So the character is merely put into the current position of the array and then printed. Of course, the cursor positioned in the array is incremented by one.

The cursor-left (subroutine 1000) and cursor-right (subroutine 1100) commands are easily implemented, as you can see from the corresponding code. The delete-character command (subroutine 1200) is implemented by shifting elements in the array down one compartment onto the character being deleted.

The insert-character command (subroutine 1400) is implemented by shifting all the characters from the current position up one compartment. Then the user enters the new character into the open position. Notice how the line is reprinted and how the cursor is repositioned in the subroutine beginning at line 1600.

☐ **FIGURE 17.6**   **Line Processor Program**

```
40 REM --- CURSOR CONTROL CHARACTERS ---
50 RT$ = CHR$(28)     : REM CURSOR RIGHT
60 LF$ = CHR$(29)     : REM CURSOR LEFT
70                                                    REM
100 GOSUB 500 : REM -- INITIALIZE SCREEN AND VARIABLES
105                                                   REM
110 REM ---------   BEGIN MAIN LOOP ---------
120 Z$ = INKEY$
130    REM ---- CASE ----
140     IF Z$ = "" THEN 120
150     IF " " <= Z$ AND Z$ <= "Z" THEN GOSUB 810 : GOTO 200
160     IF ASC(Z$) = 10 THEN GOSUB 1000 : GOTO 200
170     IF ASC(Z$) = 11 THEN GOSUB 1100 : GOTO 200
180     IF ASC(Z$) = 4  THEN GOSUB 1200 : GOTO 200
190     IF ASC(Z$) = 9  THEN GOSUB 1410 : GOTO 200
195    REM --- ENDCASE ---
200 GOTO 120
210                                                   REM
500 REM --- INTIALIZE VARIABLES & SCREEN ---
510     DIM L$(75) : REM -- ONE LINE OF CHARACTERS --
520     FOR I = 1 TO 75
530        LET L$(I) = " "
540     NEXT I
550                                                   REM
560   LET N = 0           : REM NUMBER OF CHARS IN LINE
570                                                   REM
600   CLS
602   PRINT "            **** LINE PROCESSOR ****"
604   PRINT
610   PRINT "CURSOR    : LEFT  - CTRL/J,  RIGHT  - CTRL/K"
620   PRINT "CHARACTER : DELETE - CTRL/D,  INSERT - CTRL/I"
630   PRINT "            OVERTYPE OTHERWISE"
640   PRINT
650   PRINT "TEXT:"
660   LOCATE 8,1
670   FOR I = 1 TO 75
680      PRINT L$(I);
690   NEXT I
700                                                   REM
710   LET P = 1           : REM INITIALIZE CURSOR POSITION
720   LOCATE 8,P     : REM POSITION CURSOR
740 RETURN
750                                                   REM
800 REM --- OVERTYPE ---
810     PRINT Z$;
825     IF N < P THEN N = N + 1
830     LET L$(P) = Z$
835     LET P = P + 1
840    RETURN
900                                                   REM
1000 REM --- CURSOR LEFT ---
1010    PRINT LF$;
1020    LET P = P - 1
1030   RETURN
1040                                                  REM
1100 REM --- CURSOR RIGHT ---
1110    PRINT RT$;
1120    LET P = P + 1
1130   RETURN
```

(continued)

□ **FIGURE 17.6**   **(Continued)**

```
1140                                                           REM
1200 REM --- DELETE A CHARACTER ---
1210     FOR I = P + 1 TO N        : REM SHIFT DOWN
1220       L$(I-1) = L$(I)
1230     NEXT I
1240     L$(N) = " "
1250     LET N = N - 1
1260     GOSUB 1600              : REM PRINT LINE &
1270                             : REM REPOSITION CURSOR
1295   RETURN
1300                                                           REM
1400 REM --- INSERT A CHARACTER ---
1410     FOR I = N TO P STEP -1 : REM SHIFT UP
1420       L$(I+1) = L$(I)
1430     NEXT I
1440     L$(P) = " "
1450     LET N = N + 1           : REM UP COUNT
1460     GOSUB 1600              : REM PRINT LINE &
1470                             : REM REPOSITION CURSOR
1480                             REM
1500     Z$ = INKEY$             : REM WAIT FOR CHAR
1510     IF Z$ = "" THEN 1500
1520     PRINT Z$;
1530     LET L$(P) = Z$
1540     LET P = P + 1
1550   RETURN
1560                                                           REM
1600 REM --- PRINT LINE & POSITION CURSOR ---
1610     LOCATE 8,1
1620     FOR I = 1 TO 75
1630       PRINT L$(I);
1640     NEXT I
1650     LOCATE 8,P
1660   RETURN
2000 END
```

EXERCISES

17.7. The line processor does no checking on the cursor position. Modify the program in Fig. 17.6 so that the cursor cannot move beyond the beginning or end of the line.

17.8. Inserting a word into the line is a very awkward process with the program in Fig. 17.6. Modify the program so that once you are in the insert mode, you stay there until you press another CTRL sequence, such as CTRL/X. How should the new characters be stored? Where should the characters in the line beyond the current position be stored? There are a variety of ways that this storage can be implemented. Investigate at least two different methods before proceeding to program one of them.

APPENDICES

Print Using Statement

INTRODUCTION TO APPENDIX A

The PRINT USING statement gives the programmer complete control over the form of each printed line. This statement is discussed here in the Appendix so that it can be covered at any time after the fourth chapter.

Some versions of BASIC, such as Applesoft BASIC, do not have the PRINT USING statement. In the absence of it, you can use, in the form of a subroutine, the program given in Chapter 4, Exercise 4.23, to align numeric values on the decimal point.

A.1 THE NEED FOR THE PRINT USING STATEMENT

In Section 3.5 you learned how to influence the form of the printed line by using the following:

- Commas, to align items according to zones.
- Semicolons, to print items next to each other.
- TAB( ), to align items in specific columns.

In addition, with the use of the INT( ) function, numbers can be rounded to a specific number of places.

One thing we have not insisted on is aligning columns of numbers at the decimal point. For example, an output for the program listed in Exercise 3.15 might look like the output shown in Fig. A.1. These values are not easy to read because the numbers are not aligned on the right or on the decimal point.

PRINT USING
statement

The **PRINT USING statement** will make output like that of Fig. A.1 much more readable. Specifically, two useful features of the PRINT USING statement are as follows:

1. Columns of numbers are aligned according to the decimal point.
2. Numbers are automatically rounded.

□ **FIGURE A.1**   **Printout with Numbers Unaligned at the Decimal Point**

```
                        SUMMER TRIPS
                        GAS COSTS

        NAME    MPG    DISTANCE      GAS COST

        TOM     23     2400          130.4348
        PETE    45     5000          138.8889
        KAREN   30     15000         625
        KEN     70     4900          87.5
        EDWARD  103    56            .6796116
        DOUG    9      67543         9380.972

        DONE
```

A.2 AN EXAMPLE

The program in Fig. A.2A illustrates how to control the printed results by using the PRINT USING statement. Compare the output of this program (Fig. A.2B) with that in Fig. A.1.

The crucial statements in this program are

```
120  L4$ = "\    \ ###    ####,###    #####.##"
330  PRINT USING L4$; N$, M, D, C
```

format string

format fields

The string in line 120 is called a **format string** because it specifies the format or positions of the values to be printed. The sequences of special characters are called **format fields**. Format fields have the following form:

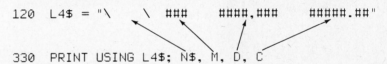

	Field 1	Field 2	Field 3	Field 4
	\ \	###	####,###	#####.##
	String format field	Numeric format fields		

This format string is used by the PRINT USING statement in line 330. When line 330 is executed, the system will first determine the one-to-one correspondence between variables and format fields:

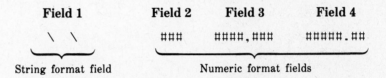

```
120  L4$ = "\    \ ###    ####,###    #####.##"


330  PRINT USING L4$; N$, M, D, C
```

Then the values of the variables will be inserted into the corresponding fields, and the string will be printed.

A number is always aligned with the decimal point in the format field. A string is always left-justified in the string format field.

Lines 100 through 120 of Fig. A.2A illustrate another good reason for using the PRINT USING statement. By using string variables to hold titles, headers, and format strings, you can easily generate attractive report forms without using printer-spacing charts.

Line 410 illustrates that the string can be included directly in the PRINT USING statement. Also notice that characters can be included in the format string to generate labels.

A.3 NUMERIC FORMAT FIELDS

numeric format field

A **numeric format field** consists of at most one decimal point and one or more # characters. A numeric format field may also contain dollar signs and commas. The features and limitations of the numeric format field are described below.

☐ **FIGURE A.2**   **Example of the PRINT USING Statement**

```
100 L1$ = "              SUMMER TRIPS"
105 L2$ = "               GAS COSTS"
110 L3$ = "NAME    MPG      DISTANCE     GAS COST"
120 L4$ = "\     \    ###     ####,###     #####.##"
125                                          REM
130 LET P = 1.25      : REM ASSUMED GAS PRICE
140                                          REM
145 LET T = 0
150 PRINT L1$
160 PRINT L2$
170 PRINT " "
200 PRINT L3$
210 PRINT " "
220                              REM
230 READ N$, M, D
240                              REM
300 IF N$ = "ZZZ" THEN 400
310    LET G = D/M
320    LET C = P * G
325    LET T = T + C
330    PRINT USING L4$;N$, M, D, C
340                              REM
350    READ N$, M, D
360 GOTO 300
370                              REM
400 PRINT " "
410 PRINT USING "TOTAL COST   $$#####,###.##"; T
420 STOP
430                              REM
800 REM --- CONSTANT DATA FILE ---
810 DATA "TOM",    23, 2400
820 DATA "PETE",   45, 5000
830 DATA "KAREN", 30, 15000
840 DATA "KEN",    70, 4900
850 DATA "EDWARD",103, 56
860 DATA "DOUG",   9, 67543
900 DATA "ZZZ",    0,  0
999 END
```

A. PROGRAM

```
RUN
            SUMMER TRIPS
            GAS COSTS

NAME    MPG     DISTANCE     GAS COST

TOM      23       2,400       130.43
PETE     45       5,000       138.89
KAREN    30      15,000       625.00
KEN      70       4,900        87.50
EDWAR   103          56         0.68
DOUG      9      67,543      9380.97

TOTAL COST      $10,363.48
```

B. OUTPUT

- When a value is assigned to a numeric field, it is right-justified if the field does not have a decimal point. The symbol b̸ is used to indicate that a blank is actually printed.

EXAMPLE

```
100   LET X = 45
200   PRINT USING "ANSWER = #####", X
999   END
RUN

ANSWER = b̸b̸b̸45
```

- When a value is assigned to a numeric field that has a decimal point, it is aligned according to the decimal point. If there are more digits to the right of the decimal point than there are # signs, the number is *rounded*.

EXAMPLE

```
100   LET X = 345.678
200   PRINT USING "ANSWER = ####.##", X
999   END
RUN

ANSWER =  345.68
```

- If a numeric format field is too small for the value that is to be printed, the number is printed but preceded by a % sign.

EXAMPLE

```
100   LET X = 345.67
200   PRINT USING "ANSWER = ##.##", X
999   END
RUN

ANSWER = %345.67
```

- One or more commas may be included in a numeric field to the left of the decimal point. The computer will insert commas every three digits to make the number easy to read.

EXAMPLE

```
100   LET X = 45638456
200   PRINT USING "ANSWER = ###,###,###", X
999   END
RUN

ANSWER =  45,638,456
```

☐ **FIGURE A.3**   **Use of String Format Fields**

```
100   LET A$ = "BASIC"
110   LET B$ = "COMPUTING"
200   PRINT USING "!" , A$
210   PRINT USING "\\" , A$
220   PRINT USING "\    \",A$
230   PRINT USING "\        \", B$
999   END
RUN


B
BA
BASIC
COMPUTING
```

■ If a numeric field begins with $$, a dollar sign will be printed immediately preceding the first digit.

☐ **EXAMPLE**

```
100   LET X = 34.70
110   LET Y = 348.45
200   PRINT USING "BALANCE = $$###.##", X
210   PRINT USING "BALANCE = $$###.##", Y
999   END
RUN

BALANCE =    $34.70
BALANCE =   $348.45
```

A.4 STRING FORMAT FIELDS

string format field   A **string format field** of one character is indicated by an exclamation point. A string format field of two or more characters is indicated by spaces between two backslashes (\) for Microsoft and PDP–11 BASIC. A percent sign (%) is used on TRS–80 computers. Each backslash or percent sign counts as a space.

　　　　String constants are left-justified in the format fields. If a string is too large for the string field, characters on the right are dropped.

　　　　Figure A.3 illustrate various string format fields. Compare the program statements with the run of the program.

Representation
of
Data

INTRODUCTION TO APPENDIX B

This appendix provides some background information that will help you understand how computers store and manipulate data. We describe how numbers and characters are stored in main memory and how numbers and characters are represented so that they may be recognized and stored by the computer.

B.1 MAIN MEMORY AND BASIC VARIABLES

The smallest data value that can be stored in a computer is represented in memory by the presence or absence of an electrical current or by one of two magnetic orientations. That is, each bit of memory is capable of being in one of two states. For convenience, the symbols 0 and 1 are used to represent these two states. Consequently, to represent any data value in a computer, we must store the data as a sequence of two states, for example, 0101101.

Rather than manipulating each bit, computers manipulate bits in groups of a fixed size. Some computers treat the bits in groups of 8. Such a computer is called an 8-bit computer. Other computers treat the bits in groups of 16, 32, 48, or 64 bits. Each group of bits is called a **word.** The **word length** is the number of bits in a word.

word
word length

If we are to reference a computer word, each memory location must have a name. If the computer has M memory locations, the numbers from 0 to $M - 1$ are customarily used to identify locations. These numbers are called **addresses:**

address

Address	←— n Bits —→	
0	010 ... 100	Word 0
1	110 ... 001	Word 1
$M - 1$	010 ... 010	Word $M - 1$

In BASIC the contents of memory compartments are referenced through variable names rather than numeric addresses. Since most microcomputers have 8-bit memory compartments, not much informa-

VARPTR

tion can be stored with so few bits. Consequently, a BASIC variable name usually corresponds to several consecutive memory compartments.

An interesting function, VARPTR, exists in Microsoft BASIC (on TRS–80 and IBM PC computers). **VARPTR** (variable) returns, for some variable types, the decimal address corresponding to the variable.

With the use of VARPTR and PEEK functions, you can verify just about all the claims made in this appendix about the representation of data in memory.

B.2 THE REPRESENTATION OF NUMBERS

Numbers are stored in memory as binary numbers. But integers and decimal numbers are stored in slightly different ways, as described in the following subsections.

Positive and Negative Integers

As mentioned above, integers are stored in computers as binary numbers. Here are some integers and their binary equivalents:

Decimal Integer	Binary Equivalent	Decimal Integer	Binary Equivalent
7	0111	−1	1111
6	0110	−2	1110
5	0101	−3	1101
4	0100	−4	1100
3	0011	−5	1011
2	0010	−6	1010
1	0001	−7	1001
0	0000	−8	1000

If a computer were limited to 4-bit words, these are all the integers that could be represented.

Had you the choice, you probably would not have used this method to represent negative numbers. For instance, in this scheme the binary representation of a negative number is larger than the binary representation of a positive number. Nevertheless, this method is very common in computers. It is called the **two's complement** representation.

two's complement

☐ RULE

To find the binary representation of a negative integer, complement (that is, change 0s to 1s and 1s to 0s) the digits in binary representation of the positive integer and add 1.

☐ EXAMPLE

The binary representation of 5 is 0101.
Complement the digits to get   1010
Add 1   +   1
The binary representation of −5 is   1011

There are advantages and disadvantages of the two's complement representation. The disadvantage is to determine which of two
numbers is the larger, the computer must first compare the leftmost
digit for the signs of the two integers. If the signs are the same, the rest
of the binary representation must be compared. Otherwise, it is clear
which is smaller.

The advantage of the scheme is that addition is the same for
both positive and negative integers. Examine the following additions to
verify this statement. (*Note:* We assume that you are familiar with
binary arithmetic.)

Human Addition	Computer Addition	
3	0011	
+2	0010	
5	0101	
−3	1101	Since only 4 bits
+3	0010	are considered, the
0	① 0000	leftmost is dropped
−1	1111	
−3	1101	
−4	① 1100	

Many inexpensive computers can perform only addition. To subtract one number from another, the computer finds the negative representation of one and then adds it to the other. Multiplication is repeated
addition. Division is repeated subtraction.

To convert a value from binary representation to integer decimal
form, we use the following expression:

8 bits

b_7	b_6	b_5	b_4	b_3	b_2	b_1	b_0

The integer decimal value is

$$b_7 * 2^7 + \cdots + b_1 * 2^1 + b_0 * 2^0$$

For example,

$$10101011 \quad \text{is} \quad 1 * 2^7 + 1 * 2^5 + 1 * 2^3 + 1 * 2^1 + 1 * 2^0 = 171$$

Fractional Decimal Numbers

The representation of fractional decimal numbers is quite involved. Essentially, the computer must convert such a number to what you might call binary scientific notation. For example, the decimal number 27.6 can first be written as $0.276 * 10^2$. To represent this number in memory, the computer must represent the base (0.276) and the exponent (2) in binary. Now given two such decimal numbers, to add them, the computer must manipulate four binary values. Consequently, decimal arithmetic takes longer than integer arithmetic.

EXERCISES

B.1.   Convert the binary number 0101010 to an integer decimal value.

B.2.   Suppose that the memory locations of a computer consist of 8 bits and that BASIC uses three memory locations per variable. What are the largest and smallest integers that can be represented in BASIC?

B.3.   Write a program that converts values from decimal to binary representation, and from binary to decimal.

B.4.   Write a program that simulates binary arithmetic bit by bit.

B.5.   Why do some versions of BASIC allow the programmer to make a distinction between integer variables, such as A%, and decimal variables?

B.3 THE REPRESENTATION OF CHARACTERS

Numbers are naturally stored in memory with their binary representation. But how is a letter like A stored? It, like any other value, must be stored as a sequence of 0s and 1s. The following subsections describe how characters and strings are coded for representation in the computer.

The ASCII Code

ASCII code

The most commonly used code for representing characters is the 7-bit **ASCII code** (American Standards Committee on Information Interchange). For example:

Decimal Equivalent of the ASCII Code	ASCII Code for the Character	Character
36	00100100	$
65	01000001	A
90	01011010	Z

The entire ASCII code is given in Table B.1. The meaning of the first 32 codes usually varies with the particular computer.

☐ **TABLE B.1**   **The 7-Bit ASCII Code**

Control Codes

ASCII Decimal Number	Character	Meaning	ASCII Decimal Number	Character	ASCII Decimal Number	Character	ASCII Decimal Number	Character
0	NUL	Null	32	SP	64	@	96	`
1	SOH	Start of heading	33	!	65	A	97	a
2	STX	Start of text	34	"	66	B	98	b
3	ETX	End of text	35	#	67	C	99	c
4	EOT	End of transmission	36	$	68	D	100	d
5	ENQ	Enquiry	37	"	69	E	101	e
6	ACK	Acknowledgment	38	&	70	F	102	f
7	BEL	Bell	39	'	71	G	103	g
8	BS	Backspace	40	(	72	H	104	h
9	HT	Horizontal tab	41	)	73	I	105	i
10	LF	Line feed	42	*	74	J	106	j
11	VT	Vertical tab	43	+	75	K	107	k
12	FF	Form feed	44	,	76	L	108	l
13	CR	Carriage return	45	–	77	M	109	m
14	SO	Shift out	46	.	78	N	110	n
15	SI	Shift in	47	/	79	O	111	o
16	DLE	Data link escape	48	0	80	P	112	p
17	DC1	Device control 1	49	1	81	Q	113	q
18	DC2	Device control 2	50	2	82	R	114	r
19	DC3	Device control 3	51	3	83	S	115	s
20	DC4	Device control 4	52	4	84	T	116	t
21	NAK	Negative acknowledgment	53	5	85	U	117	u
22	SYN	Synchronous idle	54	6	86	V	118	v
23	ETB	End of transmission block	55	7	87	W	119	w
24	CAN	Cancel	56	8	88	X	120	x
25	EM	End of medium	57	9	89	Y	121	y
26	SUB	Substitute	58	:	90	Z	122	z
27	ESC	Escape	59	;	91	[	123	{
28	FS	File separator	60	<	92	\	124		
29	GS	Group separator	61	=	93	]	125	}
30	RS	Record separator	62	>	94	^ or ↑	126	~
31	US	Unit separator	63	?	95	← or –	127	DEL

☐ **TABLE B.2**   **BASIC Functions for Converting Characters to ASCII Code**
                        and Vice Versa

Function	Meaning	Example
LET Y = ASC(Q$)	Returns the ASCII code for the first character of the string variable	100 LET Q$ = "HX4190" 110 LET Y = ASC(Q$) 120 PRINT Y 999 END RUN 72 (Code for H)
LET Z$ = CHR$(N)	Returns the character that corresponds to the ASCII code in decimal-equivalent form	100 LET N = 61 110 LET Z$ = CHR$(N) 120 PRINT Z$ 999 END RUN =

Since a memory compartment can hold 8 bits, an additional 127 characters can be represented. Again, the characters used depend on the particular computer. Usually, these characters are graphics characters.

Notice that a digit, such as 5, can be stored as a binary number or as a character. For example:

LET A = 5   Here 5 is considered a number and is stored as a binary number. Thus variable A will contain 00000101.

LET A$ = "5"   Here 5 is considered a character and is stored with its ASCII code. So variable A$ will contain 00110100.

EXERCISE

B.6. Why are arithmetic operations not allowed on digits and numbers that are stored as characters?

String Conversion Functions

Most BASIC systems have the two functions listed in Table B.2 that relate the character to the decimal equivalent of its ASCII code. The examples in the table show how these functions return the ASCII code for a character or return a character for an ASCII code.

To see the graphics characters supported by your computer, run the following program:

```
10   FOR I = 128 to 244
20     PRINT CHR$(I);
30   NEXT I
```

Representation of String Constants

A character is stored in a string variable according to its ASCII code. When more than one character is stored in a string variable, the ASCII codes are placed adjacent to each other and are left-justified. For example, if the computer executes the statement LET Z$ = "F?", then variable Z$ will contain

Variable Z$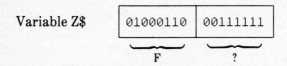

The content of variable Z$ is easier to interpret if the decimal equivalent for the ASCII code is indicated. In this case, think of its contents as

Variable Z$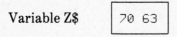

Notice that the ASCII code for nothing is 00. The ASCII code for a space is 32. To see the difference, RUN the following program:

```
100   LET A$ = " "
120   PRINT "HI";A$;"THERE"
999   END
```

Then RUN the program with line 100 changed to

```
100   LET A$ = ""
```

Comparison of Strings. When a computer compares the contents of two string variables, it compares the codes for those characters considered as binary numbers. Thus since the code for "JOHN" is less than the code for "JONES", the relation "JOHN" < "JONES" is true. In fact, from the Table B.2, given two strings, it is easy to establish the relationship between them.

☐ **TABLE B.3**   **BASIC Functions for Converting Numeric Strings to ASCII Code and Vice Versa**

Function	Meaning	Example

`LET Y = VAL(A$)`	VAL returns the numeric value corresponding to the numeric string	`100  LET Y = VAL("23.45")`
		`110  PRINT Y`
		`999  END`
		`RUN`
		
		`   23.45`

`LET Q$ = STR$(R)`	STR$ converts a numeric expression or constant to a string	`100  LET Q$ = STR$(23.45)`
		`110  PRINT Q$`
		`999  END`
		`RUN`
		
		`23.45`

Numeric Strings. A numeric string is a string composed of all digits and, at most, one decimal point. For example, "345.22" is a numeric string. Since this string is stored as a sequence of ASCII codes, the computer cannot do arithmetic on such "numbers." Some BASIC systems have special functions that convert a numeric string to its numeric value and vice versa. These functions are listed in Table B.3 along with examples that show how they operate.

EXERCISES

B.7. Is `"ZZZ"` the same as `"ZZZ "`?

Is `"XA"` the same as `" XA"`?

B.8. Write a program that produces a printout like this:

```
FIRST DATE           SECOND DATE
YEAR MONTH DAY       YEAR MONTH DAY        EARLIEST
--------------------- --------------------- -------------------
1982   04      07    1982   10      28     xxxx  xx   xx
```

First, write the program without using the VAL( ) and STR$( ) functions. Then write the program by using these functions.

A Summary
of
Basic

INTRODUCTION TO APPENDIX C

In the text the BASIC language and the program structures are necessarily described from the bottom up. That is, the various components are described. Then the way they fit together is described.

In this appendix we take the reverse approach and describe BASIC and a typical program structure from the top down. We begin by discussing program and flow control structures. Then we look at statements, expressions, and conditions in BASIC.

C.1 PROGRAM STRUCTURE

BASIC program
statement

A **BASIC program** is composed of statements. A **statement** either performs some action on the data or it controls the execution of other statements that perform actions.

main program
subroutines

A program is usually subdivided into a **main program** and **subroutines**, where each subroutine performs a well-defined task (Fig. C.1A). To document the overall structure of a program, and especially

☐ **FIGURE C.1**   **A Common Program Structure**

```
100   REM MAIN PROGRAM
      Statement
      Statement
      Statement
         GOSUB 2000
      Statement
         GOSUB 3000
      Statement
         GOSUB 4000
      Statement
      Statement
      STOP
2000  REM --- SUBROUTINE A ---
      Statement
      Statement
      RETURN
3000  REM --- SUBROUTINE B ---
      Statement
      Statement
      RETURN
4000  REM --- SUBROUTINE C ---
      Statement
      Statement
      RETURN
10000 END
```

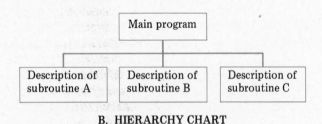

B. HIERARCHY CHART

A. PROGRAM

hierarchy chart

the relationship between the subroutines, the programmer should construct a **hierarchy chart** (Fig. C.1B).

C.2 FLOW CONTROL STRUCTURES

BASIC does not have single statements to implement the important flow control structures, such as the loop structure and the two-way and multiway selections. These flow control structures have to be implemented primarily with the IF and GOTO statements, as described in the following subsections.

Loop Control Structures

pretest loop
posttest loop

The structured-programming method requires that the exit from the loop be either at the top of the loop **(pretest loop)** or at the bottom of the loop **(posttest loop)**. These loops are implemented like this:

<table>
<tr><td>**Pretest Loop**</td><td>**Posttest Loop**</td></tr>
<tr><td>200 IF condition THEN 500</td><td>200 Statement 1</td></tr>
<tr><td>Statement 1</td><td>Statement 2</td></tr>
<tr><td>Statement 2</td><td>IF condition THEN 200</td></tr>
<tr><td>GOTO 200</td><td>500 Statement 3</td></tr>
<tr><td>500 Statement 3</td><td></td></tr>
</table>

In recognition of the loop structure as a fundamental form, some newer versions of BASIC (Microsoft and DEC BASIC) have the following pretest loop:

Pretest Loop, BASIC Extension

200 WHILE condition
    Statement 1
    Statement 2
400 WEND
    Statement 3

Two-Way Selection

Often, a selection is made between two alternatives: a student is either an undergraduate or a graduate; a person either worked 40 or more hours this week or did not. This two-way selection can be implemented in a few ways, depending on the number of statements required for each alternative. Some of the implementations are discussed below.

- If only one statement is needed to implement each alternative, the selection can be implemented like this:

```
200  IF condition THEN statement 1 ELSE statement 2
210  Statement 3
```

- If only a few statements are needed to implement each alternative, the selection can be implemented like this:

```
200  IF condition THEN 400
210  REM --- FALSE ---
220      Statement 1
230      Statement 2
     GOTO 500
390  REM --- TRUE ---
400      Statement 3
410      Statement 4
490  REM --- ENDIF ---
500  Statement 5
```

- If more than a few statements are needed to implement each alternative, then these statements can be made into subroutines and implemented like this:

```
200  IF condition THEN GOSUB 2000 ELSE GOSUB 4000
     {Subroutines at lines 2000 and 4000}
```

Multiway Selection: The Case Structure

Many selections can involve three or more alternatives. For example, a student may be an FR (freshman), SO (sophomore), JR (junior), or SE (senior). Depending on the number of actions that have to be taken for each alternative, the **case structure** (see Section 7.2) can be implemented in one of the following four common ways:

case structure

1. If the action for each alternative consists of only one or two statements, then locate the statements after the THEN, followed by a GOTO. For example:

```
200  REM --- CASE BEGIN ---
     IF condition 1 THEN statement 1 : GOTO 300
     IF condition 2 THEN statement 2 : GOTO 300
     IF condition 3 THEN statement 3 : GOTO 300
     STOP
290  REM --- CASE END ---
300  Statement 4
```

2. If there are more than a couple actions in each case, implement the case this way:

```
400  REM --- CASE BEGIN ---
        IF condition 1 THEN 600
        IF condition 2 THEN 700
        IF condition 3 THEN 800
        STOP
590  REM --- CASE: condition 1 ---
600       Statement 1
          Statement 2
          Statement 3
        GOTO 900
        REM --- CASE: condition 2 ---
700       Statement 21
          Statement 22
        GOTO 900
        REM --- CASE: condition 3 ---
800       Statement 31
          Statement 32
          Statement 33
900  REM --- CASE END ---
```

3. If each alternative involves a number of statements, then put these statements into a subroutine. For example:

```
400  REM --- CASE BEGIN ---
        IF condition 1 THEN GOSUB 1000  : GOTO 500
        IF condition 2 THEN GOSUB 2000  : GOTO 500
        IF condition 3 THEN GOSUB 3000  : GOTO 500
        STOP
500  REM --- CASE END ---
        {Subroutines at lines 1000, 2000, 3000}
```

4. If the condition is a variable that takes on small integer values, then handle the cases as you handled the case in method 3, but use a single BASIC statement:

```
400  ON X GOSUB 1000, 2000, 3000
        {Subroutines at lines 1000, 2000, 3000}
```

C.3 BASIC STATEMENTS

Most BASIC statements can be grouped into two categories: statements that take some action on data and statements that control the execution and flow of the action statements.

The statements that take an action on data can be subdivided into three categories:

Input-Related Statements	**Text Page Reference**

```
READ X$, A, C                                             59
DATA "JOE", 23.4, 5                                       59
RESTORE                                                  175
INPUT X$, A, B                                           161
INPUT "ENTER LAST NAME"; L$                              163
C$ = INKEY$ or GET C$                                    363
```
(For file statements, see Chapter 14.)

Output-Related Statements	

```
PRINT N$, A, B                                            51
PRINT TAB(23); N$                                         55
PRINT USING L1$; N$, A, B                                372
```
(For graphics statements, see Chapter 16.)

Assignment Statements	

```
LET A = 23 * H + T/Y                                      48
LET Q$ = G$ + H$                                          49
```

The following statements control the flow of statement execution:

Statement	**Text Page Reference**

```
200   IF condition THEN 400                            62, 104
200   IF condition THEN 400 ELSE 600                      137

200   GOTO 100                                         62, 108
200   ON X GOTO 400, 600, 800                            131

200   GOSUB 4000                                         143
200   ON X GOSUB 2000, 4000, 6000                        167

200   FOR I = S TO F STEP Q                              184
         Statement 1
         Statement 2
300   NEXT I

200   STOP                                                58
```

The following statements do not fit into either of the above categories:

Statement	**Text Page Reference**

```
100   DIM                                                241
100   REM                                                 50
100   RANDOMIZE                                          222
100   END                                                 51
```

C.4 DATA STRUCTURES

All programs process data. The data can have a wide variety of structures: records, fields, arrays, and files. These structures are built by the programmer out of the two primitive types of data: numbers and strings.

data value

A **data value** can have no relation to any other data. But usually, various groups of values will have some relation to other values in the group, and together these values will be thought of as a unit.

record
fields

A **record** consists of a number of values called fields. The **fields** are related in that they describe the relevant, distinctive features of an entity. The entity can be a thing, such as the owner of an automobile:

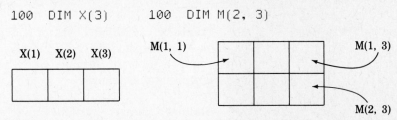

"MR. GREER",   "CHEV",   1956,   "SILVER", "234-4532-3"

└─Owner   └─Car   └─Year   └─Color   └─Registration
              make   number

field variables

These values can be held in **field variables** such as N\$ (for name), T\$ (for car make), Y (for year), C\$ (for color), and R\$ (for registration number). In BASIC a record is processed by processing the individual field variables in the record.

array

An **array** consists of a fixed number of values that are all numbers or all strings. The values are stored in an array variable. An array can be one-dimensional, two-dimensional, or of higher-dimension.

As illustrated below, the DIM statement is used to inform the BASIC system about the size of the array:

```
100  DIM X(3)       100  DIM M(2, 3)
```

X(1)   X(2)   X(3)

M(1, 1) ──→ ▢ ▢ ▢ ←── M(1, 3)

←── M(2, 3)

file

A **file** can have one of two structures on a disk: sequential or direct-access.

sequential file

A **sequential file** consists of a sequence of values that are read and written one value at a time. Some values can be numeric and others can be string. It is up to the programmer to know which type is to be read. The file is created by writing one value after another, that is, sequentially. The file is read by reading the first value, the second, the third, and so on. A sequential file has the following structure:

direct-access file   A **direct-access file** consists of numbered records. Each record must have the same form and length. For example, below we illustrate that each record has two fields. Any particular record may be read or written by specifying the record number. A direct-access file has the following structure:

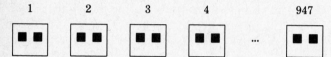

C.5 NUMERIC EXPRESSIONS

numeric expression   Some BASIC statements may contain numeric expressions. A **numeric expression** is a sequence of constants, variables, operations, and/or functions. When the expression is evaluated, it yields a numeric value. For example, the following is a numeric expression:

```
INT(A + B)/2 + 3 * Z ↑ 2
```

numeric constants   **Numeric constants** can be written in three ways: in integer, decimal, or exponential notation:

Integer constant	23
Decimal constant	34.53
Exponential	23.45E9

numeric variables   **Numeric variables** consist of a single letter or a letter followed by a digit. Most versions of BASIC now allow any number of characters for naming a variable, but usually, only the first two will be significant. Some examples are as follows:

Standard numeric variable names	A	Z4
Other allowable names	RATE	WAGE

Some versions of BASIC allow a distinction to be made between integers, single-precision decimal numbers, and double-precision decimal numbers. An integer variable name ends with a % character. Single-precision variables are those described in this text. A double-precision variable name ends with the # character.

numeric operators   The **numeric operators** consist of addition (+), subtraction (−), multiplication (*), division (/), and exponentiation (↑).

numeric functions   **Numeric functions** yield a numeric value when evaluated. The numeric functions available on most systems are listed below. The standard functions are defined on page 74. (Refer to a trigonometry book for the definition of the trigonometric functions.)

Standard Numeric Functions				Trigonometric Functions			
ABS	EXP	INT	LOG	ATN	COS	SIN	TAN
RND	SGN	SQR					

C.6 STRING EXPRESSIONS

string expression

A **string expression** is a sequence of constants, variables, concatenation operations, and/or functions. When evaluated, it yields a string value.

string constants

String constants consist of a sequence of characters enclosed in quotation marks. For example,

```
"HELLO"
```

is a string constant.

string variable names

String variable names consist of a single letter followed by a $, or a letter followed by a digit followed by a $. Most versions of BASIC now allow a string variable name to consist of any number of characters followed by a $. But only the first two are significant.

string operation

Concatenation (indicated by the +) is the only **string operation**.

string functions

String functions are functions that yield a string value when evaluated. Most of the string functions below are defined on page 86 of the text:

```
LEFT$    RIGHT$    MID$    STR$    CHR$
```

The following functions have string arguments but yield integer values. They are defined on pages 86 and 383:

```
LEN    INSTR    VAL    ASC
```

C.7 CONDITIONS

condition

A **condition** is also called a conditional expression or a Boolean expression. A condition is an expression that, when evaluated, yields a value of true or false. The two types of conditions, simple and compound, use relational operators and logical operators, as described below.

Relational Operators

simple condition
relational operator

A **simple condition** is formed when a **relational operator,** as defined below, is used between two numeric or two string expressions. The relational operators are as follows:

Relational Operator	Description	Examples
=	Equality	$A + B = 3$ $N\$ = LEFT\$(Q\$ + \text{``00''})$
<>	Inequality	$A\$ <> \text{``HELLO''}$
<	Less than	$2 < X$
<=	Less than or equal to	$A + B <= T/S$
>	Greater than	$\text{``A9''} > T\$$
>=	Greater than or equal to	$X >= Y$

Logical Operators

compound condition
logical operators

A **compound condition** is formed by joining simple conditions with the **logical operators,** as defined below. For example,

```
(AGE >= 21) AND (AVE > 70)
```

The logical operators are as follows:

Logical Operator	Example	Definition
AND	C1 AND C2	This expression is true if both simple conditions C1 and C2 are true.
OR	C1 OR C2	This expression is true if at least one of the simple conditions is true.
NOT	NOT (C1)	This expression is true if the simple expression C1 is false.

Solutions to Selected Exercises

Chapter 2

2.1. In each case the record structure is those columns that have no xxxx. The calculated results are:

(a) Cost of gas: 80.22, 2608.69, 2800, 1291.67

(b) Amount charged: 45, 75, 120

(c) Charge: 2.00, 4.50, 5.00

(d)

Gallons Needed	Cost
1.95	15.48
1.59	18.66
4.82	63.85

(e) Days between: 158, 100, 29643

2.2. Each truck file record, in addition to current fields, will have to contain the following fields: capacity in tons, bed length, day rented, day returned, dates already reserved.

2.3. The game of war:

```
Deal all the cards to two players
LOOP UNTIL one player has no cards
    Each player turns over one card
    IF both players turn over cards with same value
        FALSE: Continue on
        TRUE:  Each player turns over 5 more cards
    ENDIF
    The player with the highest card takes the pile*
ENDLOOP
Player with all the cards wins
```

*Modify this line to handle the situation when both players have cards of the same value at this point.

2.4.
```
PRINT title
PRINT headers
Get first record
LOOP UNTIL end of file
    Calculate distance traveled
    Calculate hours used
    Determine the charge
    PRINT detail line
    Get the next record
ENDLOOP
```

2.5.

Miles	Hours	Rate	Charge	Results on paper
123	4.5	5.00	53.25	53.25

2.6. (a)

C	Q	N	P	Results on paper
68	0	0	0	2 3 3
43	1			
18	2			
13		1		
8		2		
3		3		
2			1	
1			2	
0			3	

(b)

A	B	C	L	Results on paper
14	84	50	14	84
			84	

(c)

B	R	Y	P	T	Results on paper
500	.12	3	208.17	1	1 351.83
560				2	2 185.88
351.83					3 .02
394.05					
185.88					
208.19					
.02					

2.7. See figure page 399.
      Hours ← 42
      Rate ← 4.5
      IF hours > 35
          FALSE: Wage ← hours * rate
          TRUE: Wage ← rate * 35 + (hours − 35) * 1.5 * rate
      ENDIF
      PRINT wage

2.8. Credits ← ??
      IF credits < 12
          FALSE: Tuition ← 45 * credits
          TRUE: Tuition ← 50 * credits
      ENDIF
      IF tuition > 700

☐ **Flowchart for Exercise 2.7.**

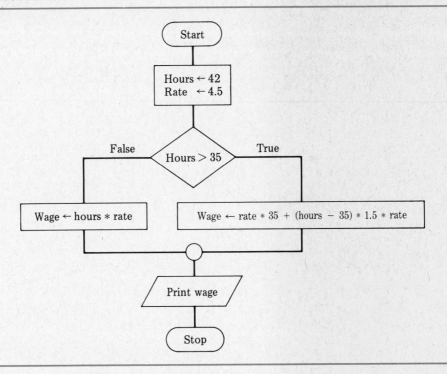

FALSE: Continue on
TRUE: Tuition ← 700
ENDIF
PRINT tuition

2.9.   (a)   C ← 68
            Q ← 0
            N ← 0
            P ← 0
            LOOP UNTIL C < 25
              C ← C − 25
              Q ← Q + 1
            ENDLOOP
            LOOP UNTIL C < 5
              C ← C − 5
              N ← N + 1
            ENDLOOP
            LOOP UNTIL C < 1
              C ← C − 1
              P ← P + 1
            ENDLOOP
            PRINT Q, N, P

       b)   A ← 14
            B ← 84
            C ← 50
            L ← A

            IF B > L
              FALSE: continue
              TRUE: L ← B
            ENDIF

            IF C > L
              FALSE: continue
              TRUE: L ← C
            ENDIF

            PRINT L

2.10.

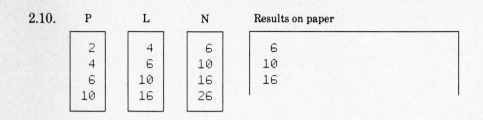

P	L	N	Results on paper
2	4	6	6
4	6	10	10
6	10	16	16
10	16	26	

Chapter 3

3.1. (a)

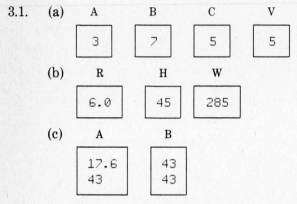

A	B	C	V
3	7	5	5

(b)

R	H	W
6.0	45	285

(c)

A	B
17.6	43
43	43

3.2. (a) Ok
   (b) Two variables on the left side of assignment operator
   (c) Z45 is illegal variable name
   (d) Variable AB is ok on most systems
   (e) Dollar sign is illegal
   (f) 2X is illegal operation or variable

3.3.

A	C	P
16	4	25

Output

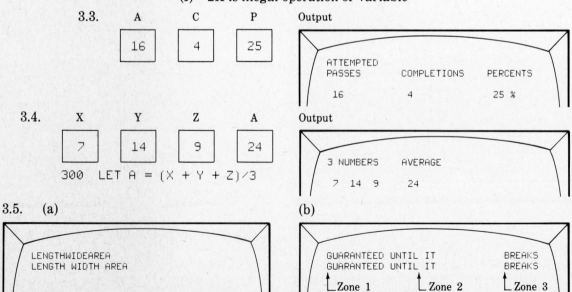

```
ATTEMPTED
PASSES         COMPLETIONS    PERCENTS
  16              4             25 %
```

3.4.

X	Y	Z	A
7	14	9	24

300 LET A = (X + Y + Z)/3

Output

```
3 NUMBERS     AVERAGE
  7  14  9      24
```

3.5. (a)

```
LENGTHWIDEAREA
LENGTH WIDTH AREA
```

(b)

```
GUARANTEED UNTIL IT                    BREAKS
GUARANTEED UNTIL IT                    BREAKS
   └─Zone 1        └─Zone 2            └─Zone 3
```

3.6.

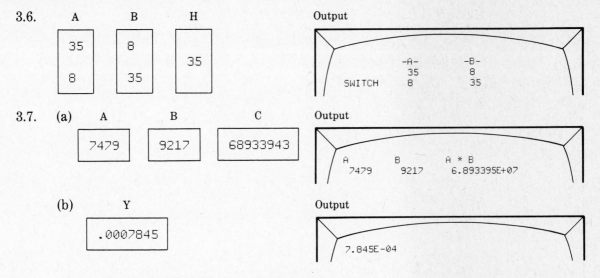

A	B	H	Output
| 35<br>8 | 8<br>35 | 35 | ```
            -A-      -B-
             35       8
   SWITCH     8       35
``` |

3.7. (a)

A	B	C	Output
| 7479 | 9217 | 68933943 | ```
  A          B         A * B
 7479       9217     6.893395E+07
``` |

(b)

Y	Output
| .0007845 | ```
 7.845E-04
``` |

3.8. Add the following statements to the program:

```
600    READ R$, W, L
610       LET A = L * W
620       PRINT R$, A
```

3.9. (a)

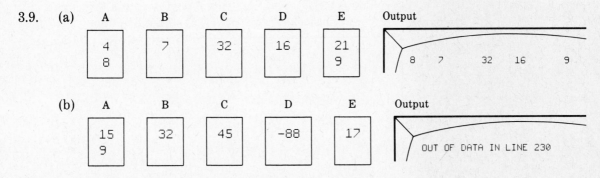

A	B	C	D	E	Output
| 4<br>8 | 7 | 32 | 16 | 21<br>9 | ```
   8    7      32    16         9
``` |

(b)

A	B	C	D	E	Output
| 15<br>9 | 32 | 45 | -88 | 17 | ```
 OUT OF DATA IN LINE 230
``` |

3.10. It is legally correct. However, the loop is not a structured loop.
The test for the exit condition is not at the top of the loop.

3.11.

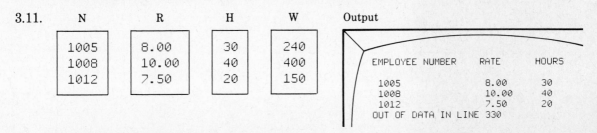

N	R	H	W	Output
| 1005<br>1008<br>1012 | 8.00<br>10.00<br>7.50 | 30<br>40<br>20 | 240<br>400<br>150 | ```
 EMPLOYEE NUMBER     RATE      HOURS

     1005            8.00       30
     1008           10.00       40
     1012            7.50       20
 OUT OF DATA IN LINE 330
``` |

To avoid the OUT OF DATA message, give the trailing record
in line 900 three numeric values.

3.12.
```
100   PRINT TAB(11); "ACME PAYROLL"
110   PRINT
120   PRINT "EMPLOYEE"
122   PRINT "NUMBER"; TAB(12);"RATE";TAB(18);
      "HOURS";TAB(26);"WAGE"

320   PRINT N; TAB(12); R; TAB(18); H; TAB(26); W
```

3.13. (a) Statements 110 and 150 should be

```
READ M, H
```

Also, the fraction $\frac{1}{2}$ in line 810 is illegal.
There is also no trailing record.

(b) The result is not printed. Line 140 should be

```
140   PRINT X, Y, S
```

There is no trailing record.

3.14. (a) The results would be calculated for every other line of data.
(b) The results for the second record will continually be printed. The computer does not read beyond the second record.
(c) The results for the first record will continually be printed.
(d) The BASIC processor will not find any data to read because it will not look beyond the END statement.

3.15.

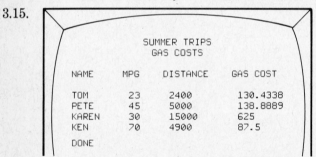

```
                SUMMER TRIPS
                 GAS COSTS

   NAME     MPG     DISTANCE     GAS COST

   TOM       23      2400        130.4338
   PETE      45      5000        138.8889
   KAREN     30     15000        625
   KEN       70      4900        87.5

   DONE
```

3.16. Use the following variables as indicated: L, length of time in days; F, food cost; T, total cost. Then lines 230 and 350 should be

```
READ N$, M, D, L
```

Two lines should be added and the third changed:

```
322   LET F = 25 * L
324   LET T = F + C

330   PRINT N$; TAB(8);M; TAB(13);D;
      TAB(23);C; TAB(30);F; TAB(38);T
```

3.17.

```
                        ACME STORES

        CUSTOMER      QUANTITY     PRICE     COST
        --------      --------     -----     ----

        JOE             34          2.34     79.56
        KAREN           10          0.53      5.30
        JILL             8          1.23      9.84
```

Chapter 4

4.1.   (a) $A/B + 5$ (e) $A \uparrow (2 * B)$

       (b) $(A + B)/C$ (f) $(Z + 8) \uparrow (.5)$

       (c) $B/(8 + H)$ (g) $B * (1 + R/N) \uparrow (N * Y)$

       (d) $(Y + 5)/(H - E)$ (h) $1/(1 - 1/(A + B))$

4.2.   (a) 4   (b) 2.5   (c) 7.3333   (d) 3.2

       (e) 2.75   (f) 284   (g) −6   (h) −18

4.3.   (a) 2   (b) 3   (c) 4

4.4.

```
      2476.937     .937     2477     2476.9     47
```

Chapter 5

5.1.

DT	N	CT	N$	D	G	C
0	0	0	GRAND CANYON	2300	92	115
2300	1	115	WORLD'S FAIR	800	32	40
3100	2	155	KENTUCKY DERBY	450	18	22.5
3550	3	177.5	ZZZ	0		

5.2.   PRINT title
       Initialize sums and counts to zero
       PRINT headers
       READ first record
       LOOP UNTIL out of data
          Accumulate total distance
          Count trip
          Calculate cost of trip
          Accumulate total cost of trips
          PRINT detail line
          READ next record
       ENDLOOP
       PRINT summaries

5.3. Before any trips are read, the total distance DT is zero.

5.4. The summary result TOTAL DISTANCE will simply be the distance of the last trip.

5.5. The TOTAL DISTANCE will not include the distance of the first trip. Also, the distance in the trailing record will mistakenly be added to the TOTAL DISTANCE.

5.6. In this program variable B may be used to hold the current balance. Instead of being inititialized to zero, it should be assigned the customer's initial balance.

5.9. The average is calculated incorrectly in line 310. Furthermore, the class total for quiz 1, quiz 2, and quiz 3 are calculated incorrectly. Line 320 should be

```
320  LET T1 = T1 + Q1
```

Lines 330 and 340 should be modified appropriately.

5.10.
```
540  LET AV = DT/N
550  PRINT "AVERAGE DISTANCE OF EACH TRIP: "; AV
560  STOP
```

Chapter 6

6.1.
```
100  PRINT "    WESTERN RHODE ISLAND COLLEGE"
110  PRINT " "
120  PRINT "STUDENT","CREDITS","STATE", "TUITION"
200  READ N$, C, S$
250  IF N$ = "ZZZ" THEN 600
300 ⎫
  .  ⎬  As in text
  .  ⎭
500 ⎭
510     READ N$, C, S$
520  GOTO 250
600  STOP
700  DATA "JOE", 14, "CT"
800  DATA "ZZZ", 0, "  "
999  END
```

6.2.

G	T	H	Output

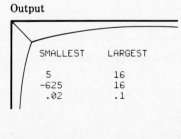

G	T	H
16	5	16
5	16	16
16	-625	.1
-625	16	
.1	.02	
.02	.1	
0	0	

Output

```
SMALLEST    LARGEST

   5          16
 -625         16
  .02         .1
```

6.4.
```
      500   IF T > 100 THEN 520
      510      REM --- FALSE ---
      511         GOTO 530
      520      REM --- TRUE  ---
      521         LET T = T - 12.00
      522      REM --- ENDIF ---
      530
```

6.5.   Let L count the number of long trips, trips over 3000 miles.

```
      235  LET L = 0 : INITIALIZE TO ZERO

      365  IF D > 3000 THEN L = L + 1

      535  PRINT "NUMBER OVER 3000 MILES:   "; L
```

6.7.   (a) Add the statement 412 GOTO 500.
        (b) Line 410 is extraneous; omit it.
        (c) This is phrased in an awkward way.

6.8.   You should test at least four situations: (1) out-of-state students,
        (2) in-state students who are full-time students; (3) in-state stu-
        dents who are part-time students, (4) an in-state student who has
        exactly 12 credits.

6.10.   In my opinion flowcharts more clearly display the logic of nested
        selection. For this reason both pseudocode and flowcharts are
        discussed in this text.

6.11.   Variable use: N, number of items; P, price of item; C, total cost.
        You might find this exercise easier to do if you first construct
        a flowchart.

```
250   READ N, P
300   IF N = 0 THEN 600 :    REM -- TERMINATION CONDITION
310     IF N <= 4 THEN 362
320     REM --- FALSE:  MORE THAN 4
330        IF N <= 10 THEN 352
340           REM --- FALSE: MORE THAN 10
342              LET C = N * P - .12 * (N * P)
344              GOTO 400
350           REM --- TRUE:  BETWEEN 5 AND 10
352              LET C = N * P - .07 * (N * P)
354              GOTO 400
356           REM --- ENDIF ---
360     REM --- TRUE: LESS THAN OR EQUAL TO 4
362        LET C = N * P
364     REM --- ENDIF ---
370                                          REM
400     PRINT N,P,C
```

Chapter 7

7.1.

L	N$	H	R	W
-1	JOE	30	4.50	135
135	MARY	40	5	200
200	FRAN	30	8	240
240	HARRY	15	5	75
	ZZZ	0	0	

7.2.   Variables: LO, largest overtime wage; OW, overtime wage.

```
142  LET LO = 0

302  IF H > 40 THEN 306
303    REM --- FALSE: NO OVERTIME
304        LET W = R * H
305        GOTO 320
306    REM --- TRUE: OVERTIME
308        LET OW = (H - 40) * 1.5 * R
310        LET W = 40 * R + OW
312        IF OW > LO THEN 316
314            GOTO 320
316        LET LO = OW
318    REM --- ENDIF ---
```

7.3.   Use a variable like NL$, which will hold the name of the person with the largest wage so far. Now add the statement

```
362  LET NL$ = N$
```

7.4.   The pseudocode for such a program will look like this:

> PRINT title
> Initialize variable to hold largest wage
> Initialize variable to hold smallest wage
> READ first record
> LOOP UNTIL no more employees
>   Calculate employee's wage
>   IF wage is larger than the largest wage
>   FALSE: Continue on
>   TRUE: Make it the largest wage
>   Save the person's name

ENDIF
IF wage is less than smallest wage
    FALSE: Continue on
    TRUE: Make it the smallest wage
             Save the person's name
ENDIF
PRINT detail line
READ next record
ENDLOOP
PRINT summaries

7.6.   So that the first value is assigned to variable S after the comparison. The first value is the smallest so far.

7.7.   The smallest string is the string that alphabetically comes before the other strings.

7.8.   You must use a weighted average to calculate the best miles per gallon. For example, the mpg for the Corvette is

$$mpg = .75 * 19 + .25 * 30$$

7.9.   *Hint:* If you do not find the problem, trace it with the following data:

```
800   DATA 34, 40, 0
```

7.12.   A nested selection involves making a selection on a branch of a two-way selection. The alternatives in a case structure are mutually exclusive.

7.13.   (a) True (b) True (c) False (d) True

7.14.   (a) (i) True (b) (i) True (c) (i) False (d) (i) False

7.15.   The two segments do not do the same thing. Draw a flowchart of each segment to see the difference.

7.16.
```
200   IF cndt 1 THEN 300
210      REM --- FALSE ---
220          IF cndt 2 THEN 250
230              REM --- FALSE ---
240                  Stmt 2
242                  GOTO 400
250              REM --- TRUE   ---
260                  Stmt 1
270                  GOTO 400
280              REM --- ENDIF ---
300      REM --- TRUE   ---
310          Stmt 1
320      REM --- ENDIF ---
```

7.17. (a) (i) To verify these equivalencies, set up a truth table:

Condition a	Condition b	NOT(a AND b)	(NOT a) OR (NOT b)
True	True	NOT(true) False ⟶	False OR False False
True	False	NOT(false) True ⟶	False OR True True
False	True	NOT(false) True ⟶	True OR False True
False	False	NOT(false) True ⟶	True OR True True

Notice that the two expressions have the same value for each possible value for condition a and condition b.

(b) (i) L >= A OR A >= U

7.18. Replace lines 310 and 360 with

```
310  IF X > L THEN L = X
```

Chapter 8

8.1. We will not show the output, just the values of the variables and the stack for the GOSUB statements:

Q$	Y	Stack
SPRING	1987	3̶3̶0̶ 3̶5̶0̶ 3̶7̶0̶ 3̶3̶0̶ 3̶5̶0̶ 3̶7̶0̶ 3̶3̶0̶ 3̶5̶0̶ 3̶7̶0̶

Notice in this case that the stack never has more than one return line number at a time.

N$	S$	R$	M$	C	R	M	T	T1
SAM	RI	T	W	12	400	800	480	1680
PETE	CT	T	W	12	400	800	960	2160
KAREN	CT	T	N	12	400	0	960	1360
ZZZ	X	X	X	0				

8.2. (a) Let variable NS hold the number of students. Then the following statements should be inserted in the program:

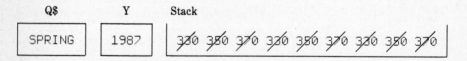

```
230  LET NS = 0
305  LET NS = NS + 1
505  PRINT "NUMBER OF STUDENTS IS: ";NS
```

8.3. The line numbers in the stack are shown here for the processing of the first record. The three dots indicate that nothing is in the stack.

8.4. The 338 would not be removed from the stack. (See the answer to Exercise 8.3.) Processing three records will cause three 338s to be in the stack, which can cause the stack to consume all available memory. Suppose line 5510 were changed to 4040. Refer again to the answer to Exercise 8.3.

8.5. The computer would execute the "print title and header" subroutine again. When it comes to the RETURN in line 2220, it will not have any value in the stack to return to. Try this program on your computer. What is the result?

8.6. Add the following line:

```
2015  IF P = 1 THEN 2100
```

Chapter 9

9.1. Suppose the string entered is A5. Then the program will print the cost as C * 5, where C will have the cost of the previous real item bought! This line should definitely be fixed!

Chapter 10

10.1. Replace line 200 with the line

```
200  REM --- TOP OF LOOP ---
```

And change the following line:

```
420  IF X > 0 THEN 200
```

10.2. As shown in the accompanying program, it is sometimes convenient to use one type of loop rather than the other.

```
10   LET S = 0
20   READ X
30   LET S = S + X
40   IF X > = 75 THEN 100
50     READ X
60     LET S = S + X
70   GOTO 40
100  PRINT S
110  STOP
120  DATA 5, 34, 20, 14, 34, 23
130  END
```

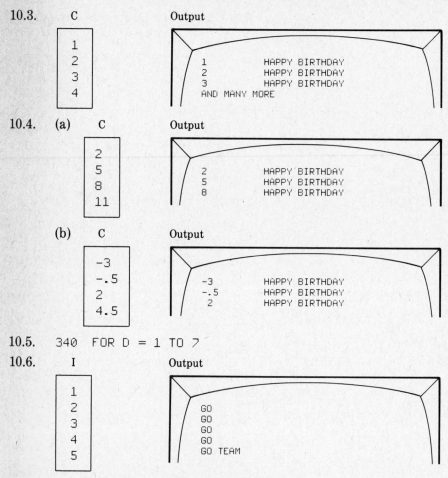

10.3.   C

10.4.   (a)   C

        (b)   C

10.5.   340   FOR D = 1 TO 7

10.6.   I

10.7.   (a)   Line 340 should be removed.

10.10. The bars of the bar graph will be continued on one line.

Chapter 11

11.1.   This exercise can be done in different ways depending on the type of computer you have. For Apple II, II+, IIe:

```
2000  PRINT "OPTION 2: OUTPUT ON SCREEN OR PRINTER (S/P)";
2002  INPUT R$
2003  IF R$ = "P" THEN PRINT PR#1
2005  PRINT "          OPTION 2: SIMULATION RUN"

2550  IF R$ = "S" THEN PRINT PR#0
```

For Microsoft BASIC this program is somewhat awkward, because the LPRINT statement must be used to print on the printer. (There is another way to do this operation in some operating systems; you have to change the contents of the IOBYTE.)

```
2000    PRINT "OPTION 2: OUTPUT ON SCREEN OR PRINTER (S/P)";
2002    INPUT R$
2003    IF R$ = "P" THEN 2700
2004    REM --- FALSE: ON SCREEN ---
2005    PRINT "        OPTION 2: SIMULATION RUN"
2010
  .
  .
  .
2600
2610    REM ------- OUTPUT TO PRINTER --------
2700    LPRINT "        OPTION 2: SIMULATION RUN"
  .
  .        Insert all lines between 2010 and 2600 with
  .        new line numbers and change all PRINTS to LPRINTS

2900    RETURN
```

11.2.   Use a posttest loop instead of the FOR–NEXT.

```
2120    LET C = L
2130    LET H = M              :REM -- INITIALIZE
2140    LET R = (L - 1) * S    :REM -- INITIALIZE
2150    REM --- LOOP TOP ---
2160       LET H = H + I
2170       LET R = R + S
2180       PRINT C, H, R
2190       LET C = C + 1
2200    IF R <= H THEN 2160
2210    PRINT
2220    INPUT "PRESS <RET> TO CONTINUE"; Z$
2230    RETURN
```

11.34.   Because the integers between 2 and 12 will be generated uniformly. That is, there will be just as many 2s as 7s, and that is not how it should be. Seven should come up more than 6, 6 more than 5, and so on.

11.35.   The D generated in the second line will always be even, which cannot realistically be the case.

Chapter 12

12.1.   Change the following statements as shown

```
100   DIM H(7), T(7)

202   FOR I = 1 TO 7

300   READ N$, R, H(1), H(2), H(3), H(4), H(5), H(6), H(7)

320    LET H = H(1) + H(2) + H(3) + H(4) + H(5) + H(6) + H(7)

410    FOR I = 1 TO 7
```

Add H(6) and H(7) to lines 510, 600. Add T(6) and T(7) to line 710.

12.2.
```
300   READ N$, R
302     FOR I = 1 TO 5
304        READ H(I)
306     NEXT I

310   IF N$ = "ZZZ" THEN 700
312     LET H = 0
314     FOR I = 1 TO 5
310        LET H = H + H(I)
312     NEXT I

510     PRINT TAB(16);
512     FOR I = 1 TO 5
514        PRINT H(I);
516     NEXT I

600     READ N$, R
602     FOR I = 1 TO 5
604        READ H(I)
606     NEXT I

710   PRINT "DAILY HRS     ";
712   FOR I = 1 TO 5 : PRINT T(I); : NEXT I
```

12.3.

I	S	X(1)	X(2)	X(3)	X(4)	X(5)	X(6)
	0	4	9	3	2		
	4
	13
	16
	18

Output

```
4  9  3  2
SUM = 18
```

Notice that you can READ, PRINT, and accumulate the sum all in one loop.

12.4.   (c)   This routine counts the number values in the array that are greater than or equal to the value in M.

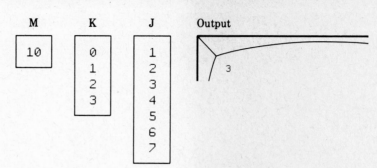

M	K	J	Output
10	0	1	
	1	2	
	2	3	3
	3	4	
		5	
		6	
		7	

12.10.   *Hint:* Let array F( ) hold the free times so far. Read the next person's free time into array X( ). Now find the free time between array F( ) and array X( ). As you compare these two arrays, put the free time in a temporary array T( ). After you complete the comparison, copy array T( ) to array F( ). Then read the next person's free time into X( ); and so on. Write the above algorithm in pseudocode before proceeding.

12.31.   (a)

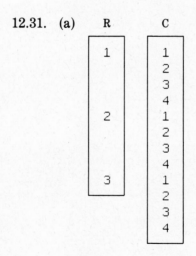

R	C
1	1
	2
	3
	4
2	1
	2
	3
	4
3	1
	2
	3
	4

Array H

3.5	-17	20	16
82	-32	14	30
16	80	-77	-66

(b)

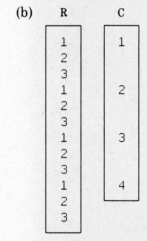

R	C
1	1
2	
3	
1	2
2	
3	
1	3
2	
3	
1	4
2	
3	

Array H

3.5	16	14	80
-17	82	30	-77
20	-32	16	-65

12.32.   Assume the values have already been read into the array. Let N
count the number of negative numbers.

```
400   LET N = 0
500   FOR R = 1 TO 3
510     FOR C = 1 TO 4
520       IF H(R, C) < 0 THEN N = N + 1
530     NEXT C
540   NEXT R
600   PRINT "NUMBER OF NEGATIVE NUMBERS:";N
```

Index

*If an entity is available only on a particular system, the system name is in parentheses.